Principled Software Development

Peter Müller • Ina Schaefer

Editors

Principled Software Development

Essays Dedicated to Arnd Poetzsch-Heffter
on the Occasion of his 60th Birthday

 Springer

Editors
Peter Müller
Department of Computer Science
ETH Zürich
Zürich, Switzerland

Ina Schaefer
Institut für Softwaretechnik und
  Fahrzeuginformatik
Technische Universität Braunschweig
Braunschweig, Germany

ISBN 978-3-030-07442-5   ISBN 978-3-319-98047-8   (eBook)
https://doi.org/10.1007/978-3-319-98047-8

Cover illustration: © Cover Photograph: Edel Modschiedler

This Springer imprint is published by the registered company Springer Nature Switzerland AG
The registered company address is: Gewerbestrasse 11, 6330 Cham, Switzerland

Preface

University professors have the great privilege that they can impact society in three major ways: by contributing scientific results and advising PhD students, by educating students, and through political and managerial work that shapes the research and education infrastructures that will allow future generations to accomplish their goals.

Arnd Poetzsch-Heffter is among the few professors who have been very successful in all three dimensions. Throughout his career, he has made major scientific contributions in a wide range of topics related to programming languages, software technology, and formal methods; he has been a passionate and demanding teacher and advisor, and he advanced TU Kaiserslautern as Department Chair and Vice President for Research, Technology, and Innovation. This book honors Arnd's achievements on the occasion of his 60th birthday.

Arnd studied Computer Science at TU Munich, where he also obtained his PhD in 1991 with a thesis on the Formal Specification of Context-Sensitive Syntax of Programming Languages. In 1997, Arnd obtained his habilitation with a thesis on the Specification and Verification of Object-Oriented Programs, also from TU Munich. He was Associate Professor at the University of Hagen from 1996 to 2002, has been Full Professor at TU Kaiserslautern since 2002, and Vice President since 2014.

This book contains articles related to Arnd's broad research interests including, among others, implementation of programming languages, formal semantics, specification and verification of object-oriented and concurrent programs, programming language design, distributed systems, software modeling, and software product lines. We collected the contributions by contacting Arnd's collaborators, colleagues, and former students. We were overwhelmed by the positive reactions. As a result, this book contains a collection of high-quality articles, presenting original research results, major case studies, and inspiring visions. Some of the work included in this book will be presented at a symposium to be held in Kaiserslautern in November 2018.

We would like to thank the authors for contributing to this book, Alexandra Bugariu, Marco Eilers, Sascha Lity, Stephan Mennicke, Tobias Runge, Sven Schuster, and Arshavir Ter-Gabrielyan for their help with copy-editing, Alexander Knüppel for compiling the LaTeX sources, Arnd's wife Edel Modschiedler for her stealth operation to take the picture on the book cover, and Annette Bieniusa for her help with the organization of the symposium. Our biggest thanks goes to Arnd Poetzsch-Heffter for being a truly exceptional PhD advisor and a role model to aspire to. Happy Birthday!

Zürich, Switzerland   Peter Müller
Braunschweig, Germany   Ina Schaefer
June 2018

Contents

Smart Contracts: A Killer Application for Deductive Source Code Verification

Wolfgang Ahrendt, Gordon J. Pace, and Gerardo Schneider

Abstract Smart contracts are agreements between parties which, not only describe the ideal behaviour expected from those parties, but also automates such ideal performance. Blockchain, and similar distributed ledger technologies have enabled the realisation of smart contracts without the need of trusted parties—typically using computer programs which have access to digital assets to describe smart contracts, storing and executing them in a transparent and immutable manner on a blockchain. Many approaches have adopted fully fledged programming languages to describe smart contract, thus inheriting from software the challenge of correctness and verification—just as in software systems, in smart contracts mistakes happen easily, leading to unintended and undesirable behaviour. Such wrong behaviour may show accidentally, but as the contract code is public, malicious users can seek for vulnerabilities to exploit, causing severe damage. This is witnessed by the increasing number of real world incidents, many leading to huge financial losses. As in critical software, the formal verification of smart contracts is thus paramount. In this paper we argue for the use of deductive software verification as a way to increase confidence in the correctness of smart contracts. We describe challenges and opportunities, and a concrete research program, for deductive source code level verification, focussing on the most widely used smart contract platform and language, Ethereum and Solidity.

W. Ahrendt (✉)
Chalmers University of Technology, Gothenburg, Sweden
e-mail: ahrendt@chalmers.se

G. J. Pace
University of Malta, Msida, Malta
e-mail: gordon.pace@um.edu.mt

G. Schneider
University of Gothenburg, Gothenburg, Sweden
e-mail: gerardo@cse.gu.se

© Springer Nature Switzerland AG 2018
P. Müller, I. Schaefer (eds.), *Principled Software Development*,
https://doi.org/10.1007/978-3-319-98047-8_1

1

1   The Blockchain and Smart Contracts

Blockchain refers to a specific data structure as well as to an architecture for maintaining that data structure. The blockchain *data structure* is essentially a list ('chain') of lists ('blocks'), but augmented with a combination of hierarchical and chained crypto hashing, in order to (1) ensure that appending blocks can only be performed by consensus; and (2) making changes on previous too computationally expensive to be tractable. The blockchain *architecture* is an open, distributed ledger that can record transactions between untrusted parties, in a permanent, transparent, and cryptographically secured way, without relying on any central authority. Bitcoin [29] was the first instantiation of blockchain, and was used for what has probably become the most widely recognised application of blockchain—that of cryptocurrencies. However, blockchain technology has a much wider and rapidly growing set of applications which are likely to play an important role in the future of the digital society. On the forefront of these are *smart contracts*.

A *smart contract* is intended to digitally facilitate and enforce the negotiation or performance of an agreement between all parties which choose to engage with it. Effectively, many smart contract implementations are computer programs which, using the blockchain, are stored in a manner that ensures immutability, i.e., they cannot be changed by any of the parties (unless mutability is implemented as part of the smart contract itself) and transparency, i.e. visible by the parties involved. The execution of smart contracts is performed in the blockchain network, by workers which earn some cryptocurrency in return, but in a manner which depends on no individual point of trust.

The by far most popular smart contract platform is *Ethereum*.[1] It was created by Vitalik Buterin and is now a community effort coordinated by the Ethereum Foundation. The Ethereum blockchain features its own cryptocurrency, Ether. Smart contracts are executed by the *Ethereum Virtual Machine* (EVM), a distributed virtual machine interpreting a bytecode-level smart contract language, called *EVM bytecode*. In order to have the code executed by workers in the blockchain network, the workers earn *'gas'* (which is traded with Ether). Each EVM instruction costs a fixed amount of gas. The caller pays for the execution by paying for the gas (in fact, in addition they also choose what gas price, in Ether, they are willing to pay), to support its execution. If a transaction runs out of gas payment, the transaction is aborted and leaves no side effect, though still losing the money used to pay for gas.

EVM code is too low-level (for most developers) to program in it directly. Similarly, it is too low level to allow inspection by (most) potential users of a contract. Instead, it is the target language for compilation from higher level languages, of which *Solidity* is the one which is used most widely. Ethereum smart contracts are largely written in Solidity, and inspected in that form by users considering to engage with a contract. The language borrows some syntactic flavour

---

[1] https://www.ethereum.org.

```
1    contract Auction {
2      bool public auctionOpen = true;
3      uint public currentBid = 0;
4      address private auctionOwner;
5      address private currentBidder = address(0);
6
7      function Auction() public {
8        auctionOwner = msg.sender;
9        ...
10     }
11
12     function placeBid() public payable {
13       // The auction must still be open
14       require (auctionOpen);
15
16       // The new bid must be higher than the current one
17       require (msg.value > currentBid, "bid too low");
18
19       // Remember the current bidder
20       address previousBidder = currentBidder;
21       uint previousBid = currentBid;
22
23       currentBidder = msg.sender;
24       currentBid = msg.value;
25
26       // If there was previous bid, return the money to that bidder
27       if (previousBidder != address(0)) {
28         previousBidder.transfer(previousBid);
29       }
30
31     }
32
33     function closeAuction() public {
34       require (msg.sender == auctionOwner);
35       auctionOpen = false;
36       ...
37     }
38
39     ...
40   }
```

Listing 1: Snippets from a smart contract regulating an auction

from JavaScript syntax. For instance, consider the smart contract snippets written in Solidity and shown in Listing 1. The Auction contract provides a protocol for regulating how the auction will take place. Once the code is set up on the blockchain (in compiled form), the participants are guaranteed that the logic of the auction process as described in the contract will be adhered to, thus ensuring certain guarantees e.g. only the auction creator may decide to close the auction.

A Solidity contract offers typically several *functions* (comparable to *methods* in the object-oriented setting) which can be called by anyone via the underlying blockchain system. For instance, in the auction smart contract, there is the function placeBid is called to make a new bid and closeAuction is used to close down the auction. More precisely, the caller is either an external account (signing the call with the private key of the account) or another contract. Any kind of information can be sent as parameter of the call, but in particular, a call can send cryptocurrency to the contract. The contract will then execute the called function, manipulating the local book-keeping data as well as transferring value, or any other kind of information, to other accounts or other contracts. For instance, the `placeBid` function will receive funds (hence marked `payable`) when called, and its logic will then (1) ensure that the new bid is higher than the current one; (2) the previous bidder (if any) will have their bid returned; (3) the new bid and the bidder's address are recorded. It is worth noting that if the argument passed to `require` does not hold, the whole execution fails and is reverted, thus not allowing the funds transfer. Reverting the execution results in rolling back the state of the smart contract to its original state to when a function was called from outside (i.e. if a function in a smart contract calls another which fails, any execution already done by the original function is also reverted). Contracts strongly encapsulate their local data. Even if a contract variable is labelled as `public`, it is still *not writable* from outside the contract. It only means that the variable is (indirectly) *readable*, through a getter-method that is generated during compilation.

The whole purpose of smart contracts is to describe and automate an agreed exchange of values and information over the internet, in a transparent way, for instance, any user knows that the auction is fair in the sense that a higher bid by *any* user is always accepted as the new winning bid. The smart contract, once enacted acts in itself as an entity on the blockchain, being able to receive or dispense funds (as regulated by its code).

The different participants are identified solely by their respective public key, which makes it easy to securely pass around encrypted or electronically signed information wherever appropriate. Whenever a function of a contract is called, the identity of the caller is sent along implicitly, and can be used by the contract in its internal bookkeeping, for call-backs, or for passing the caller identity on to some other contract.

To look further into the logic of the auction example, the code keeps track of whether the auction is open, the current winning bid, the bidder and the person who owns the auction, who corresponds to the one who enacted the contract (thus triggering the constructor of the contract). As long as the auction is open, any user may place a bid higher than the current winning one, until the owner of the auction decides to close it. Additional logic may guarantee that, for instance, the auction can only be closed after a certain period of inactivity. Transparency is the key attraction here, since inspection and analysis of the code shows that, for instance: (1) once closed, an auction may never be reopened; (2) only the owner of the auction may close it; (3) the funds stored in the auction smart contract match the value stored in the `currentBid` variable.

Relating the smart contract to the equivalent natural language legal contract one could have enacted in the real world instead, we note that: (1) unlike a legal contract, the smart contract does not only regulate behaviour, but also *performs* it— it guarantees, rather than makes illegal properties such as the fact that everyone gets to see the real highest bid, and that indeed the highest bidder (rather than a close relative) is selected as winner; and (2) the execution of the contract, in a way corresponds to a *negotiation* process, i.e., the final mutual obligations of the seller (the auction owner) and the selected winner may include or excluding certain warranties for the item sold, a warranty timeout, pre-payment before and full payment after pick-up, and so on. (At the same time, smart contracts lack many concepts which important for real legal contracts, like, for instance, prohibitions.)

Many smart contracts were created, mainly in the very recent years. The blockchain of the most popular smart contract framework, Ethereum, contains around one million smart contracts (970,898 as of December 26, 2017). Clearly, this still young technology has reached a wide spread in a short time. The applications are virtually endless, and include even integration with the Internet of Things (IoT). For instance, the Swiss company slock.it[2] offers renting of apartments, where smart contracts organise not only the agreement and payment, but also physical access through door locks that are connected to the internet and controlled by the smart contract.

There is a growing number of sectors, private as well as public, which are heavily investigating the future exploitation of blockchain and smart contracts, for innovative ways of doing business, of sharing and tracing data, of executing advanced transactions, of digital governance, of exploiting to the Internet of Things, and of executing agreements between parties, to name a few. The Enterprise Ethereum Alliance (EEA)[3] connects several hundreds of companies with Ethereum subject matter experts. (Note that this is only a fraction of the creators and users of Ethereum smart contracts.) EEA organises organisations with a particular, mostly commercial, interest in smart contracts, and include many prominent companies like American Family Insurance, AMD, BP, CISCO, Credit Suisse, HP, ING, Intel, J.P.Morgan, MasterCard, Microsoft, Rabobank, Samsung, Shell, TIBCO, and UBS, to name a few. But there are also other groupings, like R3,[4] a consortium of over 200 companies and regulators which build their own blockchain, Corda, with an according smart contract language, in order to, how they put it, *'transform the way the world does business'*. Members of the R3 partner network include (notably overlapping with the above) Amazon, HP, Intel, LG, Microsoft, and Oracle. All these developments are strong indicators that smart contracts are here to stay, and that smart contract safety is a significant issue.

2 Faulty Smart Contracts

Just like all pieces of software, smart contracts can, and do, suffer from programming errors, meaning that the code can deviate from the expected behaviour. Unlike in many software domains, the code of smart contracts is openly readable, and can be inspected by everyone before using it. And yet, it is well known that many errors are difficult to spot by inspection only. Most existing smart contract programming

---

[2]https://slock.it.
[3]https://entethalliance.org.
[4]https://www.r3.com.

languages are Turing-complete,[5] giving expressiveness and power, but making it more difficult to always understand the code fully, or to verify its correctness. There are many potential causes of programming errors, like numbers getting out of range, unintuitive semantics of certain language features, or intricate mismatches between internal bookkeeping (in the local data) and external bookkeeping (in the blockchain), to name just a few.

Erroneous behaviour may not be intended by the creator nor by the user of a contract. It is also possible that a malicious contract creator writes code to build expectations with obfuscated means to ensure that they will not be fulfilled. However, most errors are probably not intended by the creator of the contract, but discovered by a malicious user who then exploits them. In all of these scenarios, what is special in this application domain is that the parties using an erroneous smart contract can lose substantial value (typically cryptocurrency) at once, in big volumes, and that in an irreversible way (as blockchain transactions are permanent, and no authority has the power to undo them). Errors in smart contracts have already caused substantial financial damage, in some cases millions of dollars. Some famous bugs that have made the news include the DAO [37] and the Parity Wallet [10], and the two recent multi-million Ethereum bugs have led to losses equivalent to millions of dollars [1, 32]. Many more bugs have been detected and reported elsewhere [5], and some analysts claim that there are more than 30,000 buggy smart contracts on the Ethereum network [26]. All these reports just witness what many where afraid of: that it is easy to get smart contracts wrong, and that the consequences of errors can be severe.

The research community and practitioners, have already started to react to this problem by proposing different solutions. Some solutions go into the direction of creating new programming languages which are less expressive and more verification-friendly (see for instance [25] and references therein), while others propose to adapt existing or develop new verification techniques for existing programming languages. We give an overview of the latter in the next section.

3 Approaches to Smart Contract Verification: The Landscape

As argued in the previous section, given the finance-critical nature of many smart contracts, the need for verification of smart contracts is crucial, and interestingly although there is still limited foundational work and academic results addressing

---

[5]As opposed to usual Turing complete languages, executions of (Ethereum) contracts always terminate, because each external call specifies a 'gas limit', which effectively is an upper bound for the computational effort to be spent. However, as opposed to primitive recursive functions, Ethereum contracts do not themselves imply any limit on the computation. It is only the caller of the contract who provides the limit.

the challenge (perhaps because smart contracts are perceived to be no different than normal software), tool-development in the field to support smart contract developers is surprisingly active. In this section we look at the spectrum of verification techniques and tools developed for smart contract analysis and verification going beyond traditional testing and debugging support.

Dynamic analysis or runtime verification [23] have now long been touted as practical verification techniques which scale up to be used on real-world systems. There is limited research and tools applying these techniques for smart contracts, perhaps due to the overheads which runtime verification introduces on the system at runtime. On smart contract platforms such as Ethereum, these overheads translate to additional gas consumption, and hence the cost of executing the smart contract. Ellul and Pace [12] have developed CONTRACTLARVA,[6] a tool which allows for automated injection of runtime monitors into an existing smart contract written in Solidity to verify correctness at runtime. Related techniques have been developed by Idelberger et al. [16, 21, 21, 36], where the monitors are synthesised from declarative descriptions to regulate events typically coming from real-world systems rather than regulate smart contracts themselves. Similarly, García-Bañuelos et al. [14] have developed techniques using BPMN-based specifications on Ethereum, while Prybila et al. [31] have a similar solution for Bitcoin. Both approaches allow the regulation of business process models using smart contracts. Technically, although this and the previous approaches can be used to monitor events resulting from other smart contracts, they provide no automated means of instrumenting synchronisation between their monitors and the monitored contracts.

In the context of smart contracts, runtime overheads do not only cost time, but, more importantly, gas, i.e., money. In order to avoid the overheads induced by runtime monitoring, compile-time techniques may be more attractive. Moreover, compile-time techniques analyse all possible executions, rather than only the ones which were observed. Many of the tools available out there fall under the class of syntactic analysis, analysing the structure of the code with little or no semantic information to identify features which may indicate vulnerabilities in a Lint-like manner. There are various such tools out there for smart contracts written in Solidity, including Solcheck,[7] Solint,[8] Solium[9] and Solhint,[10] but many of these tools appear to simply replicate known syntactic analysis techniques from imperative languages in the context of smart contracts.

Static analysis techniques, which enrich this analysis using semantic information can be more effective in identifying potential problems with a system but require more effort to scale up for the verification of large systems. One major challenge here is that the semantics of smart contract languages are, at best, informally

---

[6]See https://github.com/gordonpace/contractLarva.

[7]See https://github.com/federicobond/solcheck.

[8]See https://github.com/SilentCicero/solint.

[9]See https://github.com/duaraghav8/Solium.

[10]See https://github.com/protofire/solhint.

explained, and typically by resorting to explaining how they work at the level of the virtual machine on which they are executed. A formal semantics for the Ethereum platform is the KEVM formal semantics [18], which formalises the bytecode assembly on the Ethereum Virtual Machine (EVM). Another formalisation was recently developed by Grishchenko et al. [17], also at the bytecode level, giving a small-step semantics in F*. Another semantics at the virtual machine level was given in [19], allowing reasoning about smart contracts to be performed using the interactive theorem prover Isabelle/HOL.

One can categorise these static techniques into two: (1) approaches which use static analysis to identify a particular class of typical vulnerabilities (e.g. gas leaks, reentrancy problems); and (2) specification-specific static analysis, particularly useful for the verification of smart contracts against a business-logic specification.

The former, typically addressing non-functional properties have been successfully deployed in many domains since they have been shown to scale up more readily—and this shows in the domain of smart contracts, where one finds a plethora of such tools. Different approaches have been taken to try to identify different types of vulnerabilities. For instance Fröwis et al. [13] try to identify cases where the control-flow of a smart contract is matable, which is typically not desirable. Luu et al. [24] have developed a tool OYENTE which uses symbolic execution to identify a whole class of possible issues, including reentrancy detection. Similarly, Mythril[11] [28] uses concolic analysis, taint analysis and control-flow analysis for security vulnerability detection. SmartCheck[12] uses a combination of lint-like and static analysis techniques to find common vulnerabilities. Many of these approaches work at the bytecode level, thus also allowing the verification of compiled contracts. In contrast, Bhargavan et al. [9] start at the source (Solidity) level and translate into F*, although they also use decompilation techniques to go from bytecode to F*. The motivation is to allow verification within F*. However, in contrast to what the title of the paper suggests, no actual verification of resulting F* is reported in the paper. The authors label their work as preliminary.

In contrast, static analysis of smart contracts at a business-logic level is still a largely neglected field of study, whether it is analysis at a code structure level (e.g. checking pre-/post-conditions or invariants of a system) or at a system-level (e.g. checking temporal logic properties which should hold along all execution paths of the system). Bai et al. [6] take a model checking approach, building a model of a particular smart contract and verifying it using the model checker SPIN. Although using this approach one can prove general temporal properties of the system, there is a huge gap between the level of abstraction of the smart contracts and the manually constructed model used for verification. Abdellatif and Brousmiche [2] model smart contracts using timed automata and verify their correctness, but take an ambitious approach of also modelling the underlying blockchain, including the mining process. Using probabilistic model checking, they verify properties such as

---

[11] See https://github.com/ConsenSys/mythril.

[12] See https://tool.smartdec.net.

the likelihood of a hacker using transaction ordering attacks. In this manner, this approach goes one step further in that they do not assume immediate writing of the information to the underlying blockchain. On the other hand, just as in the previous work, there is a gap between the smart contract model used for verification and the actual smart contract code.

While system-level temporal properties are ideal to reason at a system-wide level from an external perspective, most analysis is done post-development, with the system organisation and logic already in place. The system's architect and developers would have an understanding of how the individual parts fit together to guarantee the overall (integrated) logic of the system. Thus, finer-grained implementation-specific specifications at the code structure level, such as pre- and post-conditions and system invariants, are typically also desirable to allow developers to understand whether the parts are working as expected, and if not which parts are, in some way, broken and leading to failures. The relationship between the internal data and the transaction history is particularly desirable in the context of smart contracts, especially since smart contracts act like API calls which may be invoked independently of each other. Contrast this with monolithic systems which have a predetermined control-flow (the main function) and where user interaction affects which branches of the structure to follow. Despite this, to date we are not aware of any work done in functional verification of smart contracts at this code structure level, and this is where we position our work in this paper.

4   Towards a Deductive Source Code Verifier for Smart Contracts

Deductive program verification has been around for nearly 50 years, although a number of developments during the past 15 years have brought dramatic changes to what can be achieved. Contemporary verification tools support main-stream programming languages such as C [22], Java [3], or C# [7]. They reason directly on the source code level, support source code level specification languages (with pre/post-conditions and invariants), feature high automation (in contrast to verifiers based on higher-order logics), and provide rich graphical user interfaces.

In this section, we propose a research agenda which will provide the artefacts and tools for specification and deductive verification of smart contracts on the source code level. At this point, we aim at the by far most widely used smart contract framework, Ethereum, and at the most widely used programming language, Solidity. Clearly, these choices will have to be re-evaluated as we move forward, in the light of the very dynamic developments in this domain. Generally, targeting a wide spread platform and language is likely to boost the impact of this agenda on future smart contract practice, even more so as the Ethereum/Solidity community outspokenly asks for the involvement and contribution of formal methods.

In summary, we aim at a new specification language, a new program logic, and a new verification system for a concept (smart contract) and language (Solidity) for which comparable artefacts do not yet exist.

4.1   Challenges

Smart (Ethereum) contracts in general and Solidity in particular present various challenges to verification. We discuss these challenges in the following. Note that many of the Solidity features discussed here are also features of the underlying EVM bytecode, and partly also (at least in similar form) of other smart contract frameworks.

The Ethereum blockchain has its own *built-in cryptocurrency*, called Ether, currently the world's second biggest cryptocurrency after Bitcoin. Solidity (and the underlying EVM) supports the transfer of cryptocurrency between users and contracts, as well as among contracts. This is different from passing around other pieces of information. The attempt to transfer Ether is only accepted if the (block solving) worker can validate that the sender has a non-negative Ether balance in the blockchain after the transfer. If the validation fails, the transfer will not take place, and the entire surrounding transaction (see below) is aborted. Another difference is that the currency balance of accounts and contracts is stored as global sate, whereas other data is encapsulated in the contracts.

Solidity features a *transaction* mechanism. Each external call of a contract function starts a transaction. If during the execution of the transaction (which may include local computations, contract-triggered calls, and successful Ether transfers) some Ether transfer fails, this aborts the entire transaction. Also running out of gas, or the failure of an assertion (see `assert` in Listing 1), cause abortion of the ongoing transaction. All *local and global effects* of that transaction will be *undone*. Modelling the reverting of arbitrary computations poses a particular challenge to the proof system.

Gas analysis is an interesting challenge in smart contract verification. The limited gas budget which a smart contract user sends along with each call means that, in this domain, the resource consumption very directly affects the functionality of the contract. However, the precise consumption is defined on the level of EVM code instructions, not on the level of higher level languages translating to EVM, like Solidity. Therefore, for a quantitative gas analysis, the exact compiler version has to be considered, and analysed, to predict gas consumption of any higher-level (also Solidity) code. At the same time, out-of-gas exceptions do not generally indicate errors in the smart contract itself,[13] but rather they are caused by an insufficient gas budget provided by the caller. As the gas budget is given from outside the smart contracts, it cannot be used in static analysis.

---

[13] Although they may be the result of a *gas leak* in the code.

Cryptographic features are available as primitives in Solidity (and EVM). The Solidity programmer can heavily use (implicitly and explicitly) cryptographic primitives without mastering underlying cryptography. Our agenda does not address the verification of the underlying cryptographic algorithms. (That would belong to a different agenda, namely the verification of the underlying blockchain mechanisms.) Nevertheless, we have to formalise the guarantees cryptographic primitives make to the application level, and use them in the verification. Examples of such guarantees are the deterministic behaviour of a hash function, uniqueness of hash values, the accuracy of (the authentication with) cryptographic signatures, and so on.[14]

Solidity has *richer built-in data types* than other languages with comparable source code verification support, like Java or C. One example is mappings. (In C and Java, such data types are available only as libraries.) These data types require special reasoning support.

Solidity features *many* more *numeric types* than most languages. For instance, the programmer can use unsigned integers, the range of which can be freely configured, all the way from 2^8 to 2^{256} (in steps of 8 in the exponent). Overflow and underflow is silent, such that, for instance, 35–42 results not in -7, nor is any exception thrown, but it results in $2^{256} - 7$. Both the flexible size and the silent under- and overflow pose challenges to the verification. Admittedly, silent under- and overflow are also an issue in Java or C verification. However, underflow due to a lower bound of zero (as in Solidity) happens more easily in practice than underflow with respect to MININT (as in Java or C). Moreover, under- and overflows are particularly critical in smart contracts, where most numbers subject to arithmetic operations represent real value, like for instance amounts of cryptocurrency which one party owes another party. It makes a big difference whether A owes B a total of -7 Ether, as opposed to $2^{256} - 7$.

Solidity features a *mixture of different call mechanisms*. In addition to usual calls (building a context stack), Solidity offers some low-(EVM)-level call mechanisms. The first, `call`, is a generic function where the name of the called function is sent as an argument, together with the proper function arguments. This mechanism is not type safe. Another variant is `delegatecall`, which is similar to `call`, but effectively imports code from the called contract syntactically, thus executing it in the local, calling context. This way, some contracts act as libraries for other contracts, compensating for the lack of real libraries in the blockchain infrastructure. Furthermore, `delegatecall` is effectively a macro expansion mechanism—not type-safe, and prone to name capture. Solidity also features two different *function return mechanisms*, value return and call-by-reference (and writing to that reference instead of returning). This mixture of different call and return mechanisms poses interesting challenges to an according program logic and calculus.

As mentioned before, a smart contract strongly encapsulates its state. The contract variables can only ever be changed by other contracts or external accounts

---

[14]To be precise, some of these properties do are not strictly guaranteed, but hold with sufficiently high probability to justify relying on them.

through calls to *local* functions. At the same time, there is also contract external, global state, notably the current cryptocurrency balance of all (external and contract) accounts. Therefore, the verification needs to reason about a *combined message passing and shared memory* paradigm. At the same time, the stronger data encapsulation as compared to, say, Java or C++, is an advantage when developing compositional verification techniques.

On the other hand, it is a challenge for compositional verification that it is *not possible to pass Ether to another contract without calling it*. For instance, in Listing 1, if the address stored in `currentBidder` happens to be another contract (we cannot control whether that is the case), then `currentBidder.transfer(..)` executes the code of that contract.[15] This passing of control via seemingly elementary Ether transfer makes it more difficult to control effects locally. For instance, the execution of the Ether receiving contract may call back into the Ether sending contract. A verification methodology has to take this into account.

4.2 Approach

As argued above, the agenda we propose builds—and expands—on the state-of-the-art of deductive software verification. Concretely, we choose the KeY approach and system [3, 4] as a starting point and blueprint for a verification approach and system for Ethereum smart contracts written in Solidity. The most elaborate KeY version, KeY-Java, allows precise reasoning about practically all language features of (sequential) Java. Recently, a bug in the main sorting routine of the OpenJDK distribution of Java, `Collection.sort()`, was identified using KeY [15]. The same bug was then found to be present also in Oracle's Java and in Android. Another KeY version in the picture is KeY-ABS [11], a verification system for the distributed object language ABS. The choice of KeY is attractive because (a) KeY is among the approaches which have proven to master verification of *feature-rich mainstream languages* (like Java), (b) the KeY approach targets the object-oriented paradigm (Java, ABS) which the *contract-oriented paradigm* is building on, and (c) KeY has been used for *compositional verification of distributed objects* (ABS), which have similarities to communicating contracts with their strong data encapsulation. Note, however, that the agenda we present in this paper does not include the translation of smart contracts to another language for which a KeY version already exists. (Actually, such a work is also under the way, but will be reported elsewhere.) Rather, we describe here the version of a new KeY approach and system, for Ethereum, probably targeting Solidity, performing *source code level verification*. We give it

---

[15]In general, if c is a contract programmed in Solidity, `c.transfer(..)` behaviour can be overridden by using a fallback function which handles any function calls not defined in that contract.

the working title SolidiKeY. At the core, we aim at a new specification language, program logic, calculus, and proof system for Solidity.

Such an endeavour has to take the *examination of real smart contracts* as a point of departure. Luckily, smart contracts are openly available. (The EVM code is always stored in the blockchain. Moreover, often the corresponding source code is also publicly available, and via hash codes linked with the code in the blockchain.) One can start with those contracts which have known errors (e.g., [30]). Also, it is important to engage in discussions with the smart contract community. In the end, we want to offer to smart contract developers a method and tool which can be used *prior* to deploying a contract (irreversibly) in the blockchain.

We need to provide a new, business-logic level *specification language* for the targeted smart contract language, here Solidity. Its purpose is to formalise the desired functionality of the code units (functions and transactions), the integrity conditions on the stored data, and the relation between internal data and external communication. The specification language will share some design principles with the Java Modeling Language [20]: close integration of (non-destructive) Solidity language features into property descriptions, first-order quantification over data types, pre- and post-conditions of functions, state invariants over data stored in the contract, among others. In addition, the smart contract domain requires that the data stored in a contract reflects accurately, at each point in time, the communication between the contract and users (or other contracts). Formally, this boils down to a contract invariant, constraining the relation of the internal data to the communication history. For instance, `currentBidder` and `currentBid` (in Listing 1) must *invariantly* correspond to the sender and value of the highest bid in the *call history* of the contract. More precisely, these are the sender and value of the earliest of the calls to `placeBid()` which carries an Ether value greater or equal to the values of other calls to `placeBid()`. Such contract invariants are a cornerstone for compositional verification of a network of contracts. It must be possible to define them in the language, and the proof strategies need to support them.

From the contract and its specification, proof obligations must be generated, automatically. The logic may be a version of *dynamic logic* (DL), a modal logic for reasoning about programs on the source code level. DL extends first-order logic with two modalities, $\langle p \rangle \phi$ and $[p]\phi$, where p is a program (in source code) and ϕ is another DL formula. The formula $\langle p \rangle \phi$ is true in a state s if there *exists* a terminating run of p, starting in s, resulting in a state where ϕ holds. The formula $[p]\phi$ holds in a state s if *all* terminating runs of p, starting in s, result in a state in which ϕ holds. For deterministic programs p (like smart contract functions and transactions), the only difference between the two modalities is that termination is *stated* in $\langle p \rangle \phi$, and *assumed* in $[p]\phi$, such that the two modalities correspond to total and partial correctness, respectively. In the (Ethereum) smart contract world, a transaction will always terminate because of gas restriction. However, it is relevant to distinguish 'voluntary' termination by the business-logic and termination enforced by externally given gas limits. Also, one can redefine partial correctness to mean correctness in the absence of gas exceptions, and total correctness to mean correctness in the presence of gas exceptions. DL is the base logic for the KeY approach [8]. Hoare logic can be seen as a fragment of DL, because $\{\phi\}\texttt{foo}\{\psi\}$ can be expressed in DL as $\phi \to [\texttt{foo}]\psi$. DL and Hoare logic have in common that the logic and calculus is *specific* for the target language. We propose the development of a DL for Solidity, called Solidity DL.

For reasoning about this logic, we propose to develop a *sequent calculus*, covering all features of Solidity.[16] Given a set of formulae Γ, a program π and (post)condition ϕ the sequent $\Gamma \vdash \langle\pi\rangle\phi$ holds if π, when starting in a state fulfilling all formulae in Γ, terminates in a state fulfilling ϕ. The calculus uses the *symbolic execution* paradigm (by adding explicit substitutions to the logic, capturing the effects of a computation, see [8]). One advantages of this paradigm is that proofs advance through the source code (as opposed to flow backwards as in the weakest precondition calculus), making the proofs more intuitive. For real world languages, calculi capturing all language features tend to be large, with several hundreds of rules (including the axiomatisation of all data types). On the other hand, the full Java DL calculus realised as taclets in the KeY system provides a good starting point for axiomatising a language like Solidity. Several challenges of Ethereum/Solidity verification (see Sect. 4.1) need to be addressed in the development of such a calculus. For instance, the aforementioned transaction mechanism needs to be handled, to correctly model the roll back of all effects of a transaction once it is aborted. Here one can build on the fact that KeY-Java actually supports also JavaCard, a Java dialect featuring an abortable-transaction mechanism. Even if the transaction support of KeY-Java [27] is limited to method local transactions (whereas we need to support call-stack global transaction abortion), it provides a good starting point for smart contract transaction verification. A related issue is that the calculus must be able to verify robustness against gas-used-up exceptions. Another important aspect is that the calculus shall support *compositional* contract verification, by employing the *assume-guarantee* paradigm [33]. In our context, it means that a contract's compliance with its own specification is verified while assuming the other contracts' specification.[17] Here, one can build on concepts in KeY-ABS [11].

Finally, we aim for a *verification system*, able to perform practical source code level verification of smart contracts. Let us call that system SolidiKeY. For once, this requires the mechanisation of the aforementioned calculus. Here, one can take advantage of *taclets* [34], a domain specific language for writing and executing sequent calculus rules. In addition, what needs to be developed is the generation of proof obligations in Solidity DL from specifications, and strategies for high automation of the proof search. Such strategies are not only specific for the target language, but also for community specific programming pragmatics.

---

[16]Some deprecated and discouraged features of the language may not be supported. However, one should not exclude features simply because they are challenging for verification.

[17]But not without a small 'delay' of the considered communication, to prevent circular reasoning.

5 Discussion

In this paper, we have presented the opportunities brought forward by deductive analysis for smart contract verification. The case for the necessity of verification is increasingly being accepted in the software community, but in the case of smart contracts, the case becomes substantially stronger. Despite the typically small size of such programs (as compared to many software systems orders of magnitude larger), the fact that these contracts manipulate ownership of digital assets (typically in the form of cryptocurrency or tokens) and their immutability mean that bugs can be very costly. Ironically, unlike large systems which are typically built by teams of developers using mature software engineering practice, the small size of such contracts means that single, and not necessarily highly experienced developers, are sometimes responsible for their development.

We have argued for the need for verification at a business-logic level—ensuring that the software does what it is expected to do, and in particular, the desirability of code-structure level verification i.e. pre-/post-conditions and invariants. This is the level of abstraction at which deductive analysis gives added value. Let us contrast this with alternative means of approaching such verification.

Translate and verify: Firstly, one may ask whether building verification techniques specific to a high level language such as Solidity is necessary. Why not translate to another high level language already supported by deductive analysis tools and perform the verification on the translation? Such an approach is easier to achieve, and would still allow for verification of the types of properties we discuss in this paper—over these past months, in fact, we have been exploring the use of a Solidity-to-Java translation to verify smart contracts using the KeY verification tool for Java source code. (This will be reported elsewhere.) However, this approach comes with a number of disadvantages: (1) Verifying the translation is a major undertaking, even more so when no complete formal semantics of the source language exists. It is easy to make errors in the translation due to assumptions which may or may not hold, e.g., are the semantics of assignments in Solidity and Java equivalent?; (2) Solidity has a number of native domain-specific features, including failure and checkpointing (allowing a program to `revert` a transaction) and implicit resource management (like `payable` function calls and `transfer` of funds). Such domain specific features can be captured better by axiomatising them directly rather than coding them in syntactic sugar via another language.

Verification at a lower-level of abstraction: Given that high-level languages such as Solidity are compiled down to assembly code working on the underlying virtual machine, axiomatising the semantics of the EVM assembly and verifying at that level of abstraction comes with a number of benefits: (1) the verification is language-agnostic and can be performed on code compiled from any other high-level language; and (2) most of the smart contracts available on Ethereum *are not* accompanied by their source code, but would still be amenable to verification. Despite these advantages, VM-level code loses the structure which the developers used and which typically carries correspondence with the program's correctness logic. For instance, the condition of a while loop typically carries information which can be used to derive loop invariants, while conditional statements encode correctness corresponding to the dilemma rule. Also, this approach widens the gap between developers and the verification activity, as the verification is not performed on the source code developers write and understand. For instance, using the verification facility of KEVM, assertions must be formulated on the EVM level (see [18, Sect. 5.2]), which is very difficult, and hardly possible for source code developers. Another aspect often neglected in the literature is the need of specification languages which have at least the abstraction level of source code, ideally higher, but certainly not lower.

Despite the fact that our proposed approach will use the semantics of the language from a functional perspective, there are a number of limitations to correctness criteria which are covered by our approach. A certain class of smart contract attacks arise from transaction reordering, which may benefit a subset of the parties involved. There is little formal work addressing this issue [2, 35], but we note that it is difficult to encode within our proposed approach a formal model able to compare outcomes under malicious transaction reordering. (This would require analysis of quantitative hyper-properties, comparing the respective profit of different schedulings.) Similarly difficult to reason about (compositionally) are malicious attacks using non-functional aspects, particularly when accessing external contracts (e.g., reentrancy attacks which use gas consumption).

Despite these constraints, we believe that the correctness of smart contracts is a challenge for which no silver bullet exists. The functional correctness at the source code level is, however, an standing duck target for deductive reasoning. We believe that the limited degree of structural complexity of smart contracts, combined with the complex nature of correctness inherent to the interaction between different functions means that deductive verification can prove to be very effective in proving correctness of non-trivial intricate properties.

The outcome of the agenda we described here will contribute to the safety of the arising digital market places. By offering languages and methods for smart contract specification, users can understand better what a smart contract should do for them, and what it should not do, prior to using the contract. More importantly, the developed verification facilities provide strong guarantees to (potential) smart contract users that the specified properties are actually met, at the same time as they can warn users about incorrect contracts.

Acknowledgements The authors would like to thank Richard Bubel, Joshua Ellul, Raúl Pardo, and Vincent Rebiscoul for fruitful discussions about Solidity contracts and their verification.

References

1. A. Hern. *$300m in cryptocurrency accidentally lost forever due to bug*. Appeared at The Guardian https://www.theguardian.com/technology/2017/nov/08/cryptocurrency-300m-dollars-stolen-bug-ether. Nov. 2017.
2. T. Abdellatif and K. L. Brousmiche. "Formal Verification of Smart Contracts Based on Users and Blockchain Behaviors Models. In *2018 9th IFIP International Conference on New Technologies, Mobility and Security (NTMS)*. Feb. 2018, pp. 1–5. https://doi.org/10.1109/NTMS.2018.8328737.
3. Wolfgang Ahrendt et al., eds. *Deductive Software Verification—The KeY Book*. Vol. 10001. LNCS. Springer, 2016.
4. Wolfgang Ahrendt et al. "The KeY Platform for Verification and Analysis of Java Programs". In: *STTE'14*. Vol. 8471. LNCS. Springer, 2014, pp. 55–71. https://doi.org/10.1007/978-3-319-12154-3_4.
5. Nicola Atzei, Massimo Bartoletti, and Tiziana Cimoli. "A Survey of Attacks on Ethereum Smart Contracts (SoK)". In: *Proceedings of the 6th International Conference on Principles of Security and Trust*. Vol. 10204. LNCS. Springer, 2017. ISBN: 978-3-662-54454-9. URL: https://doi.org/10.1007/978-3-662-54455-6_8.
6. Xiaomin Bai et al. "Formal Modeling and Verification of Smart Contracts". In: *Proceedings of the 2018 7th International Conference on Software and Computer Applications*. ICSCA 2018. Kuantan, Malaysia: ACM, 2018, pp. 322–326. ISBN: 978-1-4503-5414-1. https://doi.org/10.1145/3185089.3185138. URL: http://doi.acm.org/10.1145/3185089.3185138.
7. Michael Barnett et al. "Boogie: A Modular Reusable Verifier for Object-Oriented Programs". In: *Formal Methods for Components and Objects, 4th International Symposium, FMCO 2005, Amsterdam, The Netherlands, 2005, Revised Lectures*. Ed. by Frank S. de Boer et al. Vol. 4111. LNCS. Springer, 2006.
8. Bernhard Beckert, Vladimir Klebanov, and Benjamin Weiß. "Dynamic Logic for Java". In: *Deductive Software Verification—The KeY Book*. Vol. 10001. LNCS. Springer, 2016.
9. Karthikeyan Bhargavan et al. "Formal Verification of Smart Contracts: Short Paper". In: *Proceedings of the 2016 ACM Workshop on Programming Languages and Analysis for Security*. PLAS '16. Vienna, Austria: ACM, 2016. ISBN: 978-1-4503-4574-3. https://doi.org/10.1145/2993600.2993611. URL: http://doi.acm.org/10.1145/2993600.2993611.
10. Lorenz Breidenbach et al. *An in-depth look at the parity multisig bug*. Appeared at "Hacking, Distributed" http://hackingdistributed.com/2017/07/22/deep-dive-parity-bug. June 2016.
11. Crystal Chang Din, Richard Bubel, and Reiner Hähnle. "KeY-ABS: A Deductive Verification Tool for the Concurrent Modelling Language ABS". In: *Automated Deduction - CADE-25*. Springer, 2015.
12. Joshua Ellul and Gordon J. Pace. "CONTRACTLARVA: Runtime Verification of Ethereum Smart Contracts". In: *submitted for review*. 2018.
13. Michael Fröwis and Rainer Böhme. "In Code We Trust?" In: *Data Privacy Management, Cryptocurrencies and Blockchain Technology*. Ed. by Joaquin Garcia-Alfaro et al. Vol. 10436. LNCS. 2017.
14. Luciano García-Bañuelos et al. "Optimized Execution of Business Processes on Blockchain". In: *Business Process Management*. Ed. by Josep Carmona, Gregor Engels, and Akhil Kumar. Vol. 10445. LNCS. 2017.
15. Stijn de Gouw et al. "OpenJDK's Java.utils.Collection.sort() Is Broken: The Good, the Bad and the Worst Case". In: *Computer Aided Verification - 27th International Conference, CAV 2015, San Francisco, USA, July 2015*. 2015.
16. Guido Governatori et al. "On legal contracts, imperative and declarative smart contracts, and blockchain systems". In: *Artificial Intelligence and Law* (Mar. 2018), pp. 1–33.
17. Ilya Grishchenko, Matteo Maffei, and Clara Schneidewind. "A Semantic Framework for the Security Analysis of Ethereum Smart Contracts". In: *POST*. Vol. 10804. Lecture Notes in Computer Science. Springer, 2018, pp. 243–269.

18. Everett Hildenbrandt et al. *KEVM: A Complete Semantics of the Ethereum Virtual Machine*. White paper. 2017. URL: http://hdl.handle.net/2142/97207.
19. Yoichi Hirai. "Defining the Ethereum Virtual Machine for Interactive Theorem Provers". In: *Financial Cryptography Workshops*. Vol. 10323. Lecture Notes in Computer Science. Springer, 2017, pp. 520–535.
20. Marieke Huisman et al. "Formal Specification with the Java Modeling Language". In: *Deductive Software Verification—The KeY Book*. Vol. 10001. LNCS. Springer, 2016.
21. Florian Idelberger et al. "Evaluation of Logic-Based Smart Contracts for Blockchain Systems". In: *Rule Technologies. Research, Tools, and Applications*. Ed. by Jose Julio Alferes et al. Vol. 9718. LNCS. Springer, 2016. ISBN: 978-3-319-42019-6.
22. Nikolai Kosmatov, Virgile Prevosto, and Julien Signoles. "A Lesson on Proof of Programs with Frama-C. Invited Tutorial Paper". In: *Tests and Proofs*. Ed. by Margus Veanes and Luca Viganò. Springer, 2013. ISBN: 978-3-642-38916-0.
23. Martin Leucker and Christian Schallhart. "A brief account of runtime verification". In: *The Jour. of Logic and Algebraic Progr.* 78.5 (2009). The 1st Workshop on Formal Languages and Analysis of Contract-Oriented Software (FLACOS'07), pp. 293–303. ISSN: 1567-8326.
24. Loi Luu et al. "Making Smart Contracts Smarter". In: *Proceedings of the 2016 ACM SIGSAC Conference on Computer and Communications Security*. CCS '16. Vienna, Austria: ACM, 2016, pp. 254–269. ISBN: 978-1-4503-4139-4. https://doi.org/10.1145/2976749.2978309. URL: http://doi.acm.org/10.1145/2976749.2978309.
25. Andrew Miller, Zhicheng Cai, and Somesh Jha. "Smart Contracts and Opportunities for Formal Methods". In: *ISoLA'18*. LNCS. To appear. Springer, 2018.
26. Mix. *Ethereum bug causes integer overflow in numerous ERC20 smart contracts (Update)*. Appeared at HardFork https://thenextweb.com/hardfork/2018/04/25/ethereum-smart-contract-integer-overflow/. Apr. 2018.
27. Wojciech Mostowski. "Verifying Java Card Programs". In: *Deductive Software Verification—The KeY Book*. Vol. 10001. LNCS. Springer, 2016.
28. Bernhard Mueller. "Smashing Ethereum Smart Contracts for Fun and Real Profit". In: *HITB SECCONF Amsterdam*. 2018.
29. Satoshi Nakamoto. "Bitcoin: A peer-to-peer electronic cash system". 2009. URL: http://bitcoin.org/bitcoin.pdf.
30. Ivica Nikolić et al. *Finding The Greedy, Prodigal, and Suicidal Contracts at Scale*. Unpublished, submitted, available at arXiv:1802.06038. 2018.
31. Christoph Prybila et al. "Runtime Verification for Business Processes Utilizing the Bitcoin Blockchain". In: *CoRR* abs/1706.04404 (2017). arXiv: 1706.04404. URL: http://arxiv.org/abs/1706.04404.
32. Haseeb Qureshi. *A hacker stole $31M of Ether - how it happened, and what it means for Ethereum*. Appeared at FreeCodeCamp https://medium.freecodecamp.org/a-hacker-stole-31m-of-ether-how-it-happened-and-what-it-means-for-ethereum-9e5dc29e33ce. July 2017.
33. Willem-Paul de Roever et al. *Concurrency Verification: Introduction to Compositional and Noncompositional Methods*. Cambridge University Press, 2001.
34. Philipp Rümmer and Mattias Ulbrich. "Proof Search with Taclets". In: *Deductive Software Verification—The KeY Book*. Vol. 10001. LNCS. Springer, 2016.
35. Ilya Sergey and Aquinas Hobor. "A Concurrent Perspective on Smart Contracts". In: *Financial Cryptography and Data Security*. Ed. by Michael Brenner et al. Vol. 10395. LNCS. Springer, 2017.
36. Ingo Weber et al. "Untrusted Business Process Monitoring and Execution Using Blockchain". In: *Formal Techniques for Distributed Systems*. Vol. 9850. LNCS. Springer, 2016.
37. David Z. Morris. *Blockchain-based venture capital fund hacked for $60 million*. Appeared at Fortune.com http://fortune.com/2016/06/18/blockchain-vc-fund-hacked. June 2016.

A Methodology for Invariants, Framing, and Subtyping in JML

Yuyan Bao and Gary T. Leavens

Abstract The Java Modeling Language (JML) is a specification language for describing the functional behavior of sequential Java program modules. The object-oriented features of Java make specifying invariants and framing difficult in the presence of subtyping. Using regions as a basis for a methodology, we precisely describe a technique for specifying invariants and framing in the presence of subtyping. We also extend JML by adding separating conjunction (from separation logic) for certain kinds of assertions.

1 Introduction

The Java Modeling Language (JML) [10] is a behavioral interface specification language for Java programs. Following the idea of *design by contract*, a specification is a "contract" [23] between clients and implementations. For a method, the contract is specified through *pre-, post-, and frame conditions*; for a class, the contract is specified using method contracts and *object invariants*.[1]

We use the example in Fig. 1 on the next page to introduce some of JML's specification features. The figure shows the JML specification of a class, Cell. The specification is written in the form of *annotation comments*. In JML, //@ starts a single-line annotation comment, and a longer specification can be written using /*@ ... @*/. Annotation comments just above a method definition give that

---

[1]Objects invariants are also called "class invariants" or "representation invariants".

Y. Bao
The Pennsylvania State University, University Park, PA, USA
e-mail: yxb88@ist.psu.edu

G. T. Leavens (✉)
University of Central Florida, Orlando, FL, USA
e-mail: leavens@cs.ucf.edu

© Springer Nature Switzerland AG 2018
P. Müller, I. Schaefer (eds.), *Principled Software Development*,
https://doi.org/10.1007/978-3-319-98047-8_2

```
1   public class Cell {
2     protected /*@ spec_public @*/ int val;
3
4     /*@ public invariant this.val >= 0;   @*/
5
6     /*@ public normal_behavior
7       @    assignable this.val;
8       @    ensures this.val == 0;
9       @*/
10    public Cell(){ this.val = 0;   }
11
12    /*@ public normal_behavior
13      @    requires v >= 0;
14      @    assignable this.val;
15      @    ensures this.val == v;    */
16    public void set(int v){ this.val = v; }
17
18    /*@ public normal_behavior
19      @    accessible this.val;
20      @    ensures \result == this.val;   */
21    public /*@ pure @*/ int get(){   return this.val;   }
22  }
```

Fig. 1 The JML specification of the class Cell with a model field

method's specification. Assertions in JML are written using Java expressions plus a few extensions.

Lines 12–15 in Fig. 1 specify the method set, as a **normal_behavior**, which rules out abrupt termination. The keywords **requires** and **ensures** specify pre- and postconditions respectively. The **assignable** clause specifies what the method can modify, i.e., its frame condition [9]. Similarly, the **accessible** clause on line 19 specifies the read frame of the pure method get. A *pure method*,[2] such as get, does not make any change to program states.

A class may have field names that should be hidden from its clients; e.g., the protected field val in Fig. 1 cannot be referenced by its non-privileged clients. Without such information hiding [28], when changing the field name, client code might also have to be changed. JML specifications follow the same principle [16]. For example, if val were not specified as spec_public, then one would not be able to specify set's frame condition by naming val in its assignable clause, as clients would not be able to see that field.

JML specifiers can respect information hiding by using model fields. A model field is an abstract view of an object's concrete field that can only be used in specifications. One can either declare a public model field directly, and use a **represents** clause to specify the mapping from concrete fields, or one can use the keyword **spec_public** to specify the common case where the value of the

---

[2]A pure method is also called a "query"; pure methods do not change program states, unlike commands.

model field is the same as the concrete field. For example, line 2 in Fig. 1 uses the keyword **spec_public** to implicitly declare a model field and a data group [21]. The concept of a data group will be explained shortly.

1.1 Framing Problems and Our Solutions

A goal of JML is to modularly and statically verify Java programs. Modular verification means that a program can be verified by using the specification of its components, and verified components need not be re-verified when the program adds more components [17, 24, 28]. This section focuses on JML's shortcomings for modular verification related to framing, invariants and subtyping, and sketches how we solve these problems, as described in detail in later sections of the paper.

1.1.1 Dynamically-Allocated Memory

Dynamically-allocated objects, in particular recursive data structures, are challenging for modular verification of framing, because of the difficulty in specifying the frames of such objects. Thus far, JML's solution to this problem has been to adopt the Universe Type System (UTS) [25] that structures objects into a hierarchy of disjoint groups, called *contexts*. In the UTS, there is a root context. Consider the linked list example in Figs. 2 and 3. In LinkedList, the object head owns all the nodes that constitute the list as shown in Fig. 4, which is adapted from the work of Müller et al. [25]. Those nodes are the representation of the type LinkedList.

In this ownership model, an owner object controls the access to its context; one can only access those objects through its owner. Thus, if a change happens inside

```
1   //@ model import org.jmlspecs.models.*;
2   public class Node {
3     //@ public model JMLObjectSequence values;
4     protected /*@ readonly @*/ Object elem;
5     protected Node next;//@ in values;maps next.values \into values;
6     /*@ protected represents values =
7       @    (next == null ? new JMLObjectSequence(elem)
8       @                   : next.values.insertFront(elem));   @*/
9     /*@   requires nxt != null;
10      @     ensures this.values.equals(nxt.values.insertFront(v));
11      @ also
12      @     ensures nxt == null
13      @           ==> this.values.equals(new JMLObjectSequence(v)); @*/
14    public Node(/*@readonly@*/ Object v, /*@nullable@*/ Node nxt) {
15      elem = v; next = nxt;
16    }
17  }
```

Fig. 2 JML specification of the class Node using the UTS

```
1    //@ model import org.jmlspecs.models.JMLObjectSequence;
2    public class LinkedList{
3
4       //@ public model JMLObjectSequence listValue;
5       protected /*@ rep @*/ Node head;    //@ in listValue;
6       protected int size; //@ in listValue;
7                           //@ maps head.values \into listValue;
8       //@ public invariant size() == listValue.int_size();
9
10      /*@ protected represents listValue = (head == null
11       @                      ? new JMLObjectSequence() : head.values); @*/
12
13      /*@ public normal_behavior
14       @    assignable listValue;
15       @    ensures listValue != null && listValue.isEmpty();
16       @    ensures listValue.int_size() == size();   @*/
17      public LinkedList(){   head = null;   size = 0; }
18
19      /*@ public normal_behavior
20       @    requires o != null;
21       @    assignable listValue;
22       @    ensures listValue.equals(\old(listValue.insertFront(o))); @*/
23      public void add(/*@ readonly @*/ Object o) {
24          head = new Node(o, head); size++;
25      }
26
27      public /*@ pure @*/ int size(){    return size;  }
28  }
```

Fig. 3 JML specification of the class LinkedList using the UTS

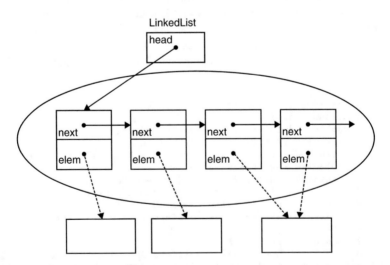

Fig. 4 An ownership model of a linked list. The oval denotes a context. The area outside the oval is its parent context. The owner object sits atop the context it owns. Nodes within the context are owned by the context's owner. The elements are outside the oval, thus, are not owned by the context's owner

one context, a property that depends on another context is preserved, as these are disjoint groups of objects.

To enforce the ownership model, JML uses the modifier **rep** to indicate that an object is a constituent of the declaring type's representation, and the invariant of the declaring type depends on the constituent object. In the example of the type LinkedList in Fig. 3, the modifier **rep** means that the context rooted by the object head is a constituent of the type LinkedList's representation. And the invariant of a list depends on the objects in this context. And these objects can be read and written through LinkedList's methods. On the other hand, JML uses the modifier **readonly** to indicate an object is not a constituent of the declaring type's representation, e.g., line 23 in Fig. 3 means those constituent objects do not contain the object o, and the invariant of a list does not depend on it either.

Problem: The UTS requires objects to be hierarchically partitioned so that the dependencies induced by object invariants do not cross ownership boundaries [6]. However, the UTS lacks flexibility to handle objects who are "friends" [6].

Consider the example in Figs. 5 and 6 adapted from the work of Drossopoulou et al. [12]. A Person has an account and a salary, and an Account has a holder, a balance and an interestRate. The invariant of the class Person depends on account.balance, but an account does not own it holder. Otherwise a person could not have more than one account. In this case, the ownership relation is not suitable.

Solution: For local reasoning about shared, mutable data structures, advances have been made by recent works, e.g., separation logic [13, 29] and dynamic frame approaches [2, 4, 14, 20, 30, 32]. In this paper, we adopt the approach of dynamic frames, but we also extend assertions with separating conjunction. In addition to using ghost fields to dynamically compute regions (sets of locations), dynamic

```
1   public class Account {
2       protected Person holder;
3       protected int balance, interestRate;
4
5
6       /*@ protected invariant balance < 0 ==>
7        @                       interestRate == 0; @*/
8
9       // constructor and other methods are omitted
10
11      public void withdraw(int amount) {
12          balance = balance - amount;
13          if (balance < 0){
14              interestRate = 0;
15              holder.getNotified();
16          }
17      }
18  }
```

Fig. 5 An account example adapted from the work of Drossopoulou et al. [12]

```
1   public class Person {
2     protected Account account;
3     protected int salary;
4
5     // constructor and other methods are omitted
6
7     /*@ protected invariant account.balance + salary > 0; @*/
8
9
10    public void spend(int amount){
11       account.withdraw(amount);
12    }
13
14    public void getNotified(){ /* ... */ }
15  }
```

Fig. 6 The class `Person` for the account example

frames can be computed implicitly by a **reads** function that returns memory locations on which the value of an assertion or a predicate may depend. A predicate is a pure Boolean method.

1.1.2 Object Invariants

Another problem for modular reasoning with JML is its visible state semantics for object invariants. JML uses the keyword **invariant** to specify invariants that impose consistency conditions on objects. JML uses the so-called *visible state semantics* [19]; this semantics means that an object invariant is intended to hold in the postcondition of each constructor and in the pre- and post-states of other (non-helper[3]) methods. For example, the invariant of the class `Account` in Fig. 5 is specified in lines 5–6. It means that if an account balance is negative, then its interest rate is 0. The invariant of the class `Person` is specified in line 5 in Fig. 6. It means that the sum of the account balance and the person's salary is greater than 0.

Problem: The visible state semantics allows an object invariant to be temporarily violated within the object's methods, but since the invariant must hold at the start of all (non-helper) methods, the invariant must be re-established before any other method may be called, so as to avoid a call back to the object finding the object in a state in which the invariant does not hold [25]. Consider the examples in Figs. 5 and 6. A person p executes its method `spend`, which invokes the method `account.withdraw`, and eventually calls back to `p.getNotified`. However, p's invariant may not hold when `p.getNotified` is called.

---

[3] A helper method in JML is one for which the invariant is not assumed and need not be established.

Solution: In this paper, instead of using the visible state semantics, we propose to use ghost fields to denote different states that an object may have in its lifetime. Each state is defined by a set of invariants. A method contract explicitly specifies the state that allows the method to be called in precondition and the state after the call ends. Our solution is inspired by the work on typestates [11]. Similar approaches have been taken by Spec♯ [7] and the KeY tool [32], which instrument a distinguished variable `inv` to state explicitly where the invariants are expected to be satisfied. We allow one to declare multiple states with meaningful state names, not just one state `inv`, so that it is helpful for improving software design [31].

1.1.3 Dynamic Method Calls

Dynamic method calls also pose challenges to modularity. *Supertype abstraction* verifies dynamically-dispatched method calls by using the specification from the receiver's static type, which may be a supertype of the receiver's exact dynamic type [18]. Validity of supertype abstraction is ensured by *behavioral subtyping* [1, 22], in which each overridden method obeys the specifications declared in its supertypes, i.e., subtype specifications refine their supertype's.

JML enforces behavioral subtyping by specification inheritance [15]. A method may be specified by a set of *specification cases*; each specification case consists of pre-, post- and frame conditions. A correct implementation must satisfy all the specification cases, which is the join of them [15]. For example, the method `set` in Fig. 7 has a specification case declared with the keyword **also**. This specification case is combined with the specification case from its supertype in Fig. 1, so that the method `set` is specified with two specification cases.

JML adopts data groups [21] to allow overriding methods to modify additional states introduced by subclasses. As described previously, the type `Cell` introduces a data group `val` in Fig. 1. The method `Cell.set`'s frame condition allows locations in the data group `val` to be modified. The data group `val` only contains one location **this**.`val` to the type `Cell`. Its subtype `ReCell` inherits the data

```
1   public class ReCell extends Cell {
2     protected /*@ spec_public @*/ int bak;   //@ in val;
3
4     /*@ also
5       @    public normal_behavior
6       @      requires v >= 0;
7       @      assignable this.val;
8       @      ensures this.bak == \old(this.val); @*/
9     public void set(int v) {
10       this.bak = this.val;
11       this.val = v;
12    }
13  }
```

Fig. 7 The JML specification of the class `ReCell`

group `val`, and adds one more location to it by using the **in** clause in line 2. The frame condition of the overriding method `set` (line 9) allows the method to change the locations in the data group `val`, which are **this**.`val` and **this**.`bak`.

Problem: The approach of data groups is sound if the additional fields added to the inherited data groups are a primitive type. A methodology is needed to handle reference types.

Solution: This paper's methodology, described in Sect. 4, addresses the case where the additional fields have a reference type.

1.2 Contribution

This section summarizes our contributions as follows:

1. Instead of using the UTS, we adopt the approach of the dynamic frames. We introduce a primitive type **region** to JML, and introduce a function **reads** that computes memory locations on which the value of an assertion or a predicate may depend. Also, we extend the assertions with separating conjunction which allows a concise way to express disjointness.
2. Instead of using a global protocol, we adopt the idea of typestates by using ghost fields. This approach provides a programmatic and flexible way to specify an object invariant.
3. We extend the approach of data groups by allowing members with a reference type to be added to an inherited data group in subtypes.

1.3 Outline

The next section presents the dynamic frame approach tailored for JML. Section 3 presents the approach to specify an object invariant. Section 4 presents the solution to allow additional fields with reference type to be modified by subclasses. Section 5 discusses the related work. Section 6 provides the conclusion of this paper.

2 Dynamic Frames in JML

This section proposes an approach to reasoning about mutable recursive data structures. It is inspired by the approach of the dynamic frames [14], region logic [2, 4] and the KeY tool [32]. We introduce a primitive type **region** to JML, and use ghost fields to track dynamically-allocated memory locations. We also extend the assertions with separating conjunction, which allows a concise way to express disjointness. In addition, we introduce a function **reads** that computes memory locations on which the value of an assertion or a predicate may depend.

2.1 New Type `region`

In this section, we define an extension of JML expressions. In Fig. 8, the syntactic category *spec-expression*, written P in this paper, denotes JML specification expressions, which are defined in the JML reference manual [19]. For convenience, we use the syntactic category E to denote a subset of JML expressions that do not depend on the heap, and on which extended expressions are well-defined.

Our extension introduces a primitive type `region` to JML as shown in Fig. 8. Over-lines indicate possible empty sequences. An expression with type `region` denotes sets of memory locations; each location is a pair of an allocated object and its field name. Heaps can be thought of mathematically as partial functions that map locations to values. The expression `region{x.f}` denotes a singleton set of location where $x.f$ is stored. The expression `region{a[i]}` denotes a singleton set of location where the ith element of the array a is stored. The expression `region{a[i..j]}` denotes the set of locations that store a range of an array from the ith element to the jth element. The expression `region{a[*]}` denotes the set of locations that store all the elements of the array a. The expression `region{x.*}` denotes the set of locations that store all the fields of the object x. The expression $E ? R_1 : R_2$ is stateful; it means that if E is true, then the expression is R_1, otherwise the expression is R_2 [4]. The operators, $+$, $-$ and $*$ denote union, difference and intersection respectively.

As the class `Object` is the root of the class hierarchy in Java, we introduce a built-in field `fpt` to the class `Object` shown in Fig. 9. The field, `fpt`, is a model field with type `region`, which stores the locations of a class's representation. The value of a model field is specified by a **represents** clause. The following is the syntax for **represents** clauses.

$$
\begin{aligned}
\textit{spec-expression}, P &::= \cdots \mid R \\
E &::= n \mid x \mid \texttt{null} \mid \texttt{true} \mid \texttt{false} \mid E_1 \oplus E_2 \mid E_1 \otimes E_2 \\
R &::= x \mid \texttt{region\{\}} \mid \texttt{region\{}\textit{SRE}\texttt{\}} \mid f(\overline{E}) \mid E \ ? \ R_1 : R_2 \mid R_1 + R_2 \\
&\quad \mid R_1 - R_2 \mid R_1 * R_2 \\
\textit{SRE} &::= x.f \mid x.* \mid x[\textit{IR}] \\
\textit{IR} &::= E_1 .. E_2 \mid * \\
\oplus &::= + \mid - \mid * \mid / \mid \% \\
\otimes &::= == \mid \ != \ \mid <= \mid >= \mid > \mid <
\end{aligned}
$$

Fig. 8 The abstract syntax of JML specification expressions, showing the new **region** expressions. We typically use P instead of *spec-expression* in this paper

```
1   public class Object {
2       //@ public model region fpt;
3       /* ... other declarations as before ... */
4   }
```

Fig. 9 The class `Object` has a built-in field `fpt`

$represents\text{-}clause$ ::= **represents** g = RCE ;
RCE ::= P | R | **reads**(P)

where g is a model field, P is an assertion and **reads** is a function that computes the locations where P's value depends. We discuss the function **reads** in Sect. 2.3.

2.2 Supporting Separating Conjunction

One drawback of specifications written in the style of dynamic frames approaches is that they lack conciseness when specifying disjoint parts of a heap. For example, $x.f \mapsto 5 * y.f \mapsto 6$ in separation logic specifies the values of $x.f$ and $y.f$ and also that these two locations are disjoint. However, in the dynamic frames style approach, it is written as $x.f == 5$ && $y.f == 5$ && (**region**$\{x.f\}$!!**region**$\{y.f\}$), where the operator ! ! means disjointness, which is less concise and tedious.

Thus, we propose to add three more assertions to JML assertions shown in Fig. 10. The assertion $R_1 <= R_2$ checks that R_1 is a subset of R_2. The assertion R_1 ! ! R_2 checks that R_1 and R_2 are disjoint. The assertion P_1 &*& P_2 means that P_1 and P_2 hold on disjoint sets of memory locations. The operator &*& is *well-defined* on a subset of JML assertions, called supported assertions [3, 5].

A supported assertion is one where, for a given heap, if the assertion is true, then there is a smallest subheap where it is true [26]. Syntactically, a supported assertion restricts the premise of an implication to be heap-independent. A heap-independent assertion is the one whose value does not rely on heaps. For example, $x.f == 5$ is not heap-independent, but $x == 5$ is. So x.f == 5 ==> z.f == 7 is not supported, but x == 5 ==> z.f == 7 is. A supported negation (!P) requires P to be heap-independent. A supported disjunction ($P_1 || P_2$) requires P_1 to be heap-independent, because $P_1 || P_2$ can be encoded to !$P_1 \Rightarrow P_2$. A supported conjunction (P_1 && P_2) requires both P_1 and P_2 to be supported. A supported existential assertion requires that the existential is witnessed by a particular field in the heap or a variable in the store. For example, $\exists y :: x.f == y$ && P is supported if P is; similarly $\exists y :: x == y$ && P is supported if P is. Assertions $R_1!!R_2$ and $R_1 <= R_2$ are both supported. Our supported assertions roughly correspond with those handled by most separation logic tools.

$$P ::= \cdots \mid R_1!!R_2 \mid R_1{<=}R_2 \mid P_1\&{*}\&P_2$$

Fig. 10 The abstract syntax of some assertions added to JML

2.3 A Read Effect Function

Recall that, from Sect. 2.1, a field `fpt` is introduced to each type to store the locations in that type's representation. Its value is defined by a **represents** clause that provides its value as a region. One way to do this is to use an expression of the form **reads**(P), where P might be the class's object invariant.

In general, the read effect of an assertion is specified by an **accessible** clause. It approximates the locations that the value of the assertion depends on. If P is a predicate, then its read effect is the read effect of the predicate body. Thus, **reads**(P) returns what P's **accessible** clause specifies. However, if a predicate's body returns the value of a supported assertion, then the read effect of its body can be syntactically computed. In this case, the **accessible** clause could be omitted.

Figure 11 defines what **reads** does for some JML expressions and assertions. We assume a partial function, α, which maps a pure method name to its read effects, which is a region expression. The read effect of a region expression is an empty set since region expressions are heap-independent. The read effect of a supported negation assertion ($!P$) is an empty set as P is heap-independent. Similarly, the read effect of a supported disjunction ($P_1 || P_2$) is the read effect of P_2 as P_1 is heap-independent. If P is not supported, then **reads**(P) is a type error.

2.4 Example

This section illustrates the above proposed approach with an example. Figures 12 and 13 specify a linked list of nodes. `LinkedList` uses the built-in model field `fpt` to abstract the concrete locations in which the representation of a list is stored. The value of the model field `fpt` is defined by the **represents** clause, where the **reads** function computes the locations where the value of the predicate `list` depends on. The predicate `list` uses separating conjunction to describe disjointness of its constituent nodes. And there is no need to specify its read effects as they are syntactically computed.

$$\mathbf{reads}(E) = \mathbf{region}\{\}$$
$$\mathbf{reads}(x.f == E) = \mathbf{region}\{x.f\}$$
$$\mathbf{reads}(R_1 <= R_2) = \mathbf{reads}(R_1) + \mathbf{reads}(R_2)$$
$$\mathbf{reads}(P_1 \,\&\&\, P_2) = \mathbf{reads}(P_1) + \mathbf{reads}(P_2)$$
$$\mathbf{reads}(P_1 \&*\& P_2) = \mathbf{reads}(P_1) + \mathbf{reads}(P_2)$$
$$\mathbf{reads}(\exists y :: x.f == y \,\&\&\, P) = \mathbf{region}\{x.f\} + \mathbf{reads}(P)[x.f/y]$$

$$\mathbf{reads}(R) = \mathbf{region}\{\}$$
$$\mathbf{reads}(R_1 !! R_2) = \mathbf{reads}(R_1) + \mathbf{reads}(R_2)$$
$$\mathbf{reads}(!P) = \mathbf{region}\{\}$$
$$\mathbf{reads}(P_1 || P_2) = \mathbf{reads}(P_2)$$
$$\mathbf{reads}(p(\overline{E})) = \alpha(p)[\overline{E}/\overline{x}]$$

Fig. 11 The read effects of expressions, region expressions, and supported assertions

```
1    //@ model import org.jmlspecs.models.*;
2    public class Node {
3      protected /*@ spec_public @*/ Object elem;
4      protected /*@ spec_public @*/ Node next;
5
6      /*@ public normal_behavior
7        @ assignable region{this.*};
8        @ ensures this.elem == v && this.next == nxt;   @*/
9      public Node(Object v, /*@nullable@*/ Node nxt){
10       this.elem = v;
11       this.next = nxt;
12     }
13   }
```

Fig. 12 A JML specification of the class Node using the new approach

The specification uses a JMLObjectSequence ghost field to store the list's abstract value.[4] The class declares one method add. Its postcondition states that the method adds the passing object to the front of the list, i.e., the assertion

```
listValue.equals(\old(listValue).insertFront(v)).
```

Moreover, the representation of the added object is not part of the list's representation, i.e., the assertion this.fpt!!v.fpt.

3   Object Invariants

An object invariant describes the consistent states of the object through several assertions. During an object's lifetime, some of these assertions may be broken. Thus, an invariant is usually specified by disjunctions of assertions [8]. The constituent assertions of the disjunction indicate the different states that the object may have in its lifetime. However, it is non-trivial to tell which state an object is in when such invariants are complex.

Our methodology uses Boolean-valued ghost fields to represent the states that an object may have. Each object's state is described by logical formulas. For example, in Figs. 14 and 15. An Account may have two states: normal and warning, and a Person may also have two states: healthyFinance or not; these states are declared with ghost fields (in line 4 of each class).

In Fig. 14, lines 6–7 mean that when an Account is in the state normal, the invariant balance >= 0 && interestRate > 0 is true. Lines 9–10 mean that when an Account is in the state warning, then the invariant for that state holds: balance < 0 && interestRate == 0. In Fig. 15, lines 8–9 mean that if the

---

[4] JMLObjectSequence is defined in the JML library.

```
1  //@ model import org.jmlspecs.models.JMLObjectSequence;
2  public class LinkedList {
3    protected   Node head;
4    //@ public ghost JMLObjectSequence listValue;
5    /*@ protected represents fpt =
6    @                   reads(list(head, listValue)); @*/
7
8    //@ public ghost boolean valid;
9    //@ protected invariant valid <==> list(head, listValue);
10
11   /*@ measured_by se.int_size();
12   @ protected predicate list(Node n,
13   @                               JMLObjectSequence se) {
14   @    return (n == null ==> se.int_size() == 0) &*&
15   @           (n != null ==> se.get(0) == n.elem &*&
16   @            list(n.next, se.removePrefix(1)));
17   @ } @*/
18   /*@ public normal_behavior
19   @    assignable region{this.*};
20   @    ensures listValue.int_size() == 0 && valid @*/
21   public LinkedList() {
22     this.head = null;
23     //@ set listValue = new JMLObjectSequence();
24     //@ set valid = true;
25   }
26   /*@ public normal_behavior
27   @    requires valid;
28   @    assignable fpt, region{this.valid};
29   @    ensures fresh(region{head.*});
30   @    ensures valid;
31   @    ensures
32   @       listValue.equals(\old(listValue).insertFront(v));
33   @    ensures this.fpt!!v.fpt;  @*/
34   public void add(Object v){
35     //@ set valid = false;
36     head = new Node(v, head);
37     //@ set listValue = listValue.insertFront(v);
38     //@ set valid = true;
39   }
40 }
```

Fig. 13 A JML specification of the class LinkedList using the new approach

invariant account.balance + salary > 0 is true, then the object is in the state healthyFinance.

Instead of using the visible state semantics, we propose following the Boogie methodology [7] where invariants must hold in all states. A method's pre- and postcondition explicitly specify which state the object is in. Line 15 in Fig. 14 means that the method withdraw can be called only when the account is in

```
1   public class Account {
2     protected Person holder;
3     protected int balance, interestRate;
4     //@ public ghost boolean normal, warning;
5
6     /*@ public invariant normal <==>
7       @   (balance >= 0 && interestRate > 0);
8       @
9       @ public invariant warning <==>
10      @   (balance < 0 && interestRate == 0); @*/
11
12    // constructor and other methods are omitted
13
14    /*@ public normal_behavior
15      @ requires normal && holder.healthyFinance;
16      @ ensures normal || warning; @*/
17    public void withdraw(int amount) {
18      //@ set normal = false;
19      //@ set holder.healthyFinance = false;
20      balance = balance - amount;
21      if (balance < 0){
22        interestRate = 0;
23        holder.getNotified();
24        //@ set warning = true;
25      } else {
26        //@ set normal = true;
27      }
28    }
29  }
```

Fig. 14 An account example adapted from the work of Drossopoulou et al. [12]. Most of specifications that describe the functional behaviors of methods are omitted

the state `normal` and its holder is in the state `healthyFinance`. We use the `set` statement to change the state of the object. For example, in the body of the method `withdraw`, the account exits the state `normal` (line 18 of Fig. 14) and the holder exits the state `healthyFinance` (line 19). And the holder's method `getNotified` can be called as it does not require it to be in the state of `healthyFinance`.

4   Dynamic Method Calls

JML enforces behavioral subtyping through specification inheritance [15]. This allows an overriding method to modify additional fields introduced in subtypes by using data groups from Leino's work [21]. However, Leino's work only addresses the problem with primitive type (e.g., an integer or a Boolean).

Our methodology enforces an *encapsulation constraint:* a location is allowed to be added to a data group in a derived class only if the location is encapsulated.

```
1   public class Person {
2     protected  Account account;
3     protected  int salary;
4     //@ public ghost boolean healthyFinance;
5
6     // constructor and other methods are omitted
7
8     /*@ protected invariant healthyFinance
9        @   <==> account.balance + salary > 0; @*/
10
11    /*@ public normal_behavior
12       @   requires healthyFinance;   @*/
13    public void spend(int amount){
14       account.withdraw(amount);
15    }
16
17    public void getNotified(){ /* ... */ }
18  }
```

Fig. 15 The class Person for the account example

```
1   public class Box {
2     protected int val;
3
4     //@ protected represents fpt = region{this.val};
5     //@ public model region eff;
6     //@ protected represents eff = region{this.val};
7
8     /*@ public normal_behavior
9        @ assignable eff;        @*/
10    public void set(int v){ this.val = v; }
11
12    /*@ public normal_behavior
13       @ accessible eff;        @*/
14    public /*@ pure @*/ int get() { return this.val; }
15  }
```

Fig. 16 The specification of the class Box with its model field eff

There are three requirements that make up this encapsulation constraint, which are motivated by three representative subclasses shown in this section. These examples use the class Box in Fig. 16 as their super class. We use a region eff to specify the write effect of the method set and the read effect of the method get. Our methodology requires the data group eff to be a subset of its footprint fpt.

Figure 17 shows a client of Box, where a method usingBox checks the return value of b2.get after b1.set is invoked. The assertion is true as the precondition b1 != b2 guarantees that b1.eff and b2.eff are disjoint, since b1.eff <= b1.fpt and b2.eff <= b2.fpt due to our methodology.

The first representative subclass involves *argument exposure*. It happens when part of a type T's representation is aliased with a client's object, which occurs as an argument of one of T's methods. In Fig. 18, we define a derived class ArgBox.

```
 1   public class Client {
 2     /*@ public normal_behavior
 3       @ requires b1 != b2;
 4       @ assignable b1.eff, b2.eff;   @*/
 5     public static void usingBox(Box b1, Box b2) {
 6       int tmp = b2.get();
 7       b1.set(1);
 8       //@ assert b2.get() == tmp;
 9     }
10   }
```

Fig. 17 A client code of the class Box

```
 1   public class ArgBox extends Box {
 2     protected Box arg;
 3
 4     /*@ protected represents
 5       @   fpt = super.fpt + region{this.arg} + arg.fpt; @*/
 6     /*@ protected represents
 7       @   eff = super.eff + region{arg.val}; @*/
 8
 9     /*@ public normal_behavior
10       @ assignable fpt;
11       @ ensures b.fpt <= this.fpt;   @*/
12     public ArgBox(Box b) { super(); this.arg = b;   }
13
14     /*@ public normal_behavior
15       @ assignable eff;   @*/
16     public void set(int v){ super.set(v); arg.set(v); }
17   }
```

Fig. 18 The Specification of the class ArgBox

The override of the method set would allow a client to modify the additional location **region**{arg.val} because this location is in the data group eff (Line 7). However, Line 7 violates the encapsulation constraint, because the field arg is aliased with the reference to an object passed through the constructor. Consequently, behavioral subtyping would be violated. The following client code shows the violation.

```
Box b=new Box(); ArgBox ab=new ArgBox(b); Client.usingBox(ab,b);
```

By the postcondition of ArgBox's constructor, we know that b.fpt <= ab.fpt. After the objects ab and b are passed to the method usingBox, the assertion in Fig. 17 would fail because ab.eff and b.fpt would be overlapping.

Another representative subclass relates to *representation exposure*. It happens when part of a type T's representation is aliased by a client through T's methods' return values. In Fig. 19, we define a derived class RepBox. The override of the method set would allow a client to modify the additional location **region**{brep.val}, because this location is in the data group eff (Line 6). However, Line 6 violates the encapsulation constraint, because the field brep

```
1   public class RepBox extends Box {
2     protected Box brep;
3     /*@ protected represents
4       @   fpt = super.fpt + region{this.brep} + brep.fpt; @*/
5     /*@ protected represents
6       @   eff = super.eff + region{brep.val}; @*/
7
8     /*@ public normal_behavior
9       @ assignable fpt;   @*/
10    public RepBox(){
11      brep = new Box();
12    }
13
14    /*@ public normal_behavior
15      @ assignable eff;   @*/
16    public void set(int v){ super.set(v); brep.set(v); }
17
18    /*@ public normal_behavior
19      @ accessible fpt;
20      @ ensures \result.fpt <= fpt;   @*/
21    public Box leak(){ return this.brep; }
22  }
```

Fig. 19 The Specification of the class RepBox

would be aliased with a client's object through the method leak. Consequently, behavioral subtyping would be violated, as the following client code shows.

```
RepBox rb=new RepBox(); Box b=rb.leak(); Client.usingBox(rb,b);
```

By the postcondition of the method leak, we know that b.fpt <= rb.fpt. After the objects rb and b are passed to the method usingBox, the assertion in Fig. 17 fails because rb.eff and b.fpt may be overlapping.

The last representative subclasses explain the problem of sharing between a superclass and its subclasses, which we call *ancestor exposure*. In Fig. 20, we define a derived class SBox. It inherits the field val, the methods set and get. In addition, it declares a new field sbb of type Box, and defines a new method get2 that returns the value of sbb.val. The specification introduces a new data group dg and lists it in the accessible clause of the new method get2.

Figure 21 shows a client of SBox, where a method usingSBox checks the return value of sb.get2 after sb.set is invoked. The assertion is true as sb.effs !! sb.dg.

Figure 22 declares a class XBox as a subclass of SBox. It has an additional field xbb, which is aliased with the inherited field sbb in the constructor. The override of the method set would allow clients to modify the location **region**{xbb.val}. Thus, this location is added to the location set eff, which violates the SBox's invariant effs !! dg. This example also violates behavioral subtyping. The following client code shows the violation.

```
XBox xb=new XBox(); Client2.usingSBox(xb);
```

```
1    public class SBox extends Box {
2      protected Box sbb;
3
4      /*@ protected represents fpt =
5        @          super.fpt + region{this.sbb} + sbb.fpt; @*/
6      //@ public model region dg;
7      //@ protected represents dg = region{sbb.val};
8      //@ public invariant effs !! dg;
9
10     /*@ public normal_behavior
11       @ assignable fpt; @*/
12     public SBox(){ sbb = new Box(); }
13
14     /*@ public normal_behavior
15       @ accessible dg; @*/
16     public /*@ pure @*/ int get2() { return sbb.get(); }
17   }
```

Fig. 20 The JML specification of the class SBox

```
1    public class Client2 {
2      /*@ public normal_behavior
3        @ requires sb != null;
4        @ assignable sb.eff;   @*/
5      public static void usingSBox(SBox sb) {
6        int tmp = sb.get2();
7        sb.set(1);
8        //@ assert sb.get2() == tmp;
9      }
10   }
```

Fig. 21 A client code of the class SBox

```
1    public class XBox extends SBox {
2      protected Box xbb;
3
4      /*@ protected represents
5        @   fpt = super.fpt + region{this.xbb} + xbb.fpt; @*/
6      /*@ protected represents
7        @   eff = super.eff + region{xbb.val};   @*/
8
9      /*@ public normal_behavior
10       @ assignable fpt;      @*/
11     public XBox(){ super(); xbb = sbb; }
12
13     /*@ public normal_behavior
14       @ assignable eff;      @*/
15     public void set(int v){ super.set(v); xbb.set(v); }
16   }
```

Fig. 22 The JML specification of the class XBox

After the objects xb is passed to the method usingSBox, the assertion in Fig. 21 would fail because xb.eff and xb.dg would be overlapping.

As method calls and assignments are the primitive actions in a language like Java, preventing these actions from breaching encapsulation will allow our methodology to assume that footprints of distinct objects do not intersect. Preventing argument and representation exposure will prevent problems arising from method calls, and preventing ancestor exposure prevents the remaining problems with assignments.

5 Related Work

In addition to the related work discussed in the introduction, Parkinson and Bierman [27] handle different types of inheritance by introducing abstract predicate families, based on the formalism of second-order separation logic. In their specification language, each method has two specifications: one static and one dynamic. Dynamic specifications follow the behavioral subtyping criteria defined in Leavens and Naumann's work [17]. Encapsulation is implicit in separation logic, due to its frame rule, in which a predicate α can be required to be separate from a predicate P when $\alpha * P$. Our methodology explicitly expresses encapsulation, which is more flexible when there is the possibility of some sharing.

6 Conclusion

We propose to replace the UTS with a refined dynamic frames approach to allow a more flexible modular verification technique. Our approach is based on the theory of dynamic frames, region logic and the KeY tool, which uses ghost fields to denote heap regions. We allow specification in the style of separation logic: separating conjunction and recursive predicates can be used in a limited way.

To avoid the drawbacks of the visible semantics for object invariants, we proposed to use ghost fields to represent the states of an object and explicitly specify the transition of the states in a method contract.

To allow an overriding method to modify additional reference type fields, the proposed methodology enforces an encapsulation constraint. This constraint prevents argument exposure, representation exposure, and ancestor exposure. We leave the soundness proof of this methodology as future work.

References

1. Pierre America. *A Behavioural Approach to Subtyping in Object-Oriented Programming Languages*. Tech. rep. 443. Revised from the January 1989 version. Nederlandse Philips Bedrijven B. V.: Philips Research Laboratories, Apr. 1989.
2. Anindya Banerjee, David A. Naumann, and Stan Rosenberg. "Local Reasoning for Global Invariants, Part I: Region Logic". In: *Journal of the ACM* 60.3 (June 2013), 18:1–18:56. ISSN: 0004-5411. https://doi.org/10.1145/2485982. URL: http://doi.acm.org/10.1145/2485982.
3. Yuyan Bao. "Reasoning About Frame Properties in Object-Oriented Programs". PhD thesis. University of Central Florida, 2017. URL: http://www.cs.ucf.edu/~ybao/tech-reports/TR_dissertation.pdf.
4. Yuyan Bao, Gary T. Leavens, and Gidon Ernst. "Conditional Effects in Fine-grained Region Logic". In: *Proceedings of the 17th Workshop on Formal Techniques for Java-like Programs*. FTfJP '15. Prague, Czech Republic: ACM, 2015, 5:1–5:6. ISBN: 978-1-4503-3656-7. https://doi.org/10.1145/2786536.2786537. URL: http://doi.acm.org/10.1145/2786536.2786537.
5. Yuyan Bao, Gary T. Leavens, and Gidon Ernst. "Unifying Separation Logic and Region Logic to Allow Interoperability". In: *Formal Aspects of Computing* 30.3 (Aug. 2018), pp. 381–441.
6. Mike Barnett and David Naumann. "Friends Need a Bit More: Maintaining Invariants Over Shared State". In: *Mathematics of Program Construction (MPC)*. Ed. by Dexter Kozen. Vol. 3125. Lecture Notes in Computer Science. Springer-Verlag, July 2004, pp. 54–84. URL: http://www.springerlink.com/content/6gt28um7j5jgra12.
7. Mike Barnett et al. "Verification of Object-Oriented Programs with Invariants". In: *Journal of Object Technology* 3.6 (2004), pp. 27–56. URL: http://tinyurl.com/m2a8j.
8. Kevin Bierhoff and Jonathan Aldrich. "Lightweight Object Specification with Typestates". In: *SIGSOFT Softw. Eng. Notes* 30.5 (Sept. 2005), pp. 217–226. ISSN: 0163-5948. https://doi.org/10.1145/1095430.1081741. URL: http://doi.acm.org/10.1145/1095430.1081741.
9. Alex Borgida, John Mylopoulos, and Raymond Reiter. "On the Frame Problem in Procedure Specifications". In: *IEEE Transactions on Software Engineering* 21.10 (Oct. 1995), pp. 785–798. URL: http://doi.ieeecomputersociety.org/10.1109/32.469460.
10. Patrice Chalin et al. "Beyond Assertions: Advanced Specification and Verification with JML and ESC/Java2". In: *Formal Methods for Components and Objects (FMCO) 2005, Revised Lectures*. Vol. 4111. Lecture Notes in Computer Science. Berlin: Springer-Verlag, 2006, pp. 342–363. URL: http://dx.doi.org/10.1007/11804192%5C_16.
11. Robert DeLine and Manuel Fähndrich. "Typestates for objects". In: *ECOOP 2004 — Object-Oriented Programming, 18th European Conference*. Vol. 3086. Lecture Notes in Computer Science. Springer Verlag, June 2004, pp. 465–490. URL: http://research.microsoft.com/apps/pubs/default.aspx?id=67463.
12. Sophia Drossopoulou, Adrian Francalanza, and Peter Müller. "A Unified Framework for Verification Techniques for Object Invariants". In: *International Workshop on Foundations of Object-Oriented Languages (FOOL'08)*. 2008. URL: http://fool08.kuis.kyoto-u.ac.jp/drossopoulou.pdf.
13. Samin S. Ishtiaq and Peter W. O'Hearn. "BI as an assertion language for mutable data structures". In: *Proceedings of the 28th ACM SIGPLAN-SIGACT symposium on Principles of programming languages*. POPL '01. London, United Kingdom: ACM, 2001, pp. 14–26. ISBN: 1-58113-336-7. https://doi.org/10.1145/360204.375719. URL: http://doi.acm.org/10.1145/360204.375719.
14. Ioannis T. Kassios. "The dynamic frames theory". In: *Formal Aspects of Computing* 23.3 (May 2011), pp. 267–288. ISSN: 0934-5043. https://doi.org/10.1007/s00165-010-0152-5. URL: http://dx.doi.org/10.1007/s00165-010-0152-5.
15. Gary T. Leavens. "JML's Rich, Inherited Specifications for Behavioral Subtypes". In: *Formal Methods and Software Engineering: 8th International Conference on Formal Engineering Methods (ICFEM)*. Ed. by Zhiming Liu and He Jifeng. Vol. 4260. Lecture Notes in Computer Science. New York, NY: Springer-Verlag, Nov 2006, pp. 2–34. URL: http://dx.doi.org/10.1007/11901433.

16. Gary T. Leavens and Peter Müller. "Information Hiding and Visibility in Interface Specifications". In: *International Conference on Software Engineering (ICSE)*. Los Alamitos, California: IEEE, May 2007, pp. 385–395. URL: http://dx.doi.org/10.1109/ICSE.2007.44.

17. Gary T. Leavens and David A. Naumann. "Behavioral Subtyping, Specification Inheritance, and Modular Reasoning". In: *TOPLAS* 37.4 (Aug. 2015), 13:1–13:88. https://doi.org/10.1145/2766446. URL: http://doi.acm.org/10.1145/2766446.

18. Gary T. Leavens and William E. Weihl. "Specification and Verification of Object-Oriented Programs Using Supertype Abstraction". In: *Acta Informatica* 32.8 (Nov. 1995), pp. 705–778. URL: http://dx.doi.org/10.1007/BF01178658.

19. Gary T. Leavens et al. "JML Reference Manual". Available from http://www.jmlspecs.org. Sept. 2009.

20. K. Rustan M. Leino. "Dafny: An Automatic Program Verifier for Functional Correctness". In: *Logic for Programming, Artificial Intelligence, and Reasoning, 16th International Conference, LPAR-16*. Vol. 6355. Lecture Notes in Computer Science. Darkar, Senegal: Springer-Verlag, 2010, pp. 348–370.

21. K. Rustan M. Leino. "Data groups: Specifying the modification of extended state". In: *OOPSLA '98 Conference Proceedings*. Vol. 33(10). ACM SIGPLAN Notices. New York, NY: ACM, Oct. 1998, pp. 144–153. URL: http://doi.acm.org/10.1145/286936.286953.

22. Barbara H. Liskov and Jeannette M. Wing. "A Behavioral Notion of Subtyping". In: 16.6 (Nov. 1994), pp. 1811–1841. URL: http://doi.acm.org/10.1145/197320.197383.

23. Bertrand Meyer. "Applying 'Design by Contract'". In: *Computer* 25.10 (Oct. 1992), pp. 40–51.

24. Peter Müller. *Modular Specification and Verification of Object-Oriented Programs*. Vol. 2262. Lecture Notes in Computer Science. Berlin: Springer-Verlag, 2002. URL: http://tinyurl.com/jtwot.

25. Peter Müller, Arnd Poetzsch-Heffter, and Gary T. Leavens. "Modular Specification of Frame Properties in JML". In: *Concurrency and Computation: Practice and Experience* 15.2 (Feb. 2003), pp. 117–154. https://doi.org/10.1002/cpe.713 URL: ftp://ftp.cs.iastate.edu/pub/techreports/TR02-02/TR.pdf.

26. Peter W. O'Hearn, Hongseok Yang, and John C. Reynolds. "Separation and Information Hiding". In: *ACM Trans. Program. Lang. Syst.* 31.3 (Apr. 2009), 11:1–11:50. ISSN: 0164-0925. https://doi.org/10.1145/1498926.1498929. URL: http://doi.acm.org/10.1145/1498926.1498929.

27. Matthew Parkinson and Gavin Bierman. "Separation Logic, Abstraction and Inheritance". In: *ACM Symposium on Principles of Programming Languages*. Ed. by Philip Wadler. New York, NY: ACM, Jan. 2008, pp. 75–86.

28. D. L. Parnas. "On the Criteria to be Used in Decomposing Systems into Modules". In: *Communications of the ACM* 15.12 (Dec. 1972), pp. 1053–1058.

29. John C. Reynolds. "Separation Logic: A Logic for Shared Mutable Data Structures". In: *Proceedings of the Seventeenth Annual IEEE Symposium on Logic in Computer Science*. Los Alamitos, California: IEEE Computer Society Press, 2002, pp. 55–74. URL: http://dx.doi.org/10.1109/LICS.2002.1029817.

30. Jan Smans et al. "Automatic verification of Java programs with dynamic frames". In: *Formal Aspects of Computing* 22.3 (2010), pp. 423–457. ISSN: 1433-299X. https://doi.org/10.1007/s00165-010-0148-1. URL: http://dx.doi.org/10.1007/s00165-010-0148-1.

31. Alexander J. Summers, Sophia Drossopoulou, and Peter Müller. "The Need for Flexible Object Invariants". In: *International Workshop on Aliasing, Confinement and Ownership in Object-Oriented Programming*. IWACO '09. Genova, Italy: ACM, 2009, 6:1–6:9. ISBN: 978-1-60558-546-8. https://doi.org/10.1145/1562154.1562160. URL: http://doi.acm.org/10.1145/1562154.1562160.

32. Benjamin Weiß. "Deductive Verification of Object-Oriented Software: Dynamic Frames, Dynamic Logic and Predicate Abstraction". PhD thesis. Karlsruhe Institute of Technology, 2011.

Trends in Relational Program Verification

Bernhard Beckert and Mattias Ulbrich

Abstract Relational program verification refers to the verification of relational properties, which relate different programs, different versions of the same program, or the same program for different inputs. Recently, there is a growing interest in relational properties. One of the main reasons for this trend is that relational properties avoid the bottleneck of having to write complex requirement specifications. Instead, the programs that are compared serve as specification of each other. In this chapter, we give an overview of current trends in relational program verification. We describe the main scenarios where relational program verification is employed to ensure dependability of systems, including regression verification and proving non-interference properties. And we discuss recent trends in how to use deductive verification to prove relational properties.

1 Introduction

Relational program verification refers to the verification of relational properties, which relate different programs, different versions of the same program, or the same program for different inputs. For relational verification several program runs need to be compared. In this chapter, we give an overview of current trends in relational program verification.

There are many interesting program properties that are relational in nature. The most prominent examples are variants of program equivalence: Two (different) programs are equivalent if they terminate in equivalent program states whenever started in equivalent states. Another important kind of a relational property is non-interference: If it is provable that any two runs of a system that differ in the initial value of some variable x result in the same output, then consequently the variable x

B. Beckert (✉) · M. Ulbrich
Karlsruhe Institute of Technology, Karlsruhe, Germany
e-mail: beckert@kit.edu; ulbrich@kit.edu

does not interfere with the output (the system does not reveal information about the initial value of x).

Recently, there is a growing interest in relational properties, and relational verification is an important trend in formal methods. One of the main reasons for this trend is that relational properties avoid the bottleneck of having to write complex requirement specifications which impedes the use of formal verification in practice. Instead, the programs that are compared serve as specification of each other. For example, one may prove that—except for intended changes—a new program version behaves as the old one (regression verification).

Even though, intuitively, relating several program runs seems to be a more complex task than just investigating single runs, relational program verification is in many cases easier than functional verification. As explained in the course of this chapter, this is in particular true if the programs resp. program runs that are being compared are similar to each other, i.e., if they run (nearly) in lockstep, produce similar results, and/or are structurally similar.

For functional verification, the effort grows with the size and complexity of the program to be verified (and its specification), while for relational program verification, the effort mainly depends on the size of the *difference* between the programs resp. program executions (and the complexity of the relational property). Thus, if the difference is small, even large and complex programs can be handled. One can exploit the fact that differences are often local and only affect a small portion of a program.

Nevertheless, relational verification is not a trivial task. It may still require complex auxiliary specifications that describe the functionality of sub-components or detail the relation between the two systems (coupling invariants).

Relational properties are a very general concept. In this chapter, we focus on scenarios

1. where the programs being compared are written in the same language—as opposed to verifying translation relations where one of the programs is an executable specification, written in a abstract language and the other is the concrete system—, and
2. where concrete programs are proved to satisfy a relational property—as opposed to proving correctness for program transformations or program generation or compilation in general.

Structure of This Chapter

First, in Sect. 2, we introduce and define the basic concepts of relational properties and relational verification. Then, in Sect. 3, we describe the main scenarios where relational program verification is employed to ensure dependability of systems, including regression verification and proving non-interference properties. In Sect. 4, we discuss recent trends in how to use deductive verification to prove relational properties. Finally, we draw some conclusions in Sect. 5.

2 Basic Notions and Definitions

The following definitions are independent of a particular programming language. We assume a set $\mathscr{P}$ of programs is given. To simplify the presentation, we assume that all programs operate on the same state space $\mathscr{S}$. The semantics of a program $P \in \mathscr{P}$ is a relation $\xrightarrow{P} \subset \mathscr{S} \times \mathscr{S}$, where $s \xrightarrow{P} s'$ means that the program P, when started in state s, may terminate in state s'. If the programming language is deterministic, the relations $\xrightarrow{P}$ are partial functions on $\mathscr{S}$. The concrete structure of states depends the declarations in the programs and on the programming language; in particular, they may contain local variables, stacks, heaps etc. The value of a program variable x in a state $s \in \mathscr{S}$ is denoted by $s(x)$. We assume that there is a special state err $\in \mathscr{S}$ to indicate a program has failed an assertion.

In the following, we define and discuss different types of functional and relational properties.

Definition 1 (Functional Safety Property) A *functional safety property* F is a set $F \subseteq (\mathscr{S} \times \mathscr{S})$, i.e., a set of state pairs.

A program $P \in \mathscr{P}$ *satisfies* F iff, for all $s, s' \in \mathscr{S}$, $s \xrightarrow{P} s'$ implies $(s, s') \in F$, i.e., $\xrightarrow{P} \subseteq F$.

Intuitively, a functional safety property F is the set of all those state pairs s, s' such that it is a correct program behaviour for P to terminate in state s' when started in s.

Example 1 The functional property that a program must either decrease the value of the variable x by 1 when started in a state with $x > 0$ or not terminate at all, can be formalised as

$$\{ (s, s') \mid \text{if } s(x) > 0 \text{ then } s'(x) = s(x) + 1 \} .$$

Note that this functional property does not place any restrictions on how a program affects other parts of the state besides the variable x.

A functional property includes those state transitions that are considered "good" or "admissible" by the property. A program is judged against the property for every state transition separately. In contrast to that, a relational property sets transitions into relation. Satisfaction of a relational property by programs P_1, P_2 is judged by considering each of the transitions in $\xrightarrow{P_1}$ in the context spanned by the state transitions of $\xrightarrow{P_2}$ and vice versa.

Definition 2 (Relational Safety Property) A *relational safety property* R is a set $R \subseteq (\mathscr{S} \times \mathscr{S}) \times (\mathscr{S} \times \mathscr{S})$, i.e., a relation on state pairs.

Two programs $P_1, P_2 \in \mathscr{P}$ *satisfy* R iff, for all $s_1, s_1', s_2, s_2' \in \mathscr{S}$:

$$\text{if } s_1 \xrightarrow{P_1} s_1' \text{ and } s_2 \xrightarrow{P_2} s_2' \text{ then } \big((s_1, s_1'), (s_2, s_2')\big) \in R .$$

Intuitively, a relational property R consists of those combinations of state transitions (s_i, s'_i) that—by definition of that property—are allowed to "co-exist" in the semantics of the two programs.

Example 2 One of the simplest but also most often used relational properties is program equivalence. If the two programs are started in the same initial state, then they terminate in the same state (if they terminate at all); if they are started in different states, their terminal state is not restricted:

$$F_{equiv} = \{((s_1, s'_1), (s_2, s'_2)) \mid \text{if } s_1 = s_2 \text{ then } s'_1 = s'_2\}$$

Example 3 Another prominent relational property is non-interference (see Sect. 3.1.1). The requirement that the input variable h does not interfere with the output variable l can be expressed as (assuming that h, l are the only variables in the state):

$$F_{non\text{-}interference} = \{((s_1, s'_1), (s_2, s'_2)) \mid \text{if } s_1(l) = s_2(l) \text{ then } s'_1(l) = s'_2(l)\}$$

Relational properties allow two dimensions of variation: transitions of the same program may be compared for *different initial states* or transitions of *different programs* may be compared for the same initial state; or both dimensions of variation may be combined. The case $P_1 = P_2$, where P_1 and P_2 are the same program, is a special case that is frequently considered in practice. Such *single-program relational properties*, which are also called *2-properties*, including non-interference, are discussed in Sect. 3.1.

The concept of relational properties is stronger and more expressive than functional properties. In fact, every functional property can also be represented as a relational property: For a functional property F, the relational property $R = F \times F$ is satisfied by a program $P = P_1 = P_2$ (Definition 2) iff F is satisfied by P (Definition 1).

The notion of relational safety properties as given in Definition 2 does not cover all interesting relational properties. Only those properties can be expressed that can be checked by looking at two state transitions at a time. However, there are many properties that require to compare three or more transitions—of the same program or of different programs.

Example 4 Consider a program *best* that chooses the "best" element from a set X according to some heuristic. Even if we may not want to or be able to specify which element is the best one in any situation, we may require *consistency of choice*: If a set X is split into two overlapping subsets X_1, X_2 (i.e., $X = X_1 \cup X_2$), and the program chooses the same element x from X_1 and from X_2 (i.e., $x = best(X_1) = best(X_2)$), then it must choose x from X as well ($x = best(X)$).

Properties such as consistency, which can (only) be defined by the comparison of three transitions, are called 3-properties. This concept can be extended to k-properties for $k \in \mathbb{N}$ by generalising Definition 2.

However, k-properties do still not cover all interesting properties. For example, termination for all initial states is a rather simple property that is not a k-property for any k. Termination is a liveness property and is existential in nature, while all k-properties are universal in nature, requiring that *all* k-tuples of state transitions are "good" in some sense.

Example 5 The relational property that, whenever P_1 terminates when started in the initial state s, the program P_2 also terminates when started in s can be formalised as:

$$\text{for all } s, s_1' \in \mathscr{S} \text{ with } s \xrightarrow{P_1} s_1' \text{ there is an } s_2' \in \mathscr{S} \text{ with } s \xrightarrow{P_2} s_2'$$

As explained above, this property (called *mutual* or *relational termination*) cannot be expressed as a relational safety property. This parallels the functional case: Termination of a single program can also not be formulated as a (functional) safety property.

The taxonomy of properties can be further extended to more complex combinations of universal and existential quantification, though such complex property types are rare in practice. Clarkson et al. [10] introduce a taxonomy of relational properties, including k-safety and k-liveness properties, considering a program semantics with traces instead of pre-/post-state pairs, which is useful for reactive systems, process algebras, etc.

So far, we have discussed the concepts of relational properties and when they are satisfied by programs. For relational verification, i.e., to prove that programs satisfy a relational property, we need a further concept, namely *coupling properties*. A coupling property is a relation on states, which intuitively holds for corresponding states during the execution of two (or more) related programs. For example, if two programs run in lockstep (i.e., their traces are the same), then identity is a trivial coupling property. Coupling properties that hold throughout program execution are also called a *coupling invariant*. Typically coupling invariants do not need to hold in all states of a trace but only at certain synchronisation points.

A *coupling predicate* is a formula (in some logic used for deductive verification) that expresses a coupling property. Coupling predicates that are inductive, i.e., for which it is possible to prove by induction on the length of the traces that the property holds throughout the execution, are a powerful tool for verifying relational properties (see Sect. 4).

3   Application Scenarios

In this section, we describe the main scenarios where relational program verification is employed to ensure dependability of systems, including regression verification and proving non-interference properties.

3.1 Single-Program Properties

Single-program properties relate runs of the same program for different inputs. Typically, they require that, if the inputs are in some relation to each other, then the outputs must be in some (other) relation.

3.1.1 Non-interference and Information-Flow Properties

For complex programs, one cannot easily tell how the input data is processed and how it affects the final state of the programs and flows into output variables. Secure information flow requires that the (public) output of a program does not depend on its (secret) inputs—resp. only to a certain degree. This is a relational safety property (Definition 2), which is also called *non-interference* as the secret input must not interfere with the public output. The non-interference property relates different runs of a program: For any two runs starting in states that only differ in the secret part of the initial state (the public part may be different), the observable (public) part of the final state must be the same (see Example 3). If a program is non-interferent, an attacker cannot learn the secret input by observing the public output—where we assume that the attacker knows the source code of the program and can control the public input.

Joshi and Leino [19] and Amtoft and Banerjee [2] were the first to give semantical definitions of information flow based on relational properties. A full definition of information flow in terms of the input-output function's equivalence kernel can be found, e.g., in [21]. The survey paper by Sabelfeld and Myers [26] gives an overview of language-based information-flow analyses.

While deductive verification of non-interference properties is a rather new development, there have been static security-enforcing techniques based on syntax or types for a long time. Type systems and program-dependency-graph-based analyses (e.g., by Hammer and Snelting [16]) allow analysis of larger programs, but are less precise than deductive methods.

3.1.2 Symmetry Properties

An important kind of relational properties are symmetry properties, which express that, if two initial states are symmetric (or in some other way similar) to each other, they lead to symmetric (similar) final states.

If the number of possible inputs for a program is large, the effort for both testing and formal verification can be greatly reduced if the state space can be partitioned using a relational symmetry property. To exploit a symmetry relation S for verifying (or testing) a program P w.r.t. a functional property F (compatible with S), it suffices

1. to show that P has the relational symmetry property S,
2. to show that P satisfies F for a small subset $X \subseteq \mathscr{S}$ of representatives, and
3. to show that X reaches all states in $\mathscr{S}$ via symmetry S.

From this it can be concluded that P satisfies the property F for all $s \in \mathscr{S}$.

Example 6 A typical symmetry property is permutation-invariance S_{perm}. Assume for this example that all states are arrays of length N (i.e., $\mathscr{S} = \mathbb{N}^N$). A program P is called permutation-invariant if its result is the same for an array a and for a permuted array $\sigma(a)$ (for some permutation $\sigma \in \text{Sym}_N$):

$$S_{perm} = \left\{ ((s_1, s_1'), (s_2, s_2')) \mid \text{if } s_1 = \sigma(s_2) \text{ for some } \sigma \in \text{Sym}_N, \text{ then } s_1' = s_2' \right\}$$

The typical set X_{perm} of representatives is the set of sorted arrays. Hence, if a program P is permutation-invariant, it suffices to prove a functional property for sorted arrays only, which reduces the search space considerably.

For the example of verifying voting rules, the use of symmetry properties is discussed extensively by Beckert et al. [7]. Voting rules are highly symmetric algorithms for fairness reasons; for example, the election result must be symmetric w.r.t. the order of voters and the order of candidates. There is also related work on breaking symmetries on the problem-specification level (e.g., by Mancini and Cadoli [23] and Cadoli and Mancini [9]).

3.2 Multi-Program Properties

Multi program relational properties compare two or more programs by their observable behaviour. Typically, the properties considered in practice are a variant of program equivalence. The programs may be required to be fully equivalent, or some relaxed version of equivalence may be used that allows for exceptions or replaces identity of results with similarity (e.g., using isomorphism of states).

Multi-program properties are not fundamentally different from single-program properties. In fact, Beckert et al. [6] show how the verification of a multi-program property can be reduced to verification of a single-program property by combining the input programs into a single program that comprises the possible behaviours of all original programs. While this reduction is theoretically possible, it is inefficient in practice.

3.2.1 Regression Verification

One of the main concerns during software evolution is to prevent the introduction
of unwanted behaviour, commonly known as *regressions,* when implementing new
features, fixing defects, or during optimisation. Undetected regressions can have
severe consequences and incur high cost, in particular in late stages of development. Currently, the main quality assurance measure during software evolution
is regression testing [1]. Regression verification—a notion coined by Godlin and
Strichman [15]—is a complementary approach that attempts to achieve the same
goals with program verification techniques. This means formally verifying that
the two programs satisfy a relational equivalence property. In the basic form of
regression verification, we try to prove that the two program versions terminate in
identical final states for any initial state. In more sophisticated scenarios, we want to
verify that the two programs (a) are equivalent only for some initial states, namely
those not affected by the evolution step (conditional equivalence), or (b) differ in a
formally specified way given by a relation on the final states that is different from
the identity (relational equivalence). If regression verification is successful, it offers
guaranteed coverage without requiring additional expenses to develop and maintain
a test suite.

Interestingly, regression verification can be applied to information-flow properties. The goal then is proving that the new program version does not leak more
secrets than the old one. This leads to a two-program 4-property; one of the rare
cases of relational k-properties with $k > 3$ that are of practical interest.

3.2.2 Translation Validation

As said in the introduction, relational program verification focuses on scenarios
where concrete programs are proved to satisfy a relational property. Ideally, one
would like to prove correctness of a program transformation in general, i.e.,
to conduct a universal proof that implies correctness of the transformation for
all programs. Then, no proof would be required for individual instances of the
transformation.

But in many cases the general proof is too complex and impractical. Then, translation validation is a useful alternative, where we show for a concrete application
of the program transformation that its result is equivalent to the original program.
During the translation, useful information (like coupling predicates, information
about applied loop unwinding, etc.) can be gathered (as witnesses) to aid the
relational verification process. An example for this approach was presented by
Lopes et al. [22] for proving correctness of optimisations in llvm code.

3.2.3 Contextual Equivalence

Contextual equivalence [24], also called *backward compatibility* [29], is a relational property of (sub-)programs requiring that they behave equivalently when included into any possible program context. This property, which is important for, e.g., evolution or refactoring of library functions, is an extension of basic program equivalence. Instead of (only) requiring two programs P_1, P_2 to be equivalent in the sense that

$$s \xrightarrow{P_1} s' \text{ iff } s \xrightarrow{P_2} s' \quad \text{for all } s, s' \in \mathcal{S} \ ,$$

contextual equivalence requires that

$$s \xrightarrow{Q[P_1]} s' \text{ iff } s \xrightarrow{Q[P_2]} s' \quad \text{for all programs } Q[\cdot] \text{ and } s, s' \in \mathcal{S} \ ,$$

where $Q[P_i]$ is the result of inserting the program P_i as a sub-program into $Q[\cdot]$.

Relational program verification to prove contextual equivalence requires an adequate semantic model for open programs. In the object-oriented setting, the program logic used for verification must account for features such as inheritance and callbacks. Welsch and Poetzsch-Heffter [29, 30] provide a solution for the context of Java and Boogie; Murawski et al. [24] show how the difficulties can be dealt with using game semantics.

3.2.4 Refinement

Refinement is a relational property between two behavioural descriptions, where usually one is more abstract and one is more concrete. Since this chapter focuses on relational program verification, we concentrate on the program verification aspects of refinement proofs. In algorithmic refinement, an abstract imperative algorithm description A is refined into a more detailed concrete description C, e.g., by defining how abstract concepts are turned into actual data structures. A distinguishing trait of refinement is that the algorithms may be non-deterministic: In the abstract program, the algorithm may have choices (like choose x such that $x > 0$) which are deliberately left open on the abstract level, whereas a refinement step may concretise the statement (e.g., into $x := 5$).

Refinement is not a relational safety property according to Definition 2 since it cannot be expressed using only universal quantification. As we have seen, program equivalence for deterministic programs, which requires that two programs started in the same state terminate in the same state (if they both terminate), can be formalised with universal quantification using the relational safety property F_{equiv} (see Example 2):

$$\text{for all } s_1, s_2, s'_1, s'_2 \in \mathcal{S} \colon \text{ if } s_1 \xrightarrow{C} s'_1 \text{ and } s_2 \xrightarrow{A} s'_2, \text{ then } ((s_1, s'_1), (s_2, s'_2)) \in F_{equiv}$$

In the presence of non-deterministic behaviour, however, this property scheme is not adequate: The abstract program A may have several different terminal states, and they cannot be all equal to the terminal state(s) of C. Instead, it must be required that s_1' is a *possible* terminal state for P_2 using a different property scheme

$$\text{for all } s_1, s_1' \in \mathscr{S} \text{ exist } s_2, s_2' \in \mathscr{S} \text{ such that:}$$

$$\text{if } s_1 \xrightarrow{C} s_1', \text{ then } s_2 \xrightarrow{A} s_2' \text{ and } \big((s_1, s_1'), (s_2, s_2')\big) \in R$$

for some refinement relation $R \subseteq (\mathscr{S} \times \mathscr{S}) \times (\mathscr{S} \times \mathscr{S})$. If the input and output coupling predicate for this refinement step is the identity (like for equivalence), then the refinement relation $R_{equiv} = \big\{((s, s'), (s, s')) \mid s, s' \in \mathscr{S}\big\}$ must be used. Interestingly, mutual termination (see Example 5) falls also into this property scheme using the relation $R_{term} = \big\{((s, s_1), (s, s_2)) \mid s, s_1, s_2 \in \mathscr{S}\big\}$.

Ulbrich [28] uses a dynamic logic to formulate and discharge refinement proof obligations. Dynamic logic [17] is a program logic like Hoare logic. But it is more general as it supports nesting of statements and supports "forall" and "exists" terminal state operators.

4 Verification of Relational Properties

Two trends in research for the verification of relational properties can be observed that lift existing successes in program verification to relational questions:

1. *Reduction of relational properties to functional safety properties that can be verified using off-the-shelf functional program verification tools.*
   This makes recent and future technological advances in functional verification automatically available for relational verification, too. Issues like modularisation, loop-handling, framing, etc. that are similar for functional and relational verification can be left to the existing functional program verification machinery.
2. *Exploiting similarities between intermediate states in the compared program runs.*
   Examining the program runs to be compared individually has serious disadvantages in many cases. For many practical application scenarios for relational verification, the program runs are related in the sense that intermediate synchronisation points in the compared programs can be identified at which the states of their runs are similar. This can ease the verification burden considerably.

These trends are not dependent on each other. But it can be observed that often they both play a role in relational verification methods.

4.1   Reduction to Functional Verification

Early approaches to verifying relational properties devised specialised logics for handling relational questions. Benton [8] first introduced the theory of a relational Hoare calculus to reason about relational properties, and Yang [31] introduced a relational separation logic with special syntactic extensions that allow the specification of separating conjunctions on two heaps instead of only one.

The seminal paper by Barthe et al. [4] introduced a general notion of *product programs* that supports a direct reduction of relational verification to standard functional verification. Product programs are not tied to a particular application scenario. To make use of single-program functional verification tools for relational two-program verification, functional verification is applied to a product program constructed from the two programs to be compared. For the construction, it is important that the two programs cannot interfere with each other. We hence assume that the two programs P_1 and P_2 operate on disjoint sets of variables. In case this assumption does not hold, e.g., for the analysis of a single-program relational property where the programs are identical, disjointness can easily achieved by variable renaming. Syntactically, a product program P operates on both the variables (heaps, stacks, memories, etc.) of P_1 and those of P_2 and consists of the statements of both P_1 and P_2. Semantically, a product program operates on the state space $\mathscr{S} \times \mathscr{S}$ and satisfies for all $s_1, s_1', s_2, s_2' \in \mathscr{S}$:

$$\text{if} \quad s_1 \xrightarrow{P_1} s_1' \text{ and } s_2 \xrightarrow{P_2} s_2' \quad \text{then} \quad (s_1, s_2) \xrightarrow{P} (s_1', s_2') \text{ or } (s_1, s_2) \xrightarrow{P} \text{err} ,$$

i.e., the result state of P consists of the result states s_1 and s_2 that would arise if P_1 and P_2 were run separately—or P may terminate in the special error state err, i.e., fail an assertion.

The concession that a product program is allowed to fail in more cases than the original programs allows us to combine programs into product programs more liberally. Assumptions about intermediate states or the synchronisation of P_1 and P_2 can be added to P using assertions in the code of P. During a proof for P, these assertions are to be proved correct, thus justifying the assumptions made during the construction of P. We will encounter product programs with additional assertions in Sect. 4.2.

Product programs pave the way for using functional program calculi to formalise and discharge relational properties. Instead of a special relational Hoare logic and calculus using quadruples $\{\phi\}\, P_1 \sim P_2 \,\{\psi\}$ to talk about two programs [8], the traditional Hoare triple $\{\phi\}\, P \,\{\psi\}$ can be analysed using a standard Hoare calculus:

$$\models \{\phi\} P \{\psi\} \quad \text{implies} \quad \models \{\phi\}\, P_1 \sim P_2 \,\{\psi\} \tag{1}$$

The challenge now is to find good principles for the construction of product programs. Most obviously, the sequential composition $(P_1\,;\,P_2)$ is a valid product program. In fact, the "implies" in implication (1) turns into an "iff" for sequential composition. Accordingly, to formulate the non-interference property for a program P as a functional proof obligation, Barthe et al. [5] and Darvas et al. [11] suggested to employ *self-composition*, i.e., to sequentially compose two copies of P.

However, this simple direct sequential composition has substantial drawbacks, as already reported by Terauchi and Aiken [27] soon after introduction of the technique of self-composition. The problem can be visualised by the following thought experiment:

Example 7 Take a (non-trivial) deterministic program P operating on a single variable x that consists of a single while-loop. In order to verify that P is equivalent to a clone P_c (with the same code, but the variable is renamed to x_c), one can try to prove the Hoare triple $\{x = x_c\}(P; P_c)\{x = x_c\}$ based on simple sequential composition. To deal with the loops, sufficiently strong loop invariants must be found for the two consecutive loops. It turns out that the *strongest possible* functional loop invariant that together with the negated guard is satisfied only by a single value (depending on the initial value of x) must be used. Any weaker loop invariant leaving freedom of choice for the values of x and x_c would not suffice to imply the required equality $x = x_c$ in the final state of $(P; P_c)$.

Loop invariants are difficult to find, automatically or manually. Hence, it is of vital importance to find better ways to construct product programs if one wants make the technique accessible to state-of-the-art automatic or interactive verification tools.

4.2 Exploiting Similarity Between Program Runs

The key to solving the problem of sequential composition exposed in Example 7 is to exploit similarities between program states that occur in the runs that are compared during the verification. This allows one to simplify the steps of the verification.

Revisiting Example 7, we see how a different execution policy makes things a lot easier: Assume the two loops were not executed consecutively but *alternatingly*, i.e., executing one iteration of the loop of P, then one of P_c, then again one of P, and so on. Then, whenever an iteration of P_c finishes, (a) both loops have iterated equally often and (b) $x = x_c$ holds. This is indeed a sufficiently strong *coupling invariant* to complete the trivial proof. Regardless of the complexity of the result that P computes, the simple coupling predicate suffices for an inductive proof.

The idea of similarity exploitation is to identify locations (e.g., line numbers) in both programs such that, when they are reached, the corresponding states of the programs are coupled. Pairs of such locations are called synchronisation points. In principle any two states can be coupled, and there is no formal definition of when two states are "similar" or "coupled". A synchronisation is well chosen (in the context of a proof) if there is a simple enough coupling predicate that can be used in program verification to abstract the states at the synchronisation point.

Figure 1 illustrates the idea of coupling states for relational verification. Figure 1a depicts the verification task $\{\phi\}(P_1 ; P_2)\{\psi\}$ for the sequential composition. The two programs must be handled separately. One needs to do verification steps to the effect of extracting functional before-after-predicates Θ_1 for P_1 and Θ_2 for P_2 (using, e.g., a weakest precondition or a Hoare calculus) and then reason that $\phi \wedge \Theta_1 \wedge \Theta_2 \rightarrow \psi$. Figure 1b shows how this can be avoided: Instead of considering a program run as one state transition, it is broken down into segments leading from synchronisation point to synchronisation point. Every segment (framed block in Fig. 1b) is verified individually. If Cpl_A, Cpl_B are coupling predicates that capture the relation between states at the synchronisation points A resp. B and θ_1, θ_2 are before-after-predicates for the transition from synchronisation point A to point B in the respective programs, then the verification condition for the segment is $Cpl_A \wedge \theta_1 \wedge \theta_2 \rightarrow Cpl_B$. The validity of the entire proof condition then follows inductively, in very much the same way as loop invariant proofs for functional programs.

A challenge here is to identify good locations at which to set synchronisation points. Most natural candidates are those points where functional program verification also applies abstraction in form of loop invariants: the entry points of loops (loop heads).

Technically, the coupling can be implemented in different ways. One possibility is to produce product programs in which the loops are iterated alternatingly. Figure 2 shows how programs in a simple while programming language (with side-effect-free expressions) can be woven into a product program. Three possibly ways to

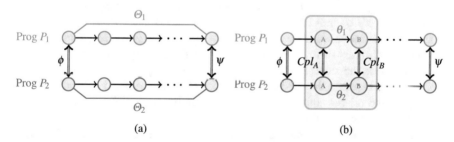

Fig. 1 Visualisation of relational verification and trace similarities. (**a**) Uncoupled analysis. (**b**) Tightly coupled runs

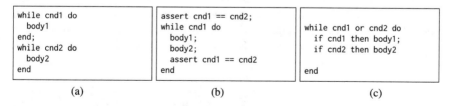

Fig. 2 Different product programs for two loops. (**a**) Sequential composition. (**b**) Perfect synchronisation. (**c**) Loose synchronisation

weave two loops are presented: Fig. 2a is the direct sequential composition which does not make use of synchronisation points. In Fig. 2b, the loop bodies are iterated alternatingly and always in pairs. Verification using this product program requires that the loops iterate equally often because otherwise the assertion that the loop conditions cnd1 and cnd2 evaluate equivalently will fail. Finally, Fig. 2c shows how the limitation of equal number of iterations can be lifted by adding conditionals that check the loop guards individually. This product loop first executes the loop bodies alternatingly and then, when one program has terminated the loop, finishes the remaining loop in an uncoupled fashion.

It is noteworthy that the verification of the perfect synchronisation scheme from Fig. 2b also implies mutual termination (see Example 5) of the two loops. The added assertion ensures that both loops iterate equally often for any input, which is sufficient for mutual termination (assuming the loop bodies have no further loops). Hence, although mutual termination is not a relational k-property, sufficient conditions can be encoded into product programs that imply the property. Elenbogen et al. [13] and Hawblitzel et al. [18] formulate more sophisticated relational safety properties that entail mutual termination.

Relational proofs for fully synchronised loops can already be conducted using the early relational calculi presented by Benton [8] and Yang [31].

4.3 More Elaborate Synchronisation Schemes

Verification by means of coupling predicates works well in many situations—but only if the two programs under inspection reach related states whenever they reach a synchronisation point. If that premise does not hold, e.g., when comparing two completely different sorting algorithms for equivalence (say, to show that the result of mergesort is the same as that of bubblesort), looking for good synchronisation points would be futile since the inner structure of the algorithms is so different that specifying the relationship between states would be more difficult than verifying that both are stable sorting functions.

The strict lockstep combination in which exactly one loop iteration of the first program corresponds to exactly one loop iteration of the second program is, in many cases, not flexible enough to account for all typical synchronization scenarios. It may very well be that for one program, a loop needs to first be unwound a number of times before entering a lockstep synchronous part; or each loop iteration of one program does not correspond to one but to k iterations of the other program; and, of course, many other synchronisation schemes are possible. Figure 3 shows

Fig. 3 Loosely coupled runs

a schematic example of loosely coupled loops in which program states are not in a 1:1 relationship.

When dealing with relational program verification by reduction to functional verification, a flexible synchronisation mechanism can be achieved by defining a set of transformation rules that can be used to weave two programs into a single program, which is a product program by construction. This has originally been suggested by Barthe et al. [4] for weaving two programs, a generalisation (that supports several programs and modular verification) has been presented by Eilers et al. [12]. Banerjee et al. [3] present a relational Hoare logic supporting flexible program weaving without necessarily producing a product program in the course.

Relational verification has a high potential for automation: Regardless of the complexity of the actual computation, the compared program runs in a relational verification task can be very closely related. For instance, in a regression verification scenario, two programs may be identical but for the assignments to a single variable x. In many cases, it is enough to specify relationally how the variable x is treated differently and assume that nothing else has changed.

If the coupling predicates between corresponding loop iterations is close to equality, it is indeed a good candidate to not have it specified by the user but to infer it automatically using inference techniques for loop invariants. Felsing et al. [14] have shown that relational coupling predicates can be inferred automatically for regression verification of non-trivial programs. The approach supports loosely coupled synchronization points and uses dynamic exploration to find loop unwinding ratios that promise a good synchronisation between programs [20]. In this approach, coupling predicates are modelled as uninterpreted predicates within constrained Horn clauses [25]. Modern SMT solvers are used to infer sufficiently strong inductive predicates such that the relational post-condition is satisfied.

4.4 Alternative Approaches

While in the previous sections, we have presented a general technique to deal with relational properties in deductive verification, it should be mentioned that product program construction (or similar techniques relating symbolic program executions) is not the only way to deal with relational properties deductively. For single-program properties, it is sometimes possible to formulate verification conditions that only require a *single* invocation of the program. However, this requires that program constructs are embedded into the logic more deeply, in particular that programs can occur in the scope of quantifiers. In Hoare logic, formulas like $\forall x \{\phi\} P \{\psi\}$ are syntactically not allowed. But, in dynamic logic [17], such a quantification is possible.

Darvas et al. [11] noted that non-interference of a (secret) variable h with a (public) variable l for a program P can be expressed using a single program invocation of P in dynamic logic:

$$\forall l \exists r \forall h \; \langle P \rangle r = l$$

Because of the order of quantifiers in this formula, it expresses that, for all input values of l, there is a *single* result value r for the public variable l that is independent of the input value for h.

5   Conclusions

Relational properties are ubiquitous, and there are many application scenarios in which they play a rule. The effort for relational program verification mainly grows with the size and complexity of the difference between the compared programs resp. program runs. As the size of the difference is a different dimension than size and complexity of the programs themselves, relational verification has the potential to be usable in cases where functional verification is infeasible. In particular, the need for writing requirement specifications can often be avoided. Thus, relational verification can extend the reach of formal methods to new application scenarios.

While—on a theoretical level—the expressiveness of relational properties is the same as that of functional properties, experience shows that some new techniques are needed in practice for relational verification, which moreover differ for different use cases. In particular, the heuristics needed to automatically find synchronisation points and coupling invariants depend on the application scenario.

References

1. Paul Ammann and Jeff Offutt. *Introduction to software testing*. Cambridge University Press, 2008. ISBN: 978-0-521-88038-1.
2. Torben Amtoft and Anindya Banerjee. "Information Flow Analysis in Logical Form". In: *Static Analysis, 11th International Symposium, SAS 2004, Verona, Italy, August 26–28, 2004, Proceedings*. Ed. by Roberto Giacobazzi. Vol. 3148. Lecture Notes in Computer Science. Springer, 2004, pp. 100–115. ISBN: 3-540-22791-1. https://doi.org/10.1007/978-3-540-27864-1_10.
3. Anindya Banerjee, David A. Naumann, and Mohammad Nikouei. "Relational Logic with Framing and Hypotheses". In: *36th IARCS Annual Conference on Foundations of Software Technology and Theoretical Computer Science, FSTTCS 2016, December 13–15, 2016, Chennai, India*. Ed. by Akash Lal et al. Vol. 65. LIPIcs. Schloss Dagstuhl Leibniz-Zentrum fuer Informatik, 2016, 11:1–11:16. ISBN: 978-3-95977-027-9. https://doi.org/10.4230/LIPIcs.FSTTCS.2016.11.

4. Gilles Barthe, Juan Manuel Crespo, and César Kunz. "Relational Verification Using Product Programs". In: *FM 2011: Formal Methods - 17th International Symposium on Formal Methods, Limerick, Ireland, June 20–24, 2011. Proceedings*. Ed. by Michael J. Butler and Wolfram Schulte. Vol. 6664. Lecture Notes in Computer Science. Springer, 2011, pp. 200–214. ISBN: 978-3-642-21436-3. https://doi.org/10.1007/978-3-642-21437-0_17.

5. Gilles Barthe, Pedro R. D'Argenio, and Tamara Rezk. "Secure Information Flow by Self-Composition". In: *17th IEEE Computer Security Foundations Workshop, (CSFW-17 2004), 28–30 June 2004, Pacific Grove, CA, USA*. IEEE Computer Society, 2004, pp. 100–114. ISBN: 0-7695-2169-X. https://doi.org/10.1109/CSFW.2004.17.

6. Bernhard Beckert, Vladimir Klebanov, and Mattias Ulbrich. "Regression verification for Java using a secure information flow calculus". In: *Proceedings of the 17th Workshop on Formal Techniques for Java-like Programs, FTfJP 2015, Prague, Czech Republic, July 7, 2015*. Ed. by Rosemary Monahan. ACM, 2015, 6:1–6:6. ISBN: 978-1-4503-3656-7. https://doi.org/10.1145/2786536.2786544.

7. Bernhard Beckert et al. "Automated Verification for Functional and Relational Properties of Voting Rules". In: *Sixth International Workshop on Computational Social Choice (COMSOC 2016)*. June 2016.

8. Nick Benton. "Simple relational correctness proofs for static analyses and program transformations". In: *Proceedings of the 31st ACM SIGPLAN-SIGACT Symposium on Principles of Programming Languages, POPL 2004, Venice, Italy, January 14–16, 2004*. Ed. by Neil D. Jones and Xavier Leroy. ACM, 2004, pp. 14–25. ISBN: 1-58113-729-X. https://doi.org/10.1145/964001.964003.

9. Marco Cadoli and Toni Mancini. "Using a Theorem Prover for Reasoning on Constraint Problems". In: *AI* IA 2005: Advances in Artificial Intelligence*. Springer, 2005.

10. Michael R. Clarkson, Stephen Chong, and Andrew C. Myers. "Civitas: Toward a Secure Voting System". In: *2008 IEEE Symposium on Security and Privacy (S&P 2008), 18–21 May 2008, Oakland, California, USA*. IEEE Computer Society, 2008, pp. 354–368. ISBN: 978-0-7695-3168-7. https://doi.org/10.1109/SP.2008.32.

11. Ádám Darvas, Reiner Hähnle, and David Sands. "A Theorem Proving Approach to Analysis of Secure Information Flow". In: *Security in Pervasive Computing Second International Conference, SPC 2005, Boppard, Germany, April 6–8, 2005, Proceedings*. Ed. by Dieter Hutter and Markus Ullmann. Vol. 3450. Lecture Notes in Computer Science. Springer, 2005, pp. 193–209. ISBN: 3–540-25521-4. https://doi.org/10.1007/978-3-540-32004-3_20.

12. Marco Eilers, Peter Müller, and Samuel Hitz. "Modular Product Programs". In: *Programming Languages and Systems - 27th European Symposium on Programming, ESOP 2018, Held as Part of the European Joint Conferences on Theory and Practice of Software, ETAPS 2018, Thessaloniki, Greece, April 14–20, 2018, Proceedings*. Ed. by Amal Ahmed. Vol. 10801. Lecture Notes in Computer Science. Springer, 2018, pp. 502–529. ISBN: 978-3-319-89883-4. https://doi.org/10.1007/978-3-319-89884-1_18.

13. Dima Elenbogen, Shmuel Katz, and Ofer Strichman. "Proving mutual termination". In: *Formal Methods in System Design* 47.2 (2015), pp. 204–229. https://doi.org/10.1007/s10703-015-0234-3.

14. Dennis Felsing et al. "Automating regression verification". In: *ACM/IEEE International Conference on Automated Software Engineering, ASE '14, Vasteras, Sweden - September 15–19, 2014*. Ed. by Ivica Crnkovic, Marsha Chechik, and Paul Grünbacher. ACM, 2014, pp. 349–360. ISBN: 978-1-4503-3013-8. https://doi.org/10.1145/2642937.2642987.

15. Benny Godlin and Ofer Strichman. "Regression verification: proving the equivalence of similar programs". In: *Softw. Test., Verif. Reliab.* 23.3 (2013), pp. 241–258. https://doi.org/10.1002/stvr.1472.

16. Christian Hammer and Gregor Snelting. "Flow-sensitive, context-sensitive, and object-sensitive information flow control based on program dependence graphs". In: *Int. J. Inf. Sec.* 8.6 (2009), pp. 399–422. https://doi.org/10.1007/s10207-009-0086-1.

17. David Harel, Dexter Kozen, and Jerzy Tiuryn. "Dynamic logic". In: *SIGACT News* 32.1 (2001), pp. 66–69. https://doi.org/10.1145/568438.568456.

18. Chris Hawblitzel et al. "Towards Modularly Comparing Programs Using Automated Theorem Provers". In: *Automated Deduction - CADE-24 - 24th International Conference on Automated Deduction, Lake Placid, NY, USA, June 9–14, 2013. Proceedings.* Ed. by Maria Paola Bonacina. Vol. 7898. Lecture Notes in Computer Science. Springer, 2013, pp. 282–299. ISBN: 978-3-642-38573-5. https://doi.org/10.1007/978-3-642-38574-2_20.

19. Rajeev Joshi and K. Rustan M. Leino. "A semantic approach to secure information flow". In: *Sci. Comput. Program.* 37.1-3 (2000), pp. 113–138. https://doi.org/10.1016/S0167-6423(99)00024-6.

20. Moritz Kiefer, Vladimir Klebanov, and Mattias Ulbrich. "Relational Program Reasoning Using Compiler IR - Combining Static Verification and Dynamic Analysis". In: *J Autom. Reasoning* 60.3 (2018), pp. 337–363. https://doi.org/10.1007/s10817-017-9433-5.

21. Vladimir Klebanov. "Precise quantitative information flow analysis - a symbolic approach". In: *Theor. Comput. Sci.* 538 (2014), pp. 124–139. https://doi.org/10.1016/j.tcs.2014.04.022.

22. Nuno P. Lopes et al. "Provably correct peephole optimizations with alive". In: *Proceedings of the 36th ACM SIGPLAN Conference on Programming Language Design and Implementation, Portland, OR, USA, June 15–17, 2015.* Ed. by David Grove and Steve Blackburn. ACM, 2015, pp. 22–32. ISBN: 978-1-4503-3468-6. https://doi.org/10.1145/2737924.2737965.

23. Toni Mancini and Marco Cadoli. "Detecting and Breaking Symmetries by Reasoning on Problem Specifications". In: *Abstraction, Reformulation and Approximation.* Springer, 2005.

24. Andrzej S. Murawski, Steven J. Ramsay, and Nikos Tzevelekos. "Game Semantic Analysis of Equivalence in IMJ". In: *Automated Technology for Verification and Analysis - 13th International Symposium, ATVA 2015, Shanghai, China, October 12–15, 2015, Proceedings.* Ed. by Bernd Finkbeiner, Geguang Pu, and Lijun Zhang. Vol. 9364. Lecture Notes in Computer Science. Springer, 2015, pp. 411–428. ISBN: 978-3-319-24952-0. https://doi.org/10.1007/978-3-319-24953-7_30.

25. Philipp Rümmer, Hossein Hojjat, and Viktor Kuncak. "Classifying and Solving Horn Clauses for Verification". In: *Verified Software: Theories, Tools, Experiments 5th International Conference VSTTE 2013, Menlo Park, CA, USA, May 17–19, 2013, Revised Selected Papers* Ed. by Ernie Cohen and Andrey Rybalchenko. Vol. 8164. Lecture Notes in Computer Science. Springer, 2013, pp. 1–21. ISBN: 978-3-642-54107-0. https://doi.org/10.1007/9783642541087_1

26. Andrei Sabelfeld and Andrew C. Myers. "Language-based information-flow security". In: *IEEE Journal on Selected Areas in Communications* 21.1 (2003), pp. 5–19. https://doi.org/10.1109/JSAC.2002.806121.

27. Tachio Terauchi and Alexander Aiken. "Secure Information Flow as a Safety Problem". In: *Static Analysis, 12th International Symposium, SAS 2005, London, UK, September 7–9, 2005, Proceedings.* Ed. by Chris Hankin and Igor Siveroni. Vol. 3672. Lecture Notes in Computer Science. Springer, 2005, pp. 352–367. ISBN: 3-540-28584-9. https://doi.org/10.1007/11547662_24.

28. Mattias Ulbrich. "Dynamic Logic for an Intermediate Language: Verification, Interaction and Refinement". PhD thesis. Karlsruhe Institute of Technology, 2013.

29. Yannick Welsch and Arnd Poetzsch-Heffter. "A fully abstract trace-based semantics for reasoning about backward compatibility of class libraries". In: *Sci. Comput. Program.* 92 (2014), pp. 129–161. https://doi.org/10.1016/j.scico.2013.10.002.

30. Yannick Welsch and Arnd Poetzsch-Heffter. "Full Abstraction at Package Boundaries of Object-Oriented Languages". In: *Formal Methods, Foundations and Applications - 14th Brazilian Symposium, SBMF 2011, São Paulo, Brazil, September 26–30, 2011, Revised Selected Papers.* Ed. by Adenilso da Silva Simão and Carroll Morgan. Vol. 7021. Lecture Notes in Computer Science. Springer, 2011, pp. 28–43. ISBN: 978-3-642-25031-6. https://doi.org/10.1007/978-3-642-25032-3_3.

31. Hongseok Yang. "Relational separation logic". In: *Theor. Comput. Sci.* 375.1-3 (2007), pp. 308–334. https://doi.org/10.1016/j.tcs.2006.12.036.

Collaborative Work Management
with a Highly-Available Kanban Board

Annette Bieniusa, Peter Zeller, and Shraddha Barke

Abstract Research group leaders and university vice presidents are responsible for tracking progress of many different projects at the same time. Kanban boards have turned into a surprisingly popular approach for project management over the last decade. Their usage spans the management of software development teams following an agile approach, business task management, and organizational development undertaken by collaborative teams. More recently, Kanban boards have also proven to be useful for personal task management. Users are required to break projects down into a collection of individual tasks. The visualization of these tasks (or a subset) helps to prioritize and focus on only a small number of tasks at a time, while tracking progress of their status. Software support for this type of task is highly desirable, but prone to data loss and corruption under concurrent updates. In this paper, we describe the functionality of software products that provide implementations of Kanban boards. We discuss how concurrent operations on these boards, such as moving entries on a board, can lead to unexpected and undesirable results. This type of bugs can be prevented by disallowing concurrent modifications of the application data. Using a formal model of a Kanban board specified in our verification tool Repliss, we show how techniques such as conflict-free replicated data types (CRDTs) can improve the programmability of highly-available systems and where their limits are.

A. Bieniusa · P. Zeller (✉) · S. Barke
TU Kaiserslautern, Kaiserslautern, Germany
e-mail: bieniusa@cs.uni-kl.de; pzeller@cs.uni-kl.de

© Springer Nature Switzerland AG 2018
P. Müller, I. Schaefer (eds.), *Principled Software Development*,
https://doi.org/10.1007/978-3-319-98047-8_4

59

Prelude

"What a week!" - The vice president for research and technology of TU Kunterbunt[1] lets out a deep sigh. *"Being a university vice president is a great job, but there are so many projects to manage with so many people involved that it is really difficult to keep track of everything. I wish there was an easy way to see how the different tasks are progressing."* – *"Have you ever heard of Kanban? We use it for managing our software development work, and it has increased our efficiency and productivity. I actually even use it for tracking my own personal projects, and it increased my personal productivity by 372,01%!"* – *"How could you possibly measure ... Anyway, what is Kanban and how does it work?"* – *"Kanban started as a scheduling system in the manufacturing system of Toyota in the 1940s. Taiichi Ohno devised it as a method for lean manufacturing in the automotive industry. But meanwhile, Kanban really took off in general project management. Software development is nowadays* the *application area for Kanban. A Kanban boards visualizes the progress of different work items (see Fig. 1). It is subdivided into a number of columns that represent the different stages of a work item. Classically, such a subdivision consists of three columns labeled todo, in progress, and done, though teams may add additional columns such as ideas or under review. Items move from left to right over time. To help focusing, each column has a limit of items it should hold."* It begins to dawn on him. *"This also allows to track inefficiencies and find bottlenecks and issues in the flow."* – *"Indeed, this was one of the original purposes of the whole Kanban idea. Further, it would make our project work flows explicit; you could track tasks, give feedback, and evaluate progress."* – *"Yeah, and it could really reduce my inbox load."* – *"Maybe indeed! There is a wide range of collaborative tools available that implement Kanban boards. Why don't you just try?"*

The vice president is convinced: Using a Kanban board will boost his productivity. It is not difficult to convince his team, and so they start off with a mobile app that allows them to collaborate on the next big tasks. The days pass by and everything works fine, his team is enthusiastic. But once in a while strange things happen: items disappear, items get duplicated, or changes are unexpectedly reverted.

The vice president starts thinking. *"What could have caused these issues? Peter was moving a task into the cancelled column at the same time when Annette was moving it to in progress. This somehow must have caused the item to get duplicated in two columns on the board. This should be prevented![2]"* His academic rigorousness is raised. *"I want to have a Kanban board that has simple, understandable semantics, even and in particular under concurrent modifications."* Being a thorough person, merely having semantics does not satisfy him: *"Actually, what I would really like are guarantees that nothing unexpected ever happens in such an app."*

---

[1] This following conversation never happened. Allusion to real-world institutes and persons is purposefully intended, though.

[2] Or at least documented.

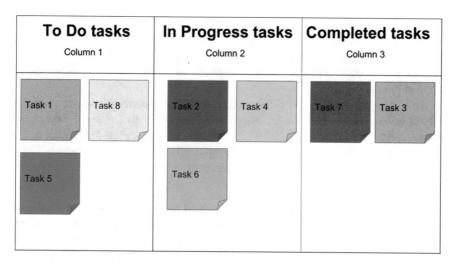

Fig. 1 Kanban board

1 Introduction

Since the release of GoogleDocs in 2006, real-time collaborative editing platforms have shown a wide-spread adoption. When interacting with such systems, users have certain expectations that these systems should satisfy [10]:

- *Convergence:* Users observe identical documents (or more generally, application state) eventually; i.e. even under concurrent modifications, the replicated app states converge to an equivalent state.
- *Causality:* If one update happens before another update, each user observes these updates in this order.
- *Intention preservation:* The intention of an operation has to be preserved at all replicas regardless of interleaving concurrent operations.

Two major technologies have been established to provide real-time collaboration fulfilling these properties. Operational transformation (OT) [4, 9] converts update operations that have been forwarded by other clients, taking into account the effects of concurrent operations which have been previously executed at this client. Conflict-free replicated data types (CRDTs) [8] are abstract data types that extend their respective sequential counterpart with a concurrency semantics such that replicas who have received the same set of updates behave in the same way.

While OT has found wide application in collaborative editing of text documents, CRDTs have proven to be useful in a variety of applications such as gambling [7], navigation coordination [6], and chats [5]. Further, several key-value stores have adopted CRDTs to improve their programmability [2, 3]. In contrast to the plain get/set interface of data stored under some key and limited consistency guarantees, CRDTs offer a data-type specific signature and stronger convergence properties.

However, convergence alone is usually an insufficient guarantee for application developers since it does not prevent anomalies like causality violations or inconsistent intermediate states. Therefore, modern databases like Antidote [1, 11] provide causal consistency and atomic transactions to simplify the development of applications.

Still, it is challenging to preserve the intention of operations and to maintain strong invariants on the data. To support developers in this, we are developing a tool called *Repliss* [14, 15]. The tool consists of a language for modeling the datastore accesses of an application and for specifying application properties. These properties can then be checked using automated testing and partially automated verification.

Outline In this paper, we will demonstrate how to derive a formal model for an application in Repliss and show how to analyze its correctness under concurrent operation. We proceed as follows: Sect. 2 introduces the system architecture. In Sect. 3, we specify the core aspects of the Kanban application in Repliss. The correctness of this model is discussed in Sect. 4 where we identify a problematic situation and its cause. Section 5 then sketches an implementation with insights on how to prevent the unanticipated concurrency bug.

2   System Model

For our Kanban board model, we assume a distributed architecture as sketched in Fig. 2. The application is locally deployed on a number of nodes, representing client devices such as personal computers or mobile devices. On each node, a replica of the data representing the shared state of the application is maintained. The application

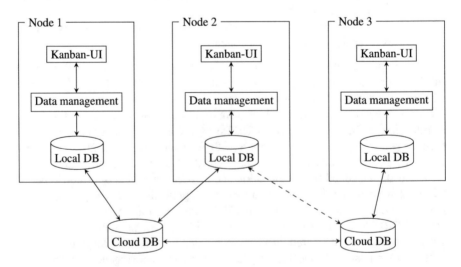

Fig. 2 System architecture

reads and updates the data by accessing the corresponding local replica. Application instances running on different nodes communicate exclusively via this shared data state.

Client-side replication of data is required for supporting an offline mode, i.e. for allowing clients to operate while being (temporarily) disconnected from the network. The local replicas asynchronously exchange data via cloud databases, which can also be replicated for fault tolerance.

To prevent surprising and unintended situations, we assume that the consistency model of the replicated data comprises session guarantees such as Read-your-writes (users observe their own updates), Monotonic Writes (writes become visible in the same order on every replica) or Monotonic Reads (every read observes at least the updates that a preceding read observed) [12]. A consistency model which provides not only sessions guarantees but additionally atomic visibility for a group of operations and convergence under concurrent updates is Transactional Causal+ Consistency [13]. The transactions provided by this model do not provide full isolation in the sense of serializability. However, this model enables high availability and low latency (even under network partitions), causal delivery of updates, and conflict resolution for concurrent updates.

For the programming model, we follow the approach described by Zeller and Poetzsch-Heffter [15]. Though the Repliss tool was initially intended to model and verify applications running on geo-replicated cloud databases, it assumes the same consistency model as described in the previous paragraphs for our client-side replication scheme.

In Repliss, each application consists of a set of procedures that comprises interaction with the shared replicated data and local computations. These procedures constitute the API of an application through which clients can interact with the system. Here, the data management layer of the application is modeled in Repliss and clients invoke procedures via the user interface (UI) of the application. Procedure invocations execute a sequence of operations sequentially. However, concurrent client sessions yield concurrent invocations of procedures (on different nodes).

The Repliss data model supports replicated data types with convergent conflict resolution semantics. For some data types, there are different variants that differ in the way how concurrent updates are handled. The selection of the respective variant is based on the required application behavior. In the next session, we will discuss in detail a data model for our Kanban board.

3   Formal Model of a Kanban Board

For the specification of a formal model, we want to focus on the aspects that are relevant to analyze the problem of the task duplication. Let us start with an informal description of the requirements. The Kanban application provides the functionality to create boards. Each board has a name and a set of columns; each column has

Fig. 3 Data model of the
Kanban application in Repliss

```
idtype BoardId
idtype ColumnId
idtype TaskId
type String

crdt board: Map_aw[BoardId, {
    name: Register[String],
    columns: Set_aw[ColumnId]
}]

crdt column: Map_aw[ColumnId, {
    name: Register[String],
    boardid: Register[BoardId],
    tasks: Set_aw[TaskId]
}]

crdt task: Map_aw[TaskId, {
    title: Register[String],
    columnid: Register[ColumnId]
}]
```

again a name and a set of associated tasks. When created, tasks are assigned to some column, but can be moved from one column to another. Other data and operations, such as modifying task descriptions, will not be covered by our core model.

Next, we discuss the two essential aspects of specifying a model for the core component of the Kanban board in Repliss [15]: the data model and the application's operations.

3.1 Data Model

Figure 3 shows the CRDT data model of our Kanban board app.

The definition starts with an introduction of the base data types. The first three lines introduce identifier types (`idtype`) for boards, columns, and tasks. Identifier types are generated by the application (using the `new`-expression) and cannot be guessed by clients. Only after[3] a client has returned an identifier, it can be used by clients in operations.

Repliss provides a data type library with different types of CRDTs. A map named `board` associates a `BoardId` with a board; similarly, there are maps `column` and `task` for the other objects. The purpose of these maps is to model a key-value store, where the data for each board, column, or task is stored under its respective identifier. The CRDT type for the map and the set refers with its postfix `aw` to the concurrency semantics of the data types, namely add-wins. The specification of an add-wins collection states that an element x is contained in the collection, if there

---

[3]Here "after" refers to global time. It could happen that the application returns a task identifier to a client and then the client uses this identifier to invoke an operation on a different replica where the task data has not yet been replicated.

was an update event `add(x)` and there is was no update event `remove(x)` that happened causally after the `add(x)`.[4]

Since we want to focus on the app's behavior when concurrently operating on tasks and columns, we restrict our data model to the essential information. A board consists of a `name` and its set of `columns`. The column name and board id are of type `Register` that resolves concurrent updates by giving precedence to the latest update (last-writer-wins semantics). A column is given as a record of `name`, a set of tasks, and the board id that the column belongs to. Finally, each task has a `title` and a reference to the column where the task currently resides in.

3.2 Operations

In Fig. 4, we show an implementation of the application API in Repliss. The application procedures use the operations on the CRDTs of the data model to manipulate the data. The synchronization of the data between replicas is done automatically using the conflict resolution implemented by the corresponding data types and need not be addressed by the developer.

The core features of the app are covered by four operations. The first operation causes the creation of a board (`createBoard`). The **new** operator generates a new *unique* identifier of type `BoardId`. In the example, the call to `board_name_assign` assigns in the map `board` to the entry `name` of record under the new id (`b`) the String value `n`. The compound name of operations on map CRDTs such as `board_name_assign` comprise the name of the map (`board`), the name of field in the value (`name`), and the operation on the respective field CRDT type (`assign`); the parameters are the key for the map entry (here, the respective identifiers) and parameters for the operation on the nested CRDT. Since no entry has been added for id `b` yet, the modification also generates the record for the new board. When adding a column to a board, both the corresponding column object and the board need to be adapted. To ensure that these modifications become visible at the same time, we use the **atomic** keyword to group these operations (similarly for `createTask`). The `moveTask` operation involves removing the corresponding `task_id` from one column and adding it to another column. In addition, the information about the current column of the task is updated.

---

[4]Since none of the modeled operations delete a board/column/task, the choice of concurrency semantics for the maps is not relevant. However, it is relevant for the add-wins sets, `Set_aw`.

```
def createBoard(n: String): BoardId {
    var b: BoardId
    b = new BoardId
    call board_name_assign(b, n)
    // add board id to list_boards
    return b
}

def addColumn(board_id: BoardId, name:String): ColumnId {
    var c: ColumnId
    c = new ColumnId
    atomic {
        call column_name_assign(c, name)
        call column_boardid_assign(c, board_id)
        call board_columns_add(board_id, c)
    }
    return c
}

def createTask(column_id: ColumnId, title: String) : TaskId {
    var t: TaskId
    t = new TaskId
    atomic {
        call column_tasks_add(column_id, t)
        call task_title_assign(t, title)
        call task_columnid_assign(t, column_id)
    }
    return t
}

def moveTask(task_id: TaskId, column_id: ColumnId) {
    var oldcolumn_id: ColumnId
    atomic {
        oldcolumn_id = task_columnid_get(task_id)
        call column_tasks_remove(oldcolumn_id, task_id)
        call column_tasks_add(column_id, task_id)
        call task_columnid_assign(task_id, column_id)
    }
}
```

Fig. 4 Operations of the Kanban application in Repliss

Interlude

"Well, this wasn't too hard, was it?" – The team members are amazed. "Actually, this model looks really neat. But, now I am actually confused?" The vice president furrows his brow. "What do you mean?" – "Well, the app that is modeled here is obviously buggy since tasks appear sometimes in two different columns. But none of the operations is actually moving a task into two columns! When creating a task, it is put into one column. And when moving the task, we take it out from one column and then add it to another column." – "As usual, concurrency is the root of all evil. The question is whether using CRDTs and atomic annotations did actually solve our problem." He ponders. "The app model is just a first step. For proving the correctness, we first need to formally specify what correctness means for this application." – "Duplications or deletions due to concurrent modifications is wrong." – "Hmm, invariants could be helpful to define this core aspect of

correctness. Can you formulate your correctness condition as invariant?" The other thinks hard. "I think a task should always be associated with exactly one column." – "Let's take this insight as a starting point for the invariant. Once we formulated them, we can run tests and even try to prove the correctness of our Kanban board model."

4 On Correctness of the Model

For our Kanban board application, it is important, that each task appears in at most one column at any point in time.

Figure 5 shows how to specify this informal invariant in Repliss. We decompose it into three formulas:

- Invariant 1 states that each task is assigned to at most one column.
- Invariants 2 and 3 together state that a task must be contained in the task list of the column that is set in the `column_id` of this task.

Invariant 1 is obviously valid in a sequential setting. However, when trying to verify these invariants on the app model, Repliss returns the counter example found in Fig. 6. Each outer box in the graphics depicts one invocation of the application API. In each invocation we can see smaller boxes representing the transaction and the individual calls made to the database. The arrows denote the happens-before relation between calls.

The produced counter example starts from the initial, empty database state. In the first four API invocations, a board with two columns and one task is created. Then this task is concurrently moved to two different columns. The final invocation observes a database state where both move-operations are visible and the invariant is violated. The two concurrent moves triggered concurrent add- and remove-calls on the database and since we used a set with add-wins semantics, our task is now present in the task-set of both columns. This clearly violates invariant 1 and since the semantics of the `Register` CRDT states that `columnid` contains the last value written, the register will contain only one of the column identifiers. For the other one, the invariant check fails.

```
// 1) Each task is assigned to at most one column.
invariant (forall c1: ColumnId, c2: ColumnId, t: TaskId ::
    column_tasks_contains(c1, t) && column_tasks_contains(c2, t) ==> c1 == c2)

// 2) If a task is in the set of column c, then the column-id of the task is c.
invariant (forall c: ColumnId, t: TaskId ::
      column_tasks_contains(c, t) ==> c == task_columnid_get(t))

// 3) If the column-id of a task is c, then the task is in the set for column c.
invariant (forall c: ColumnId, t: TaskId ::
    c == task_columnid_get(t) ==> column_tasks_contains(c, t))
```

Fig. 5 Application invariants formalized in Repliss

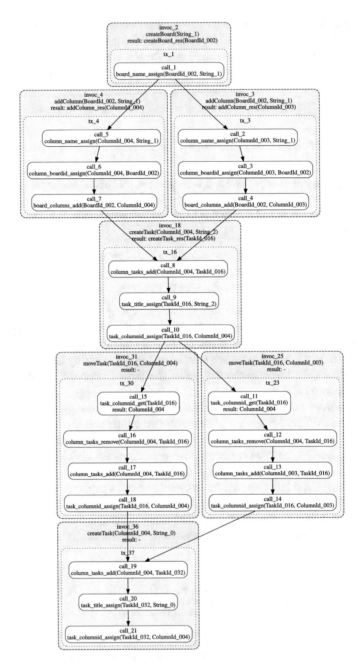

Fig. 6 Counter example found by Repliss

For invariant 3, this situation is not problematic since the add-wins set ensures that the set of tasks is always a superset of the tasks referencing the column. We can use Repliss to check invariant 3 individually and see that no violation is found.

In the next section, we will see how the knowledge about failing invariants 1 and 2 can be employed to provide the desired semantics to the user in an implementation.

5 From Model to Implementation

Now that the model is analyzed with Repliss, we know which invariants we can rely on and we can start translating the model into a corresponding program in a concrete programming language and database.

Using Antidote as the database and Java as the programming language, we can start by translating the data model from the Repliss model in Fig. 3 to the Java definitions in Fig. 7, which use the Antidote Java client. For the id-types in the Repliss model, we created individual Java classes. The top-level CRDTs in the Repliss model were maps. We can omit them in the Java implementation, since Antidote is a key-value store and therefore does not need this extra map for storing several objects under a key. Instead, we create buckets for the top-level CRDTs, which introduce namespaces in the Antidote key-value store.

```java
import static eu.antidotedb.client.Key.*;
// Buckets:
private static Bucket boards = Bucket.bucket("board-bucket");
private static Bucket columns = Bucket.bucket("column-bucket");
private static Bucket tasks = Bucket.bucket("task-bucket");

// Object representation as maps:
static MapKey boardMap(BoardId board_id) {
    return map_rr(board_id.getId());
}

private static MapKey columnMap(ColumnId column_id) {
    return map_rr(column_id.getId());
}

private static MapKey taskMap(TaskId task_id) {
    return map_rr(task_id.getId());
}

// fields of board:
private static final RegisterKey<String> f_name = register("Name");
private static final SetKey<ColumnId> f_columns = set("columns", new ColumnId.Coder());
// fields of column:
private static final RegisterKey<BoardId> f_boardId = register("BoardId", new BoardId.Coder());
private static final SetKey<TaskId> f_tasks = set("TaskId", new TaskId.Coder());
// fields of task
private static final RegisterKey<ColumnId> f_columnId = register("ColumnId", new ColumnId.Coder());
private static final RegisterKey<String> f_title = register("Title");
private static final RegisterKey<String> f_dueDate = register("DueDate");
```

Fig. 7 Data model of the Kanban application in Java

```java
public static void moveTask(AntidoteClient client, TaskId t, ColumnId c) {
    try (InteractiveTransaction tx = client.startTransaction()) {
        ColumnId old = tasks.read(tx, taskMap(t)).get(f_columnId);
        columns.update(tx, columnMap(old).update(f_tasks.remove(t)));
        columns.update(tx, columnMap(c).update(f_tasks.add(t)));
        tasks.update(tx, taskMap(t).update(f_columnId.assign(c)));
        tx.commitTransaction();
    }
}
```

Fig. 8 Implementation of moveTask in Java

For representing boards, columns, and tasks, we use maps with recursive-reset semantics from Antidote. The functions boardMap, columnMap, and taskMap, construct a corresponding key referencing that map for a given object identifier of the right type. To access the different fields of an object, we define a constant per field, which holds the name and type of the corresponding map field.

Having defined the data model, the translation of a Repliss method to Java is straightforward. As an example, Fig. 8 shows the translation of the moveTask method to Java. The atomic block is translated to an interactive Antidote transaction. Database calls can be identified in the Java code, because they have to pass the transaction tx as an argument.

One difference between the Repliss model and the implementation is that the model only reads the columnId field of the task, whereas the Java code reads the whole map from the database and then uses get to extract the field value on the client side. In general, Antidote does not (yet) support querying only parts of an object, while Repliss does not (yet) support operations that return multiple values. However, this mismatch does not affect correctness, since we can use transactions to group several queries together.

5.1 Working with Inconsistencies and Invariants

In the previous section, we have seen that invariants 1 and 2 are not valid under concurrent executions of moveTask: There can be states, where a task is stored in multiple columns. However, we do not want this inconsistency to be visible to users. For the implementation, we can use a trick by "repairing" the invariant on a view of the data when loading a column from the database as shown in Fig. 9. The method getColumn reads all tasks in a column by iterating over the tasks-field of the column. It uses the columnId stored in each task as a double-check and includes only the tasks with a matching columnId into the result set tasks. Since the columnId of a task is a single value, this ensures that a task only appears in one column at a time.

But can we be sure that getColumn includes all tasks, which actually belong to the column? To reason about this property, invariant 3 comes in handy. We have checked for our Repliss model that if the columnId of a task is c, then the task is in

```java
public static Column getColumn(InteractiveTransaction tx, ColumnId c) {
    MapReadResult column = columns.read(tx, columnMap(c));
    String columnName = column.get(f_name);
    BoardId boardId = column.get(f_boardId);
    Map<TaskId, Task> tasks = new LinkedHashMap<>();
    for (TaskId t : column.get(f_tasks)) {
        Task task = getTask(tx, t);
        if (Objects.equals(task.getColumnId(), c)) {
            // repair: only add tasks if they really are in this column
            tasks.put(t, task);
        }
    }
    return new Column(columnName, boardId, tasks);
}
```

Fig. 9 Implementation of getColumn in Java

the set for column c. Therefore, calling getColumn(c) will always include the task and thus no important task can be lost.

In the future, we plan to extend Repliss, so that it can also check functions like getColumn. The current version of the Repliss language does not include loops, so this example cannot be modeled.

Postlude

"Programming distributed systems is really hard. Considering all these weird possible interleavings and concurrency of operations is giving me a headache." His team needs a break. "Well, this was a pleasant diversion from all this administration tasks that I have to deal with day by day." The vice president leans back and admires the result. "Ah, sometimes I miss doing research on a full-time basis. There is so much to explore, so much to discover! What a pity that developers claim that it is too difficult and time consuming to verify or at least test what they are doing. Verification should be part of the curriculum for all CS students - even the freshmen would benefit from techniques like equational reasoning or the Hoare calculus. I have a new task for my Kanban board: Improve the curriculum!"

Acknowledgements The work described in this paper is based on research supported in part by the EU H2020 project "LightKone" (732505) https://www.lightkone.eu/.

References

1. Deepthi Devaki Akkoorath et al. "Cure: Strong semantics meets high availability and low latency". In: *International Conference on Distributed Computing Systems (ICDCS 2016)* Nara, Japan: IEEE, June 2016.
2. Cihan Biyikoglu. *Under the Hood: Redis CRDTs (white paper)*. 2018. URL: https://redislabs.com/docs/active-active-whitepaper/.

3. Sean Cribbs and Russell Brown. "Data Structures in Riak". In: *Riak Conference (RICON)*. San Francisco, CA, USA, Oct. 2012. URL: https://speakerdeck.com/u/basho/p/data-structures-in-riak.

4. Clarence A. Ellis and Simon J. Gibbs. "Concurrency Control in Groupware Systems". In: *Proceedings of the 1989 ACM SIGMOD International Conference on Management of Data, Portland, Oregon, May 31–June 2, 1989*. Ed. by James Clifford, Bruce G. Lindsay, and David Maier. ACM Press, 1989, pp. 399–407. https://doi.org/10.1145/67544.66963 URL: http://doi.acm.org/10.1145/67544.66963.

5. Todd Hoff. *How League of Legends Scaled Chat To 70 Million Players — It Takes Lots Of Minions*. http://highscalability.com/blog/2014/10/13/how-league-of-legends-scaled-chat-to-70-million-players-it-t.html. Oct. 2014.

6. Dmitry Ivanov and Nami Nasserazad. "Practical Demystification of CRDTs" In: *CurryOn* Rome, Italy, July 2016. URL: https://www.youtube.com/watch?v=ShiU9g5JFq8.

7. Dan Macklin. *Key Lessons Learned from Transition to NoSQL at an Online Gambling Website*. http://www.infoq.com/articles/key-lessons-learned-from-transition-to-nosql. Nov 2015.

8. Marc Shapiro et al. "Convergent and Commutative Replicated Data Types". In: *Bulletin of the EATCS* 104 (2011), pp. 67–88. URL: http://eatcs.org/beatcs/index.php/beatcs/article/view/120.

9. Chengzheng Sun and Clarence A. Ellis. "Operational Transformation in Real-Time Group Editors: Issues, Algorithms, and Achievements". In: *CSCW '98, Proceedings of the ACM 1998 Conference on Computer Supported Cooperative Work, Seattle, WA, USA, November 14–18, 1998*. Ed. by Steven E. Poltrock and Jonathan Grudin. ACM, 1998, pp. 59–68. ISBN: 1-58113-009-0. https://doi.org/10.1145/289444.289469. URL: http://doi.acm.org/10.1145/289444.289469.

10. Chengzheng Sun et al. "Achieving Convergence, Causality Preservation, and Intention Preservation in Real-Time Cooperative Editing Systems". In: *ACM Trans. Comput.-Hum. Interact.* 5.1 (1998), pp. 63–108. https://doi.org/10.1145/274444.274447. URL: http://doi.acm.org/10.1145/274444.274447.

11. *Antidote Reference Platform*. http://antidotedb.org/. Accessed 31 May 2018. 2016.

12. Douglas B. Terry et al. "Session Guarantees for Weakly Consistent Replicated Data". In: *Proceedings of the Third International Conference on Parallel and Distributed Information Systems (PDIS 94), Austin, Texas, September 28–30, 1994*. IEEE Computer Society, 1994, pp. 140–149. ISBN: 0-8186-6400-2. https://doi.org/10.1109/PDIS.1994.331722. URL: https://doi.org/10.1109/PDIS.1994.331722.

13. Marek Zawirski et al. "Write Fast, Read in the Past: Causal Consistency for Client-Side Applications". In: *Proceedings of the 16th Annual Middleware Conference, Vancouver, BC, Canada, December 07–11, 2015*. Ed. by Rodger Lea et al. ACM, 2015, pp. 75–87. ISBN: 978-1-4503-3618-5. https://doi.org/10.1145/2814576.2814733. URL: http://doi.acm.org/10.1145/2814576.2814733.

14. Peter Zeller. "Testing Properties of Weakly Consistent Programs with Repliss". In: *Proceedings of the 3rd International Workshop on Principles and Practice of Consistency for Distributed Data*. PaPoC'17. Belgrade, Serbia: ACM, 2017, 3:1–3:5. ISBN: 978-1-4503-4933-8. https://doi.org/10.1145/3064889.3064893. URL: http://doi.acm.org/10.1145/3064889.3064893.

15. Peter Zeller and Arnd Poetzsch-Heffter. "Towards a Proof Framework for Information Systems with Weak Consistency". In: *Software Engineering and Formal Methods - 14th International Conference, SEFM 2016, Held as Part of STAF 2016, Vienna, Austria, July 4–8, 2016, Proceedings*. Ed. by Rocco De Nicola and Eva Kühn. Vol. 9763. Lecture Notes in Computer Science. Springer, 2016, pp. 277–283. ISBN: 978-3-319-41590-1. https://doi.org/10.1007/978-3-319-41591-8_19.

A Case for Certifying Compilers in Industrial Automation

Jan Olaf Blech

Abstract Certifying Compilers are compilers that (1) compile programs from a source language into a target language, and (2) check their results for each compilation run by using a separate dedicated checker. In many cases, certifying compilers can guarantee compilation correctness for individual compilation runs, i.e., they guarantee that target code is a correct translation of given source code. This paper advocates the use of certifying compilers in industrial automation: It describes basic principles, potential benefits and future research directions: it connects work on certifying compilers, compiler correctness, and verification approaches in the area of industrial automation.

1 Introduction

This paper motivates the use of certifying compilers in the area of industrial automation. We motivate why industrial automation seems a good choice for the application of certifying compilers both from the perspectives of the involved research and application fields. We identify new research challenges in the intersection of these research fields, review existing work, and present and motivate new research directions.

Guaranteeing correctness of compilation has been studied for decades (see, e.g., [13] for a survey and [22] for a pioneering 1960s paper on compiler correctness). Different rigour has been applied for guaranteeing the correctness of compilers: rather lightweight methods may just focus on increased testing activity in the field of compilation, while rigorous methods require formal proofs. Compilation correctness can be achieved by using either verified compilers or certifying compilers. Both, certifying compilers and verified compilers can be seen as a kind of software engineering pattern. In an ideal world, verified compilers have been proven by mathematical means to always work correctly, whereas certifying compilers only

J. O. Blech (✉)
Altran, Munich, Germany

© Springer Nature Switzerland AG 2018
P. Müller, I. Schaefer (eds.), *Principled Software Development*,
https://doi.org/10.1007/978-3-319-98047-8_5

check compilation correctness for each individual compiler run and the checking process has been shown to work correctly. Checking individual compilation runs can be much easier. Hence, it is easier to achieve certifying compilers as opposed to verifying an entire compiler. This is especially true, when considering compiler optimizations, where much of the complexity lies in compilation algorithms aiming at the discovery of an optimal or a near optimal compilation solution, whereas the correctness of the solution can be checked using a less sophisticated algorithm.

With the advent of trends such as Industrie 4.0 [20] and the (Industrial) Internet of Things, software development for industrial automation—traditionally carried out by "classical" engineers with no special software training—has gained increased interest from disciplines such as computer science and software engineering. Traditional programmable logic controller (PLC)-based solutions and field buses used in industrial automation are increasingly combined with IT equipment and standards. Mass-produced off-the-shelf CPUs, computers, and networking technology such as ethernet have found their way into the industrial automation world.

Software development in industrial automation traditionally relies on standards such as IEC 61131–3 or the newer IEC 61499 that come with sets of languages to program PLCs. Integrated development environments with rich tool support such as the Siemens Step 7 framework[1] or tools for the ABB AC500 PLC series[2] exist. In addition, languages such as C and even Python are frequently used to program PLCs or PLC-like devices. With the exception of Python, these languages require a compiler in order to produce machine executable code, but even Python relies on compiled libraries. Academia has produced a rich set of analysis techniques and tools for IEC 61131–3-based code (see [15] for a survey) and IEC 61499-based developments (see [17] for a survey). These range from static analysis techniques (e.g., [29]) to model checking approaches (e.g., [4]) and combinations of techniques (e.g., [5]). Furthermore, tools and methods to analyse the interaction of different devices (e.g., Petri net-based approaches, such as [2]) are available, in order to analyse timing constraints.

Software in industrial automation is characterized by the facts that:

- It is usually written for a relatively small number of systems. There are few factories that are identical to each other, therefore, each PLC controlling a distinct device in a factory has to be programmed to work in this "unique" environment.
- A high degree of reliability is required. Factory downtimes are expensive, e.g., a single conveyor belt fault in a car factory can stop the entire car production of a manufacturing line, leaving potentially thousands of workers idle and disturbing the sophisticated supply and just-in-time logistic chains associated with the manufacturing line.
- In some cases, where machines work together with humans, faults in industrial automation devices can be safety critical.

---

[1]https://w3.siemens.com/mcms/simatic-controller-so retrieved 06. April 2018.
[2]http://new.abb.com/plc/automationbuilder/platform/software retrieved 06. April 2018.

Note, that the first item is fundamentally different in related disciplines such as automotive, where developments are characterized by the fact that they are deployed on sometimes millions of almost identical cars.

Guaranteeing compilation correctness in industrial automation is not a stand-alone topic. To guarantee that analysed code properties are still fulfilled in the executable code, one needs some form of verified compilation results.

Related to compiler correctness is the area of correct model transformations, where similar challenges can be found [11]. Some of the IEC 61131–3 and IEC 61499-based languages comprise features that are typically associated with model-based development such as graphical language elements and interconnected blocks, where interconnections indicate data or control dependencies.

Overview

Section 2 provides an overview on design patterns for guaranteeing compilation correctness. Standards and challenges for software development in industrial automation are discussed in Sect. 3. Section 4 presents our existing work and highlights research challenges in the intersection between certifying compilers and industrial automation and related fields of research as well as benefits. A conclusion is given in Sect. 5.

2 Certifying Compilers vs. Compiler Verification

Both, certifying compilers and compiler verification aim at guaranteeing the correctness of compilation results. We primarily advocate for solutions that provide this guarantee by using mathematical/logical proofs. These proofs are based on formal semantics of the involved source and target languages. In some settings, however, less stringent solutions are also applicable.

2.1 Semantics

Important ingredients for both certifying compilers and compiler verification is a thorough understanding of the involved source and target languages. Semantics of these languages need to be defined and related, so that one can specify a notion of correct compilation. Different classes of semantics specification mechanisms exist. For example, if we are interested in a reactive system, we may have to use an operational semantics of the involved languages.

Compilation correctness refers to the correct translation of a source into a target program. From a mathematical standing, it can be expressed as a relation $R \subseteq \mathscr{S} \times \mathscr{T}$ between source $\mathscr{S}$ and target languages $\mathscr{T}$ such that $R(s, t)$ denotes that $s \in \mathscr{S}$ and $t \in \mathscr{T}$ are semantically equivalent. Other correctness definitions based on (weak-) (bi-)simulation can be used, thereby, indicating that the source program may specify an overapproximation of behavior compared to the target program. This overapproximation manifests itself in degrees of freedom of the compilation process.

In the simplest case, the semantics specifications and their relation can be done implicit as for example:

- By writing a checker that relates source and target language, thereby, indicating if there is a correspondence. Such a checker realizes the relation R from an implementation perspective by taking a source and a target program as inputs and returning a Boolean, thereby, indicating the correctness of the compilation process.
- By textual reports such as language standards and compilation requirements that may be organized in a specification document.

Otherwise, the semantics specification can be done in a highly explicit way, by using formal description mechanisms such as mathematics and logics which can be further formalized in a proof assistant such as Coq[3] or Isabelle.[4]

2.2 Trusted Computing Base

When speaking about correctness of computations, the notion of trusted computing base (TCB) is of importance. In our compiler-case, the TCB comprises all software parts one has to trust to be convinced that the target code is indeed a correct compilation of the source code. To minimize verification efforts, we want to keep the TCB as small as possible.

2.3 Verified Compilers

The verified compiler principle is shown in Fig. 1. In the case of the verified compiler, the TCB comprises the whole compiler. This means, all algorithms, even the ones that only search through state spaces for optimal compilation solutions (e.g., register allocation, memory usage optimization, execution speed optimizations), related data structures, even the ones that only store intermediate results during the

---

[3]https://coq.inria.fr/ retrieved 12. June 2018.
[4]http://isabelle.in.tum.de/ retrieved 12. June 2018.

Fig. 1 Verified compiler

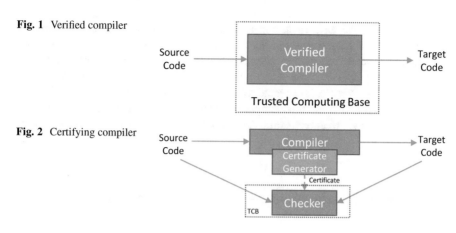

Fig. 2 Certifying compiler

compilation process have to be included in the verification process. The verified compiler principle guarantees compilation correctness for the whole compiler and, thus, for each compilation run.

2.4 Certifying Compilers

Figure 2 depicts the certifying compiler principle. In addition to the compiler, a certificate checker checks whether a compiler run was conducted correctly. This may require some instantiation of the compiler. The certificate checker may agree with the compilation, reject it, or indicate that it cannot decide whether the compilation process was correct. The certificate only guides the certificate checker, containing some clues that contain, e.g., optimization results. If the certificate is wrong, the checker will not accept the compilation. In the case of certifying compilers, the TCB comprises only the certificate checker. Thus, checking compilation correctness can be significantly simpler, since much of the complexity of the compiler such as optimization algorithms do not need to be taken into account. The certifying compiler approach guarantees compilation correctness for each successful compiler and checker run. While the verification effort is reduced, we cannot easily guarantee that there are no correct compilation runs that are rejected by the certificate checker.

Variants of the certifying compiler principle exist. They have been called proof generating compilers [28] and translation validation [24, 27]. Sometimes, only limited correctness aspects such as type safety [25] are regarded. In our work, we have used the Coq [7–9, 18] and Isabelle [6, 16] proof assistants/theorem provers as certificate checkers. The certificate is emitted by an extension of the compiler that does not belong to the TCB. The certificate is a Coq or Isabelle proof script generated by the compiler. The proof scripts guide the proof checker through the process of verifying semantical equivalence or a weaker notion of semantical correspondence of source and target program. They comprise intermediate results from the compilation process such as mappings discovered by the compiler.

Furthermore, we have looked at a certificate mechanism for verification tools [19] that feature a similar setup: a specification and a condition that is supposed to hold is formulated using a programming language-style syntax. The verification tool provides a kind of result using a target language. The complexity lies in the discovery of the verification result, whereas the checking if the result holds can be relatively simple. Transforming proved properties between languages [23] is an important approach to carry results achieved by other verification tools over to the target language.

3 Software Development for Industrial Automation

This section describes the software development prerequisites for industrial automation. We pick the IEC 61131–3 and the IEC 61499 standard as widely applied examples for programming and specification of PLC programs.

3.1 Programmable Logic Controllers

Traditionally industrial automation features the use of programmable logic controllers to control devices such as conveyor belts, machines, and to a smaller extend robots. Robots, however, typically come with their own set of controllers. PLCs focus on input and output capabilities, which are sometimes organized in a "rack-style". PLCs are increasingly often based on standard IT technology and frequently interconnected using either field buses such as Profibus or standard IT technologies such as ethernet. There is usually at least a Supervisory Control and Data Acquisition (SCADA) system to coordinate PLC activities and perform some basic form of monitoring and user interaction.

Figure 3 shows an example of standard IT technology realizing industrial automation equipment: a PLC based on a Raspberry Pi computer. It runs Linux, features ethernet and USB connectors, and has been extended with input and output boards to overcome the voltage difference between industrial sensors and actuators and the Raspberry Pi. Multiple operations are typically done in parallel, since multiple work-pieces are processed at the same time. Figure 4 shows a conveyor belt with several pick-and-place and sorting devices. It is controlled by the three boxes below each one hosting a PLC. In addition to the actuators, sensors deliver information on the state of the actuators and positions of workpieces.

Standards such as IEC 61131–3 or IEC 61499 define sets of languages to program individual PLCs. A prerequisite for guaranteeing compilation correctness is the establishment of some form of semantics for the involved languages. For example, we have formalized subsets of IEC 61131–3 in [10] using the Coq proof assistant using operational semantics. Further formal specification work for PLC programs has been carried out in safety critical domains such as nuclear facilities [31].

Fig. 3 PLC based on a Raspberry Pi (see [26])

Fig. 4 PLCs controlling parts of an example factory (see [26])

PLC programs are traditionally executed periodically in a loop within a given cycle time. This execution is repeated for the whole run-time of a system. This is shown in Fig. 5 and features a read-input phase, the execution of the actual programs, and a write-output phase. Note, when looking at compilation correctness of the actual program, one does not have to take side effects into account, since observable: input and output are restricted to the beginning and end of a program. This can simplify the required notion of compilation correctness and, thus, verification or certification effort, since the semantics of source and target languages can be less complex.

The periodical execution means that a PLC program must terminate within a given time limit so that the cycle time is met. Thus, typical PLC programs do not use constructs such as non-terminating loops or unbounded recursive function calls that can make the task of checking semantical equivalence between programs undecidable.

3.2 IEC 61131–3

The IEC 61131–3 standard comprises the following languages:

- Ladder diagrams (LD): a graphical language that resembles electric circuits.
- Function block diagrams (FBD): another graphical language, where function blocks are interconnected, each one receiving inputs from these interconnections to calculate output results that can be passed via interconnections to other function blocks. An example FBD for a simple integer arithmetic function is shown in Fig. 6.

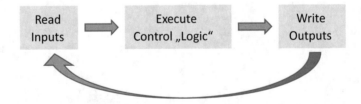

Fig. 5 PLC execution cycle

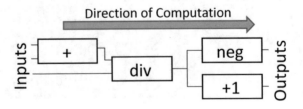

Fig. 6 Example FBD

- Structured text (ST): a textual, pascal-like language.
- Instruction lists (IL): a textual language resembling assembler.
- Sequential function charts (SFC): another graphical language, where control is passed between different steps (blocks). Actions are associated with steps which are executed once a step is activated until the step is deactivated. Multiple steps can be activated at the same time. Actions may be specified in other languages than SFC from the IEC 61131–3 standard. Figure 7 shows an SFC excerpt. Control is passed from the above step to the two parallel steps below, if the condition becomes true. The full control passing semantics of SFCs follows a petri-net-based paradigm, although this is not supported by the software tools of every PLC vendor.

3.3 IEC 61499

IEC 61499 [32] features function blocks and their interconnections as basic ingredients. A function block comes with incoming and outgoing event and data ports that trigger the execution of the function block. A key feature is the ability to distribute different function blocks over different cores or even PLCs. Code generation has to be adapted to support this feature. Figure 8 shows interconnected function blocks. Function blocks receive input on the left side, whereas the right side is the output side. One can see the event part in the upper-half of a function block and the data part in the lower-half.

Formal specifications for languages and programs in industrial automation can have additional benefits. In the work presented in [30], we have used program specifications to generate a runtime checker for IEC 61499-based programs. This

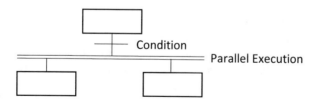

Fig. 7 Conditional parallel split

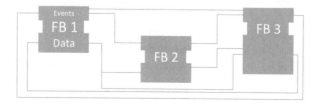

Fig. 8 Function blocks in IEC 61499

takes the certifying compiler approach one step further such that we do not even look at the compiled program, but check at runtime if it fulfills its specification.

The code generation process for industrial automation can involve different transformation steps, each one comprising well defined source and target languages. For example, in the 4DIAC tool,[5] IEC 61499 specifications are first transformed into C++ code, before a C++ compiler is invoked to generate machine code for the specific PLC.

4 Compilation Correctness in Industrial Automation

The establishment of solutions to guarantee compilation correctness for industrial automation seems to be a relatively "low hanging fruit". At least, when compared to guaranteeing compilation correctness for other application domains such as standard IT systems. Independently from the used programming language or specification language, some reasons for the relatively low complexity of guaranteeing compilation correctness in industrial automation are summarized in the first subsection below. Additional challenges for PLC verification are described afterwards. Benefits and research challenges are described in the last subsection.

4.1 Compilation Correctness as a "Low Hanging" Fruit

The involved PLC programs follow a cyclic input-processing-output pattern. This has the following impacts:

- It limits the number of programming language constructs that are used in the programs.
- It simplifies the specification of the semantics of the involved programming languages. Since observable behavior does only occur at the end of an execution cycle, we do not need full operational semantics specification of the programs.
- It allows for a relatively simple specification of the intended behavior of the program as a whole. Sometimes, an Excel sheet is enough (see our work in [1]: here, we were able to use model checkers to check IEC 61131–3-based specifications against behavior specified in Excel sheets). The relatively simple specification is often reflected in program code composed of structurally simple patterns.
- Each input-processing-output cycle is expected to terminate after a well defined cycle-time. This puts an upper limit on the number of states that a system may encounter within a single cycle and, thus, simplifies the semantics.

---

[5]https://eclipse.org/4diac/ retrieved 12. June 2018.

A typical PLC program is relatively small and can be checked for correctness individually. If programs become larger, the structural complexity is usually not increased. Typically, additional if-conditions are just added to the program, sometimes hundreds. This can make a program hard to read, but from a certifying compiler perspective, it is not difficult to deal with. For these reasons, both compiler verification and certifying compilation can be easier to achieve for PLCs.

The certifying compiler is favoured by us over the verified compiler pattern due to its lower complexity. Furthermore, in industrial automation, it seems acceptable if the checker can not come to a conclusion, since we have relatively long development cycles and there is always the possibility to modify a PLC program in the development process, so that a checker may come to a positive conclusion on the modified version.

When using general purpose programming languages, one can restrict oneself to a language subset that is actually used in the industrial automation domain. This significantly reduces specification and verification efforts compared to full classical programming languages such as Java and other imperative or object-oriented general purpose languages. Sophisticated verification techniques have been developed [14, 21] to address challenges such as unbounded stacks and relatively complicated memory heap structures as well as related type system issues which are typically not present in industrial automation.

Nevertheless, there are also some differences between the languages, language subsets, and specification mechanisms for within the industrial automation domain. We have collected some structural advantages of the newer IEC 61499 over IEC 61131–3 for verification purpose in [12].

4.2 Challenges for PLC Verification

In addition to compilation correctness, other aspects related to verification and formal methods are crucial when focusing on the correctness of an industrial automation installation. A vast amount of complexity of PLC programming lies in the coordination of multiple PLCs, e.g., in a large factory. While this is a challenging verification problem on its own, it does not affect compilation correctness. Petri-net-based approaches can be used to address these problems. There are also some aspects such as timing, that may require an additional semantics specification overhead. Again, however, this is typically not seen as a compilation correctness issue. One can rather leave timing analysis to static analysis such as tools to perform Worst-Case-Execution time analysis [3].

4.3   Benefits and Additional Research Challenges

Guaranteed correct compilation results and guaranteed correct systems are especially beneficial in the industrial automation area. Some reasons are as follows:

- Most systems are highly customized, sometimes only a single instance exists. Therefore, testing is relatively expensive and not likely to reveal all possible bugs.
- On the other hand, the correctness of such systems is crucial, since errors can lead to expensive factory down-times, e.g., if an entire production line is blocked. Safety of the involved staff can also play a role.

We believe that certifying compilers in combination with verification tools that cover

- timing behavior of individual PLCs as well as entire systems;
- analysis of the interplay between different PLCs, both, on the physical machine level as well as on the network level;
- analysis of the cyber-physical factory setups;

will deliver a powerful tool-suit to achieve verified or at least highly analysed and investigated setups, thereby, reducing down-times and improving safety.

5   Conclusion

We have motivated the use of certifying compilers in the area of industrial automation. Some arguments were presented that exemplify why the area of industrial automation is particularly suited for the use of certifying compilers. These comprise relatively simple specifications and programs, and well understood language elements. In addition, benefits which range from reducing expensive down-times to safety of involved factory staff are relevant for industrial automation. Furthermore, an overview of existing work on compiler correctness in industrial automation was given.

A related research topic are analysis and verification tools for industrial automation. Here, work on (formal) semantics and specifications of the involved programs and languages is a shared key ingredient. Furthermore, we can distinguish between:

- Tools that work PLC programs. These comprise tools that work on isolated programs such as static analysis tools that work on source code level or on compiled artifacts.
- Tools that work interconnected groups of PLCs. This comprises the analysis of the interplay between different PLCs. For example, analyzing race conditions, bottlenecks, or deadlocks in a production process.

Both certifying compilers and verification tools seem like promising topics for the future of industrial automation. Both, research areas can benefit from each other and facilitate porting analysis and verification results from source to executable code.

References

1. B. Fernandez Adiego et al. "Applying Model Checking to Industrial-Sized PLC Programs". In: *IEEE Trans. Industrial Informatics.* IEEE, 2015.
2. B. Fernandez Adiego et al "Model-based Automated Testing of Critical PLC Programs". In: *Model-based Automated Testing of Critical PLC Programs. Industrial Informatics (INDIN).* IEEE, 2013.
3. R. Wilhelm et al. "The Worst-case Execution-time Problem—overview of Methods and Survey of Tools". In: *ACM Transactions on Embedded Computing Systems (TECS).* ACM, 2008.
4. N. Bauer et al. "Verification of PLC Programs given as Sequential Function Charts". In: *Integration of software specification techniques for applications in Engineering.* Springer Berlin Heidelberg, 2004.
5. S. Biallas, J. Brauer, and S. Kowalewski. "PLC: A Verification Platform for Programmable Logic Controllers". In: *27th IEEE/ACM International Conference on Automated Software Engineering.* ACM, 2012.
6. J. O. Blech and A. Poetzsch-Heffter. "A Certifying Code Generation Phase". In: *Compiler Optimization meets Compiler Verification (COCV 2007), Braga, Portugal.* Elsevier ENTCS, 2007.
7. J. O. Blech and B. Grégoire. "Certifying Code Generation Runs with Coq: A Tool Description". In: *Compiler Optimization meets Compiler Verification (COCV 2008), Budapest, Hungary.* 2008.
8. J. O. Blech and B. Grégoire. "Certifying Code Generation with Coq". In: *Compiler Optimization meets Compiler Verification (COCV 2008), Budapest, Hungary.* 2008.
9. J. O. Blech and B. Grégoire. "Using Checker Predicates in Certifying Code Generation." In: *Compiler Optimization meets Compiler Verification (COCV 2009), York, UK.* 2009.
10. J. O. Blech and S. Ould Biha. "Verification of PLC Properties Based on Formal Semantics in Coq". In: *9th International Conference on Software Engineering and Formal Methods (SEFM).* LNCS, Springer, 2011.
11. J. O. Blech, I. Schaefer, and A. Poetzsch-Heffter. "Translation Validation for System Abstractions". In: *Runtime Verification (RV'07), Vancouver, Canada.* LCNS, Springer Verlag, 2007.
12. J. O. Blech, P. Lindgren, D. Pereira, V. Vyatkin and A. Zoitl. "A Comparison of Formal Verification Approaches for IEC 61499". In: *Emerging Technologies and Factory Automation (ETFA).* IEEE, 2016.
13. M. A. Dave. "Compiler Verification: A Bibliography". In: *ACM SIGSOFT Software Engineering Notes* ACM, 2003.
14. Drossopoulou et al. "Formal Techniques for Java-like Programs". In: *European Conference on Object-Oriented Programming* Springer, 2002.
15. G. Frey and L. Litz. "Formal Methods in PLC Programming". In: *IEEE International Conference on Systems, Man, and Cybernetics* IEEE, 2000.
16. M. J. Gawkowski, J. O. Blech, and A. Poetzsch-Heffter. "Certifying Compilers based on Formal Translation Contracts". In: *Technical Report 355–06.* University of Kaiserslautern, 2006.
17. H–M. Hanisch et al. "One Decade of IEC 61499 Modeling and Verification-results and Open Issues". In: *Reprints of the 13th IFAC Symposium on Information Control Problems in Manufacturing.* 2009.
18. J. O. Blech and B. Grégoire. "Certifying Compilers Using Higher Order Theorem Provers as Certificate Checkers". In: *Formal Methods in System Design.* Springer-Verlag, 2010.
19. J. O. Blech and M. Périn. "Generating Invariant-based Certificates for Embedded Systems". In: *Transactions on Embedded Computing Systems (TECS).* ACM, 2012.
20. H. Kagermann, W. Wahlster, and J. Helbig. *Recommendations for Implementing the Strategic Initiative INDUSTRIE 4.0 – Final Report of the Industrie 4.0 Working Group.* 2013.
21. G. T Leavens, K. R. M. Leino, and P. Müller. "Specification and Verification Challenges for Sequential Object-oriented Programs". In: *Formal Aspects of Computing.* Springer, 2007.

22. J. McCarthy and J. Painter. "Correctness Of A Compiler For Arithmetic Expression". In: *Proceedings Symposium in Applied Mathematics, Vol 19*. Mathematical Aspects of Computer Science, 1967.
23. P. Müller and M. Nordio. "Proof-transforming Compilation of Programs with Abrupt Termination". In: *Proceedings of the 2007 conference on Specification and verification of component-based systems: 6th Joint Meeting of the European Conference on Software Engineering and the ACM SIGSOFT Symposium on the Foundations of Software Engineering*. ACM, 2007.
24. G. C. Necula. "Translation Validation for an Optimizing Compiler". In: *ACM sigplan notices. Vol. 35. No. 5*. ACM, 2000.
25. G. C. Necula and P Lee. "The Design and Implementation of a Certifying Compiler". In: *ACM SIGPLAN Notices*. ACM, 1998.
26. I. D. Peake and J. O. Blech. "A Candidate Architecture for Cloud-based Monitoring in Industrial Automation". In: *2017 IEEE International Conference on Software Quality Reliability and Security Companion (QRS-C)*. IEEE, 2017.
27. A. Pnueli, M. Siegel, and E. Singerman. "Translation Validation". In: *International Conference on Tools and Algorithms for the Construction and Analysis of Systems*. Springer, 1998.
28. A. Poetzsch-Heffter and M. Gawkowski. "Towards Proof Generating Compilers". In: *Electronic Notes in Theoretical Computer Science*. Elsevier, 2005.
29. B. Schlich, J. Brauer, and S. Kowalewski. "Application of Static Analyses for State-space Reduction to the Microcontroller Binary Code". In: *Science of Computer Programming* Elsevier, 2011.
30. M. Wenger et al. "Remote Monitoring Infrastructure for IEC 61499 Based Control Software". In: *8th International Congress on Ultra Modern Telecommunications and Control Systems*. IEEE, 2016.
31. J. Yoo et al. "PLC-Based Safety Critical Software Development for Nuclear Power Plants". In: *In International Conference on Computer Safety, Reliability, and Security*. Springer, 2004.
32. A. Zoitl and R. Lewis, eds. *Modelling Control Systems using IEC 61499*. IET, 2014. ISBN: 978-1-84919-760-1.

Compositional Semantics for Concurrent Object Groups in ABS

Frank S. de Boer and Stijn de Gouw

Abstract In this paper we introduce a new compositional semantics of the Abstract Behavioral Specification (ABS) language in terms of the *observable* behavior of its concurrent dynamically generated object groups. We show that for such a compositional description we only need to observe traces of asynchronous method calls and the completion of futures. This provides a powerful abstraction from the internal details of the implementation of concurrent object groups, e.g., details concerning when methods are scheduled and futures are read.

1 Introduction

In [9] a powerful generalization of the model of active objects to concurrent components has been introduced. The Abstract Behavioral Specification (ABS) language [5] features such components by means of *concurrent object groups* (cog's, for short). These cog's form the basic run-time constituents of the underlying concurrency model: within a cog at most one thread is active which is executed in parallel with the other cog's. Active objects belonging to different cog's interact only via asynchronous method calls, whereas inside a cog synchronous calls give rise to re-entrant call stacks alike Java threads. In ABS asynchronous calls of methods which specify a return type generate a *future* which uniquely identifies the call and can be used to obtain the return value and synchronize on its completion (see also [3]).

The operational semantics of a core of ABS is also described in [5]. In this paper we introduce a new *compositional* semantics of ABS in terms of the *observable* behavior of the dynamically generated cog's. The main result of this paper is that

F. S. de Boer (✉)
CWI, Amsterdam, The Netherlands
e-mail: frb@cwi.nl

S. de Gouw
Open University, Heerlen, The Netherlands
e-mail: sdg@ou.nl

© Springer Nature Switzerland AG 2018
P. Müller, I. Schaefer (eds.), *Principled Software Development*,
https://doi.org/10.1007/978-3-319-98047-8_6

for such a compositional description we only need to observe asynchronous method calls and completion of futures. That is, for compositionality we do *not* need to observe, for example, when a method is scheduled or when a future is actually read. Synchronous method calls are also unobservable events within a cog. In the compositional semantics an asynchronous method call is modeled as a *synchronous* communication of a corresponding message between the caller and the callee. From the perspective of the callee such a call describes its reception and storage in its queue. The actual execution of the called method by the callee is an internal event which is not observable. We also only observe the completion of a future, that is, reading a future is an internal event which is not observable. Semantically, the completion of a future involves a *broadcast* of the returned value.

The synchronization between the caller and callee of sending and receiving an asynchronous method call and broadcasting the completion of futures allows for an elegant definition of the *compatibility* of the *traces* of observable events of the individual cog's (belonging to a given global system state). The main technical result of this paper is a formal justification of this notion of observable events in terms of *substitutivity* of observable equivalent cog's: we can replace the local computation of a cog without affecting the global behavior with a different local computation with the same observable behavior.

Related Work

In the works (e.g., [2, 4]) on a compositional semantics of active objects their interaction via asynchronous method calls is described by traces which include information about when the called methods are scheduled and when futures are read. This additional information requires complex well-formedness conditions on traces. As stated above, in this paper we show that we do not need such information for a compositional semantics. The above cited papers do not consider cog's. In this paper we describe the internal behavior of cog's in terms of *stacks of synchronous method calls* instead of an unstructured "soup" of processes [5] which requires additional low-level synchronization mechanisms. The use of such stacks of synchronous method calls allows for a clear and transparent structuring of the compositional semantics in terms of three distinct layers describing the sequential behavior of a stack of synchronous method calls, the interleaving of the execution of such stacks within a cog, and finally, the global communication behavior of a system of cog's.

The model of traces of synchronous communication events underlying this work is an elaboration of the trace semantics for Communicating Sequential Processes [8]. In this paper we model the completion of futures by a broadcast. A general calculus of broadcasting systems is described in [7].

Plan of the Paper

In the following section we introduce the ABS language. In Sect. 2 we introduce the basic semantic notions. Section 3 describes the operational semantics of a single thread modeled as a stack of synchronous method calls by means of a labeled transition system, where the labels indicate asynchronous method calls, completion of futures and reading futures. The interleaving of the thread within a single concurrent object group is described in Sect. 4. The computation of a global system of cog's is finally described in Sect. 5. The last Sect. 6 introduces the compositional trace semantics.

2 Preliminaries

Throughout this section and the rest of this paper we assume a given program which specifies a set of classes and a (single) inheritance relation. We distinguish between local and instance variables. The set of local variables is assumed to include the special variable "this".

We start with the following basic semantic notions. We assume for each class C given a (infinite) set O_C, with typical element o, of object references which are used at run-time to identify instances of C. Further, we assume a (infinite) set F, with typical element f, of references which are used at run-time to identify futures.

A *heap h* is formally given as a set of (uniquely) labeled object states $o : s$, where s assigns values to the instance variables of the object o. An object o *exists* in a heap h if and only it has a state in h, that is, $o : s \in h$ ($f : v \in h$), for some object state s (value v). A heap thus represents both the values of the instance variables of a group of objects. A heap is "open" in the sense that $s(x)$, for $o : s \in h$, may refer to an object that does not exist in h, i.e., that belongs to a different group. We denote $s(x)$, for $o : s \in h$, by $h(o.x)$. By s_{init} we denote the object state which results from the initialization of the instance variables of a newly created object. Further, by $h[o.x = v]$ we denote the heap update resulting from the assignment of the value v to the instance variable x of the object o. We denote by $V(e)(\tau, h)$ the value of a side-effect free expression e in the local environment τ and global heap h. In general, we have that $V(x)(s, h) = s(x)$, for a local variable x, and $V(x)(\tau, h) = h(\tau(\text{this}).x)$, for an instance variable x.

A *registry* of futures r is a set of (uniquely) labeled values $f : v$ which indicate that the future f has been resolved with value v. By $r[f = v]$ we denote the update of registry r resulting from assigning the value v to the future f.

A *thread t* is a stack of *closures* of the form (S, τ), where S is a statement and τ is a local environment which assigns values to local variables. By $\tau[x = v]$ we denote the update of the local environment τ resulting from the assignment of the value v to the local variable x.

3 Thread Semantics

In this section we describe the operational semantics of the execution of the basic statements of ABS in the context of a single thread (as introduced above).

A *thread configuration* is a pair $\langle t, h \cup r \rangle$ consisting of a thread t, a union $h \cup r$ of a heap h and a registry of futures r. A transition

$$\langle t, h \cup r \rangle \longrightarrow \langle t', h' \cup r' \rangle$$

between thread configurations $\langle t, h \cup r \rangle$ and $\langle t', h' \cup r' \rangle$ indicates

- the execution of an assignment, or
- the evaluation of a Boolean condition b of an if-then-else or while statement, or
- the execution of an internal synchronous call.

A *labeled* transition

$$\langle t, h \cup r \rangle \xrightarrow{l} \langle t', h' \cup r' \rangle$$

indicates for

$l = o!m(\bar{v})$: an asynchronous call of the method m of the object o with actual parameters $\bar{v}$.

$l = f!v$: a broadcast of the value v for future f.

$l = f?v$ reception of the value v associated with future f.

In the following structural operational semantics for the execution of a single thread, $(S, s) \cdot t$ denotes the result of pushing the closure (S, s) unto the stack t. For notational convenience, we will make use of a run-time syntax of statements by allowing values (including object and future references) as expressions. We omit the transitions for sequential composition, if-then-else, and while statements since they are standard.

Assignment Local Variables

$$\langle (x = e; S, \tau) \cdot t, h \cup r \rangle \longrightarrow \langle (S, \tau') \cdot t, h \cup r \rangle$$

where $\tau' = \tau[x = V(e)(\tau, h)]$. The assignment to a local variable thus only affects the (active) local environment.

Assignment Instance Variables

$$\langle (x = e; S, \tau) \cdot t, h \cup r \rangle \longrightarrow \langle (S, \tau) \cdot t, h' \cup r \rangle$$

where $h' = h[o.x = v]$, for $o = \tau(\text{this}).x$ and $v = V(e)(\tau, h)$.

The assignment to an instance variable only affects the heap.

Get Operation
If $V(y)(\tau, h) = f$ and $f : v \in r$, for some value v, then

$$\langle (x = y.\textbf{get}; S, \tau) \cdot t, h \cup r \rangle \longrightarrow \langle (y = v; S, \tau) \cdot t, h \cup r \rangle$$

Blocking Get Operation
To model a blocking get operation we introduce a distinguished thread configuration Δ:

$$\langle (x = y.\textbf{get}; S, \tau) \cdot t, h \cup r \rangle \longrightarrow \Delta$$

if $V(y)(\tau, h) = f$ and there does not exist a value v such that $f : v \in r$.

Awaiting a Boolean Condition

$$\langle(\mathbf{await}\ b;\ S, \tau) \cdot t, h \cup r\rangle \longrightarrow \langle(S, \tau) \cdot t, h \cup r\rangle$$

if $V(b)(\tau, h) = true$.

Awaiting a Future

$$\langle(\mathbf{await}\ x?;\ S, \tau) \cdot t, h \cup r\rangle \longrightarrow \langle(S, \tau) \cdot t, h \cup r\rangle$$

if $V(x)(\tau, h) = f$ and $f : v \in r$, for some value v.

Asynchronous Method Call

$$\langle(y = x!m(\bar{e});\ S, \tau) \cdot t, h \cup r\rangle \overset{o!m(\bar{v})}{\longrightarrow} \langle(y = f;\ S, \tau) \cdot t, h \cup r\rangle$$

where $o = V(x)(s, h)$. Further, assuming that $\bar{e} = e_1, \ldots, e_n$, we have that $\bar{v} = f, v_1, \ldots, v_n$, where f is a fresh future, and $v_i = V(e_i)(s, h)$, for $i = 1, \ldots, n$. An asynchronous call thus simply generates a corresponding message with the future that uniquely identifies the message as an additional parameter. Note that we do not distinguish between internal and external asynchronous method calls, i.e., whether the callee exists in h or not. This distinction is made at the level of cog's in Sect. 4.

Internal Synchronous Method Call

$$\langle(y = x.m(\bar{e});\ S, \tau) \cdot t, h \cup r\rangle \longrightarrow \langle(S', \tau') \cdot (y = return;\ S, \tau) \cdot t, h \cup r\rangle$$

where $V(x)(s, h) \in O_C$ is an internal object, i.e., it exists in h, and $m(\bar{x})\{S'\}$ is the corresponding method definition in class C. Further, $\tau'(this) = V(x)(\tau, h)$ and $\tau'(x_i) = V(e_i)(\tau, h)$, for $i = 1, \ldots, n$, (here $\bar{e} = e_1, \ldots, e_n$ and $\bar{x} = x_1, \ldots, x_n$). We implicitly assume here that τ' initializes the local variables of m, i.e., those local variables which are not among the formal parameters $\bar{x}$. Upon return for each type a distinguished simple variable $return$ (which is assumed not to appear in the given program) will store the return value (see the transition below for returning a value).

External Synchronous Method Call

$$\langle(y = x.m(\bar{e});\ S, \tau) \cdot t, h \cup r\rangle \overset{o!m(\bar{v})}{\longrightarrow} \langle(y = f.\mathbf{get};\ S, \tau) \cdot t, h \cup r\rangle$$

where $V(x)(s, h) \in O_C$ is an external object, i.e., it does not exist in h, and $m(\bar{x})\{S'\}$ is the corresponding method definition in class C. Further, assuming that $\bar{e} = e_1, \ldots, e_n$, we have that $\bar{v} = f, v_1, \ldots, v_n$, where f is a fresh future, and $v_i = V(e_i)(s, h)$, for $i = 1, \ldots, n$.

We thus model an external synchronous call by an asynchronous call followed by a corresponding get operation.

Class Instantiation

$$\langle (y = \text{ new } C(\bar{e}); S, \tau) \cdot t, h \cup r \rangle \longrightarrow \langle (y = o; y.C(\bar{e}); S, \tau) \cdot t, h \cup \{o : s_{init}\} \cup r \rangle$$

where $o \in O_C$ is a fresh object identity (i.e., not in h). The call of the constructor method is thus modeled by an internal synchronous call.

Cog Instantiation

$$\langle (y = \text{ new cog } C(\bar{e}); S, \tau) \cdot t, h \cup r \rangle \longrightarrow \langle (y = o; y.C(\bar{e}); S, \tau) \cdot t, h \cup r \rangle$$

where $o \in O_C$ is a fresh object identity. As above, the local variable u is used to store temporarily the identity of the new object. Note that the main difference with class instantiation is that the newly created object is *not* added to the heap h and the constructor method is thus invoked by an external synchronous call.

Return Synchronous Call

$$\langle (\text{ return } e; S, \tau) \cdot (S', \tau') \cdot t, h \cup r \rangle \longrightarrow \langle (S', \tau'[return = v]) \cdot t, h \cup r \rangle$$

where $v = V(e)(\tau, h)$. The local variable *return* here is used to store temporarily the return value.

Return Asynchronous Call

$$\langle (\text{ return } e; S, \tau), h \cup r \rangle \xrightarrow{f!v} \langle \epsilon, h \cup r[f = v] \rangle$$

where $f = \tau(dest)$ and $v = V(e)(\tau, h)$. Here *dest* is a distinguished local variable which stores the future uniquely identifying this method invocation. By ϵ de denote the empty statement which indicates termination.

In the above transitions for the creation of a fresh future, a class instance or a new cog we simply assume a mechanism for the selection of a fresh identity, the technical details of which are straightforward and therefore omitted (e.g., recording in the heap the set of created references).

Input-Enabledness Futures

$$\langle t, h \cup r \rangle \xrightarrow{f?v} \langle t, T, h \cup r[f = v] \rangle$$

We conclude the thread semantics with the above transition, which models the transmission of a value associated with a future.

4 Semantics of Concurrent Object Groups

In this section we describe the multi-threaded execution of a cog. We do so by lifting the above operational semantics of a single thread to a multi-threaded context.

A cog is a triple $\langle t, T, h \cup r \rangle$ consisting of an executing thread t, a set T of suspended threads, and a union $h \cup r$ consisting of a heap h and a registry r of futures. An object o belongs to a cog $\langle t, T, h \cup r \rangle$ if and only if it has a state in h, that is, $o : s \in h$, for some object state s.

Internal Computation Step
An unlabeled computation step of a thread is extended to a corresponding transition of the cog by the following rule:

$$\frac{\langle t, h \cup r \rangle \longrightarrow \langle t', h' \cup r \rangle}{\langle t, T, h \cup r \rangle \longrightarrow \langle t', T, h' \cup r \rangle}$$

Note that an unlabeled computation step of a thread does not affect the registry.

Internal Call
An asynchronous call of a method of an internal object is described by the rule:

$$\frac{\langle t, h \cup r \rangle \xrightarrow{o!m(\bar{v})} \langle t', h \cup r \rangle}{\langle t, T, h \cup r \rangle \longrightarrow \langle t', T \cup \{\langle S, \tau \rangle\}, h \cup r \rangle}$$

where $o \in O_C$ exists in h, and $m(\bar{x})\{S\}$ is the corresponding method definition in class C, and τ assigns the actual parameters $\bar{v}$ to the formal parameters $\bar{x}$ of m. Note that by the thread semantics of an asynchronous call as described in the previous section the first actual parameter of $\bar{v}$ denotes the future uniquely identifying the message $o!m(\bar{v})$ which is assigned to the implicit formal parameter *dest*. Moreover, τ initializes all other local variables of m (e.g., the object identity o of the callee is assigned to the implicit formal parameter "this").

External Call/Broadcast
A computation step labeled by an external asynchronous method call or a broadcast (i.e., a transmission $f!v$ or $f?v$) is extended to a corresponding transition of the cog by the following rule:

$$\frac{\langle t, h \cup r \rangle \xrightarrow{l} \langle t', h \cup r' \rangle}{\langle t, T, h \cup r \rangle \xrightarrow{l} \langle t', T, h \cup r' \rangle}$$

where in case $l = o!m(\bar{v})$, o is an external object, i.e., it does not exist in h.

Input-Enabledness Messages

We further have the following transition which describes the *reception* of an asynchronous method call to an object o which belongs to the cog $\langle t, T, h \rangle$:

$$\langle t, T, h \cup r \rangle \xrightarrow{o?m(\bar{v})} \langle t, T \cup \{\langle S, \tau \rangle\}, h \cup r \rangle$$

where, assuming that $o \in O_C$ exists in h, $m(\bar{x})\{S\}$ is the corresponding method definition in class C, and τ assigns the actual parameters $\bar{v}$ to the formal parameters $\bar{x}$ of m (as above, the first actual parameter of $\bar{v}$ denotes the future uniquely identifying the message $o!m(\bar{v})$ which is assigned to the implicit formal parameter *dest* and initializes all local variables of m (e.g., the object identity o of the callee is assigned to the implicit formal parameter "this").

Scheduling

Let $\langle t, h \cup r \rangle \not\longrightarrow$ denote that there is no transition possible from $\langle t, h \cup r \rangle$. Thus $\langle t, h \cup r \rangle \not\longrightarrow$ also excludes a transition $\langle t, h \cup r \rangle \longrightarrow \Delta$ which indicates a blocking get operation. Scheduling another thread within a given cog is then formally captured by the rule

$$\frac{\langle t, h \cup r \rangle \not\longrightarrow}{\langle t, T, h \rangle \longrightarrow \langle t', T', h \cup r \rangle}$$

where $T' = (T \setminus \{t'\}) \cup \{t\}$.

5   Semantics of Systems of Concurrent Object Groups

We next lift the above operational semantics of a single cog to the system level. A global system configuration G consists of a finite set of cog's such that for any $(t, T, h \cup r) \neq (t', T', h' \cup r') \in G$ we have that $r = r'$, that is, all cog's in G share the same registry of futures. For technical convenience we assume that all system configurations contain for every class C an infinite set of *latent* cog's $\langle \emptyset, \{o : s_{init}\} \rangle$, where $o \in O_C$ (for some class C), which have not yet been activated. The fresh object generated by the creation of a new cog, as described above in the thread semantics at this level is assumed to correspond to a latent cog.

Interleaving

An internal computation step of a cog c is extended to a corresponding transition of the global system as follows.

$$\frac{c \longrightarrow c'}{\{c\} \cup G \longrightarrow \{c'\} \cup G}$$

Note that such an internal computation step does not affect the global registry.

Asynchronous Method Call

Communication between two cog's c and d is formalized by

$$\frac{c \xrightarrow{o?m(\bar{v})} c' \quad d \xrightarrow{o!m(\bar{v})} d'}{\{c,d\} \cup G \longrightarrow \{c',d'\} \cup G}$$

Here it is worthwhile to observe that for an asynchronous call $o!m(\bar{v})$ to an object o belonging to the *same* cog there does not exist a matching reception $o?m(\bar{v})$ by a *different* cog because cog's have no shared objects. Note also that such a communication does not affect the global registry.

Broadcast

Broadcasting the value of a future is formalized by the following rules:

$$\frac{c \xrightarrow{f!v} c'' \quad G \xrightarrow{f?v} G'}{\{c\} \cup G \longrightarrow \{c'\} \cup G'} \quad \frac{c \xrightarrow{f?v} c'}{\{c\} \cup G \longrightarrow \{c'\} \cup G'} \quad \frac{G \xrightarrow{f?v} G'}{}$$

For an input $f?v$ we further have the following base case:

$$\emptyset \xrightarrow{f?v} \emptyset$$

6 Trace Semantics

In this section we describe the overall behavior of a system of dynamically generated cog's compositionally in terms of the communication behavior of the individual cog's.

A trace is a finite sequence of communications involving asynchronous method calls, e.g., $o?m(\bar{v})$ and $o!m(\bar{v})$, and futures, e.g., $f!v$ and $f?v$. For each cog c we define its trace semantics $T(g)$ by

$$\{\langle \theta, c' \rangle \mid c \xrightarrow{\theta} c'\}$$

where $\xrightarrow{\theta}$ denotes the reflexive, transitive closure of the above transition relation between cog's, collecting the input/output messages. The trace semantics thus records for each cog the set of reachable cog's and their corresponding traces. Note that the trace θ by which we can obtain from c a cog c' does *not* provide information about object creation or information about which objects belong to the same cog. In fact, information about which objects have been created can be inferred from the trace θ. Further, in general a cog does not "know" which objects belong to the same cog.

The following compositionality theorem is based on a notion of *compatible* traces which roughly requires for every input message a corresponding output message, and vice versa. We define this notion formally in terms of the following rewrite rules for sets of traces:

- $\{o?m(\bar{v}) \cdot \theta, o!m(\bar{v}) \cdot \theta'\} \cup \Theta \Rightarrow \{\theta, \theta'\} \cup \Theta$
- $\{f!v \cdot \theta\} \cup f?v \cdot \Theta \Rightarrow \{\theta\} \cup \Theta$

The first rule identifies two traces which have two matching method invocations. The second rule models a broadcast. A set of traces Θ is compatible, denoted by $Compat(\Theta)$, if we can derive the singleton set $\{\epsilon\}$, where ϵ denotes the empty trace. Formally, $Compat(\Theta)$ if and only if $\Theta \Rightarrow^* \{\epsilon\}$, where $\Rightarrow^*$ denotes the reflexive, transitive closure of $\Rightarrow$.

Theorem 1 *Let $\rightarrow^*$ denote the reflexive, transitive closure of the above transition relation between system configurations. We have*

$$G \longrightarrow^* G'$$

if and only if $G = \{c_i \mid i \in I\}$ and $G' = \{c'_i \mid i \in I\}$, for some index set I such that for every $i \in I$ there exists $\langle \theta_i, c'_i \rangle \in T(c_i)$, with $Compat(\{\theta_i \mid i \in I\})$.

Proof The proof proceeds by induction on the derivation $G \longrightarrow^* G'$.

For the base case (derivation of length zero) we have that $G = G'$. It then suffices to observe that by definition of the trace semantics $(\langle \epsilon, c_i \rangle T(c_i)$, for $c_i \in G$, and that $Compat(\{\epsilon\})$.

Next, let $G \longrightarrow G'' \longrightarrow^* G'$. By the induction hypothesis we have that $G'' \longrightarrow^* G'$ if and only if $G'' = \{c''_i \mid i \in I\}$ and $G' = \{c'_i \mid i \in I\}$, for some index set I such that for every $i \in I$ there exists $\langle \theta_i, c'_i \rangle \in T(c''_i)$, with $Compat(\{\theta_i \mid i \in I\})$.

We proceed with a case analysis of the transition $G \longrightarrow G''$.

Interleaving

Let $c_i \longrightarrow c''_i$, for some $c_i \in G$ and $c''_i \in G''$. It suffices to observe that by the above global interleaving rule we have $G'' = (G \setminus \{c_i\}) \cup \{c''_i\}$, and by the above semantics of a cog it follows that $\langle \theta_i, c'_i \rangle \in T(c''_i)$ implies $\langle \theta_i, c'_i \rangle \in T(c_i)$.

Asynchronous Method Call

Let $c_i \stackrel{o?m(\bar{v})}{\longrightarrow} c''_i$ and $d_j \stackrel{o!m(\bar{v})}{\longrightarrow} d''_j$, for some $c_i, d_j \in G$ and $c''_i, d''_j \in G''$. By the above global rule for message passing, we have that $G'' = (G \setminus \{c_i, d_j\}) \cup \{c''_i, d''_j\}$. By the semantics of cog's, $\langle \theta_i, c'_i \rangle \in T(c''_i)$ and $\langle \theta_j, d'_j \rangle \in T(d''_j)$ implies $\langle o?m(\bar{v}) \cdot \theta_i, c'_i \rangle \in T(c_i)$ and $\langle o!m(\bar{v}) \cdot \theta_j, d'_j \rangle \in T(d_j)$. Further, $Compat(\{\theta_i \mid i \in I\})$ implies $Compat(\{\theta_k \mid k \neq i, j\} \cup \{o?m(\bar{v}) \cdot \theta_i, o!m(\bar{v}) \cdot \theta_j\})$.

Broadcast

Let $c_i \stackrel{f!v}{\longrightarrow} c''_i$, for some $c_i \in G$ and $c''_i \in G''$, and $c_j \stackrel{f?v}{\longrightarrow} c''_j$, every $j \neq i$, $c_j \in G$ and $c''_j \in G''$. By the semantics of cog's, $\langle \theta_i, c'_i \rangle \in T(c''_i)$ implies $\langle f!v \cdot \theta_i, c'_i \rangle \in T(c_i)$, and $\langle \theta_j, c'_j \rangle \in T(c''_j)$ implies $\langle f?v \cdot \theta_j, c'_j \rangle \in T(c_j)$, for every $j \neq i$. Further, $Compat(\{\theta_i \mid i \in I\})$ implies $Compat(\{f!v \cdot \theta_i\} \cup \{f?v \cdot \theta_j \mid j \neq i\})$.

The above theorem states that the overall system behavior can be described in terms of the above trace semantics of the individual cog's. This means that for compositionality no further information is required.

7 Future Work

Of particular interest is the investigation of a *sound* and *complete* assertional method for reasoning about concurrent object groups in a compositional manner along the lines of the compositional semantics. This would involve the development of a trace logics for reasoning about asynchronous method calls and the completion of futures. The identification of the observable behavior of a cog and its clear distinction from its internal behavior provides a separation of concerns which is essential in mastering the complexity of reasoning about concurrent object groups and active objects in general [2].

Semantically, our work provides a promising basis for investigating a *fully abstract* semantics for cog's which captures the *minimal* information needed for compositionality. In general, asynchronous communication and networks require abstraction from certain orderings between observable events [6]. Further, as shown in [1], in an object-oriented setting the ordering of observable events also depends on the dynamically changing connectivity between the objects. How these results apply to cog's is an interesting, challenging future work.

References

1. Erika Ábrahám et al. "Object Connectivity and Full Abstraction for a Concurrent Calculus of Classes". In: *Theoretical Aspects of Computing - ICTAC 2004, First International Colloquium, Guiyang, China, September 20–24, 2004, Revised Selected Papers*. 2004, pp. 37–51.
2. Wolfgang Ahrendt and Maximilian Dylla. "A system for compositional verification of asynchronous objects". In: *Sci. Comput. Program.* 77.12 (2012), pp. 1289–1309.
3. Frank S. de Boer, Dave Clarke, and Einar Broch Johnsen. "A Complete Guide to the Future". In: *Programming Languages and Systems, 16th European Symposium on Programming ESOP 2007, Held as Part of the Joint European Conferences on Theory and Practics of Software ETAPS 2007, Braga, Portugal, March 24 April 1, 2007, Proceedings*. 2007, pp. 316–330.
4. Crystal Chang Din et al. "Locally Abstract, Globally Concrete Semantics of Concurrent Programming Languages". In: *Automated Reasoning with Analytic Tableaux and Related Methods 26th International Conference TABLEAUX 2017, Brasilia, Brazil, September 25–28, 2017, Proceedings*. 2017, pp. 22–43.
5. Einar Broch Johnsen et al. "ABS: A Core Language for Abstract Behavioral Specification". In: *Formal Methods for Components and Objects, FMCO, Graz, Austria. Revised Papers*. LNCS. Springer, 2010. DOI: 10.1007/978-3-642-25271-6_8
6. Bengt Jonsson. "A fully abstract trace model for dataflow and asynchronous networks". In: *Distributed Computing* 7.4 (May 1994), pp. 197–212. ISSN: 1432-0452.
7. K.V.S. Prasad. "A calculus of broadcasting systems". In: *Science of Computer Programming* 25.2 (1995), pp. 285–327.

8. A. W. Roscoe. *The Theory and Practice of Concurrency*. Upper Saddle River NJ, USA: Prentice Hall PTR, 1997. ISBN: 0136744095.
9. Jan Schäfer and Arnd Poetzsch-Heffter. "JCoBox: Generalizing Active Objects to Concurrent Components". In: *ECOOP 2010 - Object-Oriented Programming, 24th European Conference, Maribor, Slovenia, June 21–25, 2010. Proceedings*. 2010, pp. 275–299.

Same Same But Different: Interoperability of Software Product Line Variants

Ferruccio Damiani, Reiner Hähnle, Eduard Kamburjan, and Michael Lienhardt

This paper is dedicated to our friend and colleague Arnd Poetzsch-Heffter on the occasion of his sixtieth birthday.

Abstract Software Product Lines (SPLs) are an established area of research providing approaches to describe multiple variants of a software product by representing them as a highly variable system. Multi-SPLs (MPLs) are an emerging area of research addressing approaches to describe sets of interdependent, highly variable systems, that are typically managed and developed in a decentralized fashion. Current approaches do not offer a mechanism to manage and orchestrate multiple variants from one product line within the same application. We experienced the need for such a mechanism in an industry project with Deutsche Bahn, where we do not merely model a highly variable system, but a system with highly variable subsystems. Based on MPL concepts and delta-oriented oriented programming, we present a novel solution to the design challenges arising from having to manage and interoperate multiple subsystems with multiple variants: how to reference variants, how to avoid name or type clashes, and how to keep variants interoperable.

1 Introduction

Many existing software and non-software systems are built as complex assemblages of highly variable subsystems that coexist in multiple variants and that need to interoperate. Consider, for example, one track in a railway system. Such a track

F. Damiani · M. Lienhardt
University of Torino, Torino, Italy
e-mail: ferruccio.damiani@unito.it; michael.lienhardt@di.unito.it

R. Hähnle (✉) · E. Kamburjan
Technische Universität Darmstadt, Darmstadt, Germany
e-mail: haehnle@cs.tu-darmstadt.de; kamburjan@cs.tu-darmstadt.de

© Springer Nature Switzerland AG 2018
P. Müller, I. Schaefer (eds.), *Principled Software Development*,
https://doi.org/10.1007/978-3-319-98047-8_7

typically contains many different variants of sensors (to detect a train, its speed, etc.), and many variants of signals (of different forms or functions). The FormbaR[1] modeling project, conducted with Deutsche Bahn, aims to provide a uniform and formal model [17] of operational and technical rulebooks for railroad operations: within this project, the necessity to describe highly variable subsystems that coexist in multiple variants and that need to interoperate thus arises naturally.

In software systems, there exist several approaches to model highly variable systems, labeled as *Software Product Lines* (SPLs) [2, 5, 19, 22]. These are generalized by *Multi-Software Product Lines* (MPLs) [7, 14] that model sets of interdependent highly variable systems, typically managed and developed in a decentralized fashion by multiple stakeholders. However, MPLs do not target modeling of interoperability between multiple variants of the same SPL.

To address this issue we introduce the notion of *variant-interoperable SPL* (VPL) and propose linguistic mechanisms that support interoperability among different variants of one VPL. Each VPL encapsulates and models the variability of one system. We define a formalism that is able to reference, to generate and to compose multiple variants of one VPL in the context of its supersystem. To do so, each variant is associated with one (possibly newly generated) module and statements are able to use *variant references* instead of modules to reference classes and interfaces. During variant generation, all such variant references are replaced by the module which contains the generated variant. The final variant of the whole system contains no SPL-specific constructs. We also give a generalization of VPLs to *dependent VPLs* (DVPL). A DVPL takes variants of other product lines as parameters and is thus able to model the *composition* of variable subsystems. A VPL is obtained as the special case of a DVPL without parameters. Thus, in our approach, an MPL can be described by: (1) a set of DVPLs; and (2) a *glue program* that may contain references to different variants of the DVPLs.

Delta-Oriented Programming (DOP) [21] is a flexible and modular approach to implement SPLs. A delta-oriented SPL consists of: (1) a *feature model* defining the set of variants in terms of *features* (each feature represents an abstract description of functionality and each variant is identified by a set of features, called a *product*); (2) an *artifact base* comprising a *base program* and of a set of *delta modules* (*deltas* for short), which are containers of program modifications (e.g., for Java-like programs, a delta can add, remove or modify classes and interfaces); and (3) *configuration knowledge* which defines how to generate the SPL's variants by specifying an *activation mapping* that associates to each delta an *activation condition* (i.e., a set of products for which that delta is activated), and specifying an *application ordering* between deltas: given a product the corresponding variant is derived by applying the activated deltas to the base program according to the application ordering. DOP is a generalization of *Feature-Oriented Programming* (FOP) [3], a previously proposed approach to implement SPLs where deltas correspond one-to-one to features and do not contain remove operations.

---

[1] https://formbar.raillab.de.

In the context of the `FormbaR` project we model railway operations [17] using the Abstract Behavioural Specification (ABS) [13, 16] language, a delta-oriented modeling language. The challenge to model interoperable, multiple variants of the same subsystem that arose in this project is described in [12]. In ABS, variants are expressed in the executable language fragment Core ABS [16]. In this paper, we use railway *stations* and *signals* as a running example. We use a non-dependent VPL to model signals (which may be light or form signals and main or pre signals). A station is a DVPL that takes two signal SPLs variants as input. We illustrate the modeling capabilities by showing how one can ensure that all signals of a station are either light signals or all are form signals (generalizing the treatment of features from [7]). We also show how to model that every main signal is preceded by a pre signal.

Our contribution is the design of a delta-oriented DVPL language that can model interoperation of *multiple* variants from the *same* product line as well as from *different* product lines. We do not aim to fully explore the design space, but provide a concise system for basic functionality. However, we provide a discussion of our design decisions and how interoperability changes the role of product lines during development.

This work is structured as follows: Sect. 2 introduces FAM (Featherweight Core ABS with Modules) a foundational language for Core ABS. Section 3 introduces delta-oriented (non-dependent) VPLs on top of FAM. Section 4 generalizes to dependent interoperable product lines. Section 5 gives the reasoning behind our design decisions and how interoperability affects modeling. Section 6 gives related work and Sect. 7 concludes.

2 Featherweight Core ABS with Modules

In this section we introduce FAM (Featherweight Core ABS with Modules) a foundational language for Core ABS [16]. Following [15], we use the overline notation for (possibly empty) sequences of elements. For example, $\overline{CD}$ stands for a sequence of class declarations $CD_1 \cdots CD_n$ ($n \geq 0$)—the empty sequence is denoted by $\emptyset$. Moreover, when no confusion may arise, we identify sequences of pairwise distinct elements with sets. We write $\overline{CD}$ as short for $\{CD_1 \ldots, CD_n\}$, etc. FAM is an extension of Featherweight Core ABS [10], a previously proposed foundational language for Core ABS, that does not model modules. As seen in Sect. 3, modules play a key role in the definition of variants in VPL.

Figure 1 shows the abstract syntax of FAM. A FAM program **Prgm** consists of a set of modules **Mod**. A module has a name M, import and export clauses, a set of class definitions **CD** and a set of interface declarations **ID**. To use a class defined in one module in a different module, the defining module must export it and the using module must import it. There are no such restrictions when using a class inside its defining module. We allow wildcards ⋆ in the import/export clauses.

Prgm ::= $\overline{\text{Mod}}$	Program
Mod ::= **module** M; **import** SC **from** M; **export** SC; $\overline{\text{CD}}$ $\overline{\text{ID}}$	Module
SC ::= $\overline{\text{C}}, \overline{\text{I}}$ | * CD ::= **class** C [**implements** IR $\overline{\text{IR}}$] {$\overline{\text{AD}}$}	Selection, Class
CR ::= M.C | C IR ::= M.I | I	Class/Interface Reference
AD ::= FD | MD FD ::= T f=e MD ::= MSD{...}	Attribute (Field, Method)
MSD ::= T m($\overline{\text{T v}}$) ID ::= **interface** I [**extends** IR $\overline{\text{IR}}$] {$\overline{\text{MSD}}$}	Signature, Interface
e ::= **new** CR($\overline{\text{e}}$) | ... T ::= IR | Unit | Int | $\cdots$	Expression, Type

Fig. 1 Syntax of Featherweight Core ABS with Modules (FAM)—expressions and statements (method bodies) are left unspecified

A class definition CD consists of a name C, an optional **implements** clause and a set of method and field definitions. The references CR and IR are used respectively to reference classes and interfaces inside of modules. We assume some primitive types (including Unit, used as return type for methods without a return value) and let T range over interface names and primitive types.

Class definitions and interface definitions in ABS are similar to Java, but ABS does not support class inheritance. Our development is independent of the exact syntax of expressions e and statements s, so we leave it unspecified. We show only the object creation expression **new** CR($\overline{\text{e}}$), which creates a new instance of the class referenced by CR.

3 Delta-Oriented VPLs

We introduce Featherweight *Delta* ABS with Modules (FDAM), a foundational language for delta-oriented VPLs where variants are FAM programs. FDAM is an extension of Featherweight Delta ABS (FDABS) [10], a foundational language for standard ABS *without* variant interoperability.

3.1 Variant-Interoperable Product Lines

To handle multiple variants of an SPL and ensure their interoperability, we need to introduce several mechanisms that extend FAM:

1. We must be able to reference different variants of the same SPL. To this end, a class reference may be prefixed with a *variant reference*, i.e. a syntactic construct that identifies a specific SPL variant.
2. The notion of artifact base of a delta-oriented SPL must support interoperability of different SPL variants: specifically, different variants must be able to share common interfaces. This is achieved with a **unique** block containing the code that is common to all variants.

3. The variant generation process must generate code that can coexist and interoperate, even though the variants will necessarily have overlapping signatures. To this end, the code of each referenced variant is encapsulated by placing it in a separate module, while variant references are replaced by module references. As each variant refers to a unique module, multiple references to the same variant refer to the same module (that is, they are generated exactly once).

3.2 Syntax

Featherweight Delta ABS with Modules (FDAM) is a language for delta-oriented VPLs where variants are FAM programs. It allows to describe an MPL by a set of VPLs $\overline{\text{Vpl}}$ and a *glue program* Gprgm (i.e. a program that may contain variant references). Figure 2 gives the formal syntax of VPLs and *extended references* (i.e. the class/interface references allowed in the glue program, that may be prefixed variant references).

A Vpl has a unique name V, and a set of features $\overline{\text{F}}$, which are constrained by some feature model φ, a propositional formula over $\overline{\text{F}}$. Furthermore, a VPL has a set of deltas $\overline{\Delta}$ and configuration knowledge DConfig (comprising an ordered sequence of delta activation clauses DAC) that relates each delta to an activation condition and specifies a partial order of delta application. Finally, a VPL has a *base*

Vpl ::=**productline** V; **features** $\overline{\text{F}}$ **with** φ;	VPL
Prgm **unique** $\overline{\text{Mod}}$ $\overline{\Delta}$ DConfig	
Δ ::=**delta** D; $\overline{\text{CO}}$ $\overline{\text{IO}}$	Delta
DConfig ::=$\overline{\text{DAC}}$ DAC ::= **delta** D **when** φ;	Configuration Knowledge
CO ::=CAO | CMO | CRO | **uses** M	Class Operation
CAO ::=**adds** CD CRO ::= **removes** CR	Class Add/Remove Operations
CMO ::=**modifies** CR{AO}	Class Modifies Operations
AO ::=**adds** AD | **removes** MSD | **removes** T f	Attribute Operation
modifies AD	
IO ::=IAO | IMO | IRO | **uses** M	Interface Operation
IAO ::=**adds** ID IRO ::= **removes** IR	Interface Add/Remove Operations
IMO ::=**modifies** IR{SO}	Interface Modify Operation
SO ::=**adds** MSD | **removes** MSD	Signature Operation

CR ::=VR.M.C | M.C | C IR ::= VR.M.I | M.I | I	Extended Class/Interface Reference
VR ::=V | V[$\overline{\text{F}}$]	Variant Reference

Fig. 2 Syntax of Featherweight Delta ABS with Modules: VPLs (top) and extended references (bottom)

program as well as a **unique** block, consisting of module definitions on which the deltas operate.

Each delta has a name D and a sequence of class/interface operations. A class/interface operation may add, modify or remove a class/interface. A **uses** clause sets a module name as default prefix for further selections. During variant generation the application of the delta throws an error if the element is already in the code (if it is supposed to be added) or absent (if it is supposed to be removed or modified).[2] Adding and removing a class/interface is straightforward. In case of class/interface modification, a delta may add or remove signatures in interfaces and attributes in classes. A class modification may also modify an attribute: either replace the initialization expression of a field or replace the body of a method (the new body can call the original implementation of the method with the keyword **original** [10]).

Within a glue program class/interface references have the possibility to reference a class/interface of a variant by extended references. An extended reference is a class/interface reference that may be prefixed by a variant reference. A variant reference VR consists either of the name of the target VPL V and the features $\overline{F}$ used for variant selection; or simply the name of the target VPL V when selecting a **unique** class/interface. A variant is selected by providing a set of features $\overline{F}$ to a VPL. If that set does not satisfy the feature model φ, then an error is thrown during variant generation. All other clauses are defined as in Sect. 2.

The only form of extended references allowed in a VPL V are of the form V.C or V.I to reference *its own* **unique** block. Variant selections and references to the **unique** part of other VPLs are not allowed.

Intuitively, the generation of the variants referenced from an FDAM glue program works as follows: A new module name M is created, and modules mod from the **unique** block are added under M_mod. Next, for each referenced variant, each configured delta is applied to a copy of the base program, provided its activation condition is satisfied. All modified classes/interfaces are copied into M_mod and modified there. All added classes/interfaces are added into M_mod. Finally, all references are updated and all variant references occurring in the glue program are replaced by references to the generated modules. Figure 3 illustrates this workflow and we give a more detailed description in Sect. 3.4.

3.3 A VPL for Railway Signals

We illustrate the VPL concept with a model of railway signals, see Fig. 4. A signal is either a main or a pre signal and either a form signal (showing its signal aspects with geometric shapes) or a light signal (using colors and light patterns). This is modeled by the features Pre, Main, Light, Form, respectively. We impose the constraint that exactly one of Main and Pre and one of Form and Light must be selected.

---

[2]The ABS tool chain is equipped with a mechanism for statically detecting these errors [11].

FDAM Program   Generated FAM Program

Fig. 3 Schematic Overview over a FDAM program (representing an MPL) and the generated FAM Program

```
 1  productline SLine;
 2  features Main, Pre, Light, Form with Main↔ ¬Pre ∧ Light↔ ¬Form;
 3  module BMd;
 4  class Signal implements SLine.SMd.Sig {}
 5  unique{
 6    module SMd;
 7    interface Sig { ... }
 8  }
 9  delta SigForm;  modifies class BMd.Signal { ... } ...
10  delta SigPre;   modifies class BMd.Signal { ... } ...
11  delta SigMain;  modifies class BMd.Signal { ... } ...
12  delta SigLight; modifies class BMd.Signal { ... } ...
13
14  // Glue program
15  module main;
16  class Main{
17    Unit main() {
18      SLine.SMd.Sig s1 = new SLine[Pre,Form].BMd.Signal();
19      SLine.SMd.Sig s2 = new SLine[Main,Form].BMd.Signal();
20      s1.connect(s2);
21      SLine.SMd.Sig s3 = new SLine[Pre,Form].BMd.Signal();
22      SLine.SMd.Sig s4 = new SLine[Main,Form].BMd.Signal();
23      s3.connect(s4);
24    }
25  }
```

Fig. 4 A VPL for railway signals (configuration knowledge, which associates an activation condition to each delta and specifies the application order of the the delta, is omitted) and a glue program that uses it

The **unique** block provides an interface SMd.Sig which serves as the interface of the signal model to the outside. The base program provides an empty class BMd. Signal that implements this interface. Every variant of the VPL SLine generates a different variant of the class of Signal by adding the required functionality. We do not provide complete delta declarations. While we focus on the Signal class, each delta can add auxiliary classes (for example, a Bulb class for light signals).

The glue program contains the main module, providing the Main class with the main() method that creates a station with two main and two pre signals. After the declarations in the main() method, an expression like s1 == s2 would type check.

Observe that the `Signal` classes must be referenced with a variant selection, but this is not necessary for `Sig`, because it is **unique**. This is appropriate, because all `Signal` classes in all variants implement it. We provide a few examples to further illustrate the role of the **unique** block.

*Example 1 (Empty **unique** Block)* Consider Fig. 4, but with an empty **unique** block. The interface is added to module `BMd` in the variants instead, and the first two lines of the main method are replaced with

```
18 SLine[Pre,Form].BMd.Sig   s1 = new SLine[Pre,Form].BMd.
     Signal();
19 SLine[Main,Form].BMd.Sig s2 = new SLine[Main,Form].BMd.
     Signal();
```

Then `s1 == s2` would *not* type check, because each referenced type is added as a separate interface. However, if lines 21, 22 of Fig. 4 are changed accordingly, then `s1 == s3` *would* still type check, because the selected features identify a variant uniquely.

Example 2 (Empty Base Program) Consider again Fig. 4 but with an empty base program, where all deltas *modify* the interface and add classes that implement the modified interface. For example, replace **delta** `SigForm` with

```
delta SigForm; modifies interface SLine.SMd.Sig { ... }
adds class SMd.Signal implements SMd.Sig { ... }
```

In this case, line 18 of Fig 4 won't type check, because the `Sig` class of the variant is based on a copy of the non-variant class and is not its subtype.

3.4 Glue Program Flattening for FDAM

Glue program flattening refers to the transformation of an FDAM program that models an MPL, i.e. a glue program plus a set of VPLs, into an FAM program, see Fig. 3. This transformation involves code generation for all the variants referenced in the glue program (as outlined at the end of Sect. 3.2). Consider the MPL consisting of the glue program and the VPL in Fig. 4.

We assume an injective function *mod* mapping variant references and module names to fresh (relative to the glue program) names. We assume *mod* ignores the order of features. For each variant selection $V(\overline{F})$ and each module mod this function is used to create a new module with name $mod(V(\overline{F}), \text{mod})$ and for each VPL V and each module mod it is used to create a new module with name $mod(V, \text{mod})$.

Example 3 In Fig. 4, for each module mod in the **unique** block a module named $mod(\text{SLine}, \text{mod})$ is created, to which the unique modules and classes are added. Next, each variant reference in the glue code is processed. Let us consider `SLine [Pre,Form].BMd`. The selected feature set is checked against the constraint of the

VPL. In this case, {Pre, Form} satisfies Main ↔ ¬Pre ∧ Light ↔ ¬Form. The configuration knowledge is used to determine which deltas are applied in which order to the base program. Here, only SigPre and SigForm are applied.

For each class/interface M.C/M.I added in any delta activated to generate the selected variant, a module *mod*(SLine[Pre,Form]),M]) is created (if it does not yet exist) and the class is added there. For each class/interface reference mod.C′ in M.C, a clause **import** C′ **from** mod; is added to *mod*(SLine[Pre,Form],M). Finally, an **export** *; clause is added.

For each class/interface M.C/M.I modified in any delta activated to generate the selected variant, a module *mod*(SLine[Pre,Form],M) is created (if it does not yet exist) and the class/interface is copied there *before* any modifications are applied. In this case, all **import** and **export** clauses are also copied from their original module.

During post-processing, all variant references SLine[Pre,Form].M.C are replaced by *mod*(SLine[Pre,Form],M).C. This reference is made visible by the clause **import** C **from** *mod*(SLine[Pre,Form],M) added to the containing module.

This algorithm is applied recursively on the resulting program. If we apply the described algorithm once to the FDAM MPL in Fig. 4, then the FAM program in Fig. 5 is generated, where an obvious choice for *mod* has been adopted.

```
1  module SLine_SMd;
2  export *;
3  interface SMd { ... }
4
5  module SLine_Pre_Form_BMd;
6  import Sig from SLine_SMd;
7  export *;
8  class Signal implements SLine_SMd.Sig {...}
9
10 module SLine_Main_Form_BMd;
11 import Sig from SLine_SMd;
12 export *;
13 class Signal implements SLine_SMd.Sig {...}
14
15
16 module main;
17 import Signal from SLine_Pre_Form_BMd;
18 import Signal from SLine_Main_Form_BMd;
19 import Sig    from SLine_SMd;
20 class Main {
21   Unit main() {
22     SLine_SMd.Sig s1 = new SLine_Pre_Form_BMd.Signal();
23     SLine_SMd.Sig s2 = new SLine_Main_Form_BMd.Signal();
24     s1.connect(s2);
25     SLine_SMd.Sig s3 = new SLine_Pre_Form_BMd.Signal();
26     SLine_SMd.Sig s4 = new SLine_Main_Form_BMd.Signal();
27     s3.connect(s4);
28   }
29 }
```

Fig. 5 FAM program obtained by flattening the glue program in Fig. 4 under the assumption that no auxiliary classes or interfaces are added by the activated deltas (see the explanation in Sect. 3.3)

4 Delta-Oriented DVPLs

The VPL concept makes it possible to reference multiple variants of a product line from a glue program that is external to the product line. However, one has to know the exact product at each variant reference. If, for example, we attempt to model a station that has light signals as well as form signals, this leads to code duplication. This can be avoided by making VPLs parametric in the referenced variants: We extend VPLs to *dependent VPLs* (DVPL). A DVPL takes variants of other product lines as parameters: a product of a DVPL is identified by a set of features and a set of product lines (matching the parameters), each of them with an associated product.

4.1 Syntax

We extend the FDAM language from Sect. 3 to *Featherweight Dependent Delta ABS with Modules* (FDDAM). Figure 6 gives the formal syntax. Product lines are extended with optional product line parameters P. These parameters can be used used in the feature model, which may reference features of the passed parameters with $P.F$. Propositional formulas ψ are formulas over $P.F$ and F. A DVPL also has an optional set of DVPL names $\overline{V}$ in its **uses** clause.

The deltas and the base program may contain variant references of the form P (where P is one of the parameters) or V' (where V' is either the V itself, or one one of the DVPLs listed in the **uses** clause). In the glue program, variant references to DVPLs have the form $V[\overline{F}](VR)$: in addition to features, they may depend on variants of other product lines declared as parameters. The variants listed in the parameters VR must select products of a matching product line in accordance with the DVPL's declaration. All other clauses are defined as in Sects. 2 and 3.

A DVPL supports two kinds of dependencies:

1. It may refer to a variant associated with a parameter P by a prefix of the form $P.M$, where M is a module name.
2. It may use the **unique** part of other DVPLs: in a DVPL V, any reference to a **unique** class C or interface I from outside must be done with an extended reference of the form $V'.C$ or $V'.I$. The referenced DVPL V' (when different from V itself) must be listed in the **uses** clause of V.

$$Dvpl ::= \textbf{productline}\ V(\overline{V\ P})\,;\,[\textbf{uses}\ \overline{V}\,;]\textbf{features}\ \overline{F}\ \textbf{with}\ \psi\,; \qquad \text{DVPL}$$
$$Prgm\ \textbf{unique}\{\overline{Mod}\}\ \overline{\Delta}\ DConfig$$

$$VR ::= V\ |\ V[\overline{F}](VR)\ |\ P \qquad \text{Variant References}$$

Fig. 6 Syntax of Featherweight Dependent Delta ABS with Modules

All names occurring in the parameters declared by a DVPL are implicitly added to its **uses** clause.

Example 4 The following model uses the Sig interface of the VPL SLine in Fig. 4. The DVPL BLine has a dependency on the **unique** part of SLine, declared via **uses** SLine. As the interface Sig is from the **unique** part of the SLine VPL, it is unnecessary to refer to any *variant* of SLine. Therefore, BLine has no parameters.

```
1  productline BLine;
2  uses SLine;
3  unique {
4    module ExampleMd;
5    interface ExampleI {
6      addSignal(SLine.SMd.Sig sig);
7  }
8  ...
```

Variant generation works bottom-up: variants of DVPLs without parameters are generated first. Variants of other DVPLs are generated by instantiating their parameters with variant selections, once these have been reduced to module references. We provide a more detailed description in Sect. 4.3.

4.2 A DVPL for Railway Stations

Consider the DVPL in Fig. 7 which models a train station with two pre/main signal pairs. The signals within a pair must be implemented with the same technology, i.e. they must be both light signals or both form signals. The feature model ensures this as follows: Parameter sl1 is constrained to be a pre signal by sl1.Pre, similarly

```
1  productline BlockLine(SLine sl1, SLine sl2);
2  features Light, Form with sl1.Form ↔ sl2.Form ∧ sl1.Pre ∧ sl2.Main ∧
3                           Light ↔ sl1.Light ∧ Form ↔ sl1.Form;
4  delta AlwaysDelta;
5  adds interface BlMd.BlockI { ... }
6  adds class BlMd.Block implements BlMd.BlockI {
7      SLine.SMd.Sig s1 = new sl1.BMd.Signal();
8      SLine.SMd.Sig s2 = new sl2.BMd.Signal();
9      SLine.SMd.Sig s3 = new sl1.BMd.Signal();
10     SLine.SMd.Sig s4 = new sl2.BMd.Signal();
11     Unit Block() {
12         s1.connect(s2);
13         s3.connect(s4);
14     }
15 }
16 delta AlwaysDelta when True;
```

Fig. 7 A DVPL modeling a railway block station

```
 1  productline LineLine(BlockLine bl1, BlockLine bl2);
 2  uses SLine;
 3  delta AlwaysDelta;
 4  adds class LMd.Line {
 5    bl1.BlMd.BlockI b1 = new bl1.BlMd.Block();
 6    bl2.BlMd.BlockI b2 = new bl2.BlMd.Block();
 7    SLine.SMd.Sig s1 = b1.getRightSignal();
 8    SLine.SMd.Sig s2 = b2.getLeftSignal();
 9    Unit Line() {
10      b1.connect(s2);
11      b2.connect(s1);
12    }
13  }
14  delta AlwaysDelta when True;
```

Fig. 8 A DVPL modeling a railway block section

s12 must be a main signal. The first equivalence ensures that both feature the same technology. Finally, the features of the variants referenced in the parameters are consistently connected to the features of BlockLine. There is no **uses** dependency to SLine, as it occurs in the parameters.

The attempt to pass two main signal variants or a light pre signal and form main signal to the parameters of BlockLine causes variant generation to fail. A correct instantiation of BlockLine, for example, with light signals is:

```
BlockLine[Light](SLine[Light, Pre](), SLine[Light, Main]())
```

Dependent product lines can declare other dependent product lines as parameters. The DVPL in Fig. 8 models a railway line with two block stations that reference the neighboring signal of each other. It adds a class Line in module LMd with its block stations and their facing signals as fields. The BlockI interface from BlockLine is not unique and thus must be referenced in the products bl1, bl2. Interface Sig, however, is referenced unqualified. No parameter of LineLine is from SLine, therefore, a dependency **uses** SLine is supplied.

4.3 Glue Program Flattening for FDDAM

Flattening a FDDAM glue program is based on the procedure described in Sect. 3.4 which must be modified and extended as follows:

1. **Reference Selection.** Variant references may occur nested in FDDAM, so a variant reference or product line without parameters must be selected. That reference is either to a non-dependent VPL, or only contains **uses** dependencies.

2. **Post-Processing of a Single Iteration.** After variant generation for a VPL two additional steps are performed:

   a. If the selected VPL is a DVPL with **uses** V dependencies (but without parameters), then appropriate import clauses of the form **import** * **from** $mod(V,\text{mod})$ are added to the generated module, for each mod in the unique block of V.

   b. Variant references in the base program or deltas of the DVPL are replaced by module references as described in Sect. 3.4. However, this is not possible when the reference to be resolved is a parameter of a DVPL, because a parameter must have the syntactic shape of a variant reference, not that of a module reference. Instead, DVPLs are partially instantiated: A copy is created where the parameter corresponding to the variant reference to be resolved is instantiated. To resolve references in these copies we use an injective function dep which maps pairs of DVPL names and variant selections to fresh DVPL names. This function is used to generate the fresh names of partially instantiated DVPLs.

   For the overall flattening process we also define an auxiliary function aux that maps DVPL names to pairs of module names and class/interface names. This is used to add **import** clauses when the final variant is generated, because the **import** clauses must be added for all parameters of the DVPL. For all DVPLs present in the beginning aux is set to $\emptyset$.

   If, during post-processing, the variant reference VR to be resolved occurs in the parameter list of a DVPL, then that DVPL is copied and the following actions are performed *on the copy*:

   i. The DPVL's name V is replaced with $dep(V, VR)$.

   ii. The instantiated parameter P is removed from the parameter list.

   iii. All features of P occurring in the feature model are replaced with `True` or `False`, depending on whether the feature is selected or not.

   iv. Every reference of the form P.M in the deltas or base program of the DVPL is replaced with $mod(VR, \text{M})$.

   The auxiliary function is set to:

   $$aux(dep(V, VR)) = \{(mod(VR, \text{M}), \text{C}) \mid \text{P.M.C occurs in } dep(V, VR)\} \cup$$
   $$aux(V)$$

   The DVPL variant reference to be resolved is then replaced with $dep(V, VR)$. Figure 9 shows a copy of BlockLine after the reference to SLine[Light, Pre]() has been resolved. Please observe that the parameter sl1 is gone and the feature constraint has been simplified using sl1. Pre and ¬sl1.Form. Moreover, aux(BlockLine_SLine_Light_Pre) = {(SLine_Light_Pre_BMd, Signal)}.

```
productline BlockLine_SLine_Light_Pre(SLine sl2);
features Light, Form with ¬sl2.Form ∧ sl2.Light ∧ sl1.Main ∧ Light ∧ ¬
 Form;
delta AlwaysDelta;
adds interface BlMd.BlockI { ... }
adds class BlMd.Block implements BlMd.BlockI {
  SLine.SMd.Sig s1 = new SLine_Light_Pre_BMd.Signal();
  SLine.SMd.Sig s2 = new sl2.BMd.Signal();
  SLine.SMd.Sig s3 = new SLine_Light_Pre_BMd.Signal();
  SLine.SMd.Sig s4 = new sl2.BMd.Signal();
  Unit Block() {
    s1.connect(s2);
    s3.connect(s4);
  }
}
delta AlwaysDelta when True;
```

Fig. 9 The DVPL resulting from partial instantiation of the DVPL in Fig. 7

3. **Final Post-Processing.** For each $(m, c) \in aux(V)$, where VPL V has no parameters (is fully initialized), the clause **import** C **from** M; is added to all modules generated from V. The final processing of the example in Fig. 9 generates the following import clauses:

```
import Signal from SLine_Light_Pre_BMd;
import Signal from SLine_Light_Main_BMd;
```

5   Discussion of Design Decisions

In this section we briefly discuss and explain some central design decisions taken, including possible alternatives.

5.1   Variability, Commonality and Interoperability

We use the **unique** block to share elements common to all variants. This goes beyond the idea that product lines model *only* variability. Instead, DVPLs specify *both*, the variable and the common parts of a concept: In addition to modeling variability, DVPLs are a means to structure the overall code. We chose to place aspects of a model that do not vary over products inside a dedicated **unique** block of a DVPL. Two other possible solutions do not require such a block, but have other downsides:

- One alternative is to place common parts into the glue program. However, moving a referenced interface outside of a product line results in a less coherent overall model: The DVPL is now not a single stand-alone unit, but relies on the correct context (namely the one providing the interface).

• Another solution would be to link a DVPL (modeling the variable part of a concept) and a module (modeling the common part) with a new syntactic construct, to make the coupling explicit. Such an external coupling introduces a new concept to the language and is less elegant than coupling variablity and commonality by including and marking common parts in the DVPL.

Variant references in VPLs are similar to dynamic mixin composition in, for example, Scala. The Scala code below creates an object of class C and adds the trait/mixin T. During compilation, this is replaced by an anonymous class:

```
val o = new C with T
```

Both, VPLs and dynamic mixins, are used for on-the-fly generation of variant concepts. Despite this, both mechanisms differ in scope and aim:

• VPLs are more general, in the sense that they operate on an arbitrarily large conceptual model. Mixins are confined to single classes.
• Mixins are integrated into the type hierarchy, while the code generated by VPLs merely copies part of the type hierarchy and operates on the copy.

5.2 Implementing Interoperability

We decided to base the implementation of interoperability among different variants of a product line on ABS modules and on invariant classes/interfaces of the product line (identified by the **unique** keyword).

Modules constitute an appropriate mechanism to encapsulate different variants with overlapping namespaces. As seen above, the module mechanism cleanly separates the identifiers to access different variants while retaining considerable flexibility over what is visible via the import/export mechanism. In the Sline product line, for example, it is possible to specify that the Sig interface and the Signal class are accessible by the variants, but not by possible auxiliary classes such as a Bulb class that might be part of the implementation of a light signal.

Modules are a standard concept, available in ABS (and many other languages) that is sufficient to solve the problem of overlapping name spaces and graded visibility, without the need for dedicated special mechanisms.

As an alternative to modules and **unique** model elements it would have been possible to realize interoperability by a dedicated name space concept plus a type system. This would, however, require the introduction of new concepts that arguably are harder to comprehend.

6   Related Work

Kästner et al. [18] proposed a variability-aware module system, where each module represents an SPL that allows for type checking modules in isolation. Variability inside each module and its interface is expressed by means of #ifdef preprocessor directives and variable linking, respectively. A major difference to our proposal is their approach to implement variability (to build variants): they use an *annotative approach* (#ifdef preprocessor directives), while we use a *transformational approach* (DOP)—see [22, 26] for a classification and survey of different approaches to implement variability.

Schröter et al. [23] advocate investigating mechanisms to support compositional analyses of MPLs for different stages of the development process. In particular, they outline the notion of *syntactical interfaces* to provide a view of reusable programming artifacts, as well as *behavioral interfaces* that build on syntactical interfaces to support formal verification. Schröter et al. [24] propose *feature-context interfaces* aimed at supporting type checking SPLs developed according to the FOP approach which, as pointed out in Sect. 1, is encompassed by DOP (see [20] for a detailed comparison between FOP and DOP). A feature-context interface supports type checking of a feature module in the context of a set of features *FC*. It provides an invariable API specifying classes and members of the feature modules corresponding to the features in *FC* that are intended to be accessible. More recently, Schröter et al. [25] proposed a concept of feature model interface (based on the feature model slicing operator introduced by Acher et al. [1]) that consists of a subset of features (thus it hides all other features and dependencies) and used it in combination with a concept of feature model composition through aggregation to support compositional analyses of feature models.

Damiani et al. [9] informally outline linguistic constructs to extend DOP for SPLs of Java programs to implement MPLs. The idea is to define an MPL as an SPL that imports other SPLs. This extension is very flexible, however, it does not enforce any boundary between different SPLs: the artifact base of the importing SPL is interspersed with the artifact bases of the imported SPLs. Thus the proposed constructs are not suitable for compositional analyses. More recently, Damiani et al. [7] extended the notions proposed in [25] from feature models to complete SPLs. They propose, in the context of DOP for SPLs of Java programs, the concepts of SPL Signature (SPLS), Dependent SPL (DSPL), and DSPL-DSPL composition and show how to use these concepts to support compositional type checking of delta-oriented MPL (by relying on existing techniques for type checking DOP SPLs [4, 6, 8]). An SPLS is a syntactical interface that provides a variability-aware API, expressed in the flexible and modular DOP approach, specifying which classes and members of the variants of a DSPL are intended to be accessible by variants of other DSPLs. In contrast to feature-context interfaces [24], the concept of SPLS [7] represents a variability-aware API that supports compositional type checking of MPLs.

None of the above mentioned proposals contains a mechanism for interoperation of multiple variants from the same product line in the same application, the main goal of the present paper. The concept of DVPLs over core ABS programs proposed in this paper, formalized in the FDDAM language, is closely related to the notion of DSPL of Java programs by Damiani et al. [7], formalized in IFMΔJ—a calculus for product lines where variants are programs written in IFJ [9] (an imperative version of Featherweight Java [15]). In particular, both approaches support to model an MPL as a set of dependent product lines. The main differences are as follows:

- IFMΔJ uses SPLSs, syntactic interfaces providing variability-aware APIs, to express the dependencies of a product line. In IFMΔJ a DSPL has anonymous parameters described by SPLS names.

  - On one hand, parameters in IFMΔJ are more flexible than parameters in FDDAM, since they can be instantiated by suitable variants of any product line that implements the associated SPLS—in contrast to FDDAM, where each parameter of a DVPL is associated with a specific product line name.
  - On the other hand, parameters in IFMΔJ are less flexible than parameters in DSPL, since in IFMΔJ a DSPL cannot have more than one parameter for each SPLS and different parameters must be instantiated by variants of different product lines—in contrast to FDDAM, where each parameter has a name and it is possible to have different parameters associated to the same product line.

- FDDAM provides **unique** blocks and glue programs to write applications that reference different variants (possibly from the same product line) and make them interoperate. In contrast, IFMΔJ does not provide any mechanisms to write applications that reference different variants from the same product line.

FDDAM is more suited for our model of railway operations in FormbaR: the product line for a parameter is always known beforehand. As shown in the examples, interoperable variants occur naturally in this domain.

7 Conclusion

We proposed the concept of dependent variant-interoperable software product lines (DVPL). It provides novel linguistic mechanisms that support interoperability among different variants of one product line and enables describing an MPL by a set of DVPLs and a glue program that may contain references to different variants of the DVPLs. We have illustrated our proposal as an extension of a foundational language for ABS, a modelling language that supports delta-oriented SPLs, and outlined its application to a case study from the FormbaR project performed for Deutsche Bahn AG.

In future work we would like to fully formalize our proposal and develop a compositional type-checking analysis for MPLs described according to our proposal. The starting point for developing the analysis is represented by the work of Damiani et al. [7] (see Sect. 6). Furthermore, we plan to implement the proposal for full ABS.

Acknowledgements This work is supported by FormbaR, part of AG Signalling/DB Raillab (formbar.raillab.de); EU Horizon 2020 project HyVar (www.hyvar-project.eu), GA No. 644298; and ICT COST Action IC1402 ARVI (www.cost-arvi.eu).

References

1. Mathieu Acher et al. "Slicing feature models". In: *26th IEEE/ACM International Conference on Automated Software Engineering, (ASE), 2011*. 2011, pp. 424–427. https://doi.org/10.1109/ASE.2011.6100089.
2. Sven Apel et al. *Feature-Oriented Software Product Lines: Concepts and Implementation.* Springer, 2013, pp. I–XVI, 1–315. ISBN: 978-3-642-37520-0.
3. Don Batory, Jacob Neal Sarvela, and Axel Rauschmayer. "Scaling Step-Wise Refinement". In: *IEEE Transactions on Software Engineering* 30 (2004), pp. 355–371. ISSN: 0098-5589. https://doi.org/10.1109/TSE.2004.23.
4. Lorenzo Bettini, Ferruccio Damiani, and Ina Schaefer. "Compositional type checking of delta-oriented software product lines". In: *Acta Informatica* 50.2 (2013), pp. 77–122. ISSN: 1432-0525. https://doi.org/10.1007/s00236-012-0173-z.
5. P. Clements and L. Northrop. *Software Product Lines: Practices & Patterns.* Addison Wesley Longman, 2001.
6. Ferruccio Damiani and Michael Lienhardt. "On Type Checking Delta-Oriented Product Lines". In: *Integrated Formal Methods - 12th International Conference, IFM 2016, Reykjavik, Iceland, June 1–5, 2016, Proceedings* Vol. 9681. Lecture Notes in Computer Science. Springer, 2016, pp. 47–62. ISBN: 978-3-319-33692-3. https://doi.org/10.1007/978-3-319-33693-0_4.
7. Ferruccio Damiani, Michael Lienhardt, and Luca Paolini. "A Formal Model for Multi SPLs". In: *FSEN*. Vol. 10522. Lecture Notes in Computer Science. Springer, 2017, pp. 67–83.
8. Ferruccio Damiani and Ina Schaefer. "Family-Based Analysis of Type Safety for Delta Oriented Software Product Lines". English. In: *Leveraging Applications of Formal Methods, Verification and Validation. Technologies for Mastering Change*. Ed. by Tiziana Margaria and Bernhard Steffen. Vol. 7609. Lecture Notes in Computer Science. Springer Berlin Heidelberg, 2012, pp. 193–207. ISBN: 978-3-642-34025-3. https://doi.org/10.1007/978-3-642-34026-0_15.
9. Ferruccio Damiani, Ina Schaefer, and Tim Winkelmann. "Delta-oriented Multi Software Product Lines". In: *Proceedings of the 18th International Software Product Line Conference Volume 1*. SPLC '14. Florence, Italy: ACM, 2014, pp. 232–236. ISBN: 978-1-4503-2740-4. https://doi.org/10.1145/2648511.2648536.
10. Ferruccio Damiani et al. "A Unified and Formal Programming Model for Deltas and Traits". In: *Fundamental Approaches to Software Engineering 20th International Conference FASE 2017, Held as Part of the European Joint Conferences on Theory and Practice of Software ETAPS 2017, Uppsala, Sweden, April 22–29, 2017, Proceedings*. Vol. 10202. Lecture Notes in Computer Science. Springer, 2017, pp. 424–441. URL: https://doi.org/10.1007/978-3-662-54494-5_25.
11. Ferruccio Damiani et al. "An Extension of the ABS Toolchain with a Mechanism for Type Checking SPLs". In: *Integrated Formal Methods - 13th International Conference IFM 2017, Turin, Italy, September 20–22, 2017, Proceedings*. Vol. 10510. Lecture Notes in Computer Science. Springer, 2017, pp. 111–126. ISBN: 978-3-319-66844-4. https://doi.org/10.1007/978-3-319-66845-1_8. URL: https://doi.org/10.1007/978-3-319-66845-1_8

12. Ferruccio Damiani, Reiner Hähnle, Eduard Kamburjan, and Michael Lienhardt. "Interoperability of Software Product Line Variants". In: *Proc. 22nd Intl. Systems and Software Product Line Conference (SPLC)*. Gothenburg, Sweden: ACM, 2018.
13. Reiner Hähnle. "The Abstract Behavioral Specification Language: A Tutorial Introduction". In: *Intl. School on Formal Models for Components and Objects: Post Proceedings*. Ed. by Marcello Bonsangue et al. Vol. 7866. LNCS. Springer, 2013, pp. 1–37.
14. Gerald Holl, Paul Grünbacher, and Rick Rabiser. "A systematic review and an expert survey on capabilities supporting multi product lines". In: *Information & Software Technology* 54.8 (2012), pp. 828–852. https://doi.org/10.1016/j.infsof.2012.02.002 URL: http://dx.doi.org/10.1016/j.infsof.2012.02.002
15. A. Igarashi, B. Pierce, and P. Wadler. "Featherweight Java: A Minimal Core Calculus for Java and GJ". In: *ACM TOPLAS* 23.3 (2001), pp. 396–450. https://doi.org/10.1145/503502.503505.
16. Einar Broch Johnsen et al. "ABS: A Core Language for Abstract Behavioral Specification". In: *Formal Methods for Components and Objects - 9th International Symposium, FMCO 2010, Graz, Austria, November 29 - December 1, 2010. Revised Papers*. 2010, pp. 142–164. https://doi.org/10.1007/978-3-642-25271-6_8. URL: https://doiorg/10.1007/978-3-642-25271-6_8.
17. Eduard Kamburjan and Reiner Hähnle. "Uniform Modeling of Railway Operations". In: *FTSCS*. Vol. 694. Communications in Computer and Information Science. 2016, pp. 55–71.
18. Christian Kästner, Klaus Ostermann, and Sebastian Erdweg. "A Variability-aware Module System". In: *Proceedings of the ACM International Conference on Object Oriented Programming Systems Languages and Applications*. OOPSLA '12. Tucson, Arizona, USA: ACM, 2012, pp. 773–792. ISBN: 978-1-4503-1561-6. https://doi.org/10.1145/2384616.2384673.
19. K. Pohl, G. Böckle, and F. van der Linden. *Software Product Line Engineering Foundations, Principles, and Techniques*. Berlin, Germany: Springer, 2005.
20. Ina Schaefer and Ferruccio Damiani. "Pure delta-oriented programming". In: *Proceedings of the 2nd International Workshop on Feature-Oriented Software Development*. FOSD '10. Eindhoven, The Netherlands: ACM, 2010, pp. 49–56. ISBN: 978-1-4503-0208-1. https://doi.org/10.1145/1868688.1868696.
21. Ina Schaefer et al. "Delta-Oriented Programming of Software Product Lines". In: *Software Product Lines: Going Beyond (SPLC 2010)*. Vol. 6287. LNCS. 2010, pp. 77–91. ISBN: 978-3-642-15578-9. https://doi.org/10.1007/978-3-642-15579-6_6
22. Ina Schaefer et al. "Software diversity". English. In: *International Journal on Software Tools for Technology Transfer* 14.5 (2012), pp. 477–495. ISSN: 1433-2779. https://doi.org/10.1007/s10009-012-0253-y URL: http://dx.doi.org/10.1007/s10009-012-0253-y
23. Reimar Schröter, Norbert Siegmund, and Thomas Thüm. "Towards Modular Analysis of Multi Product Lines". In: *Proceedings of the 17th International Software Product Line Conference Co-located Workshops*. SPLC'13. Tokyo, Japan: ACM, 2013, pp. 96–99. ISBN: 978-1-4503-2325-3. https://doi.org/10.1145/2499777.2500719
24. Reimar Schröter et al. "Feature-context Interfaces: Tailored Programming Interfaces for SPLs". In: *Proceedings of the 18th International Software Product Line Conference Volume 1*. SPLC'14. Florence, Italy: ACM, 2014, pp. 102–111. ISBN: 978-1-4503-2740-4. https://doi.org/10.1145/2648511.2648522.
25. Reimar Schröter et al. "Feature-model Interfaces: The Highway to Compositional Analyses of Highly-configurable Systems". In: *Proceedings of the 38th International Conference on Software Engineering*. ICSE '16. Austin, Texas: ACM, 2016, pp. 667–678. ISBN: 978-1-4503-3900-1. https://doi.org/10.1145/2884781.2884823.
26. Thomas Thüm et al. "A Classification and Survey of Analysis Strategies for Software Product Lines". In: *ACM Comput. Surv.* 47.1 (2014), 6:1–6:45. ISSN: 0360-0300. https://doi.org/10.1145/2580950.

A Hoare Logic Contract Theory:
An Exercise in Denotational Semantics

Dilian Gurov and Jonas Westman

Abstract We sketch a simple theory of Hoare logic contracts for programs with procedures, presented in denotational semantics. In particular, we give a simple semantic justification of the usual procedure-modular treatment of such programs. The justification is given by means of a proof of soundness of a *contract-relative* denotational semantics against the standard denotational semantics of procedures in the context of procedure declarations. The suggested formal development can be used as an inspiration for more ambitious contract theories.

1 Introduction

Hoare logic [2, 5] is a well-established logic for reasoning about programs. Its judgments express what a program is intended to compute by relating the values of its variables before and after executing the program. This is adequate when the program is not interacting with its environment (i.e., when it has no side-effects), and when it is expected to terminate; mathematically speaking, from a user's view what such a program does is completely captured by a binary relation on states, initial and final ones, respectively. In Hoare logic, such a binary relation is expressed by means of a pair of logical assertions, called precondition and postcondition, respectively. These assertions are essentially first-order logic formulas over program variables and so-called logical variables; the latter are used to relate values before and after execution. The program and the two assertions form a so-called Hoare triple. What is referred to as Hoare logic is essentially a deductive proof system over Hoare triples.

D. Gurov (✉)
KTH Royal Institute of Technology, Stockholm, Sweden
e-mail: dilian@kth.se

J. Westman
KTH Royal Institute of Technology, Stockholm, Sweden

Systems Development Division, Scania AB, Södertälje, Sweden

© Springer Nature Switzerland AG 2018
P. Müller, I. Schaefer (eds.), *Principled Software Development*,
https://doi.org/10.1007/978-3-319-98047-8_8

Meyer advocated in [6] the use of Hoare-style preconditions and postconditions as *contracts* for programs under development, and a design methodology called *design-by-contract*. Contracts support *modular* development of software: if one program relies on another one, the two can be decoupled by means of a contract for the latter program; the contract is what the second program is obliged to fulfill toward the first. The first program can then be developed relying on this contract, without requiring access to, or knowledge of, the implementation of the second program (which may or may not be available). Furthermore, the first program can be *verified* to meet its own contract, under the assumption that the second program meets its contract. Besides the methodological advantages of using contracts, this has the effect that verification also becomes modular and therefore scales well with the number of modules. Many well-known tools for deductive verification, such as OpenJML [4] and VCC [3], are in fact *procedure-modular*: they expect every procedure to be accompanied by a contract, and verify each procedure in isolation.

Procedures can be mutually recursive. For instance, consider the Java program shown in Fig. 1. It consists of two procedures (or "methods"), even and odd, which call each other in order to determine whether their argument is an even number or an odd one, respectively. Both procedures are equipped with a (JML-like) contract, consisting of a precondition, expressed in a requires annotation, and a postcondition, expressed in an ensures annotation. In the latter, \result refers to the value returned by the respective procedure, while n refers to the value of the formal parameter at the time of invoking the procedure (but in classical Hoare logic this would be expressed by means of logical variables).

We can verify each procedure against its own contract in isolation, by just assuming that the procedures it calls meet their respective contracts. For instance, we can infer from the precondition of procedure even and its statements, that at the control point where it calls procedure odd, the value of variable n must be

```
public class EvenOdd {

    //@ requires n >= 0;
    //@ ensures \result == (\exists int k; n == 2 * k);
    public boolean even(int n) {
        if (n == 0) return true;
        else return odd(n-1);
    }

    //@ requires n >= 0;
    //@ ensures \result == (\exists int k; n == 2 * k + 1);
    public boolean odd(int n) {
        if (n == 0) return false;
        else return even(n-1);
    }
}
```

Fig. 1 A Java program with mutually recursive procedures

positive (since it is assumed to be non-negative in the precondition, and must be different from zero in the `else`-branch), and hence `n-1` must be non-negative. The precondition of `odd` is thus met, and we can therefore assume that upon return from this procedure call, by virtue of its postcondition, the value returned by `even` will be `true` for `n` if the value of `n-1` is odd, and *vice versa*, thus entailing the postcondition of `even`.

But is such such a circular, assume-guarantee style reasoning *sound*? It is well-known from the literature that for *partial correctness*, where termination is not required, this indeed is the case (see e.g. [8]). The usual way of showing this is based on a natural (or "big-step") operational semantics of the programming language, consisting of a set of derivation rules, and a proof system in the form of a sequent calculus over Hoare triples, also presented as a set of derivation rules. Proving soundness thus typically requires proofs by induction on the height of derivation trees, which can be rather cumbersome. We believe that an elegant, and more economic, alternative way of showing soundness could be based on *denotational semantics* and fixed-point theory. In this paper, we sketch our idea on a toy programming language with procedures, and argue that more ambitious contract theories can be developed following the suggested scheme.

Structure of the Paper We start by recalling in Sect. 2 the denotational semantics of a toy programming language without procedures. We then define, also in denotational semantics, the semantics of Hoare logic contracts. Next, in Sect. 3, we extend the programming language and its semantics with procedures. In addition to the usual denotational treatment of procedures, we propose an alternative, contract-relative semantics, and show it to be sound with respect to the former one. We conclude in Sect. 4.

2 Programs Without Procedures

We start with a toy programming language, which is imperative, has no procedures, and is sequential and deterministic.

2.1 Syntax and Denotational Semantics

The typical toy imperative programming language considered in the literature is generated by the following BNF grammar, where x ranges over (integer) program variables, a over arithmetic expressions, b over Boolean expressions, and S over statements:

$$S ::= \text{skip} \mid \text{x} := \text{a} \mid S_1; S_2 \mid \text{if } b \text{ then } S_1 \text{ else } S_2 \mid \text{while } b \text{ do } S$$

the meaning of which is well-understood.

A program *state* s is defined as a mapping from the variables of the program to their respective domains of values (in this case the integers). The set of all states shall be denoted by **State**.

The "direct style" denotation $[\![S]\!]$ of a statement S is traditionally defined as a single mathematical object, namely as a partial function on **State**, with $[\![S]\!](s) = s'$ meaning that the execution of statement S from state s terminates in the state s', and $[\![S]\!](s)$ being undefined meaning that the execution of statement S from state s does not terminate. A more general approach, which also encompasses non-determinism, is to define $[\![S]\!]$ as a binary relation on **State**, with $(s, s') \in [\![S]\!]$ meaning that there is an execution of statement S from state s that terminates in the state s'. To be able to unify the denotation of statements with that of Hoare logic contracts, we shall adopt the latter approach here.

The meaning of the program constructs is given by induction on the structure of statements, via defining equations. For instance, the meaning of sequential composition is given by the equation:

$$[\![S_1; S_2]\!] \stackrel{\text{def}}{=} [\![S_1]\!] \circ [\![S_2]\!]$$

i.e., as relation composition. The most involved case is the defining equation for the **while** loop: it is defined as the least solution to a semantic equation derived from the (intended) equality of the denotation of a loop and its unfolding. For details, the interested reader is referred to standard textbooks such as [7, 12].

2.2 Hoare Logic and Contracts

Hoare logic is based on so-called *Hoare triples* of the shape $\{P\}S\{Q\}$, where S is a statement, and where P and Q are logical formulas called *assertions*, which are interpreted over states. We denote by $s \models P$ the fact that the assertion P is true in state s.

For Hoare logic without logical variables, a Hoare triple $\{P\}S\{Q\}$ is defined to be *valid* w.r.t. partial correctness, denoted $\models_{par} \{P\}S\{Q\}$, if for every state s such that $s \models P$, if execution of S from s terminates in a state s', then $s' \models Q$. The addition of logical variables requires the semantics to be relativised on interpretations $\mathscr{I}$ that map logical variables to values; the Hoare triple is then valid if for every state s and interpretation $\mathscr{I}$ such that $s \models_{\mathscr{I}} P$, if execution of S from s terminates in a state s', then $s' \models_{\mathscr{I}} Q$. For the details of the formalization, we refer again to [12].

We refer to the pair $C = (P, Q)$ as a *Hoare logic contract*. We say that a particular implementation S *meets* the contract C w.r.t. partial correctness, denoted $S \models_{par} C$, if and only if the corresponding Hoare triple is valid, i.e., if $\models_{par} \{P\}S\{Q\}$.

2.3   The Denotational Semantics of Contracts

A natural way to define formally the semantics of a contract is to define it as the set of denotations of the programs that satisfy it. This is for instance the approach taken in [9]. In the present case, however, we can take a simpler approach and define the denotation $[\![C]\!]$ of a contract $C = (P, Q)$ in the *same domain* as the denotation of programs, namely as a binary relation on **State**. This will allow us later to give a simple definition of a contract-relative semantics for programs with procedures.

Definition 1 (Denotation of Contracts)   Let $C = (P, Q)$ be a Hoare logic contract. The *denotation* of the contract is defined as follows:

$$[\![C]\!] \overset{\text{def}}{=} \{(s, s') \mid \forall \mathscr{I}.\ (s \models_{\mathscr{I}} P \Rightarrow s' \models_{\mathscr{I}} Q)\}$$

We then obtain the following simple set-theoretic characterization of a program meeting a contract:

$$S \models_{par} C \quad \text{iff} \quad [\![S]\!] \subseteq [\![C]\!]$$

which could also be considered as an alternative definition of this notion.

Many formal frameworks express satisfaction of a contract (or specification) through set inclusion, and the theoretical implications of this are well understood. For instance, we obtain a natural notion of *precision* in the lattice of denotations.

3   Programs with Procedures

We now extend the above treatment to programs with procedures. For brevity, we shall assume that procedures do not take parameters or return values, and that they do not declare local variables; all these features can be encoded using dedicated (global) variables.

3.1   Syntax and Denotational Semantics

Consider that we extend our toy programming language with the statement call p, where p ranges over a set P of names of procedures *declared* using the syntax $p = S_p$. A *program with procedures* is a statement S in the context of a set of procedure declarations.

To give a denotational semantics of such programs, the denotation of call p needs to be defined. Considering non-recursive programs, a straightforward approach is to define $[\![\text{call } p]\!]$ to be equal to the denotation $[\![S_p]\!]$ of S_p, i.e., of the *body* of procedure p, and rely on the structural induction approach of Sect. 2.1 to give the program a meaning. However, this will not work for the general case with recursive programs, since the structural induction will become circular.

To handle the general case, a more indirect approach is taken, as in [12], by introducing: for each $p \in P$, a variable X_p ranging over **State** $\times$ **State**, and a function ρ, called *environment*, which maps each variable X_p to a binary relation on states, i.e., $\rho(X_p) \subseteq$ **State** $\times$ **State**. The denotation of statements S is relativized in terms of this environment as $[\![S]\!]_\rho$; in particular, $[\![\text{call } p]\!]_\rho \overset{\text{def}}{=} \rho(X_p)$, while the defining equations for the other language constructs remain unchanged.

Notably, this approach gives rise to a system of equations:

$$\left\{ X_p = [\![S_p]\!]_\rho \right\}_{p \in P}$$

Every solution of this system can be seen as an environment itself. Viewing ρ as a variable, we can see the whole system of equations as one equation, but over environments. Thus, semantically, the system induces a function $\xi :$ **Env** $\to$ **Env** over environments, defined by $\xi(\rho)(X_p) \overset{\text{def}}{=} [\![S_p]\!]_\rho$.

Let $\rho \sqsubseteq \rho'$ denote point-wise set inclusion over environments, and let $\rho_\perp$ be the environment mapping every variable to the empty relation. (**Env**, $\sqsubseteq$, $\rho_\perp$) can be shown to be a chain-complete partial order with bottom, in which the function ξ is continuous (i.e., ξ is monotone and respects least upper bounds of ω-chains). By the well-known Knaster-Tarski fixed-point theorem, ξ has a least and a greatest fixed point. We take the least fixed point ρ_0, which constitutes the least solution to the equation system, and define the semantics of a program with procedures S relative to this particular solution, i.e.:

$$[\![S]\!] \overset{\text{def}}{=} [\![S]\!]_{\rho_0}$$

3.2 A Contract-Relative Denotational Semantics

For a program with procedures, S, consider a contract C for the statement S and a set of contracts $\{C_p\}_{p \in P}$, one for each declared procedure p.

The set of contracts $\{C_p\}_{p \in P}$ gives rise to an alternative, *contract-relative* notion $[\![S]\!]^{cr}$ of the denotational semantics of programs with procedures. To this end, we introduce the special *contract environment* ρ_c defined by $\rho_c(X_p) \overset{\text{def}}{=} [\![C_p]\!]$, for each $p \in P$. Notice that this is only possible because of our careful choice of denotational semantics of contracts, made in Sect. 2.3. We base the semantics of programs with procedures on this environment, instead of on ρ_0, and define:

$$[\![S]\!]^{cr} \overset{\text{def}}{=} [\![S]\!]_{\rho_c}$$

Notice that this semantics is *not* recursive and does not involve fixed points: the contract-relative denotation $[\![S_p]\!]^{cr}$ of every procedure body can be computed *procedure-modularly*, i.e., independently of each other. We thus obtain an alternative, contract-relative notion of a statement meeting a contract:

$$S \models_{par}^{cr} C \quad \text{iff} \quad [\![S]\!]^{cr} \subseteq [\![C]\!]$$

The contract-relative semantics embodies an *assume-guarantee* style treatment of programs with procedures: the contract-relative denotation of a statement provides a set-theoretic "upper bound" on its standard denotation, assuming upper bounds on the denotations of the called procedures as specified by their contracts. Procedure-modular verification as used in practice essentially follows this treatment.

3.3 Soundness of the Contract-Relative Semantics

In fixed-point theory, a common technique to prove that a point x is greater than the least fixed point y of a continuous function f is to show that x is a pre-fixed point of f, i.e., that $f(x) \sqsubseteq x$. Since the least fixed point of a continuous function is also its least pre-fixed point, it follows that $y \sqsubseteq x$.

We have a similar situation here. Intuitively, the environment ρ_0, which by definition is the least fixed point of ξ, embodies the denotation (i.e., meaning) of the procedure declarations. The contract environment ρ_c embodies the denotation of the contracts of the declared procedures, while $\xi(\rho_c)$ embodies the contract-relative denotation of the procedure declarations. To show that the procedure declarations meet their contracts, we just show that their contract-relative denotation meets the contract (as we essentially do when we apply procedure-modular verification); in this way we establish that the denotation of the contracts ρ_c is a pre-fixed point of ξ.

Thus, our contract-relative semantics is *sound* w.r.t. the standard one, whenever all declared procedures meet their contracts.

Theorem 1 (Soundness) *Let S be a program with procedures as described above, and let for all $p \in P$, $S_p \models_{par}^{cr} C_p$. We have:*

$$S \models_{par}^{cr} C \quad \text{implies} \quad S \models_{par} C$$

Proof We show that $[\![S]\!] \sqsubseteq [\![S]\!]^{cr}$, from which soundness follows. Since by assumption $S_p \models_{par}^{cr} C_p$ for all $p \in P$, we have $[\![S_p]\!]^{cr} \subseteq [\![C_p]\!]$ and hence $[\![S]\!]_{\rho_c} \subseteq [\![C_p]\!]$ for all $p \in P$. Therefore, by the definitions of ξ and ρ_c, we have $\xi(\rho_c)(X_p) \subseteq \rho_c(X_p)$ for all $p \in P$. Thus, $\xi(\rho_c) \sqsubseteq \rho_c$, i.e., ρ_c is a pre-fixed point of ξ. Since ρ_0 is the least fixed point of ξ, ρ_0 is also its least pre-fixed point, and therefore $\rho_0 \sqsubseteq \rho_c$. By monotonicity of ξ, we obtain $[\![S]\!]_{\rho_0} \subseteq [\![S]\!]_{\rho_c}$, and therefore $[\![S]\!] \subseteq [\![S]\!]^{cr}$.   □

4 Conclusion

We presented a simple treatment of Hoare logic contracts in denotational semantics. It gives rise to a procedure-modular, contract-relative semantics of statements in the context of a set of procedure declarations. We showed this semantics to be sound w.r.t. the standard denotational semantics of procedural languages, which is not procedure-modular. The proof of soundness is simple, utilizing the fact that the denotations of the Hoare logic contracts of the declared procedures constitute a pre-fixed point of the semantic function used to define the standard denotational semantics, as long as all procedures meet their contracts procedure-modularly.

One concrete application of the above framework that we are currently developing is a formal justification of a technique to automatically compute procedure contracts. What the framework gives us is a notion of precision of contracts w.r.t. the (standard) denotation of their respective procedure bodies. We will use this notion to characterize the technique.

We presented here the treatment of Hoare logic contracts in the context of a toy programming language. Building on previous work [10, 11], we plan to extend our contract theory to the far more ambitious case of embedded C code. Because of the interactive nature of such code, the denotation of statements cannot be adequately defined as a binary relation on states; instead, we plan to develop the framework around the theory of nested words presented in [1].

Acknowledgement We thank Wolfgang Ahrendt for valuable comments on an earlier draft of the paper.

References

1. Rajeev Alur and Swarat Chaudhuri. "Temporal Reasoning for Procedural Programs". In: *Verification, Model Checking and Abstract Interpretation (VMCAI 2010)*. Vol. 5944. Lecture Notes in Computer Science. Springer, 2010, pp. 45–60.
2. Krzysztof R. Apt. "Ten Years of Hoare's Logic: A Survey Part 1". In: *ACM Transactions on Programming Languages and Systems* 3.4 (1981), pp. 431–483. https://doi.org/10.1145/357146.357150. URL: http://doi.acm.org/10.1145/357146.357150
3. E. Cohen et al. "VCC: A Practical System for Verifying Concurrent C". In: *Theorem Proving in Higher Order Logics (TPHOLs 2009)*. Vol. 5674. Lecture Notes in Computer Science. Springer, 2009, pp. 23–42.
4. David R. Cok. "OpenJML: JML for Java 7 by Extending OpenJDK". In: *NASA Formal Methods (NFM 2011)*. Vol. 6617. Lecture Notes in Computer Science. Springer, 2011, pp. 472–479.
5. C. A. R. Hoare. "An Axiomatic Basis for Computer Programming". In: *Commun. ACM* 12.10 (1969), pp. 576–580.
6. Bertrand Meyer. "Applying "Design by Contract"". In: *IEEE Computer* 25.10 (1992), pp. 40–51.
7. Hanne Riis Nielson and Flemming Nielson. *Semantics with Applications: An Appetizer* Berlin, Heidelberg: SpringerVerlag, 2007. ISBN: 1846286913.

8. David von Oheimb "Hoare Logic for Mutual Recursion and Local Variables". In: *Foundations of Software Technology and Theoretical Computer Science (FSTTCS 1999)*. Vol. 1738. Lecture Notes in Computer Science. Springer, 1999, pp. 168–180.
9. Dimitrios Vytiniotis et al. "HALO: Haskell to logic through denotational semantics". In: *Proceedings of POPL 2013*. ACM, 2013, pp. 431–442.
10. Jonas Westman and Mattias Nyberg. "Conditions of contracts for separating responsibilities in heterogeneous systems". In: *Formal Methods in System Design* 52.2 (2018), pp. 147–192.
11. Jonas Westman et al. "Formal architecture modeling of sequential non-recursive C programs". In: *Science of Computer Programming* 146 (2017), pp. 2–27.
12. Glynn Winskel. *The Formal Semantics of Programming Languages: An Introduction*. Cambridge, MA, USA: MIT Press, 1993. ISBN: 0-262-23169-7.

Towards Reliable Concurrent Software

Marieke Huisman and Sebastiaan J. C. Joosten

Abstract As the use of concurrent software is increasing, we urgently need techniques to establish the correctness of such applications. Over the last years, significant progress has been made in the area of software verification, making verification techniques usable for realistic applications. However, much of this work concentrates on sequential software, and a next step is necessary to apply these results also on realistic concurrent software. In this paper, we outline a research agenda to realise this goal. We argue that current techniques for verification of concurrent software need to be further developed in multiple directions: extending the class of properties that can be established, improving the level of automation that is available for this kind of verification, and enlarging the class of concurrent programs that can be verified.

1 Introduction

Software is everywhere! Every day we use and rely upon enormous amounts of software, without even being aware of it [33]. This includes the obvious applications, such as mobile phone apps and all kinds of office software, but also the software in our cars, household equipment, airplanes etc. It has become impossible to imagine what life would be like without software. What we are not aware of, is how much software is actually safety-critical or business-critical, and how big the risk is that one day software failures will bring this everyday life to a grinding halt. In fact, all software contains errors that cause it to behave in unintended ways [32, 49]. Studies have shown that software applications have on average between 1 and 16 errors per 1000 lines of code, even when tested and deployed [58, 59], and substantial research is needed to reduce this number and to make software that is reliable under all circumstances, without compromising its performance.

M. Huisman · S. J. C. Joosten (✉)
University of Twente, Enschede, The Netherlands
e-mail: m.huisman@utwente.nl; s.j.c.joosten@utwente.nl

© Springer Nature Switzerland AG 2018
P. Müller, I. Schaefer (eds.), *Principled Software Development*,
https://doi.org/10.1007/978-3-319-98047-8_9

A commonly used approach to improve software performance is the use of *concurrency* and *distribution*. For many applications, a smart split into parallel computations can lead to a significant increase in performance. Unfortunately, parallel computations make it more difficult to guarantee *reliability* of the software. The consequence is unsettling: the use of concurrent and distributed software is widespread, because it provides efficiency and robustness, but the unpredictability of its behaviour makes that errors can occur at unexpected, seemingly random moments.

As we will see below, the quest for reliable software builds on a long history, and significant progress has already been made. Nevertheless, ensuring reliability of efficient concurrent and distributed software remains an open challenge. Ultimately, it is our dream that program verification techniques are built into software development environments. When a software developer writes a program, he explicitly writes down the crucial desired properties about the program, as well as the assumptions under which the different program components may be executed. Continuously, an automatic check is applied to decide whether the desired properties are indeed established, and whether the assumptions are respected. If this is not the case, this is shown to the developer—with useful feedback on why the program does not behave as intended.

This paper outlines a research agenda, discussing what we believe are the crucial step towards reaching this goal. First, in Sect. 2 we will discuss the state-of-the-art in verification of concurrent software, focusing in particular on deductive verification techniques. In Sect. 3 we identify three main directions of research, and discusses challenges and a possible approach for each of those directions. This section discusses how abstract models can be combined with deductive verification techniques to reason about global functional correctness properties of programs. Section 4 discusses the need for and possible approaches to further increase the level of automation in deductive verification. Finally, Sect. 5 sketches the steps and chances that exist to adapt existing verification techniques to other concurrent programming models.

2 State-of-the-Art in Verification of Concurrent Software

2.1 Software Correctness

The quest for software correctness is an old tale (see Fig. 1 for a historic overview). Already in the sixties, in the early days of computing, Floyd and Hoare realised that it is actually possible to prove that a program behaves as intended [30, 37]. Given a small code fragment, and a specification of what the fragment is supposed to do, a collection of simple proof rules was devised, which can be used to establish whether a program behaves as specified. By applying the proof rules, auxiliary proof obligations in first-order logic are generated. If the proof obligations can be

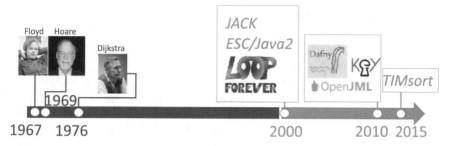

Fig. 1 Development of Sequential Software Verification

proven, we can conclude that the program satisfies its specification. This approach, called Floyd-Hoare or Hoare logic, still forms the basis for many techniques to reason about program behaviour (usually implemented using Dijkstra's predicate transformer semantics [24]).

For a long time, program verification remained a pen-and-paper activity. However, around the year 2000, several groups started working on the development of tools to support this kind of verification [8–10, 20, 38, 50]. There are several technical reasons behind the coordination of these developments:

- the emergence of Java meant that there was a popular and widely-used programming language with a reasonably well-defined semantics, amenable to formal reasoning;
- in addition, computing power had increased, which made it actually feasible to build efficient tools to reason about non-trivial programs; and
- there was tremendous progress in automated verification technology for first-order logic, which enabled automatic discharge of auxiliary proof obligations, culminating in modern, very powerful SMT solvers.

Since then, work on these program verification tools has progressed, resulting in tools such as OpenJML [21], CodeContracts [28, 47], and the most recent versions of KeY [1], which are now being used in teaching, integrated in standard development environments, and to verify or find bugs in non-trivial algorithms, such as TIMsort [23].

Despite the enormous progress that has been made, there are still many open challenges in this area [35]. One important open challenge for program verification is that it still requires a substantial level of expertise, in particular because of the high number of auxiliary annotations that have to be provided to guide the proving process (see for example the solutions to the VerifyThis program verification challenges at http://www.verifythis.org).

2.2 Verification of Concurrent Software

All techniques mentioned above focus on proving local safety properties of sequential programs, i.e., with a single thread of execution, but cannot specify or effectively prove properties on the global program behaviour of concurrent or distributed software. Thus, extending program verification techniques to enable reasoning about programs with multiple threads of execution is a necessary step to ensure the reliability of realistic programs, see Fig. 2 for a historic overview.

Already in the 70s, Owicki and Gries proposed a technique to extend program logic to reason about concurrent programs [60]. Their technique required annotations for each atomic step in the program, and a proof that these annotations could not be invalidated by any atomic step made by other program threads, thus resulting in a non-modular verification technique with an exponential number of proof obligations. In particular, if a verified program is extended with a new thread, also the existing threads have to be reverified. In 1980, Jones proposed a modular verification technique for concurrent programs, called rely-guarantee reasoning [41]. In rely-guarantee reasoning the verifier explicitly specifies the steps that are allowed for the environment, which requires thorough understanding of the application at hand.

About 10 years ago, Concurrent Separation Logic (CSL) was invented [17, 53] (Brookes and O'Hearn received the Gödel prize 2016 for this achievement). This was an important step for the verification of concurrent software, as it enabled thread-modular verification. Originally, separation logic was proposed as an extension of classical Hoare logic to reason about pointer programs, by explicitly considering which memory locations are relevant for what part of the program [54, 55]. This characteristic makes it also extremely suitable to reason about concurrent programs: if we can prove that two threads work on disjoint parts of the memory, then we know that they cannot interfere with each other.

The invention of concurrent separation logic led to a whole plethora of techniques and logics to reason about concurrent software, focusing on different aspects, see [18] for an overview.

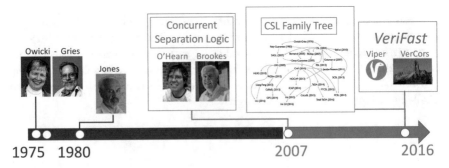

Fig. 2 Development of Concurrent Software Verification

In one line of work, more and more advanced logics are proposed, grouped in the CSL family tree [18]. This contains for example a combination of rely guarantee and separation logic [67], (impredicative) concurrent abstract predicates [25, 66], TaDa (a logic for time and data abstraction) [61, 62], fine-grained concurrent separation logic [52, 63], a combination of monoids and invariants [44, 45], and reasoning based on linearisation points [36, 68], with the aim of finding a generic logic, which can be used to verify the behaviour of all concurrent programs. So far, these approaches are still fairly theoretic, and require a high level of expertise. Some of these logics are formalised in Coq, with suitable tactics to use them inside Coq. Further, they are usually developed for relatively simple core programming languages, and focus on small but intricate examples.

In another line of work, the focus is on developing practical techniques to reason about commonly used programs, using various synchronisation methods, support for dynamic thread creation, reentrant locks etc. This has been the focus of our work on the VerCors tool set [3–5, 14], where we developed techniques (with tool support) to reason about multi-threaded Java and OpenCL programs. This is also the aim of the VeriFast tool, for verification of single- and multithreaded C and Java programs [39, 65] and the Viper framework, which provides support for separation logic-based reasoning for a low-level intermediate language [43, 51]. In particular, our VerCors tool is build on top of the Viper framework. Some of the more theoretical results on verification of concurrent software are (partially) integrated in these techniques.

By now, there is a plethora of logics to verify specific core properties about concurrent software, such as that the program is free of data races. The next challenge is to efficiently prove properties about the *global functional behaviour* of a realistic concurrent program.

2.3   Concurrent Software in Industrial Practice

Because of high demands on software performance, industry is using concurrency more and more in their daily practice. However, for many companies, reliability of the software they develop is very important: if their software is misbehaving, they risk losing the confidence of their customers. Therefore, we see that companies are often quite conservative in their use of concurrency: they use well-known programming patterns, reuse existing libraries as much as possible, and try to isolate the concurrency-related aspects to a small part of their application.

Software developers need effective verification techniques to improve the quality and reliability of their concurrent software. We believe that to develop these techniques, the ultimate challenge is not in finding a logic that can reason about all possible concurrent programs. Instead, the challenge is to develop techniques that can be used efficiently on many common concurrent programming patterns, and that can be used to detect bugs quickly and effectively, without requiring too many user interventions, and without too many false positives. This conviction is what drives our research: we aim at developing techniques that can help software developers in their daily software development practice to improve the quality of the software they are producing.

3   Abstraction Techniques for Functional Verification

One of the main open challenges for the verification of concurrent software that we consider is how to to develop techniques to *automatically verify global functional correctness properties of concurrent and distributed software*, i.e., to ensure that an application has the expected behaviour and does not experience failures.

To reach this goal, we advocate an approach where a *mathematical model* of a concurrent application is constructed, which provides an *abstract view* of the program's behaviour, leaving out details that are irrelevant for the properties being checked, see Fig. 3. The main verification steps in this approach are

1. *algorithmic verification* over the mathematical model to reason about global program behaviour, and
2. *program logics* to verify the formal connection between the software and its mathematical model.

Typically, the basic building blocks of the abstract mathematical model are *actions*, for which we can prove a correspondence between abstract actions and concrete code fragments, which is then used to prove the formal connection between the software and its mathematical model. Moreover, this has the advantage that if a global property does not hold at the abstract level, the abstract-level counterexample corresponds to a concrete candidate counterexample at the software level.

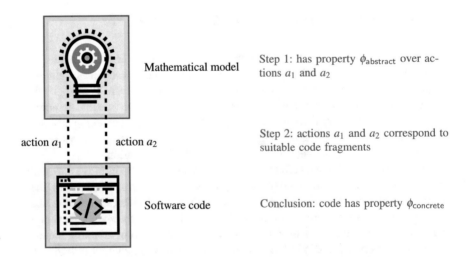

Mathematical model

Step 1: has property ϕ_{abstract} over actions a_1 and a_2

action a_1 action a_2

Step 2: actions a_1 and a_2 correspond to suitable code fragments

Software code

Conclusion: code has property ϕ_{concrete}

Fig. 3 Using abstraction for the verification of concurrent and distributed software

Within this approach, a *software designer* specifies the desired *global properties* for a given application in terms of abstract actions. The *software developer* should then specify how these *abstract actions map to concrete program state*: in which states is the action allowed, and what will be its effect on the program state. Global properties may be safety properties, e.g., an invariant relation between the values of variables in different components, or a complicated protocol specifying correct interface usage, but we believe that extensions of the approach to liveness and progress properties are also possible.

To make this approach possible, we believe the following challenges should be addressed:

1. identify a good abstraction theory,
2. extend the abstraction theory to reason about progress and liveness properties of code, and
3. use the abstraction theory to guide the programmer to develop working code through refinement.

We discuss these challenges in more detail, and discuss our first results in this direction.

3.1   The Right Mathematical Model

The purpose of a good abstraction is that it reduces the verification effort in two ways: it makes it easier for the software designer to reason about the essential parts of his program, and automated verification methods can be used, because the verification effort is used on a model that is smaller than the original program. Moreover, the abstraction should support modular and compositional verification.

To find such a level of abstraction, we need to look at what currently hinders verification. One problem is the large state space of a program, as we have to consider all possible values of all program variables. Thus, a suitable abstraction needs to be able to describe a reachable configuration of variables as a single mathematical object.

Moreover, verification of concurrent software needs to consider all possible interleavings of the threads. Thus, we need to find ways to group actions, in particular also actions that do not occur inside atomic blocks of code. The theory of linearisation points will be a good starting point [36, 68] for this, but it needs to be further generalised, as abstract actions also could correspond to method calls, and not just to memory writes.

Summarising, a good abstraction should have the following properties:

- it can accurately capture low-level implementation details,
- it is modular,
- it can abstract over a sequence of multiple actions, and
- it can abstract over a valuation of multiple variables.

When developing this abstraction theory, we use the logics in the CSL family tree [18] as an important source of inspiration. In particular, the notion of views has been advocated as a general framework that captures many commonalities in the verification of concurrent software [26], and we believe it is important that our basic abstraction theory can be described in terms of views. However, to further the state of the art in program verification, we believe there are two more additional requirements that should be considered, namely that the abstraction should be able to reason about time-dependent properties, and it should facilitate reasoning in a top-down manner, as will be motivated below.

3.2 Reasoning About Liveness and Progress

Most of program verification concerns the verification of safety properties: functional correctness is interpreted as ensuring that under a certain precondition, the postcondition will hold after executing some code. Checking that a postcondition is not violated corresponds to verifying that variable assignments that violate the postcondition are not reachable, which is a safety property. However, when designing concurrent code, safety is only one issue software designers need to deal with, they also need to make sure that their program will not deadlock, and will eventually do the right thing.

The latter property is called progress: if an action is enabled, it will eventually happen. Whether or not a progress property holds depends on a program scheduler, which depends on hardware, firmware, drivers and software. We therefore need an approach in which the assumptions about the scheduler can be made explicit.

We wish to use the abstraction theory to support reasoning about global liveness properties. This means that the abstractions need to incorporate a notion that an action must happen. This has been explored earlier by Larsen *et al.* who defined modal transition systems as an extension of standard LTSs with must- and may-transitions [6, 46].

Variant-based reasoning allows us to show that an action indeed will happen. As the actions might happen in different parts of the program, using this variant-based technique might not always be straightforward. We may develop a nested approach for variant-based reasoning, where at the lowest level we show that individual methods terminate, and at higher levels we show that a sequence of method calls terminates (assuming that the method calls themselves terminate). In the rewriting community there is a substantial amount of work on termination of rewrite systems, some of which has been applied to sequential programming languages and transition systems [16, 34, 42], and it should be investigated if and how these techniques can be used in the context of concurrent software verification.

3.3   Unification of Model and Code

Finally, we believe that if the abstraction theory is fully developed, it should also be usable in the opposite direction: if we take an abstract model as a starting point, can we use *refinement* to transform this into correct working code?

The basic refinement process can be divided into two phases. In the first phase, the global property can be separated into properties about individual processes. This might introduce some communication steps, and we need to resort here to the notion of process of equivalence under hiding of actions. The big challenge in this step is to decide how the property should be split. When verifying a concrete program, the program code dictates how this should be done. But in this case, where we wish to generate the program, we need other ways to do this. We plan to investigate different possibilities, for example maximising parallelisation, where each thread is responsible for an individual action, or even multiple threads execute the same action, all in parallel; minimising parallelisation, and grouping sets of related actions. For all these possibilities, different splitting strategies can be developed, but typically some user intervention will be necessary here to indicate the intent of the program.

In the second phase, we have process algebra terms that describe the behaviour of an individual thread. The process algebra term itself describes the control flow of the thread, and we will develop a technique to transform each process algebra term into a sequence of program instructions. The abstraction typically defines some variables, which model the synchronisation between the different threads and are used to capture the effect of the actions. These variables should be mapped into concrete program variables, and as a last step the actions are translated into concrete program code, executing the action's specified effect. Typically, the guards will be fulfilled by construction, and do not have to be incorporated in the generated program code.

In the long run, the results of these investigations might lead to a theory that unifies models and programs and removes the borders between the two. This would allow us to reason about systems where some components are already implemented, and others are only specified by a model, which later might be refined into an implementation.

3.4   First Steps Towards a Solution

In our earlier work on abstract models [13, 56, 69], we have shown that it is possible to use process algebra terms to describe the abstract control flow of a program. This allow us to show that the program behaves according to a certain protocol (for example preventing unwanted flow of information by ensuring that a send may never occur after a receive) or that a variable evolves according to a particular pattern (for example, a variable only increases, a queue never becomes empty etc.). The unique characteristic of this approach is that we can prove the correspondence between the abstract model and the program code using standard program logic, by linking the actions that are the basic building blocks of the model to concrete program statements.

Below, this approach is sketched on a very simple example. Suppose we have a shared variable x protected by a lock lck, and we have two threads that manipulate x: one thread multiplies x by 4, the other thread adds 4 to x. The specification of the thread that performs the multiplication captures that the multiplication has happened. For this we use the notion of history [13]: an abstraction of the actions a thread has taken up-to now. If before the thread is executed, the history is equal to H (written $Hist(H)$), then afterwards the action $mult(4)$ is added at the end of the history ($P.a$ is notation for a process P, followed by action a). Similarly the specification of the addition thread captures that the addition has happened. The *action* annotation inside the method body indicates the concrete code fragment that corresponds to this abstract action.

```
class Mult extends Thread {              class Add extends Thread {

//@ requires Hist(H);                     //@ requires Hist(H);
//@ ensures Hist(H.mult(4));              //@ ensures Hist(H.add(4));
public void run() {                       public void run() {
    //@ action mult(4) {                      //@ action add(4) {
    lock(lck);                                lock(lck);
    x = x * 4;                                x = x + 4;
    unlock(lck);                              unlock(lck);
    //@ }                                     //@ }
}                                         }
}                                         }
```

Next, we have action specifications that describe the effect of the actions *mult* and *add*. Using program logic, we can prove that the action implementations (in the thread bodies) indeed behave as specified.

```
//@ assume true;
//@ guarantee x == \old(x) * k;
action mult(k);

//@ assume true;
//@ guarantee x == \old(x) + k;
action add(k);
```

Suppose we have a main method, which starts the two threads and then waits for them to terminate. For this main method we can specify and verify (using a history-aware program logic) that it will execute the *mult* and the *add* action in any order (where $P + Q$ denotes a non-deterministic choice between P and Q and *empty* denotes an empty history).

```
//@ requires  Hist(empty) & x == 0;
//@ ensures  Hist(mult(4).add(4) + add(4).mult(4));
public void main(...) {
   Thread t1 = new Mult();    Thread t2 = new Add();
   t1.fork();  t2.fork();
   t1.join();  t2.join();
}
```

From the history specification of the `main` method and the action specifications, we can derive the possible values of variable x after termination of the `main` method, i.e., x can be either 4 or 16.

This example is very simple, but the same approach can be used in many different settings: for larger programs, non-terminating programs, distributed programs etc. In particular, for non-terminating programs, an abstraction can be used to predict the (abstract) behaviour, and correctness of the abstraction boils down to showing that the program flow never moves out of the predicted behaviour [56, 69]. We have used this approach to prove properties such as: in a concurrent queue, the order of elements is preserved [2]; adherence to protocols that are commonly used to capture essential security properties, such as 'no send after receive' [56]; and correctness of an active object implementation using MPI operations [70]. Our own VerCors tool set provides support to reason in this way, but also the VeriFast tool can reason about histories (personal communication by Bart Jacobs, KU Leuven).

Note that an essential difference with other existing abstraction-based approaches such as CEGAR and IC3 [15, 19, 48] is how the correctness of the abstraction is proven. Usually, the relation between the original program and the abstract program is proven as a meta-theorem, and one has to trust the implementation of the algorithm that performs the abstractions (or check it manually), while in our approach the program logic is used to prove correctness of the abstraction.

4 Automating the Verification Process

Another major challenge that we need to consider is how to automate the verification process. At the moment, program verification requires many user annotations, explicitly describing properties which are often obvious to developers. We believe that many of the required annotations can be generated automatically, using a combination of appropriate static analyses and smart heuristics. We advocate a very pragmatic approach to annotation generation, where any technique that can be used to reduce the annotation burden is applied, combined with a smart algorithm to evaluate the usability of a generated annotation, removing any annotations that do not help automation. This will lead to a framework where for a large subset of non-trivial programs, we can automatically verify many common safety properties (absence of null-pointer dereferencing, absence of array out of bounds indexing, absence of data races etc.), and if we wish to verify more advanced functional properties, the developer might have to provide a few crucial annotations, but does not have to spell out in detail what happens at every point in the program (in contrast to current program verification practice). However, it should be stressed that with this approach, we will never be able to automatically verify correctness of all programs; there will always be programs using unusual patterns, which need additional manual annotations in order to be verified.

We believe that efficient annotation generation should build on existing static analyses and heuristics [27, 29, 31, 40] extended with tailor-made new generation techniques, aiming for an optimal verification result within a minimal amount of time.

There is a plethora of tools and techniques available which can be used to derive properties about the program state. However, many of these tools work on simple idealised languages, and these results will have to be extended to a more realistic programming setting. In particular, some approaches do not consider aliasing, which is often essential for the correctness of a program.

Moreover, if we use any technique that is available, this might lead to an overload of annotations, which can have a negative impact on verifiability. We thus need to find an optimal balance in how and when to generate annotations automatically. This will be an incremental process, where we use different analyses or heuristics to generate annotations and then select those that help towards our goal. Some of the generated annotations will need other auxiliary annotations to be verified automatically, thus we need to find a suitable order in which to apply the annotation generation algorithms. For example, if an analysis is sensitive to aliasing, we might first want to use an analysis which can derive some annotations about when two variables may or may not be aliased. Note that if we use unsound heuristics to generate annotations, this may lead to conflicting annotations, which might actually give a false impression of program correctness. Therefore, we also need to investigate efficient ways to avoid conflicting annotations. In some cases, a syntactic check will be sufficient to conclude that two annotations are not conflicting. Making optimal use of these cases will help to make this conflict check efficient.

Lastly, if an annotation cannot be verified, we have to investigate how to provide the most suitable feedback. It is important to distinguish between the two following cases:

1. a counterexample exists, which thus means that the annotation is incorrect. In this case, either the annotation is removed, or if a counterexample exists for the property the developer wanted to show for the program, the counterexample has to be presented to the user. In that case, it is important that the counterexample is intelligible, and helps the developer to understand why the program does not have the intended behaviour, and how to fix this.
2. there is not sufficient information to prove the annotation. In this case, the annotation might still be kept as a candidate annotation, because when more annotations are generated, it might become possible to prove it. An intelligent strategy will be needed to keep potentially interesting annotations (for example, if the annotation would help to prove the globally desired property, it is potentially interesting), while ignoring others.

5   Verification of Programs Using Different Concurrency Paradigms

To support software developers in practice, verification techniques need to support different programming languages, and different concurrency paradigms. Most work on the verification of concurrent software focuses on shared memory concurrency with heterogeneous threading, as can be found, e.g., in Java or C. In this model, all threads have access to a shared memory, and all threads execute their own program code. However, in practice there are many other concurrency models in use (and there is also more and more hardware that supports these concurrency models directly). Therefore, we need to investigate how our verification approaches can be used for these other concurrency models as well.

In particular, we believe that it is important to investigate how to reason about programs written using the structured parallel programming model (or vector-based programming), where all threads execute the same instructions, as this model is growing in popularity. Recently, we have shown how the verification techniques for Java's shared-memory concurrency can be adapted in a straightforward manner to GPUs (including atomic update instructions) [11, 12]. On GPUs, there is a shared memory, but all threads execute the same program instructions (but operate on a disjoint part of the memory). It turns out that this restricted setting has a positive impact on verification: the same verification techniques can be used, and verification actually gets simpler. Because of the simpler concurrency paradigm, reasoning about many functional properties can be done without the need for abstraction, because the behaviour of all the other threads is more predictable. However, to reason about the interaction of the vector program in interaction with the host program, which invokes the vector program (the kernel), we are again back to the heterogeneous setting, and the abstraction theory can be used to give an abstract specification of the behaviour of the vector program. We believe that this direction should be explored further, as typical GPU programs are usually quite low-level, which makes them more error-prone. Thus, there is a high need to further develop automated techniques to reason about such applications.

It is also interesting to look at how these programs are developed. One commonly-used approach is that a developer writes a sequential program and gives compiler hints about possible parallelisations [7]. When this approach is used, a programmer is greatly helped by automated verification of these compiler directives. For basic compiler directives, we developed verification techniques to prove the correctness of these parallelisations, i.e., to prove that if the program is parallelised, its behaviour will be equivalent to the behaviour of the sequential program [11, 22], but this approach is still in its early stages, and needs to be developed further, allowing for more advanced compilation patterns.

Further, we believe that a promising line of work is to combine these techniques, in such a way that one can automatically transform a verified sequential program with annotations into an annotated vector program, which will be directly verifiable. We believe this idea can also be used for other compiler optimisations. For example, vector programs written in OpenCL (a platform-independent programming language for GPUs) can be executed both on CPUs and GPUs, but experiments have shown that to optimise performance, the data format should be different [64]. This idea can be defined as a standard compiler transformation, that transforms not only the program, but also the correctness annotations, such that the result is a (hopefully) verifiable program again. Instead of proving correctness of the transformation, both the program and the annotations are transformed, such that after the transformation the resulting program with annotations can be reverified.

Another interesting paradigm that deserves more attention is the area of distributed software, where we need techniques to reason about programs without shared memory. One particular instance of these are distributed programs, but there are also concurrency paradigms, such as the message-box concurrency model of Scala, where each parallel computation works on its own memory. We have shown that reasoning about distributed programs using the message passing interface (MPI) builds on the same principles [57] as reasoning about shared memory concurrency, but here the abstraction plays an even more important role, because it models the communication between the different computations. By adding a notion of synchronisation to the actions, we can model the communication. By defining variations in the action synchronisation, it should be possible to model other distributed programming models, such as the actor model, as well as the Scala concurrency model (on a single computer, with instantaneous send and receive), or variations of the MPI model, where the sending of messages can take time, and messages can bypass each other. It would even be possible to use this kind of reasoning at a lower level, for example to prove the correctness of an MPI implementation, where we take into account that messages might be lost.

6 Concurrent Software in 10 Years

As we have seen, over the last years, there has been enormous progress in the area of program verification, and in particular concerning the verification of concurrent software. By now, the theory behind verification of concurrent software is reasonably well understood, even though there are still open ends, but a large step is still needed to make the results usable for all programmers, in their every-day software development.

In this paper, we discussed some challenges that need to be addressed to achieve this, and we also outlined possible approaches to tackle them. In the coming years, we plan to develop techniques to address these questions, which should lead to a situation where software verification techniques will be an integral part of the software development practice, also for highly complicated concurrent software.

When verification is an integral part of software development, developing code that is formally correct will be deemed easier than developing code without formal verification. If correctness is built into the software compile chain, checking correctness and occasionally getting verification errors will be as commonplace as dealing with type checking errors. In ten years, writing code without static verification might be seen as this obscure workaround that can be okay to use if you really know what you are doing. Using automated verification will be as normal as structured programming and static type checking is now.

Acknowledgement This work is supported by the NWO VICI 639.023.710 Mercedes project.

References

1. Wolfgang Ahrendt et al. *Deductive Software Verification – The KeY Book* Vol. 10001. Lecture Notes in Computer Science. Springer International Publishing, 2016. ISBN: 9783319498126.
2. A. Amighi, S. Blom, and M. Huisman. "VerCors: A Layered Approach to Practical Verification of Concurrent Software". In: *PDP* 2016, pp. 495–503.
3. Afshin Amighi et al. "Verification of Concurrent Systems with VerCors". In: *Formal Methods for Executable Software Models 14th International School on Formal Methods for the Design of Computer Communication, and Software Systems, SFM 2014, Bertinoro, Italy June 16–20, 2014, Advanced Lectures* 2014, pp. 172–216.
4. A. Amighi et al. "Permission-based separation logic for multithreaded Java programs". In: *LMCS* 11.1 (2015).
5. A. Amighi et al. "The VerCors Project: Setting Up Basecamp". In: *Programming Languages meets Program Verification (PLPV 2012)* ACM Press, 2012, pp. 71–82. https://doi.org/10.1145/2103776.2103785
6. A. Antonik et al. "20 years of modal and mixed specifications". In: *Bulletin of the EATCS* 95 (2008), pp. 94–129.
7. R. Baghdadi et al. "PENCIL: Towards a Platform-Neutral Compute Intermediate Language for DSLs". In: *CoRR* abs/1302.5586 (2013).
8. G. Barthe et al. "JACK: A Tool for Validation of Security and Behaviour of Java Applications". In: *Formal Methods for Components and Objects (FMCO 2006)* Vol. 4709. LNCS. Springer, 2007, pp. 152–174.
9. B. Beckert, R. Hähnle, and P.H. Schmitt, eds. *Verification of Object-Oriented Software: The KeY Approach* Vol. 4334. LNCS. Springer, 2007.
10. J. van den Berg and B. Jacobs. "The LOOP compiler for Java and JML". In: *Tools and Algorithms for the Construction and Analysis of Systems* Ed. by T. Margaria and W. Yi. Vol. 2031. LNCS. Springer, 2001, pp. 299–312.
11. S. Blom, S. Darabi, and M. Huisman. "Verification of loop parallelisations". In: *FASE* Vol. 9033. LNCS. Springer, 2015, pp. 202–217.
12. S. Blom, M. Huisman, and M. Mihelvić "Specification and Verification of GPGPU programs". In: *Science of Computer Programming* 95 (3 2014), pp. 376–388. ISSN: 0167–6423.
13. S. Blom, M. Huisman, and M. Zaharieva-Stojanovski. "History-based verification of functional behaviour of concurrent programs". In: *SEFM*. Vol. 9276. LNCS. Springer, 2015, pp. 84–98.
14. S. Blom et al "The VerCors Tool Set: Verification of Parallel and Concurrent Software". In: *iFM* Vol. 10510. LNCS. Springer, 2017, pp. 102–110.
15. A.R. Bradley. "SAT-Based Model Checking without Unrolling". In: *Verification, Model Checking and Abstract Interpretation (VMCAI)* LNCS. Springer, 2011.
16. Marc Brockschmidt et al. "Certifying safety and termination proofs for integer transition systems". In: *International Conference on Automated Deduction* Springer. 2017, pp. 454–471.
17. S. Brookes. "A Semantics for Concurrent Separation Logic". In: *Theoretical Computer Science* 375.1–3 (2007), pp. 227–270.
18. Steve Brookes and Peter O'Hearn. "Concurrent Separation Logic". In: *ACM SIGLOG News* 3.3 (2016), pp. 47–65.

19. E. Clarke et al. "Counterexample-Guided Abstraction Refinement". In: *Computer-Aided Verification (CAV)* Vol. 1855. LNCS. Springer, 2000.

20. D. Cok and J. R. Kiniry. "ESC/Java2: Uniting ESC/Java and JML: Progress and issues in building and using ESC/Java2 and a report on a case study involving the use of ESC/Java2 to verify portions of an Internet voting tally system". In: *Proceedings, Construction and Analysis of Safe Secure and Interoperable Smart devices (CASSIS'04) Workshop* Ed. by G. Barthe et al. Vol. 3362. LNCS. Springer, 2005, pp. 108–128.

21. David Cok. "OpenJML: Software verification for Java 7 using JML, OpenJDK, and Eclipse". In: *1st Workshop on Formal Integrated Development Environment, (F-IDE)* Ed. by Catherine Dubois, Dimitra Giannakopoulou, and Dominique Méry. Vol. 149. EPTCS. 2014, pp. 79–92. https://doi.org/10.4204/EPTCS.149.8. URL: http://dx.doi.org/10.4204/EPTCS.149.8

22. S. Darabi, S.C.C. Blom, and M. Huisman. "A Verification Technique for Deterministic Parallel Programs". In: *NASA Formal Methods (NFM)* Ed. by C. Barrett, M. Davies, and T. Kahsai. Vol. 10227. LNCS. 2017, pp. 247–264.

23. S. De Gouw et al. "OpenJDK's java.utils.Collection.sort() is broken: The good, the bad and the worst case". In: *Proc. 27th Intl. Conf on Computer Aided Verification (CAV), San Francisco* Ed. by D. Kroening and C. Pasareanu. Vol. 9206. LNCS. Springer, July 2015, pp. 273–289.

24. Edsger W. Dijkstra. *A Discipline of Programming* Englewood Cliffs, N.J.: Prentice-Hall, Inc., 1976.

25. T. Dinsdale-Young et al. "Concurrent Abstract Predicates". In: *ECOOP* Ed. by Theo D'Hondt. Vol. 6183. LNCS. Springer, 2010, pp. 504–528.

26. T. Dinsdale-Young et al. "Views: Compositional Reasoning for Concurrent Programs". In: *POPL'13* ACM, 2013, pp. 287–300.

27. J. Dohrau et al. "Permission Inference for Array Programs". In: *Computer Aided Verification (CAV)* LNCS. Springer, 2018.

28. Manuel Fahndrich et al. "Integrating a Set of Contract Checking Tools into Visual Studio". In: *Proceedings of the 2012 Second International Workshop on Developing Tools as Plug-ins (TOPI)* IEEE, June 2012. URL: https://wwwmicrosoftcom/en-us/research/publication/integrating-a-set-of-contract-checking-tools-into-visual-studio/.

29. P. Ferrara and P. Müller. "Automatic inference of access permissions". In: *Proceedings of the 13th International Conference on Verification, Model Checking and Abstract Interpretation (VMCAI 2012)* LNCS. Springer, 2012, pp. 202–218.

30. R. W. Floyd. "Assigning Meanings to Programs". In: *Proceedings Symposium on Applied Mathematics* 19 (1967), pp. 19–31.

31. J.P. Galeotti et al. "Inferring Loop Invariants by Mutation, Dynamic Analysis, and Static Checking". In: *IEEE Transactions on Software Engineering* 41 (10 2015), pp. 1019–1037.

32. Archana Ganapathi and David A. Patterson. "Crash Data Collection: A Windows Case Study." In: *Dependable Systems and Networks (DSN)* IEEE Computer Society, Aug. 1, 2005, pp. 280–285. ISBN: 0-7695-2282-3.

33. Michiel van Genuchten and Les Hatton. "Metrics with Impact". In: *IEEE Software* 30 (4 July 2013), pp. 99–101.

34. Jürgen Giesl et al. "Proving termination of programs automatically with AProVE". In: *International Joint Conference on Automated Reasoning* Springer. 2014, pp. 184–191.

35. R. Hähnle and M. Huisman. "Deductive Software Verification: From Pen-and-Paper Proofs to Industrial Tools". In: *Computing and Software Science* Vol. 10000. LNCS. 2018.

36. Nir Hemed, Noam Rinetzky, and Viktor Vafeiadis. "Modular Verification of Concurrency-Aware Linearizability". In: *Symposium on Distributed Computing (DISC)* Springer, 2015.

37. C. A. R. Hoare. "An Axiomatic Basis for Computer Programming". In: *Communications of the ACM* 12.10 (Oct. 1969), pp. 576–580, 583. URL: http://doi.acmorg/10.1145/363235.363259.

38. Marieke Huisman. "Reasoning about Java Programs in higher order logic with PVS and Isabelle". IPA Dissertation Series, 2001-03. University of Nijmegen, Holland, Feb 2001. URL: ftp://ftpsop.inria.fr/lemme/Marieke.Huisman/thesis.ps.gz

39. B. Jacobs and F. Piessens. *The VeriFast program verifier* Tech. rep. CW520. Katholieke Universiteit Leuven, 2008.

40. M. Janota. "Assertion-based Loop Invariant Generation". In: *1st International Workshop on Invariant Generation (WING)* 2007.
41. Cliff B. Jones. "Tentative Steps Toward a Development Method for Interfering Programs". In: 5.4 (1983), pp. 596–619.
42. Sebastiaan JC Joosten, René Thiemann, and Akihisa Yamada. "CeTA–Certifying Termination and Complexity Proofs in 2016". In: *15th International Workshop on Termination* Ed. by Aart Middeldorp and René Thiemann. 2016.
43. U. Juhasz et al. *Viper: A Verification Infrastructure for Permission-Based Reasoning* Tech. rep. ETH Zurich, 2014.
44. R. Jung et al. "Iris: Monoids and invariants as an orthogonal basis for concurrent reasoning". In: *Principles of Programming Languages (POPL)* 2015.
45. R. Krebbers et al. "The Essence of Higher-Order Concurrent Separation Logic". In: *ESOP* Vol. 10201. LNCS. Springer, 2017, pp. 696–723.
46. K.G. Larsen and B. Thomsen. "A modal process logic". In: *Logic in Computer Science (LICS)* IEEE Computer Society, 1988, pp. 203–210.
47. Francesco Logozzo. "Practical verification for the working programmer with CodeContracts and Abstract Interpretation". In: *Verification, Model Checking and Abstract Interpretation (VMCAI)* Springer, 2011.
48. A. Malkis, A. Podelski, and A. Rybalchenko. "Thread-Modular Counterexample-Guided Abstraction Refinement". In: *Static Analysis (SAS)* Vol. 6337. LNCS. Springer, 2010.
49. Rivalino Matias et al. "An Empirical Exploratory Study on Operating System Reliability". In: *29th Annual ACM Symposium on Applied Computing (SAC)* Gyeongju, Republic of Korea: ACM, 2014, pp. 1523–1528. ISBN: 978-1-4503-2469-4. https://doi.org/10.1145/2554850. 2555021
50. Jörg Meyer and Arnd Poetzsch-Heffter. "An Architecture for Interactive Program Provers". In: *Tools and Algorithms for Construction and Analysis of Systems, 6th International Conference TACAS 2000* Ed. by Susanne Graf and Michael I. Schwartzbach. Vol. 1785. Lecture Notes in Computer Science. Springer, 2000, pp. 63–77.
51. P. Müller, M. Schwerhoff and A.J. Summers. "Viper A Verification Infrastructure for Permission-Based Reasoning". In: *VMCAI* 2016.
52. Aleksandar Nanevski et al. "Communicating State Transition Systems for Fine-Grained Concurrent Resources" In: *European Symposium on Programming (ESOP)* 2014, pp. 290–310.
53. P. W. O'Hearn, J. Reynolds, and H. Yang. "Local Reasoning about Programs that Alter Data Structures". In: *Computer Science Logic* Ed. by L. Fribourg. Vol. 2142. LNCS. Paris: Springer, 2001, pp. 1–19. https://doi.org/10.1007/3540448020_1
54. P. W. O'Hearn, H. Yang, and J. C. Reynolds. "Separation and Information Hiding". In: *Principles of Programming Languages* Venice, Italy: ACM Press, 2004, pp. 268–280.
55. Peter W. O'Hearn. "Resources, concurrency and local reasoning". In: 375.1-3 (2007), pp. 271–307. ISSN: 0304-3975. http://dx.doi.org/10.1016/j.tcs.2006.12.035.
56. W. Oortwijn, S. Blom, and M. Huisman. "Future-based Static Analysis of Message Passing Programs". In: *PLACES* 2016, pp. 65–72.
57. W. Oortwijn et al. "An Abstraction Technique for Describing Concurrent Program Behaviour". In: *VSTTE* Vol. 10712. LNCS. 2017, pp. 191–209.
58. Thomas J. Ostrand and Elaine J. Weyuker. "The Distribution of Faults in a Large Industrial Software System". In: *2002 ACM SIGSOFT International Symposium on Software Testing and Analysis (ISSTA)* Roma, Italy: ACM, 2002, pp. 55–64. ISBN: 1-58113-562-9. https://doi.org/10.1145/566172.566181
59. Thomas J. Ostrand, Elaine J. Weyuker, and Robert M. Bell. "Where the Bugs Are". In: *2004 ACM SIGSOFT International Symposium on Software Testing and Analysis (ISTTA)*. Boston, Massachusetts, USA: ACM, 2004, pp. 86–96. ISBN: 1-58113-820-2. https://doi.org/10.1145/1007512.1007524
60. S. Owicki and D. Gries. "An Axiomatic Proof Technique for Parallel Programs". In: *Acta Informatica Journal* 6 (1975), pp. 319–340. https://doi.org/10.1007/BF00268134

61. P. da Rocha Pinto, T. Dinsdale-Young, and P. Gardner. "Steps in Modular Specifications for Concurrent Modules". In: *Mathematical Foundations of Programming Semantics (MFPS)*. 2015.
62. P. da Rocha Pinto, T. Dinsdale-Young, and P. Gardner. "TaDA: A Logic for Time and Data Abstraction". In: *European Conference on Object-Oriented Programming (ECOOP)* LNCS. Springer, 2014.
63. I. Sergey, A. Nanevski, and A. Banerjee. "Specifying and Verifying Concurrent Algorithms with Histories and Subjectivity". In: *ESOP* Vol. 9032. LNCS. Springer, 2015, pp. 333–358.
64. J. Shen. "Efficient High Performance Computing on Heterogeneous Platforms". PhD thesis. Technical University of Delft, 2015.
65. Jan Smans, Bart Jacobs, and Frank Piessens. "VeriFast for Java: A Tutorial". In: *Aliasing in Object-Oriented Programming* Ed. by Dave Clarke, Tobias Wrigstad, and James Noble. Vol. 7850. LNCS. Springer, 2013.
66. K. Svendsen and L. Birkedal. "Impredicative Concurrent Abstract Predicates". In: *ESOP* Vol. 8410. LNCS. Springer, 2014, pp. 149–168.
67. V. Vafeiadis and M.J. Parkinson. "A Marriage of Rely/Guarantee and Separation Logic". In: *CONCUR* Ed. by Luís Caires and Vasco Thudichum Vasconcelos. Vol. 4703. LNCS. Springer, 2007, pp. 256–271.
68. Viktor Vafeiadis. "Automatically Proving Linearizability". In: *Computer Aided Verification* Ed. by Tayssir Touili, Byron Cook, and Paul Jackson. Vol. 6174. Lecture Notes in Computer Science. Springer Berlin Heidelberg, 2010, pp. 450–464. ISBN: 978-3-642-14294-9. https://doi.org/10.1007/978-3-642-14295-6_4. URL: http://dxdoiorg/10.1007/978-3-642-142956_40.
69. M. Zaharieva-Stojanovski. "Closer to Reliable Software: Verifying Functional Behaviour of Concurrent Programs". PhD thesis. University of Twente, 2015. https://doi.org/10.3990/1.9789036539241.
70. J. Zeilstra. "Reasoning about Active Object Programs". MA thesis. University of Twente, 2016.

Dynamic Software Updates and Context Adaptation for Distributed Active Objects

Einar Broch Johnsen and Ingrid Chieh Yu

Abstract Dynamic software updates enable running programs to evolve without downtime. Drivers for such updates include software enhancements, bug fixes, and maintenance for software in domains, where it is costly, impractical, or even impossible to halt the system to reconfigure. In particular, application-level services in IoT ecosystems need to adapt seamlessly to changing, heterogeneous contexts. Services need to discover, adapt to, and interact with other services already deployed in the running ecosystem, supporting autonomicity within the service life-cycle. This paper explores a formalized, type safe asynchronous system of runtime software discovery and evolution, motivated by IoT ecosystems.

1 Introduction

Your life can be automated by connecting the objects around you. Having worn out your smart socks, you automatically received a pair of ultra-smart ones from the local retailer. You have just put them in your smart washing machine and wonder if its software is compliant with the latest generation of dirty socks. While you enjoy a drink from your intelligent water dispenser, your house adjusts the lights and rolls down the window blinds of your smart home, optimizing room temperature and humidity such that the smart laundry will dry as fast as possible, given your energy-friendly parameter settings. You live a smart life.

The Internet of Things (IoT) provides the underlying technologies for such a smart life, extending the Internet into the physical realm by connecting and combining spatially distributed devices with sensing and actuating capabilities. Application areas for IoT systems include smart homes, environmental monitoring, healthcare, and Industry 4.0. IoT devices are becoming commodity, and technologies from different providers need to interact as diverse devices are dynamically

E. B. Johnsen (✉) · I. Chieh Yu
Department of Informatics, University of Oslo, Oslo, Norway
e-mail: einarj@ifi.uio.no; ingridcy@ifi.uio.no

© Springer Nature Switzerland AG 2018   147
P. Müller, I. Schaefer (eds.), *Principled Software Development*,
https://doi.org/10.1007/978-3-319-98047-8_10

assembled into one system. Going beyond low-level interoperability, the IoT poses research challenges from a software engineering and systems perspective, including programmability, scalability, self-organization, security, and semantic interoperability. If IoT devices were to act as hosts for container-like services which can interact with the actuators, third party services can be deployed much like apps on a smart phone [22], maximizing the innovation potential of the IoT. This vision of IoT is naturally supported by programming with asynchronously communicating actors [1, 15] or active objects [8], as evidenced by emerging technologies such as embedded actors[16], ELIoT [32], and Swarmlets [21].

Application-level services in IoT ecosystems need to adapt seamlessly to different contexts; we need methods to discover, deploy, and compose services at runtime, supporting autonomicity within the service life-cycle [26]. Techniques for software composition and service-oriented architectures offer a possible starting point to address these challenges based on interface encapsulation, such as design-by-contract [25], interface theories [23], and interfaces for service discovery and grouping [19]. However, a major challenge which lacks an established solution today, is the maintenance of services in this context. We can expect commodity IoT devices to need bugfixes and software enhancements after production. On the one hand, the continuous development of more advanced IoT services needs to combine with software already deployed on the devices. On the other hand, legacy devices make IoT services vulnerable to bugs and security issues. A recent study [33] reports that 45.5% of interviewed developers in the embedded software industry have no system for updating software on customers' devices beyond the physical replacement of devices; the other half have methods built in-house in the company. Although updating software on a deployed IoT device can technically be done via over-the-air firmware updates or through dynamic loading of binary modules [5], a challenge is to find high-level ways to program and orchestrate such updates at the abstraction level of the application logic.

Related Work We briefly survey existing solutions for dynamic or online updates of deployed software which aim at modular evolution; some solutions keep multiple co-existing versions of a class or schema [4, 6, 7, 10, 11, 13, 17], others apply a global update or "hot-swapping" [2, 9, 24, 27]. The approaches differ for active behavior, which may be disallowed [9, 13, 24, 27], delayed [2], or supported [17, 34]. POLUS [10] supports life-cycle management of server software and the system-level workflow of dynamic updating. It is up to operators to control the process of dynamic updates such that one update will not interfere with another update and uses state synchronization functions to support multiple versions of data. At the language level, Hjálmtýsson and Gray [17] propose proxy classes and reference indirection for C++, with multiple versions of each class. Old instances are not updated, so their activity is not interrupted. Existing approaches for Java, using proxies [27, 30] or modifying the Java virtual machine [24], use global update and do not apply to active objects. General-purpose dynamic software updating for single- and multithreaded C applications introduced in [14] updates the whole program instead of individual functions. The approach is tailored towards C developers, allowing programmer explicit control over the updating process by inserting update operations in long running loops (quiescent state), specific program points for when updates may take place as well as code to initiate data migration and redirection of execution to the new version. Automatic updates by lazy global update has been proposed for distributed objects [2] and persistent object stores [9], in which instances of updated classes are updated, but inheritance and (nonterminating) active code are not addressed, limiting the effect and modularity of the class update. In [9], the ordering of updates is serialized and in [24], invalid updates raise exceptions.

It is interesting to apply formal techniques to systems for software evolution. The engineering of dynamic system updates, addressed in [29], formalizes correctness criteria for updates, emphasizing safety in the sense that the resulting behavior after a dynamic update should be equivalent to an offline update. Interface automata have been used to characterize component-level updates [28] in terms of their interactions without considering implementation. For each kind, a state transformer indicates in which state and environment condition a component-based distributed system can be correctly updated. A runtime monitor is used to identify the matching rule and substitute the targeted component with the new version. Formalizations of programming-level runtime update mechanisms exist for imperative [34], functional [6], and object-oriented [7] languages. In a recent update system for (sequential) C [34], type-safe updates of type declarations and procedures may occur at annotated points identified by static analysis. However, the approach is synchronous as updates which cannot be applied immediately will fail. UpgradeJ [7] uses an incremental type system in which class versions are only typechecked once. UpgradeJ is synchronous and uses explicit update statements in programs. Updates only affect the class hierarchy and not running objects. Multiple versions of a class will coexist and the programmer must explicitly refer to the different class versions in the code.

Contribution of This Paper This paper explores a system of software updates for the asynchronous evolution of distributed, loosely-coupled active objects, motivated by IoT systems. Our starting point is ABS [20], a formally defined active object language, in part building on Arnd Poetzsch-Heffter's work on JCoBox [31]. We revisit previous work on dynamic class updates [18, 36]; in this paper, the mechanism is simplified for ABS by focusing on distributed devices and interface encapsulation rather than on code reuse in class hierarchies, and combined with a simple interface query mechanism for context adaptation [19].

2 A Language for Distributed Active Objects

We define a small active object language with cooperative concurrency. The language syntax is given in Fig. 1. We emphasize the differences with Java. A program P consists of interface and class definitions, followed by a main block.

$$P ::= \overline{D}\,\overline{L}\,\{\overline{T\,x}; sr\}$$
$$M_s ::= T\,m\,(\overline{T\,x})$$
$$M ::= M_s\{\overline{T\,x}; sr\}$$
$$sr ::= s;\textbf{return}\,e$$
$$b ::= \textbf{true}\mid\textbf{false}\mid x$$
$$T ::= I\mid\textbf{Bool}\mid\textbf{Fut}(T)$$

$$D ::= \textbf{interface}\,I\,\textbf{extends}\,\overline{I}\,\{\overline{M_s}\}$$
$$L ::= \textbf{class}\,C(\overline{T\,x})\,\textbf{implements}\,\overline{I}\,\{\overline{T\,x}; \overline{M}\}$$
$$s ::= x = e\mid\textbf{skip}\mid s; s\mid\textbf{if}\,c\,\{s\}\,\textbf{else}\,\{s\}\mid\textbf{suspend}\mid\textbf{await}\,g$$
$$e ::= x\mid\textbf{new}\,C(\overline{e})\mid e.\textbf{get}\mid e!m(\overline{e})\mid\textbf{null}$$
$$c ::= b\mid x\,\textbf{subtypeOf}\,I$$
$$g ::= b\mid x?\mid g\wedge g$$

Fig. 1 The language syntax. C is a class name, and I an interface name

An interface D has a name I, it extends a list $\overline{I}$ of inherited interfaces, and it contains a list $\overline{M_s}$ of method signatures. A class L has a name C, with parameters $\overline{x}$, implements a list of interfaces $\overline{I}$, defines a number of fields $\overline{x}$ typed by $\overline{T}$, and a list of methods $\overline{M}$. A method signature M_s associates a return type T and a list of formal parameters $\overline{x}$, typed by $\overline{T}$, to a method name m. A method definition M associates a method body to a method signature. The method body consists of local variables $\overline{x}$ of types $\overline{T}$ and list sr of statements to be executed; the list sr of statements ends with a final **return** statement. If a class contains a run method, this method is automatically activated on new instances of the class.

Statements s are standard apart from cooperative concurrency and interface querying. The statement **suspend** represents an unconditional suspension of the active process such that another suspended process may be scheduled. The statement **await** g represents a conditional suspension which depends on a guard g. If g evaluates to false, the statement gets preceded by a **suspend**, otherwise it becomes a **skip**. The conditional x **subtypeOf** I allows an object to be queried at runtime if it supports (a subtype of) a given interface. Such querying will be used for service discovery as software dynamically evolves.

Expressions e are standard apart from the (non-blocking) asynchronous method calls $e!m(\overline{e})$, which call method m on the object referenced by e with actual parameters referenced by $\overline{e}$, and the (blocking) operation $x.\textbf{get}$ to access the value of the future referenced by x. *Guards* g are conjunctions of Boolean expressions b and polling operations $x?$ on futures x.

Example 1 Consider a smart home, where thermostat devices, with a temperature sensor and a heating actuator, are placed in different rooms and connected to a gateway. Each room has a specified target temperature (e.g., a bedroom is typically colder than the bathroom) and may contain several devices. The gateway will try to maintain a specified temperature for each room by adjusting the target temperature on the relevant devices. For convenience, the example uses a richer syntax than the calculus, including type synonyms and basic types Int and Rat for integer and rational numbers. We also use standard operations over data types such as put and lookupDefault over maps (with constructor map[]) and appendright over lists (with constructor Nil and iterator **foreach**) from ABS [20]. Following ABS conventions, **return** statements are omitted for methods of return type Unit, variables can be declared where convenient, and write T x = **await** o!m() as

```
module SmartHome;

type Loc = Int;
type Temp = Rat;

interface TempSensor { Temp read(); }
interface HeatActuator { Unit heat(); }
interface Thermostat { Temp sensing(); }
interface Gateway { Unit register(Loc loc, Thermostat t); }

def Map<T1,List<T2>> addItem<T1,T2>(Map<T1,List<T2>> store, T1 key, T2 item)
  = put(store,key, appendright(lookupDefault(store,key,Nil),item));

class SmartHomeGateway(Temp target) implements Gateway {
  Map <Loc, List<Thermostat>> thermostats = map[];
  Map <Loc, List<Any>> unknown = map[];
  Map <Loc, Temp> targetTemp = map[];
  Map <Thermostat, Temp> currentTemps = map[];
  Temp maxTemp = 50;

  Unit register(Loc loc, Any t){
    if (t subtypeOf Thermostat) thermostats=addItem(thermostats,loc, t);
    else unknown=addItem(unknown,loc, t); }

  Unit monitor(){
    List<Thermostat> mythermostats =
      foldl((List<Thermostat> v, List<Thermostat> a) =>
        concatenate(v, a))(values(thermostats),Nil);
    foreach (sensor in mythermostats){
      Temp tmp = sensor.sensing();
      if (tmp > maxTemp) ⟨...⟩; } } // Raise alarm...

  Unit updateTemperature(Thermostat t,Temp val){
    currentTemps=put(currentTemps,t,val);}

  Unit run(){ this.monitor(); this!run(); }
}

class Thermostat(Gateway gw, Temp targetTemp, Loc loc, TempSensor sensor,
  HeatActuator heater) implements Thermostat{

  { gw.register(loc, this); } // Init block:

  Rat sensing() { Temp t = await sensor!read(); return t; }

  Unit run(){
    Temp currentTemp = this.sensing();
    if (targetTemp > currentTemp) heater!heat(); // Activate heater
    this!run(); }
}
```

Fig. 2 The basic smart home example in ABS

syntactic sugar for the standard programming pattern T x; **Fut**(T) f; f = o!m(); **await** f?; t = f.**get**. The interface Any is the supertype of all interfaces.

We program the smart home by two classes SmartHomeGateway and Thermostat, shown in Fig. 2. In SmartHomeGateway, a method register is called by new devices to get connected. Note the use of interface querying to identify devices of type Thermostat, which are stored per location in a map, other devices are stored in the map unknown. The gateway monitors registered thermostats and receives their temperature values to, e.g., raise an alarm if the temperature exceeds a maximum temperature or collect statistics. The active method run calls itself asynchronously, allowing the cooperative scheduling of other processes between each monitoring cycle, so the gateway can register new sensors. The class Thermostat is connected to the IoT device through the TempSensor and HeatActivator interfaces. In Thermostat, the init block registers a new instance with the gateway. The Thermostat objects are active objects, i.e., their run method is automatically started to activate the heater, whenever the target temperature is not reached.

3   Programming Dynamic Software Updates

Software evolution may be perceived as a series of dynamic software updates injected into a running system, gradually modifying class definitions which interact the active objects. To enhance programmability, we consider operations U using the structuring concepts of the language, as given by the following syntax:

$$U ::= \textbf{newclass}\ C(\overline{T\ x})\ \textbf{implements}\ \overline{I}\ \{\overline{T\ x};\ \overline{M}\}\ \mid \textbf{newinterface}\ I\ \textbf{extends}\ \overline{I}\ \{\overline{M_s}\}$$
$$\mid\ \textbf{update}\ C\ \textbf{implements}\ \overline{I}\ \{\overline{T\ x};\ \overline{M}\}$$

The **newclass** declaration adds a new class C to the system, **newinterface** extends the type system with the new interface I, and **update** extends an existing class with new fields $\overline{x}$ and methods $\overline{M}$, *redefining* existing methods in the class in the case of name capture. Updates propagate *asynchronously* at runtime. They first modify classes, then the instances of those classes. We here ignore *state transfer* from an old to a new object state and initialize fields with default values; in a real system, an initialization block in the update could extend an old initialization block to give initial values to new fields in terms of the old fields.

Example 2 We consider how to dynamically modify and add new services and devices into the smart home ecosystem of Example 1. Let us install smart window blinds in the smart home by introducing an active object to the interface WindowActuator. A class SmartWindow with a new interface WindowBlind allows each window blind at location loc to be connected to the gateway. The gateway can open and close blinds through method adjustBlind.

```
newinterface WindowBlind { Unit adjustBlind(); }
newinterface WindowActuator { Unit moveBlind(); }

newclass SmartWindow(ThermalComfort gw, Loc loc, WindowSensor sensor,
  WindowActuator controller) implements WindowBlind {

  { gw.register(loc, this); }

  Unit adjustBlind() { controller!moveBlind(); }
}
```

Example 3 Home owners may want to dynamically change the target temperature
(e.g., 5 hours before coming home from a holiday). We update class **Thermostat**
with a new method **adjustTargetTemp** which changes the target temperature of
the thermostat device. The run method in class **Thermostat** will then use this new
temperature setting in its next execution cycle.

```
newinterface Thermostat2 extends Thermostat { Unit adjustTargetTemp(Rat amount); }

update Thermostat implements Thermostat2{
  Unit adjustTargetTemp (Rat amount) { targetTemp = targetTemp + amount; }
}
```

Example 4 **SmartHomeGateway** needs to receive sensor values from the different
thermostats and adjust the window blinds at different locations. The update operation in Fig. 3 shows modifications to class **SmartHomeGateway**. New mappings
blinds and open will store the registered window blinds for each location and the
state of the window blinds, and **theromostats2** the enhanced thermostats. Method
register is extended to recognize the new interfaces, and store devices accordingly.

The updated run method will monitor the old thermostats as before, but also
monitor new thermostats and update currentTemps with the current sensor readings
before calling adjustBlinds(loc) to adjust blinds at location loc. The new method
adjustBlinds will open or close blinds for a given location, triggered by the
temperature. The new method changeTargetTemp will allow home owners to
change target room temperatures through the gateway.

By combining new interfaces, a new class **WindowBlind**, and updating the
classes **Thermostat** and **SmartHomeGateway**, we obtain a very flexible dynamic
update mechanism. However, modifications should not compromise the type safety
of the running program. For example, class **WindowBlind** must be available before
code to create objects of the class can run. Similarly, objects of class **Thermostat**
must support adjustTargetTemp before the new **SmartHomeGateway** method
changeTargetTemp can be called on these objects. In a distributed setting, where
updates are not serialized but propagate asynchronously through the network,
objects of different versions may coexist. Consequently, the order in which updates
are applied at runtime may differ from the order in which they are type checked and
inserted into the runtime system.

```
newinterface BlindController { Unit adjustBlind(); }
newinterface TempController { Unit changeTargetTemp(); }

update SmartHomeGateway implements BlindController, TempController {
  Map <Loc, List<Thermostat2>> thermostats2 = map[];
  Map <Loc,List<WindowBlind>> blinds = map[];
  Map <WindowBlind, Bool> open = map[];

  Unit register(Loc loc, Any t){
    if (t subtypeOf Thermostat2) thermostats2=addItem(thermostats2,loc, t);
    else { if (t subtypeOf Thermostat) thermostats=addItem(thermostats,loc, t);
          else if (t subtypeOf WindowBlind) blinds=addItem(blinds,loc, t);
              else unknown=addItem(unknown,loc, t); }}

  Unit adjustBlinds(Loc loc){
    List<Thermostat> sensors = lookupDefault(thermostats,loc,Nil);
    Temp targetLoc = lookupDefault(targetTemp,loc,target);
    List<WindowBlind> blinds = lookupDefault(blinds,loc,Nil);
    foreach (sensor in sensors){
      Temp current = sensor.sensing();
      currentTemps = put(currentTemps,sensor,current); }
    List<Temp> temps = map((Thermostat sensor)=>
                              lookupDefault(currentTemps,sensor,0))(sensors);
    Temp avg = average(temps);
    if (average(temps) <targetLoc)
      foreach (blind in blinds){
        if(lookupDefault(open,blind,False)){ blind.adjustBlind(); put(open,blind,True); }}
    else
      foreach (blind in blinds){
        if(lookupDefault(open,blind,True)){ blind.adjustBlind(); put(open,blind,False); }}}

  Unit changeTargetTemp(Loc loc, Int newTemp){
    List<Thermostat2> ts = lookupDefault(thermostats2,loc,Nil);
    targetTemp=put(targetTemp, loc, newTemp);
    foreach (t in ts){ t!adjustTargetTemp(newTemp); }}

  Unit newDevices(){
    foreach (loc in elements(keys(unknown))) {
      foreach (t in lookupDefault(unknown,loc,Nil)){
        if (t subtypeOf Thermostat2) thermostats2=addItem(thermostats2,loc,t);
        if (t subtypeOf WindowBlind) blinds=addItem(blinds,loc, t); }}}

  Unit run(){
    this.newDevices();
    this.monitor();
    foreach (loc in elements(keys(targetTemp))) {
      foreach (t in lookupDefault(thermostats,loc,Nil));{
        Temp newtemp = t.sensing();updateTemperature(t,newtemp);adjustBlinds(loc);}
      foreach (t in lookupDefault(thermostats2,loc,Nil)){
        Temp newtemp = t.sensing();updateTemperature(t,newtemp);adjustBlinds(loc);}}
    this!run();}
}
```

Fig. 3 Updating the gateway

4   Type Checking for Asynchronous Software Updates

To statically track dependencies to different versions of code, we consider a type
and effect system [3, 35] developed in the context of a *mapping family*.

Definition 1 Let n be a name, δ a declaration, $i \in \mathscr{I}$ a mapping index, and $[n \mapsto_i \delta]$ the binding of n to δ indexed by i. A *mapping family* Γ is built from the empty mapping family $\emptyset$ and indexed bindings by the constructor $+$. The *extraction* of an indexed mapping Γ_i from Γ and *application* for the indexed mapping Γ_i, are defined as follows

$$\emptyset_i \qquad\qquad = \varepsilon$$
$$(\Gamma + [n \mapsto_{i'} \delta])_i \quad = \textbf{if } (i = i') \textbf{ then } \Gamma_i + [n \mapsto_i \delta] \textbf{ else } \Gamma_i$$

$$\varepsilon(n) \qquad\qquad\qquad = \bot$$
$$(\Gamma_i + [n \mapsto_i \delta])(n') = \textbf{if } (n = n') \textbf{ then } \delta \textbf{ else } \Gamma_i(n').$$

Our typing context uses four indexes; the mappings $\Gamma_{\mathscr{I}}$ and $\Gamma_{\mathscr{C}}$ map interface and class names to interface and class declarations, and Γ_v maps program variable names to types. In a static setting, $\Gamma_{\mathscr{I}}$ and $\Gamma_{\mathscr{C}}$ correspond to the *static tables* which can usually be omitted from the type system, but this is not the case with dynamic software updates. For the purposes of dynamic updates, there is a mapping of *dependencies* $\Gamma_d : \mathsf{Dep} \to \mathsf{Set[Dep]}$, where the type Dep consist of pairs of class names and natural numbers. A version of a class C can be uniquely identified by a natural number; e.g., $\langle C, 5 \rangle$ represents the fifth update of C. Elements in $\Gamma_d(\langle C, u \rangle)$ will represent versions of classes on which an update u of a class C depends; these dependencies are inferred from the current class table by the type analysis, and exploited for dynamic classes in Sect. 5.

We assume for simplicity that variable declarations $T\,x$ have unique names and known types, and denote by $[\overline{x} \mapsto_v \overline{T}]$ the mapping (built from the bindings $[x \mapsto_v T]$). The auxiliary function *implements*(C, I, Γ) matches signatures for methods declared in an interface I to those in C, in order to check that the class provides method bodies for the method declarations of its interfaces. We omit the (straightforward) definitions of other auxiliary functions on Γ; e.g., *curr*(C, Γ) denotes the current version of C in Γ.

Typing of the Base Language The (static) base language uses a standard type system for object-oriented languages with explicit futures (e.g., [20]), decorated with effects. Subtyping $T_1 \preceq T_2$ is defined by interface inheritance: If I extends J then $J \preceq I$. The type rules are given in Fig. 4. Judgments have the form $\Gamma \vdash e : T \langle \Sigma \rangle$ and $\Gamma \vdash s \langle \Sigma \rangle$, where Γ is the typing environment and $\Sigma : \mathsf{Set[Dep]}$ the effect. To simplify the presentation, we assume that method declarations in interfaces are unique and well-typed and omit the analysis of interfaces. In rule CONDITIONAL2, the interface query for x changes the type of x in s_1. Note that in NEW, the current version of the instantiated class is recorded in the effect (highlighted). These effects are collected for each method, and assembled to update the dependency mapping (highlighted) of the class in CLASS and again collected in PROGRAM (highlighted).

$$\frac{\text{(SUSPEND)}}{\Gamma \vdash \textbf{suspend} : \text{ok}} \qquad \frac{\text{(SKIP)}}{\Gamma \vdash \textbf{skip} : \text{ok}} \qquad \frac{\text{(NULL)}}{\Gamma \vdash \textbf{null} : I} \qquad \frac{\text{(VAR)}}{\dfrac{\Gamma(x) = T}{\Gamma \vdash x : T}}$$

$$\frac{\text{(POLL)}}{\dfrac{\Gamma \vdash x : \textbf{Fut}(T)}{\Gamma \vdash x? : \textbf{Bool}}} \qquad \frac{\text{(GET)}}{\dfrac{\Gamma \vdash x : \textbf{Fut}(T)}{\Gamma \vdash x.\textbf{get} : T}} \qquad \frac{\text{(ASSIGN)}}{\dfrac{\Gamma \vdash e : \Gamma(x) \langle \Sigma \rangle}{\Gamma \vdash x := e : \text{ok} \langle \Sigma \rangle}} \qquad \frac{\text{(AWAIT)}}{\dfrac{\Gamma \vdash g : \textbf{Bool}}{\Gamma \vdash \textbf{await } g : \text{ok}}}$$

$$\frac{\text{(CALL)}}{\dfrac{\Gamma \vdash \bar{e} : T \langle \Sigma_1 \rangle \qquad \Gamma \vdash e : I \langle \Sigma_2 \rangle}{\begin{array}{c} match(m, T \to T', I) \\ \hline \Gamma \vdash e!m(\bar{e}) : \textbf{Fut}(T') \langle \Sigma_1 \cup \Sigma_2 \rangle \end{array}}} \qquad \frac{\text{(COMPOSITION)}}{\dfrac{\Gamma \vdash s : \text{ok} \langle \Sigma_1 \rangle \quad \Gamma \vdash s' : \text{ok} \langle \Sigma_2 \rangle}{\Gamma \vdash s; s' : \text{ok} \langle \Sigma_1 \cup \Sigma_2 \rangle}} \qquad \frac{\text{(AND)}}{\dfrac{\Gamma \vdash g_1 : \textbf{Bool} \quad \Gamma \vdash g_2 : \textbf{Bool}}{\Gamma \vdash g_1 \wedge g_2 : \textbf{Bool}}}$$

$$\frac{\text{(NEW)}}{\dfrac{T \in interfaces(\Gamma_{\mathscr{C}}(C)) \qquad \Gamma \vdash \bar{e} : type(\Gamma_{\mathscr{C}}(C).param)}{\Gamma \vdash \textbf{new } C(\bar{e}) : T \ \langle (C, curr(C, \Gamma)) \rangle}} \qquad \frac{\text{(CONDITIONAL1)}}{\dfrac{\Gamma \vdash b : \textbf{Bool}}{\dfrac{\Gamma \vdash s_1 : \text{ok} \langle \Sigma_1 \rangle \qquad \Gamma \vdash s_2 : \text{ok} \langle \Sigma_2 \rangle}{\Gamma \vdash \textbf{if } b \ \{s_1\} \ \textbf{else}\{s_2\} : \text{ok} \langle \Sigma_1 \cup \Sigma_2 \rangle}}}$$

$$\frac{\text{(SUB)}}{\dfrac{T \preceq T' \qquad \Gamma \vdash e : T'}{\Gamma \vdash e : T}} \qquad \frac{\text{(CONDITIONAL2)}}{\dfrac{\Gamma[x \mapsto_v I] \vdash s_1 : \text{ok} \langle \Sigma_1 \rangle \qquad \Gamma \vdash s_2 : \text{ok} \langle \Sigma_2 \rangle}{\Gamma \vdash \textbf{if } x \ \textbf{subtypeOf } I \ \{s_1\} \ \textbf{else}\{s_2\} : \text{ok} \langle \Sigma_1 \cup \Sigma_2 \rangle}}$$

$$\frac{\text{(METHOD)}}{\dfrac{\Gamma' = \Gamma + [\bar{x} \mapsto_v \bar{T}, \bar{x'} \mapsto_v \bar{T'}]}{\dfrac{\Gamma' \vdash e : T' \langle \Sigma_1 \rangle \qquad \Gamma' \vdash s : \text{ok} \langle \Sigma_2 \rangle}{\Gamma \vdash T' \ m \ (\overline{T \ x})\{\overline{T' \ x'}; s; \textbf{return } e\} : \text{ok} \langle \Sigma_1 \cup \Sigma_2 \rangle}}} \qquad \frac{\text{(PROGRAM)}}{\dfrac{\Gamma[\bar{x} \mapsto_v \bar{T}] \vdash s : \text{ok}}{\dfrac{\forall L \in \bar{L} \cdot \Gamma + \Gamma_d^L \ \vdash L : \text{ok}}{\Gamma + \bigcup_{L \in \bar{L}} \Gamma_d^L \vdash \bar{L} \ \{\overline{T \ x}; s\} : \text{ok}}}}$$

$$\frac{\text{(CLASS)}}{\dfrac{\forall I \in \bar{I} \cdot implements(C, I, \Gamma)}{\dfrac{\forall M \in \bar{M} \cdot \Gamma[\textbf{this} \mapsto_v C, \bar{x} \mapsto_v \bar{T}, \bar{x'} \mapsto_v \bar{T'}] \vdash M : \text{ok} \langle \Sigma^M \rangle}{\Gamma + [\langle C, 0 \rangle \mapsto_d \bigcup_{M \in \bar{M}} \Sigma^M] \ \vdash \textbf{class } C(\overline{T \ x}) \ \textbf{implements } \bar{I} \ \{\overline{T' \ x'}; \bar{M}\} : \text{ok}}}}$$

Fig. 4 The type and effect system. Judgments for the Boolean constants true and false are similar to SUSPEND. We omit empty effects; e.g., $\Gamma \vdash e \langle \emptyset \rangle$ is written $\Gamma \vdash e$

Typing of Dynamic Class Extensions Dynamic class operations $U_1, U_2, \ldots$ are type checked in a *sequence* of typing environments $\Gamma^0, \Gamma^1, \ldots$, which extend each other; Γ^0 is the typing environment for the original program and Γ^i the current static view of the system. We describe the construction of Γ^{i+1} for the next well-typed update U. The type system for judgments $\Gamma^{i+1} \vdash U$ is shown in Fig. 5. We here omit the analysis of **newinterface** and focus on class updates, and assume that new interfaces are well-typed and that $\Gamma_{\mathscr{J}}^i$ is correctly extended for each update. (As before, we omit the straightforward analysis of superinterfaces and method signatures.)

Rule NEW-CLASS for class additions requires a fresh name, type checks like a class in the original program, and extends $\Gamma_{\mathscr{C}}^i$. The version number of the new class differs from those of the program's original classes (highlighted). This reflects that the new class may depend on other dynamic system changes.

$$(\textsc{New-Class})$$

$$\Gamma' = [C \mapsto_C (\overline{T\,x}, \overline{I}, \overline{T'\,x'}, \overline{M})] \quad \forall I \in \overline{I} \cdot implements(C, I, \Gamma + \Gamma')$$

$$\frac{C \notin dom(\Gamma_{\mathscr{C}}^i) \quad \forall M \in \overline{M} \cdot \Gamma^i + \Gamma'[\mathbf{this} \mapsto_v C, \overline{x} \mapsto_v \overline{T}, \overline{x'} \mapsto_v \overline{T'}] \vdash M : \mathrm{ok} \langle \Sigma^M \rangle}{\Gamma^i + \Gamma' + [\langle C, 1 \rangle \mapsto_d \underset{M \in \overline{M}}{\bigcup} \Sigma^M] \vdash \mathbf{newclass}\ C(\overline{T\,x})\ \mathbf{implements}\ \overline{I}\ \{\overline{T'\,x'}; \overline{M}\}}$$

$$(\textsc{Class-Extend})$$

$$\Gamma_{\mathscr{C}}^i(C) = (\overline{T'\,x'}, \overline{I'}, \overline{T''\,x''}, \overline{M'}) \quad \forall I \in \overline{I} \cdot implements(C, I, \Gamma^i + \Gamma')$$

$$refines(\overline{M}, \overline{M'}) \quad \Gamma' = [C \mapsto_C (\overline{T'\,x'}, \overline{I'}; \overline{I}, \overline{T''\,x''}; \overline{T\,x}, (\overline{M'} \oplus \overline{M}))]$$

$$\frac{vs = curr(C, \Gamma_d^i) \quad \forall M \in \overline{M} \cdot \Gamma^i + \Gamma'[\mathbf{this} \mapsto_v C, \overline{x} \mapsto_v \overline{T}] \vdash M \langle \Sigma^M \rangle}{\Gamma^i + \Gamma' + [\langle C, vs+1 \rangle \mapsto_d \underset{M \in \overline{M}}{\bigcup} \Sigma^M \cup \{(C, vs)\}] \vdash \mathbf{update}\ C\ \mathbf{implements}\ \overline{I}\ \{\overline{T\,x}; \overline{M}\}}$$

Fig. 5 The type system for dynamic class extensions. Judgments have the form $\Gamma^{i+1} \vdash U$, where Γ^i is the current typing environment before the operation U

Rule CLASS-EXTEND obeys a substitutability discipline captured by the predicate $refines(\overline{M}, \overline{M'})$; if $M \in \overline{M}$ redefines $M' \in \overline{M'}$, the signature of M must be a subtype of the signature of M'. When retrieving the old version of the class from Γ_C^i, we represent the class compactly as a tuple and we denote by $\overline{M'} \oplus \overline{M}$ the union operation which retains methods in $\overline{M}$ in case of name conflicts. The new definition of C replaces the old one in $\Gamma_{\mathscr{C}}^i$ by the binding Γ'. The function $curr(C, \Gamma_d^i)$ identifies the current version number of a class C by inspecting the dependency mapping. The new methods of the updated class are type checked in a similar way as rule CLASS and the resulting dependencies, accumulated by the type analysis of methods, are bound to the new version $curr(C, \Gamma_d^i) + 1$ of the class in Γ_d^{i+1} (highlighted). Since type checking assumes the current version of the class to be present, the current version is included in this mapping.

In the asynchronous distributed setting, updates may be delayed or bypass each other. The *static view* of the system, reflected by the current typing environment, may differ considerably from the running system. To ensure that execution is type safe, inferred dependencies in Γ^i are imposed as constraints on the applicability of the i'th update at runtime. The constraints ensure that updates which depends on each other will be applied in the correct order; otherwise, they may be applied in any order, or in parallel.

5 Context-Reduction Semantics

The semantics is given by a small-step reduction relation $rcf \rightarrow rcf'$ over configurations. *Configurations* consist of objects, futures, and a class table CT (see Fig. 6). A *class* has a version number, parameters, a list of interfaces, a set of fields with default values, and a set of methods, bound to the class id in CT. Default values for types are given by a function *default* (e.g., *default*(bool) = false, and

$$
\begin{aligned}
rcf &::= CT \rhd cf & object &::= o(n,a,active,q) \\
CT &::= C \mapsto \langle n,\bar{x},\bar{I},a,mtds\rangle \mid CT \circ CT & a &::= x \mapsto \langle T,v\rangle \mid a \circ a \\
cf &::= \varepsilon \mid object \mid future \mid msg \mid cf\, cf & active &::= pr \mid \mathtt{idle} \\
future &::= f \mid f(v) & q &::= \varepsilon \mid pr \mid q \circ q \\
msg &::= bind(C,m,\bar{v},o,f) \mid bound(o,pr) & pr &::= \{a|sr\} \mid \mathtt{error} \\
mtd &::= T\ m(\overline{T\ x})\{a|sr\} & v &::= o \mid f \mid \mathtt{null} \mid b \\
mtds &::= \varepsilon \mid mtd \mid mtds\ mtds
\end{aligned}
$$

Fig. 6 Syntax for runtime configurations; o and f are object and future identifiers

$default(I) = default(\mathbf{Fut}(T)) = \mathbf{null})$. An *object* has an id o, version n, fields a, an active process, and a queue q of suspended processes. The $\mathtt{idle}$ process indicates that no method is active in the object and $\mathtt{error}$ that method binding has failed. A *future* has an id f, which becomes $f(v)$ when the future's reply value v has been received. Denote by $\overline{I}^*$ the transitive closure of $\overline{I}$ over the subtype relation (i.e., if $I \in \overline{I}$ and $J \preceq I$, then $I, J \in \overline{I}^*$). The *initial configuration* of a program $\overline{L}\ \{\overline{T}\ x;\ sr\}$, with classes and one *main* object, is defined as follows:

Definition 2 (Initial Configuration) Let P be a program and let *Main* $=$ *classOf(main)*. The initial configuration for P, denoted $[\![P]\!]$, is defined as:

$$
\begin{aligned}
[\![\overline{D}\ \overline{L}\ \{\overline{T}\ \bar{x};\ s\}]\!] \quad &= Main \mapsto \langle \mathbf{this} \mapsto \langle Main, \mathbf{null}\rangle, \epsilon\rangle \circ [\![\overline{L}]\!] \\
&\rhd main(0, \mathbf{this} \mapsto \langle Main, \mathbf{null}\rangle, \{[\![\overline{T}\ \bar{x}]\!]|s\}, \epsilon) \\
[\![L\ \overline{L}]\!] \quad &= [\![L]\!] \circ [\![\overline{L}]\!] \\
[\![\mathbf{class}\ C(\overline{T\ x})\ \mathbf{implements}\ \overline{I}\ \{\overline{T'\ x'};\ \overline{M}\}]\!] \quad & \\
&= C \mapsto \langle 0, \bar{x}, \overline{I}^*, \langle \mathbf{this} \mapsto \langle C, \mathbf{null}\rangle \circ [\![\overline{T\ x}, \overline{T'\ x'}]\!], [\![\overline{M}]\!]\rangle \\
[\![T\ x, \overline{T\ x}]\!] \quad &= [\![T\ x]\!] \circ [\![\overline{T\ x}]\!] \\
[\![T\ x]\!] \quad &= x \mapsto \langle T, default(T)\rangle \\
[\![M\ \overline{M}]\!] \quad &= [\![M]\!]\ [\![\overline{M}]\!] \\
[\![T\ m(\overline{T\ x})\{\overline{T'\ x'};\ sr\}]\!] &= T\ m(\overline{T\ x})\{\mathrm{destiny} \mapsto \langle \mathbf{Fut}(T), \mathbf{null}\rangle \circ [\![\overline{T\ x}, \overline{T'\ x'}]\!]|sr\}
\end{aligned}
$$

We consider a context reduction semantics [12], which decomposes a statement into a reduction context and a redex, and reduces the redex. The main reduction rules are given in Fig. 7. *Reduction contexts* are method bodies M, statements S, expressions E, and guards G with a single hole denoted by $\bullet$:

$$
\begin{aligned}
M &::= \bullet \mid S;\ \mathbf{return}\ e \mid \mathbf{return}\ E & S &::= \bullet \mid v = E \mid S;\ s \mid \mathbf{if}\ G\ \{s_1\}\ \mathbf{else}\ \{s_2\} \\
E &::= \bullet \mid E.\mathbf{get} \mid E!m(\bar{e}) \mid o!m(\bar{v}, E, \bar{e}) & G &::= \bullet \mid E?\ \mid G \wedge g \mid b \wedge G \mid E\ \mathbf{subtypeOf}\ I
\end{aligned}
$$

Redexes reduce in their respective contexts; i.e., body-redexes in M, stat-redexes in S, expr-redexes in E, and guard-redexes in G. Redexes are defined as follows:

$$
\begin{aligned}
\textit{body-redexes} \quad &::= \mathbf{skip} \mid \mathbf{return}\ v \\
\textit{stat-redexes} \quad &::= x = v \mid \mathbf{await}\ g \mid \mathbf{skip};\ s \mid \mathbf{if}\ b\ \{s\}\ \mathbf{else}\ \{s\} \mid \mathbf{suspend} \\
\textit{expr-redexes} \quad &::= x \mid f.\mathbf{get} \mid o!m(\bar{v}) \mid \mathbf{new}\ C(\bar{v}) \\
\textit{guard-redexes} \quad &::= f? \mid b \wedge g
\end{aligned}
$$

$$\frac{\text{(Red-Assign1)}}{l^T(x)=T}$$
$$\frac{l^T(x)=T}{o(n,a,\{l|M[x=v]\},q)}$$
$$\to o(n,a,\{l[x\mapsto\langle T,v\rangle]|M[\textbf{skip}]\},q)$$

$$\text{(Red-Assign2)}$$
$$\frac{x\notin dom(l)\quad a^T(x)=T}{o(n,a,\{l|M[x=v]\},q)}$$
$$\to o(n,a[x\mapsto\langle T,v\rangle],\{l|M[\textbf{skip}]\},q)$$

$$\text{(Red-Cond1)}$$
$$o(n,a,\{l|M[\textbf{if true }\{s\}\textbf{ else }\{s'\}]\},q)$$
$$\to o(n,a,\{l|M[s]\},q)$$

$$\text{(Red-Cond2)}$$
$$o(n,a,\{l|M[\textbf{if false }\{s\}\textbf{ else }\{s'\}]\},q)$$
$$\to o(n,a,\{l|M[s']\},q)$$

$$\text{(Red-Skip1)}$$
$$o(n,a,\{l|M[\textbf{skip};s]\},q)$$
$$\to o(n,a,\{l|M[s]\},q)$$

$$\text{(Red-Skip2)}$$
$$o(n,a,\{l|\textbf{skip}]\},q)$$
$$\to o(n,a,\text{idle},q)$$

$$\text{(Guard1)}$$
$$o(n,a,\{l|M[\text{true}\wedge G]\},q)$$
$$\to o(n,a,\{l|M[G]\},q)$$

$$\text{(Guard2)}$$
$$o(n,a,\{l|M[\text{false}\wedge G]\},q)$$
$$\to o(n,a,\{l|M[\text{false}]\},q)$$

$$\text{(Red-New)}$$
$$o'\text{ is fresh}\quad CT(C)=\langle n,\bar{x},\bar{I},a,mtds\rangle$$
$$\frac{C=classOf(o')\quad a''=[\textbf{this}\mapsto\langle C,o'\rangle,\bar{x}\mapsto\langle a^T(\bar{x}),\bar{v}\rangle]}{CT\triangleright o(n',a',\{l|M[\textbf{new }C(\bar{v}))]\},q)}$$
$$\to CT\triangleright o(n',a',\{l|M[o']\},q)\,o'(n,a;a'',\text{idle},\varepsilon)$$

$$\text{(Red-Query1)}$$
$$C=classOf(v)\quad I\in\bar{I}$$
$$\frac{CT(C)=\langle n',\bar{x},\bar{I},a',mtds\rangle}{CT\triangleright o(n,a,\{l|M[v\textbf{ subtypeOf }I]\},q)\,f(v)}$$
$$\to CT\triangleright o(n,a,\{l|M[\text{true}]\},q)\,f(v)$$

$$\text{(Red-Query2)}$$
$$C=classOf(v)\quad I\notin\bar{I}$$
$$\frac{CT(C)=\langle n',\bar{x},\bar{I},a',mtds\rangle}{CT\triangleright o(n,a,\{l|M[v\textbf{ subtypeOf }I]\},q)\,f}$$
$$\to CT\triangleright o(n,a,\{l|M[\text{false}]\},q)\,f$$

$$\text{(Red-Poll1)}$$
$$o(n,a,\{l|M[f?]\},q)\,f(v)$$
$$\to o(n,a,\{l|M[\text{true}]\},q)\,f(v)$$

$$\text{(Red-Call1)}$$
$$\frac{o'\neq\textbf{this}\quad C=classOf(o')\quad f\text{ is fresh}}{o(n,a,\{l|M[o'!m(\bar{v})]\},q)}$$
$$\to o(n,a,\{l|M[f]\},q)\,bind(C,m,\bar{v},o',f)\,f$$

$$\text{(Red-Poll2)}$$
$$o(n,a,\{l|M[f?]\},q)\,f$$
$$\to o(n,a,\{l|M[\text{false}]\},q)\,f$$

$$\text{(Red-Call2)}$$
$$\frac{C=classOf(o)\quad f\text{ is fresh}}{o(n,a,\{l|M[\textbf{this}!m(\bar{v})]\},q)}$$
$$\to o(n,a,\{l|M[f]\},q)\,bind(C,m,\bar{v},o,f)\,f$$

$$\text{(Red-Await)}$$
$$o(n,a,\{l|M[\textbf{await }g]\},q)$$
$$\to o(n,a,\{l|M[\textbf{if }g\ \{\textbf{skip}\}\textbf{ else }\{\textbf{suspend};\textbf{ await }g\}]\},q)$$

$$\text{(Red-Bound)}$$
$$o(n,a,\text{idle},q)\,bound(o,pr)$$
$$\to o(n,a,\text{idle},q\circ pr)$$

$$\text{(Red-Get)}$$
$$o(n,a,\{l|M[f.\textbf{get}]\},q)\,f(v)$$
$$\to o(n,a,\{l|M[v]\},q)\,f(v)$$

$$\text{(Red-Bind)}$$
$$CT(C)=\langle n,\bar{x},\bar{I},a,mtds\rangle$$
$$\frac{lookup(m,\bar{v},f,mtds)=pr}{CT\triangleright bind(C,m,\bar{v},o,f)}$$
$$\to CT\triangleright bound(o,pr)$$

$$\text{(Red-Return)}$$
$$\frac{l^V(destiny)=f}{o(n,a,\{l|\textbf{return }v]\},q)\,f}$$
$$\to o(n,a,\text{idle},q)\,f(v)$$

$$\text{(Red-Context1)}$$
$$\frac{cf\to cf'}{CT\triangleright cf\to CT\triangleright cf'}$$

$$\text{(Red-Reschedule)}$$
$$n=n'$$
$$\frac{CT(C)=\langle n',\bar{x},\bar{I},a',mtds\rangle}{CT\triangleright o(n,a,\text{idle},pr\circ q)}$$
$$\to CT\triangleright o(n,a,pr,q)$$

$$\text{(Red-Suspend)}$$
$$o(n,a,\{l|M[\textbf{suspend}]\},q)$$
$$\to o(n,a,\text{idle},q\circ\{l|M[\textbf{skip}]\})$$

Fig. 7 The context reduction semantics

Filling the hole of a context M with a redex r is denoted $M[r]$. Before evaluating the expression e in the method body s; **return** e, the body will be reduced to **skip**; **return** e. For simplicity, we elide the **skip** and write just **return** e.

Statements. In Red-Assign1 and Red-Assign2, values are assigned to local and program variables. In Red-Cond1, the boolean condition evaluates to true so the evaluation of s is chosen. Otherwise, evaluate s' in Red-Cond2.

In RED-QUERY1, the given interface is found among the interfaces in the class definition of an object, reducing the query to true. Otherwise, reduce to false in RED-QUERY2.

Expressions and Guards. In RED-CALL1 and RED-CALL2, external and internal asynchronous calls add a future to the configuration, and return its id to the caller. In RED-GET, the future's reply value is read. In RED-NEW, a new instance of class C is placed in the configuration. The new object's fields are given by the class table $CT(C)$ and the active process is initiated with the idle process. We use $classOf(o) = C$ to retrieve the class name C from the object id o. In RED-POLL1 and In RED-POLL2, a future is polled to see if a call has been executed.

Suspension and Rescheduling. Guards determine whether a process should be suspended. In RED-AWAIT, a process proceeds if its guard is true and suspends otherwise. When a process is suspended, its guard is reused to reschedule the process. When a process is suspended in RED-SUSPEND or terminates, it is replaced by the idle process, which allows a process from the process queue to be scheduled for execution in RED-RESCHEDULE.

Method Calls and Returns. A method call results in an activation on the callee's process queue. There is a delay between the asynchronous call and its activation, represented by a future without any reply value and a bind request to the callee's class. In RED-BIND, the method is retrieved from the class, resulting in a *bound* message to the callee, which is loaded into the process queue in RED-BOUND. When the process terminates, the result is stored by RED-RETURN in the future identified by the destiny variable. This future now carries a reply value and the active process becomes idle. Finally, RED-CONTEXT1 reduces subconfigurations.

Semantics of Dynamic Software Updates To support updates, we consider update messages by extending the runtime syntax of Fig. 6 as follows:

$$
\begin{aligned}
msg &::= \ldots \mid upd \\
upd &::= new(C, \overline{x}, \overline{I}, a, mtds, dep) \mid ext(C, \overline{I}, a, mtds, dep) \\
dep &::= \overline{(C, n)}
\end{aligned}
$$

An update message for a new class or class extension has a class name C, class parameters $\overline{x}$ for new class, a list $\overline{I}$ of interfaces, a list a of new fields, a set *mtds* of new (or redefined) methods, and a set *dep* of constraints to classes in the runtime system. If a message injected into the runtime configuration is well-typed in an environment Γ^i, then *dep* is $\Gamma_d^i(\langle C, curr(C, \Gamma_d^i)\rangle)$. Thus, the static dependencies of the current update are introduced into the runtime configuration. The semantics for dynamic class operations consist of the rules in Fig. 8.

Dynamic software updates are initiated by injecting a message *upd* into the configuration by rule UPDATE. For the *extension* of a class C, this message is $ext(C, \overline{I}^*, a, mtds, dep)$ which cannot be applied unless the constraints in *dep* are satisfied; these are checked by DEP. Thus, the update is delayed at runtime until other updates have been applied. When the constraints are satisfied, the fields and methods of the runtime class definition are extended and the version number

$$(\text{Dep1})$$
$$\frac{n' \geq n \quad CT(C') = \langle n', \bar{x}, \bar{I}', a', mtds \rangle}{CT \rhd new(C, \bar{x}, I, a, mtds, ((C', n) \cup dep))}$$
$$\to CT \rhd new(C, \bar{x}, I, a, mtds, dep)$$

$$(\text{Dep2})$$
$$\frac{n' \geq n \quad CT(C') = \langle n', \bar{x}, \bar{I}', a', mtds \rangle}{CT \rhd ext(C, \bar{I}, a, mtds, ((C', n) \cup dep))}$$
$$\to CT \rhd ext(C, \bar{I}, a, mtds, dep)$$

$$(\text{Obj-State})$$
$$C = classOf(o)$$
$$\frac{CT(C) = \langle n', \bar{x}, \bar{I}, a', mtds \rangle}{n' > n \quad a'' = transf(a')}$$
$$\frac{CT \rhd o(n, a, \texttt{idle}, q)}{\to CT \rhd o(n', a'', \texttt{idle}, q)}$$

$$(\text{Extend-Class})$$
$$\frac{CT(C) = \langle n, \bar{x}, \bar{I}', a', mtds' \rangle}{CT \rhd ext(C, \bar{I}, a, mtds, \emptyset)}$$
$$\to CT[C \mapsto \langle n+1, \bar{x}, (\bar{I}', \bar{I}), a' \circ a, mtds' \oplus mtds \rangle]$$

$$(\text{New-Class})$$
$$CT \rhd new(C, \bar{x}, \bar{I}, a, mtds, \emptyset)$$
$$\to CT[C \mapsto \langle 1, \bar{x}, \bar{I}, a, mtds \rangle]$$

$$(\text{Update})$$
$$config \xrightarrow{upd} config\ upd$$

$$(\text{Red-Context2})$$
$$\frac{rcf \to rcf'}{rcf\ cf \to rcf'\ cf}$$

Fig. 8 The context reduction semantics for dynamic software updates

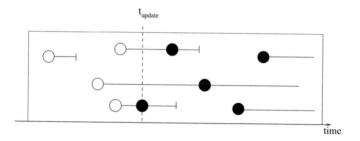

Fig. 9 Asynchronous object update

increased in EXTEND-CLASS. (For the operator $\oplus$, see Sect. 4.) Similarly, when the constraints are satisfied, NEW-CLASS creates a new runtime class with all implemented interfaces and its version number set to 1 (only classes in the original program have the version numbers initially set to 0).

Figure 9 illustrates the update mechanism for objects after an update has been applied to the objects' class. Fields must be updated *before* new code is allowed to execute. New instances of the class (i.e., objects created after time t_{update}) automatically get the new fields, but the update of existing objects must be controlled; if new or redefined methods were executed that rely on fields that are not yet available in the object errors may then occur. For recursive or nonterminating methods, objects cannot generally be expected to reach a state without any pending processes, even if one postpones the activation of new method calls. Waiting for the completion of all processes before applying an update is, therefore, too restrictive. However, objects may reach *quiescent* states when the processor has been released and before any pending process has been activated, which is when the active process is `idle`. Objects which do not deadlock will eventually reach such state and we have that at least one quiescent state is reached in each cycle if nonterminating activity is defined by recursion. At this point, objects can be updated. This update mechanism is asynchronous meaning that some objects may be updated before others in a non-deterministic order. The updated objects may execute a new implementation of some methods, while other objects are still running the old method implementation.

A class update propagates to its objects in two steps. For EXTEND-CLASS, the version number of the class increases then the object gets an update the next time it interacts with its class. Before the new process is activated, the active process must become `idle`, in which case OBJ-STATE applies (abstracting from a more asynchronous locking scheme). The *transf* function returns the new state, retaining the values of old fields. A class may be updated several times before the object reaches a quiescent state, meaning that the object may miss some updates. In this case, a single update suffices to ensure that the object is a complete instance of the present version of its class.

6   Conclusion

This paper presents a system of software updates for the asynchronous evolution of distributed, loosely-coupled active objects, motivated by IoT systems. The system emphasizes programmability, yet ensures type safety at runtime for the gradually evolving system. We have combined dynamic software updates with an interface query mechanism to facilitate context adaptation. A characteristic feature of our system is the use of type and effect analysis to identify dependencies between different updates, which are checked at runtime to ensure that the runtime view of the system is sufficiently close to the static view for updates to apply.

References

1. Gul A. Agha. *ACTORS: A Model of Concurrent Computations in Distributed Systems* Cambridge, Mass.: The MIT Press, 1986.
2. Sameer Ajmani, Barbara Liskov, and Liuba Shrira. "Modular Software Upgrades for Distributed Systems". In: *Proc. 20th European Conf on Object-Oriented Programming (ECOOP'06)* Ed. by Dave Thomas. Vol. 4067. Lecture Notes in Computer Science. Springer, 2006, pp. 452–476.
3. Torben Amtoft, Flemming Nielson, and Hanne Riis Nielson. *Type and Effect Systems: Behaviours for Concurrency* Imperial College Press, 1999.
4. Joe Armstrong. *Programming Erlang: Software for a Concurrent World* Pragmatic Book-shelf, 2007.
5. Emmanuel Baccelli et al. "Scripting Over-The-Air: Towards Containers on Low-end Devices in the Internet of Things". In: *IEEE PerCom 2018* Mar 2018. URL: https://hal.inria.fr/hal01766610.
6. Gavin Bierman, Matthew Parkinson, and James Noble. "UpgradeJ: Incremental Typechecking for Class Upgrades". In: *Proc. 22nd European Conf on Object-Oriented Programming (ECOOP'08)* Vol. 5142. Lecture Notes in Computer Science. Springer, 2008, pp. 235–259. ISBN: 978-3-540-70591-8.

7. Gavin Bierman et al. "Formalizing Dynamic Software Updating". In: *Proc. 2nd Intl. Work-shop on Unanticipated Software Evolution (USE)* Apr 2003.
8. Frank De Boer et al. "A Survey of Active Object Languages". In: *ACM Comput. Surv* 50.5 (Oct. 2017), 76:1–76:39.
9. Chandrasekhar Boyapati et al. "Lazy modular upgrades in persistent object stores". In: *Proc. Object-Oriented Programming Systems, Languages and Applications (OOPSLA'03)* Ed. by Ron Crocker and Guy L. Steele Jr ACM Press, 2003, pp. 403–417.
10. Haibo Chen et al. "POLUS: A POwerful Live Updating System". In: *Proceedings of the 29th International Conference on Software Engineering* ICSE '07. IEEE Computer Society, 2007. ISBN: 0-76952828-7. DOI: 10.1109/ICSE.2007.65 URL: http://dx.doi.org/10.1109/ICSE.2007.65
11. Dominic Duggan. "Type-Based Hot Swapping of Running Modules". In: *Proc. 6th Intl. Conf on Functional Programming (ICFP'01)* Ed. by Cindy Norris and Jr. James B. Fenwick. Vol. 36, 10. ACM SIGPLAN notices. New York: ACM Press, Sept. 2001, pp. 62–73.
12. Matthias Felleisen and Robert Hieb. "The Revised Report on the Syntactic Theories of Sequential Control and State". In: *Theor Comp. Sci.* 103.2 (1992), pp. 235–271.
13. Deepak Gupta, Pankaj Jalote, and Gautam Barua. "A Formal Framework for On-line Software Version Change." In: *IEEE Trans. Software Eng* 22.2 (1996), pp. 120–131.
14. Christopher M. Hayden et al. "Kitsune: Efficient, General-Purpose Dynamic Software Updating for C". In: *ACM Trans. Program. Lang Syst.* 36.4 (2014). ISSN: 0164-0925. DOI: 10.1145/2629460 URL: http://doi.acm.org/10.1145/2629460
15. Carl E. Hewitt. "Viewing Control Structures as Patterns of Passing Messages". In: *Journal of Artificial Intelligence* 8.3 (1977), pp. 323–364.
16. Raphael Hiesgen, Dominik Charousset, and Thomas C. Schmidt. "Embedded Actors Towards distributed programming in the IoT". In: *IEEE Fourth International Conference on Consumer Electronics Berlin (ICCE-Berlin 2014)* IEEE, 2014, pp. 371–375.
17. Gisli Hjálmtýsson and Robert S. Gray. "Dynamic C++ Classes: A Lightweight Mechanism to Update Code in a Running Program". In: *Proc. USENIX Tech. Conf (USENIX '98)* May 1998.
18. Einar Broch Johnsen, Marcel Kyas, and Ingrid Chieh Yu. "Dynamic Classes: Modular Asynchronous Evolution of Distributed Concurrent Objects". In: *Proc. 16th International Symposium on Formal Methods (FM'09)* Ed. by Ana Cavalcanti and Dennis Dams. Vol. 5850. Lecture Notes in Computer Science. Springer, Nov. 2009, pp. 596–611.
19. Einar Broch Johnsen et al. "A formal model of service-oriented dynamic object groups". In: *Sci. Comput. Program.* 115–116 (2016), pp. 3–22.
20. Einar Broch Johnsen et al. "ABS: A Core Language for Abstract Behavioral Specification". In: *Proc. 9th International Symposium on Formal Methods for Components and Objects (FMCO 2010)* Ed. by Bernhard Aichernig, Frank S. de Boer, and Marcello M. Bonsangue. Vol. 6957. LNCS. Springer, 2011, pp. 142–164.
21. Elizabeth Latronico et al. "A Vision of Swarmlets". In: *IEEE Internet Computing* 19.2 (2015), pp. 20–28.
22. Edward A. Lee et al. "The Swarm at the Edge of the Cloud". In: *IEEE Design & Test* 31.3 (2014), pp. 8–20.
23. Marten Lohstroh and Edward A. Lee. "An Interface Theory for the Internet of Things". In: *Proc. 13th International Conference on Software Engineering and Formal Methods (SEFM 2015)* Ed. by Radu Calinescu and Bernhard Rumpe. Vol. 9276. Lecture Notes in Computer Science. Springer, 2015, pp. 20–34.
24. Scott Malabarba et al. "Runtime Support for Type-Safe Dynamic Java Classes". In: *Proc. 14th European Conf on Object-Oriented Programming (ECOOP'00)* Ed. by Elisa Bertino. Vol. 1850. Lecture Notes in Computer Science. Springer, June 2000, pp. 337–361.
25. Bertrand Meyer. "Applying "Design by Contract"". In: *IEEE Computer* 25.10 (1992), pp. 40–51.
26. Daniele Miorandi et al. "Internet of things: Vision, applications and research challenges". In: *Ad Hoc Networks* 10.7 (2012), pp. 1497–1516.

27. Alessandro Orso, Anup Rao, and Mary Jean Harrold. "A Technique for Dynamic Updating of Java Software". In: *Proc. Intl. Conf. on Software Maintenance (ICSM'02)* IEEE Computer Society Press, Oct. 2002, pp. 649–658.
28. Valerio Panzica La Manna. "Local Dynamic Update for Component-based Distributed Systems". In: *Proceedings of the 15th ACM SIGSOFT Symposium on Component Based Software Engineering* CBSE '12. ACM, 2012. ISBN: 978-1-4503-1345-2. DOI: 10.1145/2304736.2304764. URL: http://doi.acm.org/10.1145/2304736.2304764
29. Valerio Panzica La Manna et al. "Formalizing Correctness Criteria of Dynamic Updates Derived from Specification Changes". In: *Proceedings of the 8th International Symposium on Software Engineering for Adaptive and Self-Managing Systems* SEAMS '13. IEEE Press, 2013. ISBN: 978-1-4673-4401-2. URL: http://dl.acm.org/citation.cfm?id=2487336.2487349
30. Luis Pina, Luis Veiga, and Michael Hicks. "Rubah: DSU for Java on a Stock JVM". In: *Proceedings of the 2014 ACM International Conference on Object Oriented Programming Systems Languages & Applications* OOPSLA '14. ACM, 2014. ISBN: 978-1-4503-2585-1. DOI: 10 1145 / 2660193 2660220. URL: http://doi.acm.org/10.1145/2660193.2660220.
31. Jan Schäfer and Arnd Poetzsch-Heffter. "JCoBox: Generalizing Active Objects to Concurrent Components". In: *Proceedings of the 24th European Conference on Object-Oriented Programming (ECOOP 2010)*. Ed. by Theo D'Hondt. Vol. 6183. Lecture Notes in Computer Science. Springer, 2010, pp. 275–299.
32. Alessandro Sivieri, Luca Mottola, and Gianpaolo Cugola. "Building Internet of Things software with ELIoT". In: *Computer Communications* 89–90 (2016), pp. 141–153.
33. Eystein Stenberg. "Key Considerations for Software Updates for Embedded Linux and IoT". In: *Linux J* 2017.276 (Apr 2017). ISSN: 1075-3583.
34. Gareth Stoyle et al. "*Mutatis Mutandis*: Safe and predictable dynamic software updating". In: *ACM TOPLAS* 29.4 (2007), p. 22. ISSN: 0164-0925.
35. Jean-Pierre Talpin and Pierre Jouvelot. "Polymorphic Type, Region and Effect Inference". In: *Journal of Functional Programming* 2.3 (1992), pp. 245–271.
36. Ingrid Chieh Yu, Einar Broch Johnsen, and Olaf Owe. "Type-Safe Runtime Class Upgrades in Creol". In: *Proc. 8th Intl. Conf on Formal Methods for Open Object-Based Distributed Systems (FMOODS'06)* Ed. by Roberto Gorrieri and Heike Wehrheim. Vol. 4037. LNCS. Springer, June 2006, pp. 202–217.

Using CSP to Develop Quality Concurrent Software

Derrick G. Kourie, Tinus Strauss, Loek Cleophas, and Bruce W. Watson

Abstract A method for developing concurrent software is advocated that centres on using CSP to specify the behaviour of the system. A small example problem is used to illustrate the method. The problem is to develop a simulation system that keeps track of and reports on the least unique bid of multiple streams of randomly generated incoming bids. The problem's required high-level behaviour is specified in CSP, refined down to the level of interacting processes and then verified for refinement and behavioural correctness using the FDR refinement checker. Heuristics are used to map the CSP processes to a GO implementation. Interpretive reflections are offered of the lessons learned as a result of the exercise.

1 Introduction

In software engineering, the functional requirements state *what* the system should do. Non-functional requirements are stated in terms of quality attributes that characterise *how* these functional requirements are to be attained. Examples of such attributes include maintainability, portability, security, etc. Many authors include correctness—the extent to which the software agrees with its specification—as a

D. G. Kourie (✉) · T. Strauss
Department of Information Science, Stellenbosch University, Stellenbosch, South Africa
e-mail: dkourie@fastar.org; tinus@fastar.org

L. Cleophas
Department of Information Science, Stellenbosch University, Stellenbosch, South Africa

Department of Mathematics and Computer Science, Eindhoven University of Technology, Eindhoven, The Netherlands
e-mail: loek@fastar.org

B. W. Watson
Department of Information Science, Stellenbosch University, Stellenbosch, South Africa

Centre for Artificial Intelligence Research, CSIR Meraka Institute, Pretoria, South Africa
e-mail: bruce@fastar.org

© Springer Nature Switzerland AG 2018
P. Müller, I. Schaefer (eds.), *Principled Software Development*,
https://doi.org/10.1007/978-3-319-98047-8_11

quality attribute. The overall *quality* of a given system is measured by the extent to which these quality attributes are attained.

A spectrum of relatively mature software development strategies has evolved over time that are aimed at ensuring high quality software systems. Some are programming-in-the-small strategies such as correctness-by-construction (CbC) and post-hoc verification. These aim principally at producing error-free code. Others may be thought of as programming-in-the-large strategies. They are represented by an array of software methodologies (such as Agile or RUP, etc). These are oriented towards ensuring that functional requirements are met in such a way that pre-specified levels of a broad range of quality attributes are met.

However, most of these strategies are aimed primarily, if not exclusively, at producing *sequential* software systems. One might have expected that the proliferation of multiprocessor hardware systems (such as multicore chips and graphical processing units) would have spawned an array of comparable strategies for developing *concurrent* systems, but this has not materialised to any significant extent.

The pioneering attempt of Owicki and Gries [8] to extend CbC to concurrent contexts has not gained traction. Neither have various proposals for concurrent software development methodologies[1] gained a significant foothold in industry. Examples of such proposals include [4, 7, 9, 11, 12, 16].

Ironically, quite a number of languages have emerged, both for *specifying* and *implementing* concurrent software systems. Specification languages include Estelle (ISO standardised); process algebras such as LOTOS (also ISO standardised), CCS and CSP; and finite automaton-based notations such as Harel's State Charts (used in UML). Programming languages with significant support for concurrency include Ada, Esterel, Occam, concurrent C++, concurrent Java, Erlang, Go, etc.

In this chapter, a small concurrent software system is formally specified, refined and then eventually implemented. The specification's development style is "iterative incremental". It starts with an abstract high-level CSP specification of the overall system whose behaviour very broadly conforms with the product requirements. FDR (a tool for analysing CSP specification refinements) is used to verify the correctness of each refinement step. When the iteratively refined specification has sufficiently exposed an architectural and logical structure for the problem's solution, the specification is mapped to a system of interacting *software processes*, expressed in the Go programming language.

The next section provides the background needed in respect of CSP and FDR, and suggests heuristics for mapping CSP to Go. Section 3 then describes the functional requirements for the system to be developed. Section 4 walks through the process of incrementally refining an initial abstract CSP specification and verifying the

---

[1]The notion of a "concurrent software development methodology" is ambiguous. It could refer to a methodology aimed at developing *concurrent software*, or to a methodology that advocates *concurrent execution of tasks* in the software development life cycle (sometimes referred to as concurrent engineering). Here the term is used in the former sense.

refinement steps. Section 5 outlines how the refined specification was mapped to an implementation in Go. Some interesting results obtained from the implemented system are displayed in Sect. 6. We conclude in Sect. 7 with some reflective comments about our experience.

2 Background

Since being open-sourced in 2009, the Go language has surged in popularity, climbing on the TIOBE index from 65th in 2015 to 14th at the time of writing.[2] Its developers aimed at a language that not only compiles efficiently to produce object code that runs efficiently, but that also supports concurrency. To achieve the latter objective, they based aspects of the language on CSP. They justified this choice as follows:

> Concurrency and multi-threaded programming have a reputation for difficulty. . . . One of the most successful models for providing high-level linguistic support for concurrency comes from . . . CSP. Go's concurrency primitives derive from . . . the powerful notion of channels as first class objects. Experience with several earlier languages has shown that the CSP model fits well into a procedural language framework.[3]

The foregoing confirms and motivates our choice of CSP, FDR and Go as a trilogy of technologies upon which to rely in our quest to evolve a concurrent software methodology.

Below we briefly introduce CSP and the notion of refinement in that context, we introduce relevant features of the FDR tool as well as the syntax of CSP variant used by the tool, indicated as CSP_M. Finally, features of Go that are pertinent to this study are introduced as well as the guidelines that were used to map CSP_M specifications to Go.

2.1 CSP and Refinement

CSP (Communicating Sequential Processes) is a process algebra that was originally proposed by Hoare as a language for specifying the behaviour of concurrent systems. Over time various modifications and extensions have been proposed (e.g. to model real time systems or asynchronous and shared memory systems). A comprehensive introduction and reference volume for CSP is available in [10].

CSP envisages that a process interacts with its environment (one or more other processes) in terms of *events* from an alphabet. It is essentially a notation for concisely describing the set of event sequences (called *traces*) that characterise a

---

[2]https://www.tiobe.com/tiobe-index/.
[3]https://golang.org/doc/faq.

process's interaction with its environment. Events are abstractions that are regarded as *atomic*—i.e. they have no duration and thus cannot occur simultaneously, but only before or after one another.

The trace set of process P is denoted by traces(P). It includes all prefixes of all traces of P. Such a trace set can be regarded as the semantics of P. Process Q is said to trace-refine process P iff traces(Q) ⊆ traces(P).

CSP includes a more elaborate notion of refinement based on so-called *failures*. To briefly explain the notion of a failure, let P/s represent process P after trace s. A *refusal set* of P/s is *any* set of events, say X, that P/s can fail to accept from its environment, irrespective of how long one or more events in that set are offered. If X is a refusal set of P/s, then the pair (s,X) is called a *failure* of P.[4] The set of all failures of P over all of its traces is denoted by failures(P). Process Q is said to failure-refine process P iff failures(Q) ⊆ failures(P) and traces(Q) ⊆ traces(P). If Σ is the alphabet of P and (s,Σ) is a failure of P, then P has a deadlock after executing trace s.

There is yet another CSP notion of refinement related to so-called *divergences*. In order to remain concise, we will not discuss divergences in detail here. Nevertheless, we note that the definition for divergence-refinement is similar to that of failure-refinement. We furthermore note that divergences are associated with starvation (livelock).

2.2   FDR and CSP$_M$

In this text, a keyboard friendly syntactical variant of CSP known as CSP$_M$ will be used. This allows us to make use of FDR (version 4), an open source tool for analysing CSP specifications [2, 3, 10]. The tool can be used to automatically check for certain correctness attributes in a specification. It can also be used to generate the labelled transition diagram that visualises a specification.

Figure 1 summarises the CSP$_M$ operators that will be used in subsequent text. An informal explanation of these operators and their operands follows. Formal operator semantics and laws for their manipulation are available in various texts such as [5, 6, 10].

a -> P represents an **unnamed** process that does nothing until its environment offers event a, at which point the process engages with that event and thereafter behaves as the **named** process, P. The unnamed process may be named Q by writing Q = a -> P.

---

[4]Note that X does not have to be maximal to be a refusal set of P/s. There can therefore be many refusal sets of P/s. The set of such refusal sets at P/s is denoted by refusals(P/s), each such refusal set giving rise to an additional failure of P.

a -> P	event *a* **then** process *P*
P [] Q	**External choice** between P and Q
P |~| Q	**Internal choice** between P and Q
P [|A|] Q	P in **shared parallel** with Q
	Synchronize on events in the set A
P ||| Q	P **interleaved** with Q
	Equivalent to P |{}| Q; P and Q run independently
P ; Q	P **followed by** Q
C!x	**Output** the value x to channel C
C?t	**Input** into variable t from channel C
P\\{|C|}	**Hide** events in P *except* those on channel C
Op a:A @ P(a)	P(a1) Op P(a2) Op ... P(an) where Op is |~| or |||
	and A = {a1, a2, ..., an}

Fig. 1 Selected CSP$_M$ operators and operands

Using the notation Q/s to reference process Q after engaging in trace s, the foregoing means that Q/<a> references process P. Note, however, that Q/s is not part of FDR syntax.

Named processes may have zero or more parameters (e.g. Q or P(x,y)). The **let...within** clause is used to assign a name and initialise the parameters of a subprocess that is only known locally to some exteriorly defined process.

SKIP designates a special process that simply terminates successfully without engaging in further events.

In Rext = (a -> P) [] (b -> Q) two unnamed processes serve as operands to the **external choice** operator.[5] If its environment offers event a then Rext engages with a and the behaves thereafter as P. Conversely, if its environment offers event b then it engages with b then behaves as Q. The behaviour thus depends on which event is offered first by other processes in the environment. If P and Q are both replaced by SKIP, then traces(Rext) = {<>,<a>,<b>} where <> is the empty trace.

In contrast, Rint = (a -> P) \|~\| (b -> Q) has the same two unnamed processes, but these serve as operands to the **internal choice** operator. Rint *may* engage with event a if offered by the environment and then behave as P, but may also refuse to engage with a. Likewise, Rint *may* engage with event b if offered by the environment and then behave as Q, but may also refuse to engage with b. Externally, the behaviour of Rint manifests as non-deterministic. Its behaviour is determined by internal considerations. Its traces correspond to those of Rext but its failures do not.

FDR provides for various ways of expressing parallel synchronisation between two (or more) processes. Synchronisation is with respect to an explicit or implied set of events. R = P [\|A\|] Q represents a process that synchronises on any element

---

[5]Equivalence relationships indicate what occurs if operands are unguarded. For example, if an operand is SKIP then Rext would be equivalent to the SKIP process.

in the set A. Thus, if the environment offers a ∈ A, and both P and Q are ready to
engage with a, then R/<a> = P/<a> [|A|] Q/<a>. However, if P and/or Q
is not ready to engage with a, then **deadlock** occurs. If the environment offers a ∉
A, and P is ready to engage with a but Q is not, then R/<a> = P<a> [|A|] Q,
and similarly if Q is ready to engage with a, but not P.

The process R = P ||| Q represents the interleaving of P and Q and is simply
another way of writing R = P [|||] Q. Here, P and Q respond to what the
environment offers entirely independently of one another. Normally, it is assumed
that their alphabets are disjoint.

In the process specification R = P;Q, the **followed by** operator is used. R
behaves as P until it terminates successfully (i.e. evolves into SKIP). Thereafter,
process R behaves as Q.[6]

CSP relies on the notion of **channels** as part of a process's environment. Channels
synchronously connect processes to one another. Each channel has a specific
alphabet determining events (or messages) that are communicated across it. If C
designates a channel and x is an element of its alphabet, then the notation C!x
indicates that x is to be output on C (or equivalently, the event C.x is offered to the
environment.) Dually, C?t indicates that any one of the events in the alphabet of C
may be input (received) into variable t.

Process Q = P\{|C|} is a process whose traces are the traces of P except
that all events not in the alphabet of channel C are **hidden**. Thus, if t is a trace of
P and t′ is t but stripped of all events except those that occur on C, then t′ is a
trace of Q.

The following notation is used to express the external choice or interleaving over
n parameterised processes: Op a:A @ P(a) = P(a1) Op ... OP P(an),
where Op is either |~| or ||| and A = {a1, a2, ..., an}

The syntax **if** Bexp **then** P **else** Q specifies a process that behaves as process
P if the Boolean expression Bexp is true and behaves as process Q otherwise.

The FDR assert statement takes an FDR predicate as argument and appropriately returns true or false (together with debugging information). We used
assert with the following predicates, P and Q being process names.

P [T= Q	Q trace-refines P
P [FD= Q	Q failure-divergence-refines P
P : [deadlock-free]	P is deadlock free
P : [divergence-free]	P is divergence free
P : [deterministic]	P is deterministic

---

[6]Again, equivalence relationships indicate what occurs under various conditions. For example, if
P does not terminate successfully (i.e. it does not terminate, or terminates in the deadlock process,
STOP, then P;Q ≡ P.

2.3 Go

Although Go is in the tradition of the C/Java family of languages, there are several differences: for example, declaration syntax differs and features such as generics, pointer arithmetic and inheritance are absent. Below, a very brief account is given of Go features that are relevant in this text. For more information, refer to standard documentation sources.[7]

In mapping CSP_M to Go, we use a number of heuristics and special Go features.

- CSP_M processes are mapped to Go functions that are subsequently launched as so-called goroutines. Each time the command `go somefun()` is issued, a goroutine instance of the function called `somefun` is allocated to one of the available cores on a multicore machine and runs to completion on that core. A goroutine may therefore be viewed as a process that runs concurrently with other goroutines / process, the allocation of processes to processors being sorted out automatically by the runtime environment.
- In general, the state of a CSP_M process at any given point is reflected by the process's actual (as opposed to formal) parameters. The corresponding Go process's state is naturally stored in variables that were declared as local in the Go function's definition.
- Since Go supports channels, we map CSP_M channels to Go channels. An instance of a channel, say `c`, that is to convey messages of a given type, say `<T>`, is created by the call `c := make(chan <T>)`. In our implementation, all channels were of type `int`.
- The CSP_M command `C!a` (i.e. transmit a on channel C) is mapped to Go as `C <- a`.
- Similarly, `C?x` (read from a channel c into variable x) is mapped to Go as `x := <-C`.
- Since Go channels optionally may be buffered, there is no need to explicitly map every CSP_M FIFO buffer process to a goroutine. For example, the command `C := make(chan int, 10)` creates the channel C that stores up to 10 integers in a FIFO buffer.
- Additionally, multiple goroutines can write to and/or read from the same Go channel. This feature was relied upon in constructing the multiplexing FIFO buffer described below in CSP_M.
- The Go for-loop construct `for e := range c {...}`, repeatedly reads a value from channel c into variable e, and then executes the body of the loop. Once the channel C is closed using the call `close(C)`, attempts to read from the channel are discontinued. This convenient Go feature was used in our implementation to ensure graceful closure of processes.
- CSP_M's external choice is mapped to Go's `select` statement.

---

[7]For example https://golang.org/doc/.

It should be emphasised that the foregoing mappings are merely heuristics. They should not be mechanistically applied.

3   A Least Unique Bid Game Simulation

The least unique bid (LUB) game is generally played for charity fund raising purposes. Bids for a prize are solicited. All bids have to be paid over to the fund raising entity. Once bidding is closed, the bidder who has submitted the *least unique* bid wins the prize. If there is no unique least bid, then no prize is awarded.

The algorithmic task of finding the LUB of a given set of bid values is relatively straightforward. One approach is to sort the values, and then traverse the sorted values in ascending order until the first entry is found that differs from both its predecessor and its successor entries.

However, a simulation of the LUB game is to be developed that is more elaborate than merely computing the LUB of a given set of bid values. This simulation serves as a small case-study to illustrate the proposed CSP-based strategy for developing quality concurrent software. The simulation system's functional description is as follows:

- Several streams of independent random bids (representing, for example, random bids coming into a call centre) serve as input to a LUB calculator.
- The LUB calculator keeps track of the LUB (if it exists) with respect to all the bids it has received to date.
- Upon request from the user of the system, the LUB calculator returns the LUB most recently computed. If no LUB is present in the bids offered to date, it returns a special signal instead.

The system may be viewed abstractly as three interacting processes as loosely described below.   GEN generates random bids that are offered to LUB. LUB processes all the received bids and offers results to USER.

```
System = GEN  ||  LUB  ||  USER
```

4   Refining System Processes

The informal abstract of System given above glosses over several details. For example, it ignores the fact that the output from GEN derives from several streams of independent random bids. Neither does it indicate the specific operations that LUB has to carry out. Nor does it name channels connecting the processes.

Below, CSP_M will be used to describe the behaviour of each of the interacting processes of System. The CSP_M description will then be incrementally refined. The FDR system is used to ensure that the refinements are consistent. Once the refinements are sufficiently detailed to expose an overall system architecture and execution logic to allow for easy heuristic mapping to GO structures, then the system is further developed in GO.

4.1 Refining LUB

The CSP$_M$ defined process below, LUB1, is a first approximation description of LUB.

```
LUB1(in,out) =
 let
   RandOut(Bids) =  |~| b:Bids @ out!b -> P(Bids)
   P({}) = in?b -> P({b})
   P(Bids) = in?b -> P(union({b},Bids))
           [] RandOut(Bids)
 within
   P({})
```

Channel in acquires bids from its environment (represented above by GEN). Channel out offers bids to its environment (represented above by USER). The internal process P has a set parameter (initially the empty set) that describes the set of bids received to date. The built-in FDR function union is used to update this set parameter. Another internal process, RandOut, copies to the out channel a randomly selected member from the set of received Bids. To express this random selection, the internal choice operator, $|\sim|$, is distributed over multiple unnamed processes, each process outputting a different element of Bids.

Even though LUB1 is highly simplified—it does not even select a *unique* bid, let alone the *least* unique bid—it has the advantage of exposing the skeletal outline of what we hope will emerge as the final refined version of the CSP$_M$ specification for LUB.

LUB2 is our next iteration refinement of LUB1. It ensures that a bid emitted on the out channel is a random representative of the set of *unique* bids received to date on the in channel. It therefore accomplishes the task of isolating unique bids, but avoids the task of identifying the *least* unique bid.

```
LUB2(in, out) =
 let
   RandOut(UBids,Bids) =  |~|b:UBids @ out!b -> P(UBids,Bids)
   P({},{}) = in?b -> P({b},{b})
   P(Bids,{}) = in?b -> (if member(b,Bids) then P(Bids,{})
                         else P(union({b},Bids),{b}))
   P(Bids,UBids) =
        in?b -> (if member(b,Bids) then P(Bids,diff(UBids,{b}))
                 else P(union({b},Bids), union({b},UBids)))
   [] RandOut(UBids,Bids)
 within
   P({},{})
```

In order to keep track of unique bids, an internal process of LUB2, namely P, maintains *two* set parameters. The first, called Bids, is the set of received bids. The second, called UBids, is the set of unique bids received to date. Again built-in FDR functions, namely member, union and diff, are used to update these sets. The internal process, RandOut is modified to offer randomly selected members from the set of *unique* bids on the out channel.

LUB3 refines LUB2 so that the *least* of all unique bids is emitted upon request. Again, the same CSP_M structure as LUB2 can be retained. However, UBids is now maintained as a *sorted sequence* instead of as a set.

```
LUB3(in, out) =
  let
    P({},<>) = in?b -> P({b},<b>)
    P(Bids,<>) =
        in?b -> (if member(b,Bids) then P(Bids,<>)
                 else P(union({b}, Bids), <b>))
        [] out!Null -> P(Bids,<>)
    P(Bids,UBids) =
        in?b -> (if member(b,Bids) then P(Bids,remove(b,UBids))
                 else P(union({b}, Bids), insert(b,UBids)))
        [] out!head(UBids) -> P(Bids,UBids)
  within
    P({},<>)
```

The definition of P(Bids,UBids) achieves this by relying on two user-defined sequence functions, remove and insert (not reproduced here), instead of using the built-in set functions diff and union, respectively.

1. remove(b,UBids) returns the largest subsequence of UBids that excludes b.
2. insert(b,UBids) returns the smallest sorted super-sequence of UBids that includes b.

Furthermore, LUB3 no longer needs the internal function, RandOut. Instead, an FDR built-in sequence function, head, is used to offer the head of the sorted sequence UBids to a request on channel out.

Note that LUB3 returns Null on channel out if no LUB is present in bids processed to date. In contrast, LUB1 and LUB2 never offer a Null signal on the out channel. In this respect, LUB3 is not a strict refinement of LUB2 because it relies on an enriched alphabet for channel out.

However, the FDR tool affirms that LUB3 trace-refines LUB2 provided that the Null event is excluded from LUB3's traces. It also affirms that LUB2 trace-refines LUB1. It does so by verifying the following assertions:

```
assert LUB2(in, out) [T= LUB3(in,out)\{out.Null}
assert LUB1(in, out) [T= LUB2(in,out)
```

Note that the LUB processes above do note terminate. The matter of graceful process termination was ignored in the interests of clarity and brevity. LUB1T below shows how LUB1 may be changed to specify graceful termination upon receipt of a sentinel signal, End, received on the in channel, that is then relayed to the out channel before shutting down.

```
LUB1T(in,out) =
  let
    RandOut(Bids) =  |~| b:Bids @ out!b -> P(Bids)
      P({}) = in?b -> if b != End then P({b})
                          else out!End -> SKIP
      P(Bids) = in?b -> if b != End then P(union({b},Bids))
                            else out!End -> SKIP
                  [] RandOut(Bids)
  within
    P({})
```

Similar adaptations are easily made to the other LUB variants. These adaptations do not disturb any of the refinement arguments.

4.2 Refining GEN

A first approximation for a CSP$_M$ definition of GEN would be a process, GEN1, whose definition is substantially the same as that of RandOut that was defined locally in LUB1 above. However, instead of generating an infinite stream of random numbers from the interval Range, as does RandOut, GEN1 generates only Max such numbers and outputs them to the channel out. The process therefore has the parameters GEN1(Max,Range,out).

While such a process GEN1 produces what LUB3 expects from GEN—a stream of random bids on a single channel—the stated system requirement is that these bids should derive from *multiple independent streams*.

GEN2 is therefore defined as a refinement of GEN1. It can be modelled as a set of M independent instances of GEN1, collectively named as the process MGEN, each instance sending its output to a *multiplexing* buffer that we will call MBuff. Using Mchans to denote the set of channels connecting each instance of GEN1 with Buff, GEN2 and MGEN may be defined as follows:

```
GEN2 = MGEN [|{|Mchans|}|] MBuff(Size, Mchans, out)|\{|out|\}
MGEN = |||i:ID @ GEN1(Max, Range, Mchans.i)
```

Here ID = {1, ...M}, indicating that there are M instances of GEN1. The ith instance of GEN1 outputs on channel Mchans.i, an element of Mchans.

Note that the expression with the hide operator at the end of GEN2's definition, |\ {|out|}|, means that GEN2's traces only contain events that occur on

channel out—events occurring on channels Mchans.1...Mchans.M are hidden
when FDR generates a trace description of GEN2.

In the interests of brevity, the full definition of the multiplexing buffer, MBuff,
is not given here. It is an adaptation of a CSP$_M$ specification of a FIFO buffer that
may be found in [10]. The first parameter of MBuff indicates its size and the third
parameter is the single channel feeding bids to LUB3.

The FDR system affirms that the following two assertions are true:

```
assert GEN1(Max * M, Range, out) [FD= GEN2
assert GEN2 [FD= GEN1(Max * M, Range, out)
```

Thus, if an instance of GEN1 outputs to the same output channel as GEN2, and
generates Max * M random integers in the same range as the M subprocesses in
GEN2, and if the M subprocesses in GEN2 each generate Max random integers,
then those instances of GEN1 and GEN2 are trace-, failure- and divergent-equivalent
processes. This is in line with expectations.

4.3   Checking the System

The USER process can be modelled at various levels of detail. At its simplest, it
can be seen as a process that merely consumes everything sent to it. USER(in)
defined below is a slightly more elaborate model. It relies on a subtly defined local
process, P, consisting of the external choice between two unnamed processes. The
first receives input on channel in and then recurses to P but with its parameter
overwritten by the received input, y. The second engages in the event use.x, and
then recurses to P with no change in P's parameter. To start off, P is parameterised
as Null.

```
USER(in) =
  let
    P(x) = in?y:Range -> P(y) [] use.x -> P(x)
  within
    P(Null)
```

Rather than connecting the USER process directly to LUB3, a standard FIFO
buffer, BUFF(Cap,in,out) (as defined in [10]) between them will temporarily
store the output from LUB3 until USER is ready to consume it. The buffer's
parameters indicate its capacity, its input channel and its output channel. The overall
system can therefore be modelled as follows in FDR.

```
System =
  (((GEN2 [|{|in|}|] LUB3(in,out))
           [|{|out|}|] BUFF(UserMax,out,uin))
           [|{|uin|}|] USER(uin))
```

Here, GEN2's output channel, named out in its definition above, should be renamed to in and serve as the input channel to LUB3 whose output is placed on channel out. The buffer, whose capacity is designated UserMax, receives its input from channel out and offers its data to USER on the channel parameterised here as uin.

The first two assert statements below verified that the system is deadlock and divergence (livelock) free. Subsystem1 in the third assert statement refers to the concurrent interaction of the LUB3, BUFF and USER processes. This assert statement verifies that if we remove the nondeterministic bid generators in GEN2, then the remainder of the system behaves deterministically.

```
assert System  : [deadlock-free]
assert System  : [divergence-free]
assert Subsystem1 : [deterministic]
```

The foregoing has presented *some* of the CSP_M specifications that we developed and tested. When we judged that the CSP_M models had reached a sufficient level of refinement maturity, and given us sufficient insight into the solution approaches, we used the specifications together with the heuristics mentioned in Sect. 2.3 as a guide to evolve a GO implementation.

5 Implementation

The overall architecture of System as specified in CSP_M is visualised in Fig. 2. It was carried over as the basic architecture for the GO implementation, making adaptations appropriate for the GO environment.

The CSP_M LUB subprocess was mapped to a corresponding GO function and then launched as a goroutine from within GO's main program. Two different versions were considered, for reasons explained below. The CSP_M USER subprocess was implemented as final code of GO's main process.

Instead of a separate GO process matching the CSP_M BUFF process that buffers messages from the out channel to the uin channel, the GO processes implementing LUB and USER are linked by a single buffered GO channel.

In the GO implementation, GEN2 does not exist as an explicit goroutine. Its functionality was realised by mapping the CSP_M subprocess GEN1 to a GO function,

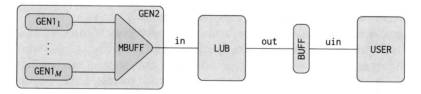

Fig. 2 Diagram of System

Gen1, and then launching multiple instances of Gen1 as separate goroutines from within a loop of Go's main program. All Gen1 goroutines output to the *same* buffered channel. That channel, in turn, is used for input by the Go implementation of the LUB process. The CSP_M multiplexing buffer process, MBUFF, is therefore redundant in the Go implementation.

The parameters of Gen1 specify, *inter alia*, the number of integers to be generated, the range within which they should fall, and the channel to which they should be sent. Based on these parameters, Gen1 generates and outputs random integer values from a given uniform distribution. Between every generation of a random number, the function sleeps for a short period.

The two different Go versions of the LUB process were Lub3 and Lub4 respectively. Lub3 corresponds to the previously given CSP_M process LUB3. Lub4 corresponds to a CSP_M process, LUB4, whose specification—though omitted above in the interests of brevity—had been verified to be a trace refinement of LUB3.

In accordance with our heuristics, Lub3 was implemented using a select statement that has two cases: one for receiving a new bid; and another for emitting the current LUB on the output channel. Note that the Lub3 implementation does indeed conform to Sect. 3's requirement that, upon request from the user of the system it is to return the most recently computed LUB. However, it would fail to meet a more stringent requirement, namely that the USER process should be able to record *every* LUB value as the sequence of bids evolves over time.

The Lub4 process meets this requirement by requesting a new bid from its inbound channel only *after* not only processing the previous bid, but also communicating the resulting LUB to its outbound channel. An outline of Lub4's implementation is given in lines 1–22 of Fig. 3. The for-loop header in line 3 reads a bid from the input channel, in, and lines 4–15 of the loop's body update local data structures (bids and ubids) according to the logic already worked out in the CSP_M specification. Lines 16–20 emit resulting LUB information on the out channel.

The for construct of line 3 allows for simple but graceful termination of Lub4. When all the GEN1 processes have terminated, an anonymous goroutine-(see below) is prompted to close the in channel. The for loop is exited (at line 22) if and only if the buffer of channel in is both empty *and* the channel has been closed. Code in the omitted sections (line 2) ensures that channel out will be closed before Lub4 terminates.

The main function of the Go program sets up the process network and dispatches the goroutines. It is shown in lines 24–44 of Fig. 3.

Lines 28–31 show the launching of multiple instances of the Gen1 function, all parameterised to send output to the same channel, namely bids.

Line 34 launches an anonymous function as a goroutine. Without showing the details of this code, we note that its task is to close the bids channel when all Gen1 processes have shut down. The Lub3 implementation requires a modification in this function so that it receives a sentinel from this process, sends the sentinel downstream and then terminates.

```
1    func Lub4(in <-chan int, out chan<- int) {
2       ...
3       for bid := range in {
4          if ubids.Len() <= 0 { // No unique bid
5             if bids.Contains(bid) {// Change nothing
6             } else {
7                bids.Insert(bid); ubids.Insert(bid)
8             }
9          } else { // At least one unique bid
10            if bids.Contains(bid) {
11               ubids.Remove(bid)
12            } else {
13               bids.Insert(bid); ubids.Insert(bid)
14            }
15         }
16         if ubids.Len() <= 0 {
17            out <- NULL
18         } else {
19            out <- ubids.GetHead()
20         }
21      }
22   }
23
24   func main() {
25      // Instantiate channels.
26      bids := make(chan int, 10); clubs := make(chan int, 10)
27      ...
28      for i := 0; i < GENS; i++ { // Start all instances of Gen1.
29         wg.Add(1)
30         go Gen1(bids, BIDSPERGEN, LOW, HIGH, rng, &wg)
31      }
32
33      // Close channel bids when all Gen1 instances terminate
34      go func(w *sync.WaitGroup) {...}
35
36      go Lub4(bids, clubs) // Start the LUB process.
37
38      // The USER process.
39      for current := range clubs { // Receive a LUB
40         fmt.Println(current) // Use a LUB
41      }
42   }
```

Fig. 3 Extracts of Go code

Line 36 launches Lub4 using bids and club as the actual parameters for Lub4's formal parameters in and out respectively.

Lines 38–41 implement the CSP_M USER process's functionality. The for-loop reads repeatedly from channel clubs and then sends out the received data to the console. When Lub4 closes clubs and its buffer is cleared, then the loop, and consequently also main, terminate.

6   Results

Though the Go implementation described above is no more than a prototype for a more comprehensive simulator for the LUB game, it can already be deployed to discover characteristics of the game of potential interest to someone wanting to use it for fund generation.

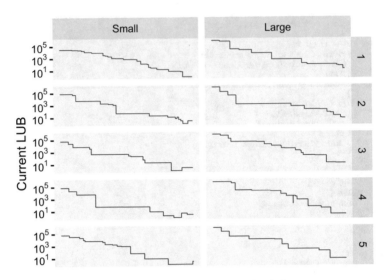

Fig. 4 LUBs over time for five runs for two scenarios of the simulation

As an example of its use, we carried out an experiment to find out how the LUB varies over time as the number of random bids increases. Ten `Gen1` goroutines, each generating 10^5 bids, were launched. Two scenarios dubbed 'Small' and 'Large', respectively, were considered. For the 'Small' scenario, random values were drawn from the interval $[1; 10^5)$ and for the 'Large' scenario the interval was $[1; 10^6)$. In each case, `Lub4` was used to determine the LUBs. Figure 4 shows graphs of the results of five runs of the implementation for the two respective scenarios.

The graphs neatly illustrate that, while the LUB tends to decline as increasingly more bids come in, the decline is not always monotonic. The graphs also show that the possibility of the LUB increasing is greater under the 'Small' scenario than under the 'Large'.

Clearly, similar experiments could investigate the impact of random data that is not drawn from a uniform distribution, different intervals could be used, expected income for different modes of charging for bids could be computed, etc. Such information could be used for decision support with respect to the size of the prize on offer, the expected amount of income to generate, etc.

7   Reflections

It is well-known that "...errors generate significant software development costs if their resolution requires system redesign..." [17]. The risk of needing to redesign a system will be mitigated by using a specification language to articulate, analyse and explore different architectural solutions before committing to an implementation in code. That, at least, has been the assumption underlying the work described here and elsewhere.

In order to *effectively* support such analysis and exploration in the context of *concurrent* software development, the specification language has to be able to express the notions of concurrent processes and their interactions. For the language to do so *efficiently*, it has to allow for abstraction away from irrelevant details. But there is a certain tension between expressiveness and abstraction: too much abstraction might elide over relevant details; too much expression of detail risks bogging the user down in time-consuming matters better addressed during implementation. Language support for refinement is intended to provide a structured pathway from an efficiently produced abstract specification to a more effective concrete specification.

In previous work [13–15], we used CSP to derive appropriate software architectural specifications, and then mapped the specifications to Go implementations. However, in the interests of efficiency, we used CSP in an informal, *lightweight* fashion. This meant that we ignored specification details such as types and ranges; where needed, we simply assumed the existence of utility functions instead of specifying their details; refinements were informal and were made *in situ*, as it were, by simply overwriting parts of an earlier version of a specification until we deemed it to be sufficiently detailed; etc. Even so, this approach to *efficiently* (ab)using CSP proved to be sufficiently *effective* for our purposes in that context.

The present study represents our first practical exposure to FDR. For this reason we chose an illustrative problem of limited scope for study. Although this limits the inferences we can draw from using the tool, we nevertheless consider that some valuable lessons have been learned, both in regard to the advantages of specification prior to implementation in general, and in regard to perceived strengths and weaknesses of FDR.

Unsurprisingly, FDR requires attention to details that we previously ignored. For example, precise type and range specifications are needed for variables. In previous exercises, we would simply assume that utility functions such as `insert` and `remove` exist (for inserting a value into its sorted position in a sequence or removing a value from a sequence) and reference them in a specification; in FDR, we had to write (and therefore also debug) such functions. In return for this additional effort, FDR allowed us to automatically verify assertions about refinements, deadlock freedom and divergence freedom. While the value-add of being able to automate these verifications might not be particularly spectacular for our relatively small problem, being able to do this for larger problems could be very useful indeed.

An important prerequisite for successfully evaluating these FDR assertions was to ensure that the state space to be searched was kept sufficiently small. For example, we verified that the system is deadlock-free if there are three independent bid generators, each generating exactly two random bids, and we inductively infer that `SYSTEM` is generally deadlock free for any number of generators and bids. It is not self-evident that such inductive inferences are *always* valid. Furthermore, we found that FDR rapidly overloads as the problem size increases. The question of how well

FDR would scale up in the face of a much larger "industrial scale" problems is an issue that requires further investigation.

What has been our constant experience, though, is that the intellectual effort put into articulating a system in CSP (whether or not for subsequent FDR analysis) offers significant returns: relevant processes and their interactions are identified, leading to an inherently modular architecture; various potential problems and pitfalls in the actual implementation may be suggested; alternative architectural or algorithmic possibilities may suggest themselves; the need to reformulate the initial functional specification might be realised; etc. Here is a non-exhaustive list of some such fruitful ideas that arose while developing the CSP_M specifications for the current problem:

- The need for a modular pipelined architectural structure having a multiplexed FIFO buffering function between GEN and LUB was apparent from the start. However, the need for a FIFO buffer between LUB and USER was unanticipated, emerging only when we revised the functional specification.
- The initial impulse for finding the LUB of an incoming data stream was to maintain a list of received values in ascending sorted order, and to traverse the list from the bottom upwards whenever a LUB is requested. While refining LUB1, an innovative notion came to mind: store on separate lists a *single exemplar* of each bid received, as well a list of each *unique* bid received. For each new bid, update both these lists appropriately. LUB3 then introduced a further refinement of maintaining the unique bid list in ascending order so that its head is, by default, the LUB. (Note that LUB3 left as an implementation detail the decision about whether or not to maintain the list of received bids in ascending order.)
- While contemplating the LUB3 solution, the question naturally arose: what if we wanted to capture *every* LUB generated during a simulation? This led to a change in functional requirements as well as to the formulation of LUB4 and implementation of its counterpart in GO, Lub4. The implementation example in Sect. 5 illustrated the interesting information that could be gleaned from this change in functional specification.
- While specifying LUB at various refinement levels, the matter of graceful termination also naturally arose. The specification of LUB1T and its refinements indicated one approach, subsequently implemented by relying on a sentinel. In the case of Lub4, a for...range loop provided a neat implementation solution.

Our collective experience in using CSP and FDR (only partially outlined above) provides *prima facie* evidence to support the incorporation of an early phase of abstract specification in a comprehensive concurrent software development methodology. In some circumstances, CSP used in lightweight fashion appears as a suitable candidate for such specification. Elsewhere there are claims that "FDR has made a significant impact ...across industrial domains, such as high-tech manufacturing, telecommunications, aerospace, and defence"[3]. Yet others report on the benefits of generating CSP traces for test cases in the software development life-cycle [1].

Notwithstanding such evidence, it would be difficult to prove empirically to a cynic that the benefits attributed to the use of CSP would not accrue in any case, even if a hack-and-attack approach has been taken to writing the software. A meta-study to settle such issues would be valuable.

References

1. Gustavo Carvalho et al. "NAT2TEST tool: From natural language requirements to test cases based on CSP". In: *Software Engineering and Formal Methods* Springer, 2015, pp. 283–290.
2. Thomas Gibson-Robinson et al. "FDR: From Theory to Industrial Application". In: *Concurrency Security and Puzzles: Essays Dedicated to Andrew William Roscoe on the Occasion of His 60th Birthday* Ed. by Thomas Gibson-Robinson, Philippa Hopcroft, and Ranko Lazić Cham: Springer International Publishing, 2017, pp. 65–87. ISBN: 978-3-319-51046-0. DOI: 10.1007/978-3-319-51046-0_4. URL: https://doi.org/10.1007/978-3-319-51046-0_4
3. Thomas Gibson-Robinson et al. "FDR3 — A Modern Refinement Checker for CSP". In: *Tools and Algorithms for the Construction and Analysis of Systems*. Ed. by Erika Ábrahám and Klaus Havelund. Vol. 8413. Lecture Notes in Computer Science. 2014, pp. 187–201.
4. Hassan Gommaa. *Software Design Methods for Concurrent and Real-Time Systems* Addison-Wesley Professional, 1993.
5. C. A. R. Hoare. *Communicating Sequential Processes*. Ed. by Jim Davis. (Electronic version). 2004. URL: http://www.usingcsp.com/cspbook.pdf (visited on 09/16/2016).
6. C. A. R. Hoare. "Communicating sequential processes". In: *Communications of the ACM* 26.1 (1983), pp. 100–106.
7. J. Magee and J. Kramer. *Concurrency: State models and Java Programs*. 2nd ed. John Wiley, 2006.
8. Susan Owicki and David Gries. "An axiomatic proof technique for parallel programs I". In: *Acta Informatica* 6.4 (Dec. 1976), pp. 319–340. ISSN: 1432-0525. DOI: 10.1007/BF00268134. URL: https://doi.org/10.1007/BF00268134.
9. Carl G. Ritson and Peter H. Welch. "A Process-Oriented Architecture for Complex System Modelling". In: *Concurrency and Computation: Practice and Experience* 22 (Mar. 2010), pp. 182–196. DOI: 10.1002/cpe.1433 URL: http://wwwcs.kent.acuk/pubs/2010/3066.
10. A. W. Roscoe. *Understanding Concurrent Systems*. 1st. New York, NY, USA: Springer Verlag New York, Inc., 2010. ISBN: 9781848822573.
11. Marlene Maria Ross. "Unity-inspired object-oriented concurrent system development". PhD thesis. University of Pretoria, 2001.
12. Adam T. Sampson. "Process-oriented Patterns for Concurrent Software Engineering". D.Phil thesis. University of Kent, 2008.
13. Marthinus David Strauss. "Process-based Decomposition and Multicore Performance: Case Studies from Stringology". PhD thesis. University of Pretoria, 2017.
14. Tinus Strauss et al. "A Process-Oriented Implementation of Brzozowski's DFA Construction Algorithm". In: *Proceedings of the Prague Stringology Conference 2014, Prague Czech Republic, September 1–3, 2014*. Ed. by Jan Holub and Jan Zdárek. Department of Theoretical Computer Science, Faculty of Information Technology, Czech Technical University in Prague, 2014, pp. 17–29. ISBN: 978-80-01-05547-2.
15. Tinus Strauss et al. "Process-Based Aho-Corasick Failure Function Construction". In: *Communicating Process Architectures 2015. Proceedings of the 37th WoTUG Technical Meeting 23–26 August 2015, University of Kent, UK*. Ed. by Kevin Chalmers et al. Open Channel Publishing Ltd., 2015, pp. 183–206. ISBN: 0993438504. URL: http://wotug.org/cpa2015/programme.shtml.

16. Peter H. Welch and Jan B. Pedersen. "Santa Claus: Formal Analysis of a Process-oriented Solution". In: *ACM Transactions on Programming Languages and Systems* 32.4 (Apr 2010), 14:1–14:37. ISSN: 0164-0925. DOI: 1.1145/1734206.1734211 URL: http://doi.acm.org/10.1145/1734206.1734211.
17. J. Christopher Westland. "The cost of errors in software development: evidence from industry". In: *Journal of Systems and Software* 62 (2002), pp. 1–9.

Modular Verification Scopes via Export Sets and Translucent Exports

K. Rustan M. Leino and Daniel Matichuk

Abstract Following software engineering best practices, programs are divided into modules to facilitate information hiding. A variety of programming-language constructs provide ways to define a module and to classify which of its declarations are private to the module and which are available to public clients of the module.

Many declarations can be viewed as consisting of a signature and a body. For such a declaration, a module may want to export just the signature or both the signature and body. This translucency is particularly useful when formally verifying a program, because it lets a module decide how much of a declaration clients are allowed to depend on.

This article describes a module system that supports multiple export sets per module. Each export set indicates the translucency of its exported declarations. The module system is implemented as part of the verification-aware programming language Dafny. Experience with the module system suggests that translucency is useful.

1 Introduction

Software engineers constantly have to manage the complexity of the software they are writing. One fundamental principle to follow is to try to isolate different pieces of functionality and to limit the interfaces to the details of that functionality [9]. Programming languages provide various features for such *information hiding*, for example, procedures that separate the what from the how, and classes and modules that hide both implementations and internal state.

K. R. M. Leino
Amazon Web Services, Seattle, WA, USA
e-mail: leino@amazon.com

D. Matichuk (✉)
Data61 CSIRO, Canberra, ACT, Australia
e-mail: daniel.matichuk@data61.csiro.au

© Springer Nature Switzerland AG 2018
P. Müller, I. Schaefer (eds.), *Principled Software Development*,
https://doi.org/10.1007/978-3-319-98047-8_12

When doing verification of software, the concerns are similar. But for verification, the concerns go deeper than the concerns involved during compilation or type checking. A compiler needs to know about the existence of certain methods and other declarations in a module interface, and a type checker additionally needs to know the type signatures of such declarations. For verification, a module interface may choose to either reveal or keep hidden a part of the definition of a declaration. For example, it makes a difference if the verifier is able to use the body of a function or just the signature and specification of the function. So, there is a need for finer-granularity control of information hiding during verification.

In this paper, we motivate and explain the design of the module system in the verification-aware programming language Dafny [4, 5]. Conspicuous among various influences on the design are ML [6] and Modula-3 [8]. One of the contributions is the way our module system lets exported declarations be either "provided" or "revealed". Another contribution is the working implementation of the module system, which has now been in use for a couple of years.

While the module system provides considerable flexibility, one of our design goals was to keep simple things simple. Our presentation also follows that format, starting off with the obvious features and moving into the more advanced.

Finding ways to write modular specifications of programs, so that one can reason about the programs modularly, has been one of the research agendas of Arnd Poetzsch-Heffter (e.g., [7, 10–12]). It is therefore our privilege to contribute this article in the Festschrift honoring Arnd Poetzsch-Heffter.

2 Preliminaries

We start by explaining the names introduced in modules and how modules can refer to names declared in other modules.

2.1 Modules and Imports

A rudimentary chore that a module system helps with is organizing the names of declarations in a program. Consider the following two modules.

```
module A {
  type S = set<char>
}
module B {
  function S(x: int): int {
    x + 1
  }
}
```

Each of these modules introduces a declaration S, in A being a type synonym for sets of characters and in B being a successor function on the integers. To make use of these modules, a client module, say C, has to import them.

```
module C {
  import A
  import B
  function CardPlusOne(s: A.S): int {
    B.S(|s|)
  }
}
```

With the fully qualified names A.S and B.S, there is no ambiguity as to what they are referring to.

A module that imports another can pick a new local name to refer to the imported module. This lets modules have long, meaningful names while clients can choose abbreviations. To illustrate, the following module D introduces the local name M to refer to the imported library MathLibrary.

```
module MathLibrary {
  function Abs(x: int): nat {
    if x < 0 then -x else x
  }
}
module D {
  import M = MathLibrary
  function AbsDiff(m: int, n: int): nat {
    M.Abs(m - n)
  }
}
```

In fact, the import declarations in module C above are abbreviations for import declarations that use as the local name the same name as the imported module. That is, import A is simply an abbreviation for import A = A.

2.2 Nested Modules

Modules can be nested. The enclosing module refers to the declarations in the nested module in the same way as for an imported module. It is also possible to import a nested module, which provides the dubious pleasure of giving it an alias.

```
module Outer {
  module Inner {
    type T = int
  }
```

```
import I = Inner
function Double(x: I.T): Inner.T {
  2 * x
}
}
```

The names `Inner.T` and `I.T` refer to the same declaration (and since that declaration is a type synonym, both of those qualified names refer to the type `int`).

As we have seen, a module can import "sibling modules", that is, modules declared at the same level of lexical nesting. However, it is never possible for a nested module to refer to the enclosing module itself. This makes a module blissfully unaware of how deeply nested it is, giving it a kind of contextual independence.

Just like a declaration of a function or type, an `import` declaration also introduces a new name. And like the names of other declarations, such a name has to be unique. The name of the import can be used in prefixes of qualified names, as the following example illustrates:

```
module G {
  type T = string
}
module H {
  import HereComesG = G
}
module I {
  import H
  function WelcomeString(): H.HereComesG.T {
    "greetings"
  }
}
```

The qualified name `H.HereComesG.T` gives `I` a way to refer to the type `T` declared in `G`. But since `I` does not import `G` directly, the qualified name `G.T` is not defined in `I`.

As a final example of playing around with names, note that the right-hand side of an `import` declaration can be a qualified name, provided that, as for all qualified names, each part of the prefix is defined.

```
module J {
  import H
  import GG = H.HereComesG
  function FarewellString(): GG.T {
    "this has gone on for too long"
  }
}
```

In other words, without the `import H`, the import declaration that refers to H in its right-hand side would not be legal.

2.3 Imports Are Acyclic

We define an *import relation* on modules. A module X is related to a module Y in the import relation if X contains an import declaration whose right-hand side designates Y. This relation is in general not transitive, but it has to be acyclic, which is enforced by the compiler or linker.

2.4 Opened Imports

Since an import declaration can introduce any local name for an imported module, qualified names don't have to get too long. However, there are situations where even two extra characters (like M.) feel too long. In those cases, which should be kept to a minimum, it is possible to import a module as opened. This causes the names of the imported module to be poured into the set of names declared directly by the importing module. Almost. The names declared directly in the importing module get preference over any opened-imported names. Furthermore, names of different opened-imported declarations are allowed to overlap, but trying to refer to them generates an error.

For illustration, consider the following modules.

```
module K {
  function Fib(n: nat): nat {
    if n < 2 then n else Fib(n-2) + Fib(n-1)
  }
  const G := 9.81
  function U(x: int): int {
    x | 2
  }
}
module L {
  function U(x: int): int {
    x - 2
  }
}
module N {
  import opened LocalNameForK = K
  import opened L
  function G(n: nat): nat {
    Fib(n) + LocalNameForK.Fib(n)
  }
  function H(): nat {
    G(12)   // G refers to the local function G,
            //      not to LocalNameForK.G
```

```
    }
    function V(): int {
        L.U(50)
    }
}
```

Module N imports K and L under the local names LocalNameForK and L, respectively. Both of the imports are opened, so the names declared in those modules are also available in N without qualification. Consequently, both the unqualified and qualified mention of Fib in function G are legal and refer to the Fib function declared in module K. Using the unqualified name G in N refers to the function declared in N, not to the constant G defined in K, since locally declared names are preferred over opened-imported names. Finally, it is not an error to opened-import both K and L, despite the fact that both of them declare a name U. However, an attempt to refer to U without a qualification (e.g., by changing L.U to just U in function V) would result in an "ambiguous name" error.

By preferring local names over opened-imported names and allowing duplicate opened-imported names as long as these are not referred to without qualification, our module design remains true to the motto that "declarations are unordered" in Dafny. This is in contrast to, for example, ML-based languages, which resolve similar ambiguities by ordering imports.

3   Export Sets and Translucency

So far, the set of names introduced in a module has been available indiscriminately to any importer. This does not promote the use of information hiding. To make it possible to limit what an importing module gets to know, Dafny makes use of *export sets*. In its simplest form, an export set lets a module indicate which of its names are available to importers. This makes it easy to encode the common idiom that categorizes declarations as being either *public* (that is, available to importers) or *private* (that is, for internal use only) to a module.

3.1   Export Sets

A module uses an export declaration to make manifest which declarations are available to importers. For example:

```
module M {
    export
        reveals F
    function F(x: int): int { x + 1 }
```

```
  function G(x: int): int { x - 1 }
}
module Client {
  import M
  function H(x: int): int {
    M.F(x) + M.G(x)   // error: unresolved identifier: G
  }
}
```

As indicated by the `reveals` clause of M's `export` declaration, only one of M's two functions (F) is revealed to importers. In general, the `reveals` clause contains a list of names. Analogously to the use of other kinds of clauses in Dafny, an `export` declaration can have several `reveals` clauses, with the same meaning as concatenating their lists of names into just one `reveals` clause.

An export set must be *self-consistent*. The essential idea is that if you project the module's declarations onto those that are exported, then all symbols must still resolve and type check. This is most easily understood through an example.

```
module BadExportSet {
  export
    reveals T, Inc, Identity
  type U = T
  type T = int
  function Inc(x: T): T { x + 1 }
  function Identity(x: U): U { x }
    // error: U undeclared in export set
}
```

This module is not self-consistent, because it attempts to reveal function `Identity` while keeping private the type U, which appears in the function's signature. The projection of BadExportSet onto its export set would look like:

```
module BadExportSet {
    // projection of the module onto its export set
  type T = int
  function Inc(x: T): T { x + 1 }
  function Identity(x: U): U { x }
}
```

It is clear from this projection that the export set was not self-consistent, since U is nowhere declared.

3.2   Translucent Exports

Even export declarations with selectively revealed declarations can give away more information than intended to importers. This is because most declarations can be considered to have two parts. For example, a function has a signature and a body. A `reveals` clause that mentions a function reveals both the signature and body of that function to importers. Dafny's `export` declarations also have `provides` clauses. Mentioning a function in a `provides` clause provides only the signature, not the body, of the function to importers.

For the purpose of export sets, we think of every Dafny declaration as having a *signature* part and a *body* part. Together, the signature and body parts make up the entire declaration. What is included in the signature part depends on what kind of declaration it is. For a function, the signature part includes the function's name, its type signature (that is, its type parameters, the in-parameters and their types, and the result type), and the function's specification (that is, its pre- and postcondition and its frame specification). For a type declaration, the signature part is the name of the type, its type parameters (including any variance annotations), and any type *characteristics* that can be declared (e.g., supports equality, contains no references). For a constant, the signature is the name and type of the constant, but not its defining expression. For a method or a lemma, the signature includes the name, its type signature (type parameters, in- and out-parameters and their types), and its specification.

The following example shows a mix of `provides` and `reveals` clauses.

```
module Accumulator {
  export
    provides T, Zero, Add, Get, Behavior
    reveals GetAndAdd
  datatype T = Nil | Cons(int, T)
  function Zero(): T {
    Nil
  }
  function Add(t: T, x: int): T {
    Cons(x, t)
  }
  function Get(t: T): int {
    match t
    case Nil => 0
    case Cons(x, tail) => x + Get(tail)
  }
  function GetAndAdd(t: T, x: int): (int, T) {
    (Get(t), Add(t, x))
  }
  lemma Behavior(t: T, x: int)
    ensures Get(Zero()) == 0
```

```
    ensures Get(Add(t, x)) == x + Get(t)
  {
    // proof follows trivially from the function
    definitions
  }
}
```

Again, the export set has to be self-consistent. The projection of module Accumulator onto its export set looks like this:

```
module Accumulator {  // projection of the module onto
    its export set
  type T
  function Zero(): T
  function Add(t: T, x: int): T
  function Get(t: T): int
  function GetAndAdd(t: T, x: int): (int, T) {
    (Get(t), Add(t, x))
  }
  lemma Behavior(t: T, x: int)
    ensures Get(Zero()) == 0
    ensures Get(Add(t, x)) == x + Get(t)
}
```

In this projection, we have indicated that T is exported as an opaque type—the fact that it denotes a datatype and has a certain list of constructors is kept private to the module. To an importing module, functions Zero, Add, and Get are just arbitrary functions. By calling lemma Behavior, an importer learns some properties of these functions, but the importer has no way to prove these properties directly. In this way, this lemma serves as an exported contract of the otherwise opaque functions.

By only providing, not revealing, type T, the Accumulator module retains the ability to change the representation of the type without affecting any clients. For example, the module can replace its declarations of T, Zero, Add, and Get by

```
type T = int
function Zero(): T { 0 }
function Add(t: T, x: int): T { t + x }
function Get(t: T): int { t }
```

or by

```
type T = int
function Zero(): T { 3 }
function Add(t: T, x: int): T { t + 2 * x }
function Get(t: T): int { (t - 3) / 2 }
```

without having to reverify any modules that import Accumulator.

Unlike the other declarations in `Accumulator`, function `GetAndAdd` is revealed in the export set. This means that the function's behavior is fully known to any exporter. For example, this lets an importer prove assertions like

```
assert Accumulator.Get(t) == Accumulator.GetAndAdd(t, 5).0;
```

In Dafny, the verifier always reasons about calls to methods and lemmas in terms of their specifications, never in terms of their bodies. Thus, there would be no difference between providing and revealing a method or lemma in an export set, so we decided to reduce confusion by disallowing methods and lemmas from being mentioned in `reveals` clauses (accompanied by a useful error message, of course).

Similarly, a name introduced by an `import` declaration can only be provided in an export set, not revealed.

If a declaration happens to be mentioned in both a `reveals` clause and a `provides` clause, it is the same as just revealing it. That is, the export set is like a set of declaration signature parts and declaration body parts, so the export set is the union of all of the parts added on behalf of `reveals` and `provides` clauses.

An export declaration can use the clause `provides` *, which is a shorthand for providing all declarations in the module. Similarly, the clause `reveals` * is a shorthand for revealing all declarations in the module that can be revealed and providing the rest (that is, `reveal` * provides methods, since methods cannot be revealed).

3.3 Effect of Import Aliases in Export Sets

Export sets are only allowed to mention names declared in the module itself. For example,

```
module P {
    type T = int
}
module Q {
    export
        provides P
        reveals U, V
    import opened P
    import R = P
    type U = P.T
    type V = T
}
```

is allowed, but adding `T` or `P.T` to either of the export clauses would not be allowed. Note that `T` cannot be exported, despite the fact that the opened import allows it to be mentioned unqualified inside Q. Stated differently, by marking an import as `opened`, the ability to mention the imported declarations as unqualified is not inherited by further importers.

Furthermore, neither U nor V could be revealed if the export set didn't provide P. More precisely, module Q declares three aliases to the module P, namely P and R and the opened-import alias. The self-consistency check is not performed textually, but uses these import aliases. Therefore, it is more correct to say that neither U nor V could be revealed if Q's export set didn't provide some alias for the module where T (which is mentioned in the body parts of U and V) is declared. So, module Q would still be fine if `provides` P were replaced by `provides` R.

3.4 Default Export Set

If a module does not contain any `export` declaration, everything is revealed as an export. This makes it simple to start learning about modules and imports, like we did in Sect. 2 before we had mentioned the `export` declaration. In other words, without any explicit `export` declaration, Dafny acts as if the module had been declared with

```
export
  reveals *
```

As soon as a module gives some `export` declaration, only what is explicitly exported is made available to importers. This makes it easy to go from the implicit "everything is revealed" to an explicit "nothing is revealed": simply add the empty export declaration

```
export
```

That is, one keyword is all it takes.

4   Multiple Export Sets

Not all importers are alike. For instance, in some cases, a module may have some declarations that all users will want to know about, whereas some others are useful for companion modules, so-called *friends* modules. To support this, Dafny allows a module to have multiple export sets, each providing its own *view* of the module.

4.1 Named Export Sets

The following module defines two export sets, named `Public` and `Friends`.

```
module R {
  export Public
    provides Combine
  export Friends
    reveals Combine
  function Combine(x: set<int>, y: set<int>): set<int> {
    x + y - (x * y)
  }
}
```

The export set `Friends` reveals the signature and body of function `Combine`, whereas the export set `Public` only provides the signature of `Combine`. Hence, an importer of the `Public` view of the module is not able to verify an assertion like

```
assert R.Combine({2,3}, {3,5}) == {2,5};
```

whereas an importer of the `Friends` view is.

Each export set is checked separately to be self-consistent.

4.2 Importing a Named Export Set

When a module has several export sets, an importer indicates which export set to import by appending to the module name a back-tick and the name of the desired set. Here are two such client modules:

```
module R_PublicClient {
  import R = R`Public
  lemma Test() {
    assert R.Combine({2,3}, {3,5}) == {2,5};
      // error: not provable here
  }
}
module R_FriendClient {
  import R`Friends
  lemma Test() {
    assert R.Combine({2,3}, {3,5}) == {2,5};
  }
}
```

Note that if the local name for the module is omitted, it defaults to the name of the module, without the name of the selected export set. That is, `import R`Friends` is the same as `import R = R`Friends`.

The back-tick notation is not new to import declarations in Dafny. Dafny uses the back-tick notation in a similar way in frame specifications, where an expression denoting one or a set of objects can be further restricted to a field of that object or objects. Dafny borrows this use of back-tick in frame specifications from Region Logic [1]

4.3 *Eponymous Export Sets*

When an `export` declaration omits a name, as in all of our examples before Sect. 4, then it defaults to the name of the module itself. This eponymous export set is also what gets imported if an `import` declaration omits the back-tick and the export-set name. While most modules tend to have an eponymous export set, there is no requirement to have one. For example, module R above does not have an eponymous export set.

4.4 *Example*

A common idiom is to use the eponymous export set to stand for the most common view of the module. This means that most importers only need to mention the imported module in their `import` statement—no need for a back-tick and a specific export-set name. Any additional export sets are then given names.

For example, module `Accumulator` in Sect. 3.2 defined an export set:

```
export
  provides T, Zero, Add, Get, Behavior
  reveals GetAndAdd
```

It can also define a `Friends` view that reveals how the type `T` is represented:

```
export Friends
  provides Zero, Add, Behavior
  reveals T, Get, GetAndAdd
```

Using the `Friends` view, a new module can augment the `Accumulator` functionality, like this:

```
module AccumulatorMore {
  export
    provides A, Mul, Behavior
  import A = Accumulator
```

```
  import Acc = Accumulator`Friends
  function Mul(t: Acc.T, c: int): Acc.T {
    match t
    case Nil => Acc.Nil
    case Cons(x, tail) => Acc.Cons(c * x, Mul(tail, c))
  }
  lemma Behavior(t: Acc.T, c: int)
    ensures Acc.Get(Mul(t, c)) == c * Acc.Get(t)
  {
  }
}
```

This module needs to know the full definition of T to implement `Mul` and needs to know the full definition of `Get` to prove the lemma about `Mul`. Therefore, it imports the `Friends` view of `Accumulator`. To be self-consistent, the module's export set must provide a way to understand the type `Acc.T`, which appears in the signatures of the provided declarations `Mul` and `Behavior`. Adding `Acc` to the `provides` clause would make the export set self-consistent. However, this would provide all `AccumulatorMore` clients with the information entailed by the `Friends` view of `Accumulator` (e.g., the full definition of `T`), which results in less information hiding than desired. Therefore, module `AccumulatorMore` also declares an import for the eponymous export set of `Accumulator`, here with the local name A. Providing A instead of `Acc` in the export set makes it self-consistent without passing on any of the `Accumulator` information that only friends need.

Here is a module that uses both the original and augmented functionality of `Accumulator`:

```
module AccTest {
  import A = Accumulator
  import M = AccumulatorMore
  lemma Test() {
    var z := A.Zero();
    var e := A.Add(z, 8);
    A.Behavior(z, 8);
    M.Behavior(e, 3);
    assert A.Get(M.Mul(e, 3)) == 24;
  }
}
```

A module decides which export sets to define and which parts of which declarations to include in these export sets. However, the module does not control where these export sets can be imported. That is, unlike in C++ [2], where a class defines which other classes are its "friends", the export sets in Dafny are more like the "friends interfaces" in Modula-3 [8], where each importer gets to decide whether or not it is a friend.

4.5 Combinations of Export Sets

If a module imports several views of a module, it obtains the parts from the union of those views. Syntactically, an imported declaration can only be qualified by the local name of an import that provides or reveals that declaration. But what is known about the imported declaration (that is, only its signature part or both its signature and body parts) is derived from the union of the imported parts, not just the import used to qualify the declaration.

For example, consider the following two modules.

```
module S {
  export AB reveals a, b
  export B provides b
  export AC provides a reveals c
  const a := 10
  const b := 20
  const c := 30
}
module T {
  import S0 = S`AB
  import S1 = S`B
  import S2 = S`AC
  lemma Test() {
    assert S0.a == S2.a;
    assert S0.a + S1.b == S2.c;
  }
}
```

Module T can refer to S's constant a as either S0.a or S2.a, since both the imports S0 and S2 include the signature part of a, but trying to say S1.a in T would give an "unresolved identifier" error. Because T imports the export set AB, the body part of a (that is, the fact that a is defined to be 10) is known in T, regardless of if a is syntactically referred to as S0.a or as S2.a (see the first assertion in the example). Similarly, despite the fact that S1 only imports the signature part of b, S1.b is known in T to equal 20 on account of import S0.

It is also possible to combine several imported views of a module into a single local name for the module. This is done by following the back-tick with a set of names. For example, the local names S0, S1, and S2 in module T can be combined into the one local name S as follows:

```
module T' {
  import S`{AB,B,AC}
  lemma Test() {
    assert S.a == S.a;
    assert S.a + S.b == S.c;
  }
}
```

4.6 Building an Export Set as an Extension of Another

When a module defines several export sets, it is often the case that one is a superset of another. For example, export set `Friends` is a superset of the eponymous export set in module `Accumulator` in Sect. 4.4. To make such superset relations easier to maintain, an export set can be declared to *extend* another. This is done by following the name of the new export set by `extends` and the list of export sets that are being extended.

So, instead of spelling out all the provided and revealed declarations of `Friends` in Sect. 4.4, the `Friends` export set can be defined to extend the eponymous export set:

```
export Friends extends Accumulator
  reveals T, Get
```

5 The Road We Traveled

The module system in Dafny has gone through several major revisions. Ostensibly, it seems that a module system just provides a way to carve up the namespace of a program, which gives the illusion that the task of designing it would be trivial. Our struggle with the design tells a different story.

Part of our difficulty stemmed from trying to rely on Dafny's features for *refinement* [3], which are also based on modules, to be the mechanism for hiding declarations and parts of declarations. Because every new refinement module creates a copy of the module being refined (to allow several different refinements of a module), it was difficult to determine when two imported declarations were the same and when they were different copies of some previously defined declaration. After experimenting with this and finally declaring the attempt a failure, our next quagmire became trying to deal gracefully with the legacy programs that had grown out of our experiments.

Our experience shows that the need to be able to decide separately about exporting a declaration's signature and exporting the declaration's body is fundamental for verification. This rendered an otherwise convenient keyword like `public` inadequate. Would we have more than one flavor of the keyword, like `public_sig` and `public_body`? Or would we have a single keyword `public` that could designate different parts of a declaration, depending on where in the declaration the keyword was placed? Searching for a consistent way to deal with this issue for different kinds of declarations caused us to look at what subsets of parts of each declaration could make sense to make visible. We were surprised to find that essentially every declaration had a signature part and a body part, and we were delighted that no declaration needed more than two parts.

There was also a design choice of how many visibility levels (like `private` and `public`) to provide. Remembering Modula-3's interfaces, we knew we could let the program (as opposed to the programming language) make this choice if we introduced named export sets in the language. This and the "every declaration has two parts" realization eventually led us to `export` declarations with `provides` and `reveals` clauses.

With export sets, our implementation of Dafny needed to be careful about what information to use when resolving names, when type checking, and when producing logical verification conditions. The aliasing of imports with different views made this issue quite delicate, and all in all it added up to a substantial implementation effort.

The current module system has seen two years of use without major issues.

6   Concluding Remarks

A module system that supports information hiding is important for any programming language. For a verification-aware language like Dafny, a good module system not only explicates the things clients of a module can rely on versus the things the module is free to change without affecting clients, but also enables modular verification. We have described the Dafny module system and given examples of how its features can be applied when specifying and verifying programs. The module system is characterized by its multiple export sets, its translucent `provides` exports, and its transparent `reveals` exports.

Acknowledgements This work was done in 2016 when both of us were at Microsoft Research. We are grateful to the Ironclad team at Microsoft Research, especially Chris Hawblitzel, Jay Lorch, and Bryan Parno, who went through the pains of using the (several!) previous module systems of Dafny, and offered constant feedback and valuable suggestions. Jason Koenig and Michael Lowell Roberts were instrumental in experimenting with various module-system features that influenced the current design.

References

1. Anindya Banerjee, David A. Naumann, and Stan Rosenberg. "Regional logic for local reasoning about global invariants". In: *Jan Vitek, editor ECOOP 2008, Object-Oriented Programming 22nd European Conference* Springer, 2008.
2. Margaret A. Ellis and Bjarne Stroustrup. "The Annotated C++ Reference Manual". In: Addison-Wesley Publishing Company, 1990.
3. Jason Koenig and K. Rustan M. Leino. "Programming language features for refinement". In: *In John Derrick, Eerke A. Boiten, and Steve Reeves, editors, Proceedings 17th International Workshop on Refinement, Refine@FM 2015* EPTCS, 2016.
4. K. Rustan M. Leino. "Accessible software verification with Dafny". In: *IEEE Software* IEEE, 2017.
5. K. Rustan M. Leino. "Dafny: An automatic program verifier for functional correctness". In: *Edmund M. Clarke and Andrei Voronkov editors, LPAR-16* Springer, 2010.
6. Mark Lillibridge. "Translucent Sums: A Foundation for Higher-Order Module Systems". In: *PhD thesis* Carnegie Mellon University, 1997.
7. Peter Müller, Arnd Poetzsch-Heffter, and Gary T. Leavens "Modular invariants for layered object structures". In: *Science of Computer Programming* 2006.
8. Greg Nelson. "Systems Programming with Modula-3". In: *Series in Innovative Technology* Prentice-Hall, Englewood Cliffs, NJ, 1991.
9. D. L. Parnas. "On the criteria to be used in decomposing systems into modules". In: *Communications of the ACM* ACM, 1972.
10. Arnd Poetzsch-Heffter and Jan Schäfer. "Modular specification of encapsulated object-oriented components". In: *Formal Methods for Components and Objects, 4th International Symposium, FMCO 2005* Springer, 2005.
11. Ina Schaefer and Arnd Poetzsch-Heffter. "Compositional reasoning in model-based verification of adaptive embedded systems". In: *Sixth IEEE International Conference on Software Engineering and Formal Methods (SEFM)* IEEE Computer Society 2008.
12. Ina Schaefer and Arnd Poetzsch-Heffter. "Using abstraction in modular verification of synchronous adaptive systems". In: *Workshop on Trustworthy Software of OASICS* Inter nationales Begegnungs- und Forschungszentrum für Informatik (IBFI), Schloss Dagstuhl, 2006.

The Binomial Heap Verification Challenge in Viper

Peter Müller

Abstract Binomial heaps have interesting invariants that constrain the shape of and the values stored in the data structure. A challenge of the VSComp 2014 verification competition was to find a fault in a given Java implementation of binomial heaps that leads to a violation of the invariants, to fix the error, and to verify the corrected version. In this paper, we present the first solution to this challenge. Using an encoding of the verification problem into Viper, we identified and fixed the known and a previously-unknown fault in the Java code and then successfully verified the implementation. Our case study illustrates the degree of automation that modern program verifiers achieve for complex invariants; it also demonstrates how modular verification techniques can be used to iteratively strengthen the verified properties, allowing the developer to focus on one concern at a time.

1 Introduction

The program verification community regularly engages in verification competitions such as SV-COMP, VerifyThis, and VSComp. The participants attempt to solve a set of challenges using verification tools of their choice. These competitions allow tool developers to assess the strengths and weaknesses of their tools and identify techniques and tool features that are useful to handle challenging verification problems. It is common for participants to work on their solutions even beyond the end of the official competition, and to publish their results [11].

In this paper, we present our solution to one of the challenges of the VSComp 2014 competition. The challenge is to detect a fault in the Java implementation of a binomial heap data structure [4], to fix the error, and to verify that the corrected code maintains the invariants of binomial heaps. VSComp 2014 was organized by Ernie Cohen, Marcelo Frias, Natarajan Shankar, and the author of this paper. The binomial

P. Müller (✉)
Department of Computer Science, ETH Zurich, Zurich, Switzerland
e-mail: peter.mueller@inf.ethz.ch

© Springer Nature Switzerland AG 2018
P. Müller, I. Schaefer (eds.), *Principled Software Development*,
https://doi.org/10.1007/978-3-319-98047-8_13

heap challenge was proposed by Marcelo Frias. Out of 14 teams that had registered for the competition, 8 submitted solutions to some of the challenges. None of them solved the binomial heaps problem; to the best of our knowledge, it has also not been solved in the aftermath of the competition.

We solved this challenge using our verification infrastructure Viper [16]. We translated the Java program into the Viper intermediate verification language, annotated the Viper program with suitable specifications, and verified it using Viper's symbolic-execution-based verification back-end. The solution uses access permissions and recursive predicates in the style of separation logic to describe the shape of the binomial heap data structure, and heap-dependent abstraction functions to specify value invariants such as sortedness of lists. The method specifications and loop invariants necessary for the verification include a mix of complex shape and value properties. Our case study illustrates the degree of automation that modern program verifiers achieve for such properties; it also demonstrates how modular verification techniques can be used to iteratively strengthen the verified properties, thereby allowing the developer to focus on one concern at a time.

A noteworthy outcome of our verification effort is that we did not only find and fix the defect that was detected earlier by Marcelo Frias using bounded model checking. We also identified a second (very similar) fault that was previously undetected. Both faults are present in Java implementations of binomial heaps that are available online, for instance, at https://www.sanfoundry.com/java-program-implement-binomial-heap.

Outline We provide the necessary background on binomial heaps in Sect. 2. We reproduce the challenge in Sect. 3 and explain the intended behavior of the faulty method in Sect. 4. We summarize our formalization of the main invariants in Sect. 5 and explain in Sect. 6 how we found the fault, fixed it, and verified the corrected code. Section 7 provides a quantitative and qualitative evaluation of our solutions and Sect. 8 concludes. The challenge statement including the given Java source code as well as our solution are available online [14].

2   Binomial Heaps

A *binomial heap* stores a multiset of keys, here, integers. Important operations are very efficient: finding a minimum value, deleting a minimum value, decreasing a key, and merging two binomial heaps all work in logarithmic amortized time; insertion has constant amortized time.

Binomial heaps are sets of binomial trees. A *binomial tree* is defined as follows: a binomial tree of degree 0 is a single node. A binomial tree of degree k has k children, which are the roots of binomial trees of degrees $k - 1, k - 2, \ldots, 1, 0$. The list of children is ordered in descending order. Consequently, a binomial tree of degree k has 2^k nodes. Figure 1 shows binomial trees.

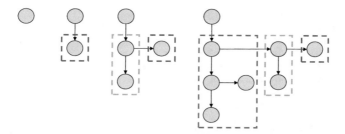

Fig. 1 Binomial trees of degrees 0, 1, 2, and 3. The children of a node are stored in a singly-linked list. Horizontal arrows depict the `sibling`-references between the children of a node. Vertical arrows depict `child`-references from a parent to its first child. We omit `parent`-references in the diagrams for simplicity. The dashed boxes visualize the structure. For instance, the children of a tree of degree 3 are three trees of degrees 2, 1, and 0

A binomial heap contains at most one binomial tree of each degree. Each tree must satisfy the minimum-heap property, that is, the key of each node is less or equal to the keys of each of their children. Consequently, the minimum key of each tree is stored in its root. Figure 4a shows a binomial heap with trees of degrees 0, 2, and 3.

3 Verification Challenge

The verification challenge addressed in this paper was presented at VSComp 2014 as follows.

We present a compilable excerpt from classes BinomialHeap and BinomialHeapNode modeling binomial heaps [4]. Method extractMin has a fault that allows for the class invariant to be violated. Your goals towards solving this problem are:

1. Find and describe the above-mentioned fault.
2. Provide an input binomial heap that exercises this fault, and describe the technique used to find the input (automated techniques are preferred to human inspection).
3. Provide a correct version of method extractMin.
4. Provide a suitable class invariant.
5. Verify that method extractMin indeed preserves the provided class invariant or at least a meaningful subset of properties from the class invariant.

Hints can be obtained from the organizers in exchange for penalties in the final score.

The given Java implementation of tree nodes, class BinomialHeapNode, is presented in Fig. 2. For binomial heaps, Fig. 3 presents an outline of class BinomialHeap including the method extractMin, which is mentioned in the challenge. We provide the complete source code from the competition problem online [14].

```
1   public class BinomialHeapNode {
2      public int key;
3      public int degree;
4      public BinomialHeapNode parent;
5      public BinomialHeapNode sibling;
6      public BinomialHeapNode child;
7
8      public BinomialHeapNode() {}
9
10     public BinomialHeapNode reverse(BinomialHeapNode sibl) {
11        BinomialHeapNode ret;
12        if (sibling != null)
13           ret = sibling.reverse(this);
14        else
15           ret = this;
16        sibling = sibl;
17        return ret;
18     }
19  }
```

Fig. 2 The provided Java implementation of class BinomialHeapNode

4   Algorithm

The challenge states that method extractMin has a fault. In this section, we explain the intended behavior of the method on a concrete example. The method is supposed to find a minimum key in a given binomial heap and remove it. It achieves that in five main steps, which we explain in the following and illustrate in Fig. 4.

Figure 4a shows the input heap; we assume that node 6 contains the minimum key to be removed. Note that the implementation used in the challenge requires the trees in a binomial heap to be sorted by degree in ascending order.

Step 1: Removing the Minimum Node Method extractMin traverses the list of binomial trees and identifies the tree with the minimum key (via the call to findMinNode in line 9 of Fig. 3). Due to the minimum-heap property, this method needs to compare only the keys at the roots. Lines 10–16 of extractMin remove the tree with the minimum from the binomial heap. The remaining elements of the original binomial heap are then split between the remainder of the heap and the children of the removed minimum node, as illustrated in Fig. 4b.

Step 2: Reversing the Children List The children list of the removed minimum node is itself a binomial heap, but sorted in descending rather than ascending order. The next step of extractMin (lines 30 and 36 in Fig. 3) is to reverse this list, resulting in the state shown in Fig. 4c.

Step 3: Merging the Heaps The next step (call to unionNodes in line 36) merges both binomial heaps into one sorted list of trees as shown in Fig. 4d. This merge operation is implemented by a method merge, which is called at the beginning of method unionNodes. Note that the resulting list is not a binomial heap since it may

```java
public class BinomialHeap {
  public BinomialHeapNode Nodes;
  public int size;

  public BinomialHeapNode extractMin() {
    if (Nodes == null)  return null;

    BinomialHeapNode temp = Nodes, prevTemp = null;
    BinomialHeapNode minNode = findMinNode(Nodes);
    while (temp.key != minNode.key) {
      prevTemp = temp;
      temp = temp.sibling;
    }

    if (prevTemp == null) { Nodes = temp.sibling; }
    else                  { prevTemp.sibling = temp.sibling; }
    temp = temp.child;
    BinomialHeapNode fakeNode = temp;

    // remove the parent-pointers pointing to the minimum
    while (temp != null) {
      temp.parent = null;
      temp = temp.sibling;
    }

    if ((Nodes == null) && (fakeNode == null)) {
      size = 0;
    } else {
      if ((Nodes == null) && (fakeNode != null)) {
        Nodes = fakeNode.reverse(null);
        size--;
      } else {
        if ((Nodes != null) && (fakeNode == null)) {
          size--;
        } else {
          unionNodes(fakeNode.reverse(null));
          size--;
        }
      }
    }
    return minNode;
  }

  void merge(BinomialHeapNode binHeap) { ... }
  void unionNodes(BinomialHeapNode binHeap) { ... }
  static BinomialHeapNode findMinNode(BinomialHeapNode arg) { ... }
}
```

Fig. 3 Excerpt from the provided Java implementation of class BinomialHeap. The complete version is available online [14]

contain up to two trees for each degree. In our example, it includes two trees of degree 0 and two of degree 2.

Step 4: Combining the Trees To re-establish the invariant of a binomial heap, method unionNodes traverses the list resulting from merge and iteratively combines

Fig. 4 Example execution of method `extractMin`. For illustration purposes, each node has a unique number; for some binomial trees, we indicate their degree in red. We assume that the minimum value to be extracted is stored in node 6. We show the states before and after each of the four steps of the algorithm. The diagram shows the result of a correct implementation, not the code provided in the challenge. (**a**) The initial binomial heap. (**b**) State after removing the minimum node 6. (**c**) State after reversing the children list of the removed minimum node. (**d**) State after merging the two lists. (**d**) Final binomial heap

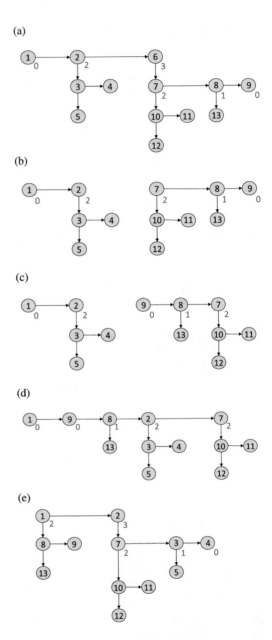

two consecutive trees of degree k into one tree of degree $k + 1$. This traversal relies on the fact that the trees of a binomial heap (and consequently the list produced by merging two heaps) are sorted in ascending order. If that is the case, it produces a well-formed binomial heap as shown in Fig. 4e. Here, the two trees of degree 0 were merged into a tree of degree 1, which is then merged with the other tree of degree 1 into a tree of degree 2, resulting in a list with three trees of degree 2. The two trees at the back of the list are then merged into one tree of degree 3.

5 Formalization of Invariants

We solved the verification challenge by manually encoding the given Java implementation and its specification into the intermediate verification language Viper [16]. Viper uses a program logic based on implicit dynamic frames [22], a permission logic akin to separation logic [17, 21]. Viper associates an *access permission* with each heap location. A method may read or write the location only if it holds the corresponding permission. Permissions may be passed between method executions, but cannot be duplicated or forged. Permissions to an unbounded number of memory locations can be represented by recursive predicates [18]. Viper's permission logic offers various advanced features such as fractional permissions [2, 9], magic wands [21], and quantified permissions (iterated separating conjunction) [15], but these features were not needed for the binomial heap challenge.

In contrast to separation logic, implicit dynamic frames separate permission specifications from value properties. For instance, separation logic's points-to predicate $x.f \mapsto y$ is expressed in Viper as the conjunction of two assertions $acc(x.f)$ && $x.f == y$, where the former conjunct denotes the access permission to location $x.f$ and the latter constrains the value stored in the location. This separation carries over to other specification constructs. In particular, Viper uses recursive predicates to abstract over the permissions to a data structure and supports heap-dependent abstraction functions to abstract over its values [8]. Viper's conjunction && behaves like separating conjunction when applied to assertions that denote permissions. In particular, $acc(x.f)$ && $acc(y.f)$ implies $x \neq y$.

We formalize the invariants of binomial trees using two mutually recursive predicates tree and heapseg, which are presented in Fig. 5. The tree predicate takes as argument a reference to a tree node; it provides access permission to the four fields of this node. The subsequent conjuncts express that a tree's degree is non-negative (line 4), that the child field points to a null-terminated list (line 5), and that the degree is the length of this list (line 6). Here, lists are represented as so-called list segments, encoded via the heapseg predicate described below. segLength is a function that yields the length of a list segment; the definition is straightforward and, therefore, omitted. The remaining conjuncts express properties of the children list: the first child's degree is one less than the current node's (lines 7 and 8); the boolean function validChildren (line 9) encodes that each child's degree is one larger than its sibling's. Finally, the first child's parent is the current node (line 10).

The heapseg predicate represents the empty list segment when its arguments are equal. Otherwise, it provides a tree predicate for each node in the list segment and access permission to its sibling field (line 15), and requires all nodes in the segment to have the same parent (lines 17 and 18).

```
 1   predicate tree(this: Ref) {
 2     acc(this.key) && acc(this.degree) &&
 3     acc(this.child) && acc(this.parent) &&
 4     0 <= this.degree &&
 5     heapseg(this.child, null) &&
 6     this.degree == segLength(this.child, null) &&
 7     (0 < this.degree ==>
 8                   segDegree(this.child, null, 0) == this.degree - 1) &&
 9     validChildren(this.child, null) &&
10     (this.child != null ==> segParent(this.child, null) == this)
11   }
12
13   predicate heapseg(this: Ref, last: Ref) {
14     this != last ==>
15       tree(this) && acc(this.sibling) &&
16       heapseg(this.sibling, last) &&
17       (this.sibling != last ==>
18                   treeParent(this) == segParent(this.sibling, last))
19   }
```

Fig. 5 Mutually recursive predicates describing binomial trees

```
 1   predicate heap(this: Ref) {
 2     acc(this.Nodes) &&
 3     heapseg(this.Nodes, null) && sorted(this.Nodes, null) &&
 4     (this.Nodes != null ==> segParent(this.Nodes, null) == null) &&
 5     acc(this.size) && this.size == segSize(this.Nodes, null)
 6   }
```

Fig. 6 Predicate describing binomial heaps

Together, these predicates encode the invariant of binomial trees explained in Sect. 2: The access permissions ensure that the data structure is a tree since they prevent aliasing. Moreover, since the first child of a tree with degree k has degree $k - 1$ (lines 7 and 8), and since there are k children (line 6), which are binomial trees (line 15) whose degrees decrease by one from child to child (function validChildren in line 9), we express that the children are the roots of binomial trees of degrees $k - 1, k - 2, \ldots, 1, 0$, as required.

The heap predicate in Fig. 6 describes the invariant of a binomial heap. It provides access permission to the Nodes field, which points to the root of the first binomial tree (line 2). The trees in a binomial heap form a null-terminated list; function sorted expresses that the trees in this list are sorted by degrees in strictly increasing order (line 3). The trees in this list have no parent (line 4). Finally, the code provided in the verification challenge has a size field that is supposed to store the number of elements in a binomial heap. This field is not read in the provided Java implementation. We included it, nevertheless, together with an invariant that size contains the actual number of elements as determined by the recursive function `segSize` (line 5).

6 Verification

The verification challenge (see Sect. 3) states that method `extractMin` violates the invariant of a binomial heap. We can check this property by verifying the following method specification in Viper: If the receiver object `this` is a well-formed binomial heap in the pre-state of the method (that is, satisfies the `heap` predicate), it will also be a well-formed heap in the post-state:

```
method extractMin(this: Ref) returns (res: Ref)
  requires heap(this)
  ensures  heap(this)
```

Verifying the method implementation against this specification requires suitable specifications for all methods (transitively) called by `extractMin`. These specifications are available online [14]. Here, we focus on method `merge`, which is the method that contains the fault. As part of Step 3 of the `extractMin` algorithm (see Sect. 4), `merge` merges two sorted lists of binomial trees as illustrated by the transition from Fig. 4c, d.

The Viper specification of method `merge` is shown in Fig. 7. The first two preconditions require the receiver to be a non-empty binomial heap (lines 2 and 3). Viper distinguishes between a predicate and its body [23]. In order to prevent automatic provers from unrolling recursive definitions indefinitely, exchanging a predicate for its body and vice versa is done manually via `unfold` and `fold` statements. The first two preconditions include the unfolded version of the `heap(this)` predicate. The third precondition requires parameters `binHeap` to point to a null-terminated list of

```
1   method merge(this: Ref, binHeap: Ref)
2     requires acc(this.Nodes) && this.Nodes != null
3     requires heapseg(this.Nodes, null) && sorted(this.Nodes, null)
4     requires heapseg(binHeap, null) && sorted(binHeap, null)
5     requires binHeap != null ==>
6             segParent(this.Nodes, null) == segParent(binHeap, null)
7
8     ensures acc(this.Nodes) && this.Nodes != null
9     ensures heapseg(this.Nodes, null) && presorted(this.Nodes, null)
10    ensures segSize(this.Nodes, null) ==
11            old(segSize(this.Nodes, null))+old(segSize(binHeap, null))
12    ensures segParent(this.Nodes, null)==old(segParent(this.Nodes, null))
```

Fig. 7 Viper specification of method `merge`

binomial heaps (line 4), and the last precondition requires the trees in both lists to have the same parent (line 5).

Similarly, the first two postconditions ensure that after the method execution, the Nodes field of the receiver will point to a non-empty, null-terminated list of binomial trees. Note, however, that this list will in general not satisfy the sorted property. As we explained in Sect. 4 and illustrated in Fig. 4d, the resulting list is sorted, but, in contrast to a binomial heap, may contain up to two trees of each degree. We express these properties using the presorted function (lines 8 and 9). The third postcondition expresses that the size of the merged list is the sum of the sizes of the input lists (lines 10 and 11), and the last postcondition ensures that the parent of the trees in the lists is not modified by the method (line 12).

This specification illustrates one of the main benefits of implicit dynamic frames over traditional separation logic. By separating access permissions from value properties, one can conveniently describe different constraints over the same data structure. Our heapseg predicate describes the permissions to the trees in a list segment, whereas different sorting criteria can be specified separately using functions. In the specification of method merge, we use sorted to express sortedness without duplicates and presorted to allow degrees to occur at most twice. During the combination of binomial trees (Step 4 in Sect. 4), there may even be states where a list can contain up to one element up to three times. For instance, after combining the first two trees in Fig. 4d and then combining the result with the third tree, the list includes three trees of degree 2. Viper allows one to use the same heapseg predicate in all three situations and to combine it with different value constraints. In contrast, separation logic would require either a complex parameterization of the predicate or a mapping from list segments to a mathematical sequence of degrees that can then be constrained appropriately; however, reasoning about sequences in SMT solvers is often flaky.

The Java implementation of method merge is presented in Fig. 8; its Viper encoding is available online [14]. Verifying this method requires a complex loop invariant consisting of 26 lines of Viper code. Besides various access permissions and sortedness criteria, which we discussed above, it requires that the degree of the last tree in the list starting at temp1 is at most the degree of the tree pointed to by temp2, unless temp1 points to the first tree, this.Nodes. This constraint is violated by the implementation given in the verification challenge.

Figure 9 shows the execution of the given faulty implementation of method merge for the example from Fig. 4. As shown by Fig. 9b, already the first loop iteration does not preserve this invariant: Here, the last tree in the listed starting at temp1 has degree 2, which is larger than the degree of temp2, which is 1. A careful inspection of the executed branch of the loop (lines 5–9) reveals that the assignment temp1 = tmp.sibling in line 9 is wrong. The correct assignment is temp1 = tmp, which would let temp1 point to node 9 in Fig. 9b and, thus, preserve the loop invariant. The smallest counterexample that reveals this error has 13 nodes in the initial binomial heap, as in Fig. 4a. We confirmed the detected fault also by running the Java implementation on that example.

```
1    private void merge(BinomialHeapNode binHeap) {
2      BinomialHeapNode temp1 = Nodes, temp2 = binHeap;
3      while ((temp1 != null) && (temp2 != null)) {
4        if (temp1.degree == temp2.degree) {
5          BinomialHeapNode tmp = temp2;
6          temp2 = temp2.sibling;
7          tmp.sibling = temp1.sibling;
8          temp1.sibling = tmp;
9          temp1 = tmp.sibling;
10       } else {
11         if (temp1.degree < temp2.degree) {
12           if ((temp1.sibling == null)
13                || (temp1.sibling.degree > temp2.degree)) {
14             BinomialHeapNode tmp = temp2;
15             temp2 = temp2.sibling;
16             tmp.sibling = temp1.sibling;
17             temp1.sibling = tmp;
18             temp1 = tmp.sibling;
19           } else {
20             temp1 = temp1.sibling;
21           }
22         } else {
23           BinomialHeapNode tmp = temp1;
24           temp1 = temp2;
25           temp2 = temp2.sibling;
26           temp1.sibling = tmp;
27           if (tmp == Nodes) {
28             Nodes = temp1;
29           }
30         }
31       }
32     }
33
34     if (temp1 == null) {
35       temp1 = Nodes;
36       while (temp1.sibling != null) {
37         temp1 = temp1.sibling;
38       }
39       temp1.sibling = temp2;
40     }
41   }
```

Fig. 8 Provided implementation of the auxiliary method `merge`, which is called from `unionNodes`, which is in turn called from `extractMin`

Re-verifying the code after fixing this fault reveals a second one: the assignment in line 18 has the same fault and can be fixed in the same way. The smallest counterexample we found is a binomial input heap with 25 nodes: trees of degrees 0, 3, and 4, where the minimum is extracted from the tree of degree 3; we also confirmed this fault in the given Java implementation. After applying the second fix, the example verifies.

Fig. 9 States before and after each loop iteration in the faulty implementation of method merge. The initial state is the same as in Fig. 4d. Fig. 4e shows the final state of the corrected implementation. The faulty implementation incorrectly removes nodes 8 and 13 from the list. (**a**) State at the beginning of method merge. (**b**) State after the first loop iteration (executing lines 5–9). (**c**) State after the second loop iteration (executing lines 23–29). (**d**) State after the third loop iteration (executing line 20). (**e**) State after the last loop iteration (executing lines 5–9)

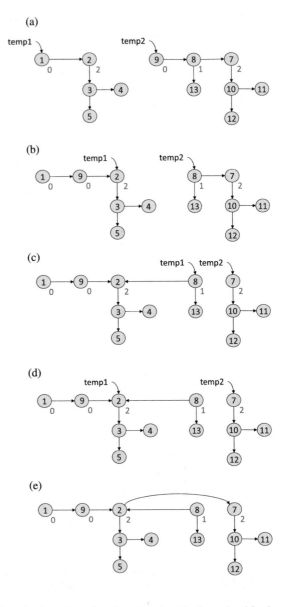

It is interesting to observe that the loop invariant implies that the last else-block (lines 23–29) is reachable only when temp1 == this.Nodes, a property that we verified. So the condition in line 27 is always true and the if-statement could be omitted.

7 Discussion

We solved all five tasks given in the verification challenge (see Sect. 3). The input required for Task 2 was found manually when trying to understand why the loop invariant in method merge is not preserved. Note that our solution goes beyond the challenge in two major ways. First, Viper's permission logic ensures the absence of run-time errors and data races. That is, our solution is correct even in a concurrent setting. Second, before he proposed the verification challenge, Marcelo Frias used bounded model checking and detected the first of the two errors. However, the second error, which is triggered by a larger input (25 instead of 13 nodes) remained undetected. We found both errors and verified the fixed version of the code for unbounded inputs.

Quantitative Evaluation Table 1 provides an overview of our encoding. The 141 lines of Java code were encoded into 170 lines of Viper code; the slight increase is caused by the fact that Viper is an intermediate language. The translation from Java to Viper could be performed completely automatically using a suitable front-end such as VerCors [1]. The specification of the program consists of 117 lines, 80 lines for the definition of recursive predicates and heap-dependent abstraction functions, and 37 lines for the preconditions and postconditions of the five methods. In addition, our solution required 128 lines of ghost code for the unfolding and folding of recursive predicates, 112 lines of loop invariants, and 13 local assertions to help the SMT solver, for instance, to unroll function definitions.

In total, the ratio of annotations to code is $370/170 = 2.2$, which is significantly lower than the numbers reported for other SMT-based verification efforts, which report an overhead factor around 5 [6, 7], and much lower than verification efforts in interactive theorem provers, which often have overhead factors between 10 and 20 [5, 10, 12, 25]. Note, however, that these are very rough comparisons since the complexity of programs and verified properties differ between these case studies; moreover, verification in interactive provers such as Coq can provide foundational guarantees, whereas soundness of our approach depends on the correct implementation of Viper.

Table 1 Summary of solution. "Lines" excludes empty lines and comments

Content	Lines
Program code	170
Predicate and function declarations	80
Method specifications for 5 methods	37
Ghost code including specification of ghost method	128
Loop invariants	112
Local assertions	13
Total overall	540
Total annotations	370

We measured the verification time on an Intel Core i7-4770 CPU (3.40 GHz, 16 Gb RAM) running Windows 10 Pro using a warmed-up JVM. Averaged over ten runs, Viper's verification back-end based on symbolic execution requires slightly under 23 s for the verification.

Qualitative Evaluation Viper's modular verification technique allowed us to verify the example incrementally. We started with the verification of memory safety, using recursive predicates that mostly specified access permission. We then iteratively strengthened the invariants, first by including more properties of binomial heaps and trees, and then by including the parent and size fields. Due to Viper's support for heap-dependent abstraction functions, we were able to strengthen the verified properties without substantial changes to the recursive predicates. This iterative process greatly reduced the complexity of the verification tasks.

During the verification, we simplified the code in three minor ways. First, we moved line 16 in method reverse (Fig. 2) into the conditional statement, which allowed us to fold the heapseg predicate before the recursive call in line 13. Second, we simplified the condition of the loop in lines 10–13 of method extractMin (Fig. 3) to temp = minNode!, which is equivalent because findMinNode yields a node with a minimal key. This change simplifies the specification of findMinNode. Third, we execute this loop only if minNode is not the first node of the list and otherwise set this.Nodes to temp.sibling. This change simplifies the loop invariant significantly. Besides these changes, the code we verified is a direct translation of the Java implementation. Note that we consider the second and third change to improve the clarity of the code, whereas the first change merely simplifies verification.

The manipulation of predicates via manual folding and unfolding gives a lot of control over the proof search, but introduces a very high overhead. Most of this overhead is needed to manipulate list segments during iterative traversals. Possible remedies are support for loops that are specified with pre- and postconditions instead of loop invariants [24], support for automatic folding and unfolding [3, 19], or a specification based on iterated separating conjunction rather than recursive predicates [15]. We plan to explore these options as future work.

Our solution requires 13 local assertions to make the SMT solver succeed. These local assertions provide expressions that trigger quantifier instantiations or temporarily unfold predicates to extract information from their bodies. Both usages should be automated.

Finally, the case study demonstrated the importance of a good development environment that parallelizes verification and caches verification results [13]. We have implemented both features since we completed the case study.

8 Conclusion

We presented the first solution to the Binomial Heap verification challenge from the VSComp 2014 competition. Our solution uses Viper's permission logic and makes heavy use of recursive predicates and heap-dependent abstraction functions.

The solution suggests several directions for future work. First, it requires a significant amount of annotations, especially loop invariants and ghost code to manipulate recursive predicates. It will be interesting to explore whether at least some of these annotations can be inferred. Second, our solution required 13 local assertions to help the SMT solver prove certain obligations; we will explore strategies to eliminate those. Third, we plan to encode the example using magic wands or iterated separating conjunction instead of list-segment predicates in order to reduce the overhead of manipulating these predicates.

This paper is a contribution to a book in honor of Arnd Poetzsch-Heffter's 60th birthday. One of my first scientific discussions with Arnd was about the role of object invariants in specifying object-oriented programs, especially, about the difference between invariants and well-formedness predicates as part of method specifications [20]. This discussion was the starting point of my PhD work and many more years of research on various forms of invariants. I hope Arnd will enjoy reading this case study about the verification of object invariants. I would like to take this opportunity to thank him for the tremendous support he has given me as my PhD advisor and beyond.

Acknowledgements We thank Marcelo Frias for proposing the Binomial Heaps verification challenge and for clarifying the results of previous verification attempts. We are grateful to Malte Schwerhoff for his help with the verification effort and to Alex Summers for the performance measurements.

References

1. S. Blom, S. Darabi, M. Huisman, and W. Oortwijn. The VerCors tool set: Verification of parallel and concurrent software. In N. Polikarpova and S. Schneider, editors, *Integrated Formal Methods (IFM)*, volume 10510 of *LNCS*, pages 102–110. Springer, 2017.
2. J. Boyland. Checking interference with fractional permissions. In *Static Analysis Symposium (SAS)*, volume 2694 of *LNCS*, pages 55–72. Springer, 2003.
3. C. Calcagno, D. Distefano, P. W. O'Hearn, and H. Yang. Compositional shape analysis by means of bi-abduction. In Z. Shao and B. C. Pierce, editors, *Principles of Programming Languages (POPL)*, pages 289–300. ACM, 2009.
4. T. H. Cormen, C. E. Leiserson, R. L. Rivest, and C. Stein. *Introduction to Algorithms, 3rd Edition*. MIT Press, 2009.
5. M. Doko and V. Vafeiadis. Tackling real-life relaxed concurrency with FSL++. In H. Yang, editor, *European Symposium on Programming (ESOP)*, volume 10201 of *LNCS*, pages 448–475. Springer, 2017.
6. C. Hawblitzel, J. Howell, M. Kapritsos, J. R. Lorch, B. Parno, M. L. Roberts, S. T. V. Setty, and B. Zill. Ironfleet: proving practical distributed systems correct. In E. L. Miller and S. Hand, editors, *Symposium on Operating Systems Principles (SOSP)*, pages 1–17. ACM, 2015.

 7. C. Hawblitzel, J. Howell, J. R. Lorch, A. Narayan, B. Parno, D. Zhang, and B. Zill. Ironclad apps: End-to-end security via automated full-system verification. In J. Flinn and H. Levy, editors, *Operating Systems Design and Implementation (OSDI)*, pages 165–181. USENIX Association, 2014.
 8. S. Heule, I. T. Kassios, P. Müller, and A. J. Summers. Verification condition generation for permission logics with abstract predicates and abstraction functions. In G. Castagna, editor, *European Conference on Object-Oriented Programming (ECOOP)*, volume 7920 of *LNCS*, pages 451–476. Springer, 2013.
 9. S. Heule, K. R. M. Leino, P. Müller, and A. J. Summers. Abstract read permissions: Fractional permissions without the fractions. In *Verification, Model Checking, and Abstract Interpretation (VMCAI)*, volume 7737 of *LNCS*, pages 315–334, 2013.
10. J. Kaiser, H. Dang, D. Dreyer, O. Lahav, and V. Vafeiadis. Strong logic for weak memory: Reasoning about release-acquire consistency in Iris. In P. Müller, editor, *European Conference on Object-Oriented Programming (ECOOP)*, volume 74 of *LIPIcs*, pages 17:1–17:29. Schloss Dagstuhl - Leibniz-Zentrum fuer Informatik, 2017.
11. V. Klebanov, P. Müller, N. Shankar, G. T. Leavens, V. Wüstholz, E. Alkassar, R. Arthan, D. Bronish, R. Chapman, E. Cohen, M. Hillebrand, B. Jacobs, K. R. M. Leino, R. Monahan, F. Piessens, N. Polikarpova, T. Ridge, J. Smans, S. Tobies, T. Tuerk, M. Ulbrich, and B. Weiss. The 1st Verified Software Competition: Experience report. In M. Butler and W. Schulte, editors, *Formal Methods (FM)*, volume 6664 of *LNCS*, pages 154–168. Springer, 2011.
12. G. Klein, K. Elphinstone, G. Heiser, J. Andronick, D. Cock, P. Derrin, D. Elkaduwe, K. Engelhardt, R. Kolanski, M. Norrish, T. Sewell, H. Tuch, and S. Winwood. sel4: formal verification of an OS kernel. In J. N. Matthews and T. E. Anderson, editors, *Symposium on Operating Systems Principles (SOSP)*, pages 207–220. ACM, 2009.
13. K. R. M. Leino and V. Wüstholz. Fine-grained caching of verification results. In *Computer Aided Verification (CAV)*, volume 9206 of *LNCS*, pages 380–397. Springer, 2015.
14. P. Müller. The binomial heap verification challenge in Viper: Online appendix. viper.ethz.ch/onlineappendix-binomialheap, 2018.
15. P. Müller, M. Schwerhoff, and A. J. Summers. Automatic verification of iterated separating conjunctions using symbolic execution. In S. Chaudhuri and A. Farzan, editors, *Computer Aided Verification (CAV)*, volume 9779 of *LNCS*, pages 405–425. Springer, 2016.
16. P. Müller, M. Schwerhoff, and A. J. Summers. Viper: A verification infrastructure for permission-based reasoning. In B. Jobstmann and K. R. M. Leino, editors, *Verification, Model Checking, and Abstract Interpretation (VMCAI)*, volume 9583 of *LNCS*, pages 41–62. Springer, 2016.
17. P. W. O'Hearn, J. C. Reynolds, and H. Yang. Local reasoning about programs that alter data structures. In *Computer Science Logic (CSL)*, pages 1–19. Springer, 2001.
18. M. Parkinson and G. Bierman. Separation logic and abstraction. In J. Palsberg and M. Abadi, editors, *Principles of Programming Languages (POPL)*, pages 247–258. ACM, 2005.
19. R. Piskac, T. Wies, and D. Zufferey. Automating separation logic with trees and data. In A. Biere and R. Bloem, editors, *Computer Aided Verification (CAV)*, volume 8559 of *LNCS*, pages 711–728. Springer, 2014.
20. A. Poetzsch-Heffter. Specification and verification of object-oriented programs. Habilitation thesis, Technical University of Munich, Jan. 1997. https://softech.cs.uni-kl.de/homepage/en/publications.
21. M. Schwerhoff and A. J. Summers. Lightweight support for magic wands in an automatic verifier. In J. T. Boyland, editor, *European Conference on Object-Oriented Programming (ECOOP)*, volume 37 of *LIPIcs*, pages 614–638. Schloss Dagstuhl, 2015.
22. J. Smans, B. Jacobs, and F. Piessens. Implicit dynamic frames: Combining dynamic frames and separation logic. In *European Conference on Object-Oriented Programming (ECOOP)*, volume 5653 of *LNCS*, pages 148–172. Springer, 2009.
23. A. J. Summers and S. Drossopoulou. A formal semantics for isorecursive and equirecursive state abstractions. In G. Castagna, editor, *European Conference on Object-Oriented Programming (ECOOP)*, volume 7920 of *LNCS*, pages 129–153. Springer, 2013.

24. T. Tuerk. Local reasoning about while-loops. In R. Joshi, T. Margaria, P. Müller, D. Naumann, and H. Yang, editors, *VSTTE 2010. Workshop Proceedings*, pages 29–39. ETH Zurich, 2010.
25. V. Vafeiadis and C. Narayan. Relaxed separation logic: a program logic for C11 concurrency. In A. L. Hosking, P. T. Eugster, and C. V. Lopes, editors, *Object Oriented Programming Systems Languages & Applications (OOPSLA)*, pages 867–884. ACM, 2013.

Abstract and Concrete Data Types
vs Object Capabilities

James Noble, Alex Potanin, Toby Murray, and Mark S. Miller

Abstract The distinctions between the two forms of procedural data abstraction—abstract data types and objects—are well known. An abstract data type provides an opaque type declaration, and an implementation that manipulates the modules of the abstract type, while an object uses procedural abstraction to hide an individual implementation. The object-capability model has been proposed to enable object-oriented programs to be written securely, and has been adopted by a number of practical languages including JavaScript, E, and Newspeak. This chapter addresses the questions: how can we implement abstract data types in an object-capability language? and, how can we incorporate primitive concrete data types into a primarily object-oriented system?

1   Introduction

> Objects and abstract data types are not the same thing, and neither one is a variation of the other. They are fundamentally different and in many ways complementary.
>
> On Understanding Data Abstraction, Revisited,
> William Cook [3].

William Cook's "On Understanding Data Abstraction, Revisited" [3] emphasises a dichotomy between abstract data types, on one hand, and objects on the other.

Based on facilities originating in Alphard [30] and CLU [10], Cook defines an Abstract Data Type (ADT) as consisting of "a public name, a hidden representation,

J. Noble · A. Potanin (✉)
Victoria University of Wellington, Wellington, New Zealand
e-mail: kjx@ecs.vuw.ac.nz; alex@ecs.vuw.ac.nz

T. Murray
University of Melbourne, Melbourne, VIC, Australia
e-mail: toby.murray@unimelb.edu.au

M. S. Miller
Agoric, San Francisco, CA, USA

© Springer Nature Switzerland AG 2018
P. Müller, I. Schaefer (eds.), *Principled Software Development*,
https://doi.org/10.1007/978-3-319-98047-8_14

and operations to create, combine and observe values of the abstraction". The identification of a "public name" emphasises the fact that ADTs are not first class—certainly ADTs are not first class in most subsequent modular programming languages [2, 11, 28, 29]. An ADT has a hidden representation: this representation is not of the (non-first-class, singleton) ADT itself, but of the *instances* of the ADT—the values of the abstraction that are manipulated by the ADT's operations. ADTs encapsulate their implementations using type abstraction: all the instances of an ADT are instances of the same (concrete) type, and the language's (static) type system ensures that the details of the instance's implementations cannot be accessed outside the lexical scope of the ADT's definition. The exemplary ADTs are generally stacks, queues, lists, but crucially numbers, strings, and machine level values can also be modelled as ADTs.

In contrast, objects are essentially encapsulated individual components that use procedural abstraction to hide their own internal implementations [3]. "Pure" objects do not involve a hidden type, or indeed any form of type abstraction: rather an object is a self-referential record of procedures. Whereas ADTs are typically supported in statically typed languages (because they depend on type abstraction), objects are as common in dynamically typed languages as in statically typed languages.

According to Cook, ADTs and objects have complimentary strengths and weaknesses. Objects are organised around data, so it is easy to add a different representation of an existing interface, and have that implementation interoperate with every other implementation of that interface. On the other hand, it is easier to add a new operation to an ADT, but hard to change an ADT's representation.

A crucial difference, however, is that ADTs offer support for what Cook calls "complex operations": that is, operations that involve more than one instance. Complex operations may be low-level, such as arithmetic operations on two machine integers, or higher level operations, such as calculating the union of two or more sets, or a database style join of several indexed tables. The distinguishing factor is that these operations are complex in that implementations must "inspect multiple representations" i.e. representations of other instances [3]. Complex operations are easy to support with ADTs: all the instances of the ADT are encapsulated together in the ADT, and the code in the ADT has full access to all the instance's representations. In contrast, pure object-oriented programming does not support complex operations: each object is individually encapsulated and only one instance's representation can be accessed at any time.

This is particularly the case in object-capability systems—pure object-oriented systems designed for security [16]. Following Butler Lampson [9], Miller [14] defines the key design constraint of an object-capability system: *"A direct access right to an object gives a subject the permission to invoke the behaviour of that object"*. A programming language or system that grants one object privileged access to the representation or implementation of another object does not meet this criterion.

This, then, is the first question addressed by this chapter (and the workshop paper that preceded it [21]): how can we implement Abstract Data Types, in pure object-oriented languages with object capabilities, while still permitting complex operations across multiple instances? The key design question is: how do we model the boundary between the protected outside interface of an ADT and the shared inside implementation, and how do we manage programs that cross that boundary? [5, 12, 13, 15, 18, 23]

Then, we take our discussion further and propose a way to support primitive/concrete data types in a fully object-oriented language in the later part of this chapter.

2 Mint as an Abstract Data Type

Let us consider the well known Mint/Purse (or Bank/Account) example [12–14] used in the object capability world. A Mint (a Bank) can create new Purses (Accounts) with arbitrary balances, while a purse knows its balance, can accept deposits from another purse, and can also sprout new empty purses. Figure 1 shows the interface of the Mint/Purse example as an Abstract Data Type. Here, **makePurse** creates a new purse with a given balance, **deposit** transfers funds into a destination purse from a source purse, and **balance** returns a purse's balance. We also have an auxiliary operation **sprout** that makes a purse with a zero balance.

Figure 2 shows how one can define the type's behaviour axiomatically. These axioms reduce the ADT to a normal form where each purse is just created by **makePurse** with its balance. The nature of the Mint/Purse design as an ADT is shown by the **deposit** method which must update the balances of both the source and destination purses. As we will see, this is a key difficulty when implementing the Mint/Purse system in a pure object-capability language, because such a language cannot permit methods to access the representation of more than one object [3].

This description of Mint/Purse as an ADT obscures a couple of important issues. The first of these is that some of the operations on the ADT are more critical than others: notably that **makePurse** operation "inflates the currency" [13], that is it increases the total amount of money in the system—i.e. the overall sum of all the

1. **makePurse**(Number) $\longrightarrow$ Purse
2. **deposit**(Purse, Number, Purse) $\longrightarrow$ (Purse, Purse, Boolean)
3. **balance**(Purse) $\longrightarrow$ Number
4. **sprout** $\longrightarrow$ Purse

Fig. 1 Mint/purse abstract data type

1. **deposit**(**makePurse**(D), A, **makePurse**(S)) = **true** $\rightsquigarrow$
   (**makePurse**($D+A$), **makePurse**($S-A$), true) $(A > 0) \wedge (S >= A)$
2. **deposit**(**makePurse**(D), A, **makePurse**(S)) = **true** $\rightsquigarrow$
   (**makePurse**(D), **makePurse**(S), false) $(A <= 0) \vee (S < A)$
3. **sprout** $\rightsquigarrow$ **makePurse**(0)
4. **balance**(**makePurse**(N)) $\rightsquigarrow N$

Fig. 2 Mint/purse axioms

balances of all the ADT's purses. This operation must be protected: it should only be invoked by components that, by design, should have the authority to create more money. The other operations can be called by general clients of the ADT to transfer funds between purses but not affect the total money in the system.

This is why there is the auxiliary **sprout** operation which also creates a new purse, but which does not create additional funds—even though the semantics are the same as **makePurse**(0). In an object-oriented system, particularly an object-capability system, this restriction can be enforced by ensuring that the **makePurse** operation is offered as a method on a distinguished object, and access to that object is carefully protected. Languages based on ADTs typically use other mechanisms (such as Eiffel's restricted imports, or Modula-3's multiple interfaces, C++'s friends) to similar effect. These approaches are rather less flexible than using a distinguished object, as typically they couple the ADT implementation to concrete client modules—on the other hand, the extra object adds complexity to an object-oriented system's design.

The second issue is that, in an open system, particularly in an open distributed system, programs (and their programmers) cannot assume that all the code is "well behaved". This is certainly the case for a payments system: the point of a payment system is to act as trusted third party that allows one client to pay another client, even though the clients may not trust each other; one client may not exist at the time another client is written. In that sense, the notion of an "open system" as a system is, at best, ill-defined: where new components or objects can join and leave a system dynamically, questions such as what is the boundary of the system, which components comprise the system at any given time, or what are the future configurations of the system are very difficult to answer.

The question then is: how best can we implement such an ADT in a pure object-oriented language, particularly one adopting an object-capability security model, within an "open world": where an ADT may have to interoperate with components that are not known in advance, and that cannot be trusted by the ADT?

3   Implementing the Mint

We now try and answer that question, considering a number of different designs to support ADTs in object-oriented languages. We will present various different Grace implementations of the "Mint and Purse" system ubiquitous in object-capability research [13] to illustrate different implementation patterns.

3.1   Sealer/Unsealer

Our first implementation is based on the "classic" Mint in E, making use of sealer/unsealer brand pairs [13]. The sealer/unsealer design encodes the Mint/Purse

ADT into two separate kinds of objects, Mints and Purses (see Fig. 3). The Mint capability (i.e. the Mint object) must be kept secure by the owner of the whole system, as it can create funds. On the other hand, Purses can be communicated around the system: handing out a reference to a Purse risks only the funds that are deposited into that purse, or that may be deposited in the future.

This design is based on brand pairs [13, 17]. Brand pairs are returned from the `makeBrandPair` method, which returns a pair of a `sealer` object and an `unsealer` object. The sealer object's `seal` method places its argument into an opaque sealed box: the object can be retrieved from the box only by the corresponding unsealer's `unseal` method. The sealer/unsealer pairs can be thought of as modelling public key encryption, where the sealer is the public key and unsealer the private key (see Fig. 4).

We can implement these two types using two nested Grace classes (see Fig. 5, which follows the nesting in the E implementation [13]). The outer class implements the Mint type, with its **purse** method implemented by the nested **class** purse. Thanks to the class nesting, this implementation is quite compact. The Mint class itself is straightforward, holding a `brandPair` that will be used to maintain the integrity of the ADT, i.e. the whole Mint and Purse system. Anyone with access to a `mint` can create a new purse with new funds simply by requesting the `purse` class. (Grace doesn't need a **new** keyword to create instances of classes—just the class

```
type Mint = interface {
  purse(amount : Number) —> Purse
}

type Purse = interface {
  balance —> Number
  deposit(amount : Number, src : Purse) —> Boolean
  sprout —> Purse
}
```

Fig. 3 Mints and purses

```
type Sealing = interface {
  makeBrandPair —> interface {
    sealer —> Sealer
    unsealer —> Unsealer
  }
}

type Sealer = interface { seal(o : Object) —> Box }

type Unsealer = interface { unseal(b : Box) —> Object }

type Box = interface { }
```

Fig. 4 Brand pairs

```
class mint —> Mint is public {
  def myMint = self
  def brandPair = sealing.makeBrandPair

  class purse(amount : Number) —> Purse {
    var balance := amount

    method decr(amt : Number) —> Boolean is confidential {
    if ((amt < 0) || (amt > balance)) then {
       return false }
    balance := balance − amt
    return true }

    method getDecr
      {brandPair.sealer.seal { amt —> decr(amt) } }

    method deposit(amt : Number, src : Purse) —> Boolean {
    if (amt < 0) then { return false }
    var srcDecr
    try { srcDecr := brandPair.unsealer.unseal(src.getDecr) }
      catch { _ —> return false }
    if (srcDecr.apply( amt )) then {
       balance := balance + amt
       return true }
    return false }

    method sprout { purse(0) }
  }
}
```

Fig. 5 Sealer/unsealer based mint

name is enough.) There is a sprout method at the end of the purse class so that
clients with access to a purse (but not the mint) can create new empty purses (but
not purses with arbitrary balances).

The work is all done inside the purses. Each purse has a *per-instance private*
variable balance, and a deposit method that, given an amount and a valid source
purse which belongs to this Mint/Purse system (i.e. which represents an instance
of this ADT) adjusts the balance of both purse objects to perform the deposit. The
catch is that the deposit method, here on the destination purse, must also modify the
balance of the source purse. In a system that directly supported ADTs (such as many
class-based OO languages [3]) this is simple: the balance fields would be *per-class
private* and the deposit method could just access them directly (see Fig. 6).

This is not possible in an object-capability language because objects are encapsulated individually. The brokenDeposit method could only work if each purses'
balance field was publicly readable and writable: but in that case, any client could
do anything it wanted to any purse it could access. Rather, in this design, the decr
and getDecr and deposit methods, and the sealer/unsealer brandPair, collaborate

```
method brokenDeposit(amt : Number, src : Purse) -> Boolean
{ if ((amount >= 0) && (src.balance >= amount))
    then {
        src.balance := src.balance - amount
        balance := balance + amount
        return true
    } else {return false}
}
```

Fig. 6 ADT deposit method (per-class private)

to implement deposit without exposing their implementation beyond the boundary of the ADT. First, the decr method can decrease a purse's balance: this method is annotated as confidential, that is, *per-instance* private. Second, the public getDecr wraps that method in a lambda expression "{ amt -> decr(amt) }" and then uses the brandPair to seal that lambda expression, putting it into an opaque box that offers no interface to any other object. Although getDecr is public, meaning that it can be called by any object that has a reference to a purse, an attacker does not gain any advantage by calling that method, because the result is sealed inside the opaque box. Finally, the deposit method will use the matching unsealer from the *same* brand pair to unseal the box, and can then invoke the lambda expression to decrement the source purse. This remains secure because each instance of the mint class will have its own brand pair, and so can only unseal its own purses' boxes—the unseal method will throw an exception if it is passed a box that was sealed by a different brand pair.

3.2 Generalising the Sealer/Unsealer

The previous section's Mint/Purse design works well enough for, well, purses and mints, but sealing a single lambda expression only works when there is just one operation that needs to access two (or more) instances in the ADT. We can generalise the sealer-unsealer design by sealing a more capable object to represent the instances of the ADT.

In this design, we have an ExternalPurse that offers no public methods, and an InternalPurse that stores the ADT instance data, in this case the purse's balance (see Fig. 7).

Because the external purses are opaque, we need a different object to provide the ADT operations—effectively to reify the ADT as a whole. Rather than making requests to the ADT instance objects directly ("dst.deposit(amt, src)") we will pass the ADT instances to the object reifying the ADT, e.g.:

```
mybank.deposit(dstPurse, amt, srcPurse)
```

```
type ExternalPurse = interface { }

type InternalPurse = interface {
  balance --> Number
  balance:= ( n : Number )
}
```

Fig. 7 External and internal purse interfaces

```
type Issuer = interface {
  balance(of : ExternalPurse) --> Number
  deposit(to : ExternalPurse,
       amount : Number,
       from : ExternalPurse ) --> Boolean
  sprout --> ExternalPurse
}

type Mint = interface {
  purse(amount : Number) --> ExternalPurse
  issuer --> Issuer
}
```

Fig. 8 Splitting the issuer from the mint

In fact, to deal with the difference in privilege between creating new purses containing new money, versus manipulating existing purses with existing money, this design needs two objects: an Issuer that presents the main interface of the ADT, and which can be publicly available, and a Mint that permits inflating the currency, and consequently must be kept protected (see Fig. 8).

These interfaces can be implemented with a generalisation of the basic mint design (see Fig. 9). Each mint again has a brand pair, and auxiliary (confidential) methods to seal and unseal an InternalPurse within an opaque sealed box: these boxes will be used as the ExternalPurse objects. A new internal purse is just a simple object with a public balance field; an external purse is just an internal purse sealed into a box with the brand pair. Implementing the ADT operations is quite straightforward: any arguments representing accessible proxies for ADT instances (external purses) are unsealed, yielding the internal representations (internal purses) and then the operations implemented directly on the internal representations. An invariant of this system, of course, is that those internal representation objects are confined with the object reifying the whole ADT, and so can never be accessed outside it.

```
class mint -> Mint {

  def myBrandPair = sealing.makeBrandPair

  method seal(protectedRep : InternalPurse) -> ExternalPurse
    is confidential { myBrandPair.sealer.seal(protectedRep) }

  method unseal(sealedBox : ExternalPurse) -> InternalPurse
    is confidential { myBrandPair.unsealer.unseal(sealedBox) }

  method purse(amount : Number) -> ExternalPurse {
    seal( object { var balance is public := amount } ) }

  def issuer is public = object {

    method sprout -> ExternalPurse { purse(0) }

    method balance(of : ExternalPurse) -> Number {
      return unseal(of).balance}

    method deposit(to : ExternalPurse,
             amount : Number,
             from : ExternalPurse) -> Boolean {
      var internalTo
      var internalFrom
      try {
         internalTo := unseal(to)        // throws if fails
         internalFrom := unseal(from)  // throws if fails
      } catch { _ -> return false }

      if ((amount >= 0) && (internalFrom.balance >= amount))
        then {
          internalFrom.balance := internalFrom.balance - amount
          internalTo.balance := internalTo.balance + amount
          return true
        } else {return false}
    }
  }
}
```

Fig. 9 Generalised sealer/unsealer based mint

3.3 Hash Table

A similar design can employ a hash table, rather than sealer/unsealer brand-pairs to map from external to internal representations (see Fig. 10). This has the advantage that the external versions of the ADT instances have to be the sealed boxes themselves, and can offer interfaces so that they can be used directly as the public interface of the ADT. This means we do not need to split the ADT object into two

```
type ExternalPurse = interface {
  balance --> Number
  deposit(amount : Number, src : ExternalPurse) --> Boolean
  sprout --> ExternalPurse
}

type Mint = interface {
  purse(amount : Number) --> ExternalPurse
  deposit(to : ExternalPurse,
          amount : Number,
          from : ExternalPurse) --> Boolean
  balance(of : ExternalPurse) --> Number
  sprout --> ExternalPurse
}

type InternalPurse = interface {
  balance --> Number
  balance:= (Number) --> Done
  deposit(amount : Number, src : ExternalPurse) --> Boolean
}
```

Fig. 10 Interfaces for hash table based mint

objects to distinguish between a public interface ("Issuer") and a private interface ("Mint").

The implementation of this design (in Fig. 11) is more straightforward than the sealer/unsealer design (Fig. 9). The mint class contains a map (here instances) from external to internal purses; we also have a couple of helper methods to check if an (external) purse is valid for this mint, and to get the internal purse corresponding to an external purse.

To actually make a new purse, the mint makes a pair of objects (one internal and one external purse) stores them into the instances map, and returns the external purse. As in the sealer/unsealer based design, here the Mint object reifying the ADT must still offer methods implementing the ADT operations. These operations are used by the external purses to implement the ADT: they cannot generally be used by the ADT's clients as the reified ADT object (the mint) can inflate the currency by creating non-empty purses, so that capability must be kept confined.

The internal purse implementation is also straightforward. We could have used just objects holding a balance field, or even stored the balance directly in the map, but here we add some additional behaviour into the representation objects (see Fig. 12).

Finally, the externalPurse class implements the ADT instances—the public purses—as "curried object" proxies that delegate their behaviour back to the mint object that represents the whole ADT. Here we give the external purses their mint as a parameter: this would work equally well by nesting the external purse class within the mint (see Fig. 13).

```
class mint −> Mint {

  def instances = collections.map[[ExternalPurse,InternalPurse]]

  method valid(prs : ExternalPurse) −> Boolean
    { instances.contains(prs) }

  method internal(prs : ExternalPurse) −> InternalPurse
    { instances.get(prs) }

  method purse(amount : Number) −> ExternalPurse {
    def ext = externalPurse(self)
    def int = internalPurse(amount)
    instances.put(ext, int)
    return ext
  }

  method deposit(to : ExternalPurse,
          amount : Number,
          from : ExternalPurse) −> Boolean {
    if ((valid(to)) && (valid(from))) then {
      return internal(to).deposit(amount, internal(from))}
    return false
  }
  method balance(prs : ExternalPurse) −> Number
    { internal(prs).balance }

  method sprout −> ExternalPurse {purse(0)}
}
```

Fig. 11 Hash table based mint

```
class internalPurse(amount : Number) −> InternalPurse {
  var balance is public := amount
  method deposit(amount : Number, src : InternalPurse)
        −> Boolean
    { if ((amount >= 0) && (src.balance >= amount)) then {
      src.balance := src.balance − amount
      balance := balance + amount
      return true }
    return false
    }
}
```

Fig. 12 Internal purse for hash table based mint

```
class externalPurse(mint' : Mint) —> ExternalPurse {
  def mint = mint'
  method balance {mint.balance(self)}
  method sprout —> ExternalPurse { mint.sprout }
  method deposit(amount : Number, src : ExternalPurse)
    —> Boolean { return mint.deposit(self, amt, src)  }
}
```

Fig. 13 External purse for hash table based mint

4 Owners as Readers

In earlier work we have argued that an owners-as-readers discipline can provide an alternative formulation of ADTs [20]. Owners-as-readers depends on object ownership rather than type abstraction to encapsulate the implementations of the ADT instance [24]. In this model, all the instances are owned by an additional object that reifies the whole ADT, and the ownership type system ensures that they can only be manipulated within the scope of that object. Where owners-as-readers differs from other ownership disciplines is that other objects outside the ADT can hold references to the ADT instance objects, but those outside references appear opaque, and any requests on those objects from outside raise errors.

A range of ownership systems can be characterised as providing an owners-as-accessors discipline [4, 7, 8, 19, 27]: we have discussed these in more detail elsewhere [20]. Owners-as-readers systems clearly **do not** meet the key requirement of an object-capability system, precisely because owned objects are opaque outside their owners—although they would meet the following modified criterion: *"A direct access right to an object gives a subject the permission to invoke the behaviour of that object from inside that object's owner"*.

The resulting design is most similar to the sealer/unsealer version, because outside the mint ADT the internal purses are opaque. This means clients need to interact with the object reifying the ADT, and so we must split that object to separate the privileged capability (again, Mint) from the general capabilities to use the rest of the ADT operations (again, Issuer). On the other hand, we do not need an explicit split between internal and external purses (see Fig. 14).

Implementing this really should be straightforward by now. We make a purse class that only holds a balance: crucially that class is annotated is owned. The main ADT operations are defined inside the issuer object—the methods implementing these operations can just access the owned purse objects directly because they are within the mint: the owners-as-readers constraint ensures that the purses cannot be accessed from outside the ADT's boundary (see Fig. 15).

From the perspective of the owners-as-readers design, we can consider that both the sealer/unsealer or the map-based designs embody an ad-hoc form of ownership: in both cases there are internal capabilities—the internal purses—that must be confined within the ADT implementation, and the ownership—the control of the

```
type Mint = interface {
  purse(amount : Number) —> Purse
  issuer —> Issuer
}

type Issuer = interface {
  balance(of : Purse) —> Number
  deposit(to : Purse,
        amount : Number,
        from : Purse) —> Boolean
  sprout —> Purse
}

type Purse = interface {
  balance —> Number
  balance:= ( n : Number )
}
```

Fig. 14 Interfaces for owners-as-readers based mint

```
class mint —> Mint {

  class purse(amount : Number) —> Purse is owned {
    var balance is public := amount
  }

  def issuer is public = object {

    method sprout —> Purse { purse(0) }

    method deposit(to : Purse is owned, amount : Number,
          from : Purse is owned) — > Boolean {
      if (
        (amount >= 0) && (from.balance >= amount))
      then {
        from.balance := from.balance — amount
        to.balance := to.balance + amount
        return true
      } else {return false}
    }

    method balance(of : Purse is owned) —> Number {
      return of.balance}
  }
}
```

Fig. 15 Owners-as-readers based mint

ADT's boundary—is embodied in the sealer/unsealer's brand-pair, or in the map from external to internal purses: here that ownership is supported directly in the programming language.

We can also speculate on whether there is an obvious way to provide a public ADT interface via the purses, rather than again requiring operations to be addressed to the object reifying the ADT (here the Issuer and the Mint). The answer is both yes and no: yes, because a language could e.g. distinguish between ADT-public and ADT-private operations on those instance objects, and no, because that takes us right back to ADT oriented languages with per-class access restrictions, that is, right away from the object-capability model.

5   Primitive Data Types

Object-oriented languages must also integrate another type of data item into their object models. Machine-level primitive types such as integers, floating point numbers, Booleans, may be provided directly by the underlying CPU; other types such as Strings or Symbols should be implemented directly by a virtual machine. Different languages tackle this problem in different ways:

- C++ & Java objects and primitives are in different universes. The languages' static type systems ensure primitives and objects cannot be mistaken for each other— although different types of conversions can be applied to "box" a primitive into an object, and "unbox" it as necessary.
- Smalltalk objects have a primitive part and an "object-oriented" part [6]. The primitive part stores e.g. the value of a number as a primitive double, while the object-oriented part holds the objects' variables and methods The body of each method of each object can designate virtual machine primitive operations that should be invoked using data stored in the objects' primitive parts.
- Self objects also have a primitive part and an object-oriented part (the same data model as Smalltalk) [26]. In Self, primitive code is invoked by syntactically differentiated messages (requests, method calls) rather than by designated method bodies.
- Newspeak objects again have primitive and object-oriented parts, but primitive code is invoked via a VM proxy object, rather than distinguished methods or messages [1].

5.1   External Primitives

Figure 16 shows the kind of code Newspeak uses to invoke operations on primitive objects (albeit expressed using Grace syntax). A request on integers ("1 + 2") resolves to one of these method definitions, resulting in a request such as ("vm.addInteger(1,2)") to the vm object that reifies the virtual machine.

```
class integer { // construction is magic
    method +(other : Number) { vm.addInteger(self, other) }
    method −(other : Number) { vm.subtractInteger(self, other) }
    method *(other : Number) { vm.multiplyInteger(self, other) }
    method /(other : Number) { vm.divideInteger(self, other) }
    method prefix− { vm.negateInteger(self) }
}
```

Fig. 16 Newspeak primitive invocations via VM proxy

The key here is to compare the code for integers in Fig. 16 with the code for the external purses in the mint implemented with a hash table in Fig. 13. Both of these figures exhibit the same pattern: a method is called on an "instance object"— generally a method that takes more than one instance to implement a complex operation and the receiver and arguments to that message are passed in to a third party (the mint or vm proxy) which effectively retrieves the data and executes the operation.

This model certainly makes the route to invoke VM primitives clear—and, in accordance with Newspeak's pure object-object design, does so without any language support for primitive methods or messages. This model is still asymmetric, however: although the behaviour is moved out of the objects, the primitive data still remains in their primitive parts. This is most obvious when asking how instances of the integer class in Fig. 16 are created—the answer is: they have to be created by the VM or language implementation itself, either from literals in the source code or operations on other integers or other primitive types.

5.2 Object-as-Readers Primitives

Perhaps the cleanest model is to follow William Cook's distinction between objects and ADTs to its logical conclusion [3]. We can treat all low-level primitive types as (interlinked) sets of ADTs provided by the VMs—rather than objects. Individual instances of these ADTs offer no methods in their own rights, not even equality. To other code, they are opaque 'magic cookies' that can be stored in object's fields, stored in variables, passed as arguments, but that offer no behaviour themselves: the only way to operate on the instances is to pass them into the VM or another object reifying the ADT, as in the code in Fig. 17.

Behaviour for these ADTs is again provided by a VM object—or, perhaps, a set of singleton objects: one per ADT. The methods e.g. on the vmIntegerADT class take and return those magic cookies, which cannot be manipulated any other way. All the language-level behaviour for primitives is then written as normal code that manipulates the magic cookies. In Fig. 17, the integer class can be written in completely normal code.

```
class integer(cookie' : VmInteger) −> Number  { // construction is normal
  def cookie is public = cookie'

  method +(other : Number) −> Number {
    integer(vmIntegerADT.addInteger(cookie, other.cookie))}
  method −(other : Number) −> Number {
    integer(vmIntegerADT.subtractInteger(cookie, other.cookie))}
  method *(other : Number) −> Number {
    integer(vmIntegerADT.multiplyInteger(cookie, other.cookie))}
  method /(other : Number) −> Number {
    integer(vmIntegerADT.divideInteger(cookie, other.cookie))}
  method prefix− −> Number {
    integer(vmIntegerADT.negateInteger(cookie)) }
}
```

Fig. 17 Objects-as-readers primitive invocations

This design results in a clear interface to the VM ADTs, a clearer data model—as objects are either all primitive, or all language-level objects, but with nothing in between. There is also a clear interface to the VM support for the primitive types—the interface supported by objects like vmIntegerADT module object. Other information or behaviour can be added in to the wrapper classes—perhaps to add provenance information, or taint tracking—without affecting the interface to the underlying ADT.

This model need not necessarily be slower or more memory intensive than one based on primitive parts and inheritance. Raw CPUs, and high-performance VMs both end up implementing primitive types by allocating implementation fields in the representation of the object. This is as true for a machine code implementation as it is for an implementation in a higher level VM or even a translation to a dynamic language such as Javascript.

5.3 Primitives for All Objects

The remaining issue is that in many object-oriented languages, all objects are to some extent primitive objects. Just as class Object in Smalltalk or Java provides language level methods that apply to all objects, so it also relies on a small number of primitive methods that also apply to all objects. In these object models, we can consider that—conceptually—each object has a primitive data part that can be thought of as holding its identity (at least), perhaps also its class, lock, type, etc. Again, as with other kinds of primitives, primitive behaviours can be invoked by an appropriate mechanism to access that primitive data part. Because every object has that primitive data, those primitives apply to all objects. Figure 18 shows how this could be implemented in the explicit-ADT style.

```
class graceObject —> Object {

  def cookie is public = vmObjectADT.newUniqueIdentity

  method ==(other : Object) —> Boolean
    { boolean( vmObjectADT.eq(cookie, other.cookie) ) }
  method hash —> Number
    { integer( vmObjectADT.hash(cookie) ) }
  method synchronized (block : Block[Done]) —> Done
    { with (vmObjectADT.lock(cookie).acquire) do (block) }
}
```

Fig. 18 Identity ADT at the top of the hierarchy

```
trait abstractEquality {
  method ==(other) { isMe(other) }
  method !=(other) {! (self == other) }
  method hash { identityHash }

  method isMe(other) is required { }
  method identityHash is required { }
}
```

Fig. 19 Abstract equality trait

```
trait identityEquality {
  use equality

  def cookie is public = vmObjectADT.newUniqueIdentity

  method ==(other : Object) —> Boolean
    { boolean( vmObjectADT.cq(cookie, other.cookie) ) }
  method hash —> Number
    { integer( vmObjectADT.hash(cookie) ) }
}
```

Fig. 20 Identity equality trait

This design, though, gives objects an identity-based hash, and identity-based equality whether they want it or not—e.g. "functional" objects (basically records) may not want this equality; a proxy may want both identity and hash code to be delegated to the object they are proxying.

Time, then, to go to one last remove. Figure 19 shows an abstractEquality trait that defines a suite of "left-handed" equality operators in terms of two abstract operations, isMe and hash [22]. Objects can either provide those operations directly, or if they do want identity semantics, they can additionally inherit from the identityEquality trait shown in Fig. 20 which provides a ready-made identity-based implementation.

6 Conclusion

In this chapter we have considered issues in designing and implementing abstract data types in purely object-oriented systems, and in object-capability systems in particular. We show how primitive instances can be treated as abstract data types in object-oriented systems, and extend that treatment to encompass even explicit object identity.

The first design we considered used sealer/unsealer brand pairs to encapsulate the ADT's shared state, but kept that state within the individual purse objects. Dynamic sealing is an established example that captures the essence of the abstractions involved when working with capabilities [25]. The code that implemented the system is also primarily in the purses—a mint object primarily exists to provide a separate capability to inflate the currency.

Our second design also encapsulates the ADT implementation using sealer/unsealer pairs, but generalises the design, to split each logical purse into two different capabilities, that is, into two separate objects, one of which is accessible from outside the ADT, and the second accessible only from inside. In this design, the external purse objects are opaque, so in effect we also split the mint object representing the whole ADT into an unprivileged Issuer, and the privileged Mint.

Our third design retains the split between internal and external purses, but uses a hash table rather than sealer/unsealer brand pair to provide the encapsulation boundary. This has the advantage that the external purses do not have to be the sealed boxes, and so we can return to a more "object-oriented" style API, where clients interact with the purse objects directly, rather than via the issuer object; this means we no longer need to split the mint capability. The catch, of course, is that this is probably the most complex design that we consider in this chapter.

Our last design revisits our owners-as-readers encapsulation model, which tries to build in minimal support for ADTs in a dynamic, object-oriented setting. This is the smallest implementation, because owners-as-readers renders the purses opaque outside the ADT, and so the purse objects no longer need to be split in any way. On the other hand, because the purses are opaque to all the clients of the system, we again need an issuer offering the classic ADT-style interface.

Finally, we show how primitive objects, and primitive operations across all objects can be encompassed within these designs.

We note that aliasing issues arise pervasively in these object-capability implementations. Wherever we have to split objects to divide public and private capabilities (i.e. those capabilities on the inside and outside of the ADT's boundaries) then there will be an implicit aliasing relationship between those objects. These designs also involve confinement or ownership relationships, implicitly or explicitly, in that the internal object-capabilities must not be accessible from outsides.

As with much object-capability research, we have once again tackled the mint/purse system. The abstract data type perspective can explain why this example is so ubiquitous: because the mint/purse system is about as simple an abstract data type as you can get: the data held in each ADT instance is just a single natural number. We hypothesise that many of the examples used in object-capability systems may be better modelled as ADTs, rather than objects, and that much of the difficulty in implementing those examples in object-capability systems stems directly from this incompatibility in underlying model. We hope the object-capability designs that we have presented here, however, should be able to cope with a range of more complex abstract data types.

Acknowledgements We thank the anonymous reviewers for their comments. This work was supported in part by a James Cook Fellowship, by the Royal Society of New Zealand Marsden Fund, by Oracle Labs Australia, and by the US Department of Defense.

References

1. Gilad Bracha. *Newspeak Programming Language Draft Specification Version 0.05*. Tech. rep. Ministry of Truth, 2009.
2. Luca Cardelli et al. "Modula-3 language definition". In: *SIGPLAN Not.* 27.8 (Aug. 1992), pp. 15–42. DOI: https://doi.org/10.1145/142137.142141 URL: http://doi.acm.org/10.1145/142137. 142141.
3. William R. Cook. "On understanding data abstraction, revisited". In: *OOPSLA Proceedings.* 2009, pp. 557–572.
4. Christos Dimoulas et al. "Declarative Policies for Capability Control". In: *Proceedings of the 27th IEEE Computer Security Foundations Symposium*. June 2014.
5. Sophia Drossopoulou, James Noble, and Mark. S. Miller. "Swapsies on the Internet". In: *PLAS* 2015.
6. Adele Goldberg and David Robson. *Smalltalk-80: The Language and its Implementation*. Addison-Wesley, 1983.
7. Donald Gordon and James Noble. "Dynamic Ownership in a Dynamic Language". In: *DLS Proceedings*. 2007, pp. 9–16.
8. Olivier Gruber and Fabienne Boyer. "Ownership-Based Isolation for Concurrent Actors on Multi-core Machines". In: *ECOOP*. 2013, pp. 281–301.
9. Butler W. Lampson. "Protection". In: *Operating Systems Review* 8.1 (Jan. 1974), pp. 18–24.
10. Barbara Liskov et al. "Abstraction Mechanisms in CLU" In: *Comm. ACM* 20.8 (Aug. 1977), pp. 564–576.
11. David MacQueen. "Modules for Standard ML". In: *LISP and Functional Programming* Austin, Texas, United States: ACM, 1984, pp. 198–207. DOI: https://doi.org/10.1145/800055.802036 URL: http://doi.acm.org/10.1145/800055.802036.
12. Mark S. Miller, Tom Van Cutsem, and Bill Tulloh. "Distributed Electronic Rights in JavaScript". In: *ESOP*. 2013.
13. Mark Samuel Miller, Chip Morningstar, and Bill Frantz. "Capability-Based Financial Instruments: From Object to Capabilities". In: *Financial Cryptography*. Springer, 2000.
14. Mark Samuel Miller. "Robust Composition: Towards a Unified Approach to Access Control and Concurrency Control". PhD thesis. Baltimore, Maryland, 2006.
15. Mark Samuel Miller. "Secure Distributed Programming with Object-capabilities in JavaScript". Talk at Vrije Universiteit Brussel, mobicrant-talks.eventbrite.com. Oct. 2011.
16. James H. Morris Jr "Protection in Programming Languages". In: *CACM* 16.1 (1973).
17. James H. Morris Jr. "Protection in Programming Languages". In: *Commun. ACM* 16.1 (Jan. 1973), pp. 15–21. ISSN: 0001-0782. DOI: https://doi.org/10.1145/361932.361937 URL: http://doi.acm.org/10.1145/361932.361937.
18. James Noble. "Iterators and Encapsulation". In: *TOOLS Europe*. 2000.

19. James Noble, David Clarke, and John Potter "Object Ownership for Dynamic Alias Protection". In: *TOOLS Pacific 32*. 1999.
20. James Noble and Alex Potanin. "On Owners-as-Accessors". In: *IWACO Proceedings*. 2014.
21. James Noble et al. "Abstract Data Types in Object-Capability Systems". In: *IWACO Proceedings*. 2016.
22. James Noble et al. "The left hand of equals". In: *Onward! ACM International Symposium on New Ideas, New Paradigms, and Reflections on Programming and Software*. 2016, pp. 224–237. DOI: https://doi.org/10.1145/2986012.2986031.
23. James Noble et al. "Towards a Model of Encapsulation". In: *IWACO Proceedings*. Ed. by Dave Clarke. UU-CS-2003 030. Utrecht University, July 2003.
24. Alex Potanin, Monique Damitio, and James Noble. "Are Your Incoming Aliases Really Necessary? Counting the Cost of Object Ownership". In: *International Conference on Software Engineering (ICSE)*. 2013.
25. Eijiro Sumii and Benjamin C. Pierce. "A Bisimulation for Dynamic Sealing". In: *SIGPLAN Not.* 39.1 (Jan. 2004), pp. 161–172. ISSN: 0362-1340. DOI: https://doi.org/10.1145/982962.964015 URL: http://doi.acm.org/10.1145/982962.964015
26. David Ungar and Randall B. Smith. "SELF: The Power of Simplicity". In: *Lisp and Symbolic Computation* 4.3 (June 1991).
27. Erwann Wernli, Pascal Maerki, and Oscar Nierstrasz. "Ownership, Filters and Crossing Handlers". In: *Dynamic Language Symposium (DLS)*. 2012.
28. Williaam A. Whitaker. "Ada - The Project: The DoD High Order Language Working Group". In: *HOPL Preprints*. 1993, pp. 299–331.
29. Niklaus Wirth. *Programming in Modula-2*. isbn 0-387-15078-1. Springer Verlag, 1985.
30. William A. Wulf, Ralph L. London, and Mary Shaw. "An Introduction to the Construction and Verification of Alphard Programs". In: *IEEE Trans Softw. Eng.* SE-2.4 (1976), pp. 253–265.

A Personal History of Delta Modelling

Ina Schaefer

Abstract Delta modelling is a transformational approach to represent variability of software systems through change operations to transform one software variant to another variant realizing different functionality. The term *delta* for a container of those change operations was coined by Arnd Poetzsch-Heffter in early 2009. This article gives a personal account of the achievements in delta modelling since then by a collection of quotes from collaborators, students and friends.

1 Introduction

The history of delta modelling starts in spring 2009 at TU Kaiserslautern when my then Master student Alexander Worret and I were working on a paper publishing the results of his Master thesis. This paper [17] appeared at the MAPLE workshop held at SPLC 2009 in San Francisco. While we were working on the final version, we were discussing how to name the modules containing changes to a base variant of the code. And Arnd said: *Well, the Americans would just call them delta.* And when Alexander and I left Arnd's office, the term *delta modelling* was born.

Delta modelling is a transformational approach [15] to modelling variability of a system, as considered in software product lines (SPLs). The main idea is to represent one particular variant as a core module. This variant can be developed with standard software engineering principles to ensure its quality. A set of delta modules captures changes that can be applied to the core module in order to realise further features or other system variants. Deltas as containers for changes can add, remove or modify elements of the core module. To derive a variant, they can be applied in sequence to perform a number of change operations to the core module. Of course, the sequence of deltas has to be chosen such that the resulting variant is well-formed.

I. Schaefer (✉)
Technische Universität Braunschweig, Institute of Software Engineering and Automotive Informatics, Braunschweig, Germany
e-mail: i.schaefer@tu-braunschweig.de

© Springer Nature Switzerland AG 2018
P. Müller, I. Schaefer (eds.), *Principled Software Development*,
https://doi.org/10.1007/978-3-319-98047-8_15

Deltas can be connected to features in a feature model [10], such that variants can be automatically derived for a given feature configuration. In this context, deltas (or combinations of deltas) capture the impact a feature has on the core module. The notion of the core module was removed later [14], giving rise to the notion of *pure delta modelling*, where variant derivation starts from an empty core module in order to make the formulation of the approach more uniform. The main benefit of delta modelling as a variability modelling approach is the flexible notion of change, while still being modular, in contrast to annotative variability modelling as in preprocessors [4]. Furthermore, delta modelling allows the seamless integration of evolutionary changes in contrast to compositional variability modelling [1], by allowing to remove entities from variants again.

Delta modelling started as an approach to automatically generate variants of a system and then unfolded into a variability modelling approach spanning numerous modelling and programming languages, such as Simulink [2] or Java [5], and was extended to also model and reason about system evolution [11, 18]. Based on the notion of delta modelling, a number of testing [8], performance analysis [6], and verification [19] techniques for variable systems and software product lines were developed. Furthermore, approaches how to obtain delta models from a set of existing variants are extensively considered in the context of family mining and reengineering of software product lines [20].

My main goal for this paper is to provide a historical perspective on delta modelling. I have asked collaborators and past and present PhD and Master students to provide their personal history of delta modelling answering how they got involved with delta modelling, what they like or dislike about it and where they see future challenges for delta modelling. You will read what they said in the following sections.

2   The Beginnings of Delta Modelling

Ferruccio Damiani is one of my first collaborators on delta modelling. In particular, we worked on delta-oriented programming [13] as an alternative modular implementation approach for variability.

> I first heard about delta modelling in March 2009, when Ina Schaefer visited Torino in the context of a research project (funded by the German-Italian "Vigoni" Exchange Program) between the research group of Arnd in Kaiserslautern and my group in Torino. During Ina's first visit to Torino, we immediately realised that the notion of *deltas* could be used for designing innovative languages for implementing SPLs. The first outcome of this collaboration has been the SPLC 2010 paper "Delta-Oriented Programming of Software Product Lines". [13] In the ten years before, I had been working on programming constructs for making Java-like programming languages more declarative and flexible—in particular with respect to code reuse. Deltas provided a way for realising both these goals at a system level, providing a shortcut connection between foundational research and industrial applications.

What I liked (and still like) about deltas is that it is very natural to think/design/program in terms of them and that they are a very general concept (e.g., not confined to a particular programming/modelling paradigm for variants). The flexibility of deltas soon raised interesting research challenges (e.g., for the design of analysis techniques for delta-oriented software product lines): it has been (and still is) a pleasure to work on them. I think that the potential of deltas in not yet fully unveiled. Although people from industry generally like them, the adoption barrier is an issue. DSL languages, like the ABS modelling language [3], are currently the most suitable candidates to put deltas at work. (Ferruccio Damiani, University of Turin)

While I was still waiting to hear back from a few colleagues in early 2009 if they would host me as a postdoc, Arnd called Reiner Hähnle and 2 hours later I had a postdoc position. So, I enjoyed working in Reiner's group at Chalmers University in Gothenburg and in the HATS project.

In 2010, I was leading an EC FP6 project that was about to define the new modelling language ABS [3] that was supposed to handle product variability. Arnd was part of that project and suggested that Ina might spend some time as a postdoc in my group. She brought their idea of delta-oriented programming (DOP) with her, which had just been published in the previous year. It became quickly clear that DOP was exactly the mechanism we needed for ABS and we decided to adopt it. DOP is intuitive, simple, and powerful: the hallmarks of a useful language concept. "We use it every day in academic as well as in industrial modelling projects performed with the ABS language, which features perhaps the most mature implementation of DOP to date." (Reiner Hähnle, then Chalmers University)

At a HATS project meeting in Gothenburg in 2009, I met Dave Clarke. It was on a plane to a HATS meeting in Leuven, hosted by Dave, when I worked out the idea for the VaMoS10 paper [12] that remained my only single author paper so far.

I first encountered delta modelling when the HATS project started and Ina Schaefer presented her work on the topic. I immediately saw the potential of delta modelling as a key ingredient in expressing variability in the ABS programming language developed within HATS. Delta modelling provides a clear separation between the base software artifacts, the variability model, and the changes implementing each variant. Unfortunately, it is sometimes difficult to get a good overview of the totality of changes any delta makes and consequently understanding the effect of a delta or a collection of deltas can be difficult, especially if there are many different overlapping deltas. Delta modelling has certainly made an impact on programming, and it has been successfully applied to numerous programming paradigms and formalisms to produce delta-oriented versions of such formalisms. I think the key challenge that remains is related to understanding the models. How can delta models be developed and maintained while preserving a high degree of comprehensibility? And what tool support can be developed to help with this problem? (Dave Clarke, then KU Leuven)

3 Delta Modeling and Model-Based Development

One of my first papers [12] on delta modelling was about model-based development and the independent refinement of core and delta models in different modelling layers. Bernhard Rumpe shared the excitement on delta modelling in a series of papers with his group where we used delta modelling to express architectural variability.

Delta modelling is a promising approach to connect variability and model-based development. Early attempts of deriving deltas have shown, however, that reuse is limited. Considerable effort is necessary to generalise deltas (as a special form of transformations) such that they can be applied on a variety of different models. The more I have been thinking about deltas, the more I think higher-order generalised deltas share some characteristics with graph transformations. (Bernhard Rumpe, RWTH Aachen)

Christoph Seidl and I met at the FOSD meeting that I organised in Braunschweig in 2012 and again at the VaMoS workshop in Pisa in 2013. It was there that we started discussing about variability realisation techniques that are also suitable to deal with evolution. This resulted in Christoph's PhD thesis, and Christoph became my postdoc in Braunschweig in 2015.

I first came in contact with delta modelling at the Feature-Oriented Software Development (FOSD) Meeting 2012 as "the other way" of realizing variability in Software Product Lines (SPLs) by transforming realisation artifacts (instead of just adding or removing). When looking for a way to integrate variability in space (configuration) and variability in time (evolution) in SPLs, delta modelling seemed like an ideal fit and soon thereafter became one of the pillars of my dissertation as well as the tool suite DeltaEcore [18]. Today, my working group is involved in multiple topics revolving, among others, around delta modelling, e.g., to research ways to leverage its power as a white-box composition technique while still permitting peaceful co-existence with other, more gray-box composition techniques. (Christoph Seidl, PhD 2016, TU Dresden)

Matthias Kowal was my first team member when I started at TU Braunschweig towards the end of 2010, first as student assistant, then as Master student and finally as PhD student. Matthias worked on variability and delta modelling for automation systems as well as efficient performance analyses.

I came in contact with delta modelling during the end of 2012 by reading a DFG project proposal. It was a decisive encounter as this proposal described my potential PhD thesis and, thus, the first job in my life after graduating from university. While I like [delta modelling's] flexibility and expressiveness, these aspects are also great challenges. Developers can do all kinds of mischief with delta operations and it is sometimes very difficult to keep track of the changes considering a sequence of delta modules.
"With great power comes great responsibility" (from Spiderman).
(Matthias Kowal, PhD 2017)

Michael Nieke, among my second generation of PhD students, in his work focuses mainly on evolution of software production lines and detecting and preventing errors introduced by evolution of variability models. His tool suite Darwin-SPL [11] uses delta modelling for a model-based representation of change.

I first encountered delta modelling during the software product line engineering lecture at TU Braunschweig. After dealing with feature-oriented programming (FOP) and aspect-oriented programming (AOP), delta modelling seemed to be a sensible alternative. Compared to FOP, I valued the ability of delta modelling to remove and modify elements, and compared to AOP, I was not overwhelmed by the complex concept and syntax. My most impressive moment with delta modelling was when we let students develop a product line using a preliminary version of DeltaJ [5]. We introduced the syntax of DeltaJ in half an hour and another half an hour for an introduction to feature models. During the student project, the students organised themselves, directly understood how to use and define deltas, automatically introduced modularity because of a proper delta module application and were finally able to create a product line with more than 15 features in only three weeks. (Michael Nieke, Master Thesis 2015)

4 Delta Modelling for Testing and Analysis

Having applied delta modelling to model-based software development, we started considering how delta models can be used to make product line analysis and testing more efficient. In particular, we looked at testing and formal verification of software product lines with the help of delta modelling. The ideas of delta testing were published in the 2012 TAP paper [9] that I co-authored with Malte Lochau and Sascha Lity when I just had started at TU Braunschweig.

- How you got to know delta modelling: via our joint work for the TAP paper and the Master thesis of Sascha [Lity], and then a number of follow-up papers.
- What you like about it: simplest and most intuitively accessible way to think about variability and a superset of other approaches.
- What you dislike about it: delete is boon and bane at once.
- What you think about achievements and challenges: There are a number of beautiful (and especially formally founded) works on delta modelling, it is still open however how delta modelling can be applied in practice. (Malte Lochau, TU Darmstadt)

Sascha Lity, now my PhD student, continued working on delta modelling for capturing the evolution of variable systems, and came up with the notion of higher-order delta models [7] where a delta can modify a whole delta model. This higher-order delta then captures the evolution of a software product line from one point in time to the next. Based on this notion of higher-order delta models, Sascha develops techniques to efficiently test evolving software product lines, i.e., variants and versions at the same time.

My first contact with delta modelling was during my Master's thesis, where its concept was adopted to facilitate incremental product-line testing. Since then, deltas have become my daily work as a PhD student. I really like the idea behind delta modelling to exploit the commonality between variants and to solely focus on the differences between them. In my recent work, I extended delta modelling to also capture the evolution of product lines by means of deltas specifying the differences between consecutive version-specific delta models. This extension is then utilised to allow for regression testing of evolving product lines which will be the topic of my PhD thesis. However, sometimes, especially for evolution, the usage of delta modelling can get complex as a modeller has to have in mind how the potentially huge set of variants and also their versions differ to specify respective deltas. But, this is a challenge for variability modelling techniques in general. (Sascha Lity, Master Thesis 2012)

Remo Lachmann started his Master thesis on delta-oriented testing approaches very shortly after our first paper on delta testing had been published. Remo focused on architectural integration testing and expanded that in his PhD to a more general approach towards efficient and effective testing of variants and versions.

In software testing, we are able to use delta modelling to identify changes between variants on a very detailed level, e.g., using architecture diagrams we are able to identify changes on interface level. In particular, regression deltas allow us to guide the testers focus and avoid redundancy for a certain order of product variants. Delta modelling is an elegant way to avoid discussions about "What has changed between variants?" as we exactly know the places which might cause us troubles. Of course, we cannot know where a failure will be but we can make some good guesses using deltas. (Remo Lachmann, PhD 2017)

After Martin Wirsing introduced us, Mirco Tribastone and I wrote a joint project proposal for the DAPS project on efficient performance analysis approaches for variable and evolving software systems. Our joint work [6] is one of the first approaches towards constructive performance modelling and analysis for software product lines, while most other approaches only work empirically.

Since our collaboration within the DAPS project, I found delta modelling an appropriate language to reason about variability not only in programs but also in quantitative models of programs. In this context, the construction of a super-model that contains all the information about each possible variant is a powerful idea that has allowed us to perform family-based performance analysis of software models in an efficient manner. However, currently I see two main limitations. The first limitation concerns the assumption, in the delta modelling work I have been involved in so far, that one is given all possible variants of a system: this can be a large set in realistic situations, hence I feel we need higher-level formalisms that represent variants in an implicit way. The second limitation is not so much about delta modelling per se, but it is about the feasibility of variant-aware performance analysis. At present, we are limited in the types of software behaviours that can be modelled; more research is needed to be able to extend delta-based methods to expressive performance models such as layered queuing networks. (Mirco Tribastone, IMT Lucca)

5   Extractive Product Line Engineering

Delta modelling shows its main strengths compared to compositional approaches for realising variability when we want to extract variably from a set of existing variants. Thomas Thüm and I collaborated a lot on efficient analysis and verification of software product lines, leading to a survey article where Thomas proposes a classification of product line analyses techniques [19] and classified the state-of-the-art.

When I heard about delta-oriented programming for the first time, I noticed the potential for extractive creation of product lines. Simply take an existing program as input and then write your deltas around it. If you have even multiple program variants that have been created using clone-and-own or with branching, you can take one program as the core and automatically compute regression deltas to all other program variants. The migration from clones to a delta-oriented product line can thus be done completely automatically. Another advantage is that you can use state-of-the-art tools to develop the core, similar to aspect-oriented programming. Furthermore, delta-oriented programming is so flexible that you can have an empty core, a small core, or a large core and deltas can be large regression deltas or small units increasing the sharing.

While delta-oriented programming is quite flexible, the flexibility is boon and bane at the same time. When considering the research literature, the flexibility is often restricted to make certain analyses feasible. Some approaches require to have an empty core, while others assume monotonicity of deltas requiring either a small or a large core. This is problematic as the advantage of developing the core using standard tools is dependent on the choice of the core. If we take an empty core, the advantage is gone. Especially the discussion of monotonicity is interesting, because requiring monotone deltas only adding functionality is essentially known as feature-oriented programming, a programming technique much older than delta-oriented programming, which has been well researched. Similarly, while the automated transition of clones into a core and regression deltas sounds great, we have to be clear about the fact that those regression deltas have no sharing (i.e., we only share the core) and we are able to generate only the migrated clones and no new products. The process of retrieving deltas that are easy-to-understand, free of redundancies, and can be combined in multiple ways by means of reusable parts requires a large manual effort. A process which is likely to be only manageable with proper tool support. (Thomas Thüm, PhD 2015 U Magdeburg)

David Wille was a Bachelor and Master student at TU Braunschweig and is also among my second generation of PhD students. David's main research area evolves around re-engineering of software product lines by family mining approaches.

I first came in contact with delta modelling during a lecture on Automotive Software Engineering. After finishing my Master's degree and starting as a PhD student, delta modelling became part of my daily life. Personally, I am more of a late adopter as my main research evolves around reverse-engineering of variability from existing variants. Thus, I started using delta modelling only after realising algorithms to identify the variability that should be encoded in the created SPL. What I like most about delta modelling is its flexibility (i.e., the ease of extending the SPL and the possibility to use basically one variant as core of the SPL), the possibility of high modularity and, given a well designed delta language, the tight integration of the delta operations with the underlying programming language. While the flexibility and modularity are big advantages over other SPL mechanisms, developers should use the provided techniques in a well reflected manner as otherwise these advantages can easily turn into disadvantages. For instance, the potentially high invasiveness of delta modelling can easily become a hurdle as developers easily lose the overview over the encoded variability. Overall, I would recommend delta modelling for realizing SPLs in companies as, from my experience, even people with low or no programming knowledge and managers can understand the general idea and see its benefits. Although, with DeltaEcore [18] already a very mature implementation of delta modelling exists for Ecore models, the approach will hopefully gain additional momentum (not only in research) when a stable version of DeltaJ [5] is available in the near future. (David Wille, Master thesis 2014)

Tobias Runge, also a student at TU Braunschweig, already used delta modelling in his Bachelor's thesis. He continued in my group as a Master's student and now as a PhD student, but is one of the few who moved away from delta modelling as his main research topic.

My first contact with delta modelling was in my Bachelor's thesis. I had to extend a family mining approach for state charts. Starting with the family model of two or more variants, I generated deltas between the variants. The deltas contained operations to add or remove states and transitions. Modify operations were only used to change names. To apply deltas, the DeltaEcore framework [18] was used. I was very impressed how well the delta approach worked. I compared two variants and collected all differences which I translated to add and remove operations. If I then executed the deltas on the core variant, the other variant was created accordingly. The only problem arose if more variants are compared and smaller deltas for subparts are created. It was complicated to remove repetition without violating the correctness. (Tobias Runge, Bachelor Thesis 2016)

While attending the meetings of IFIP Working Group 2.4 on program implementation technology, which also Arnd is a member of, I learnt about software
taxonomies as a different way to structure families of software variants. In a joint
paper [16], we explored how to bridge the gap from software taxonomies to software
product lines realised by delta modelling.

> My first exposure to deltas was via discussion with Arnd at various IFIP Working Group
> 2.4 meetings. It took several such discussions to highlight that they were the solution
> to software engineering problems I'd encountered while architecting and programming a
> wide variety of software product lines, including compilers/interpreters, security products
> (including hardware), and silicon-chip optimisers & simulators. In all of those contexts,
> my teams used an assortment of hacks which could've been much cleaner (also with more
> supportive languages). As for what I like to see in ongoing and future research – my own
> background in correctness-by-construction (CbC, Dijkstra-style) motivates the integration
> of all such programming paradigms (including deltas) into correctness preserving calculi
> for program (family) derivation. Similarly, (nominally CbC) taxonomies of algorithms and
> data-structures have been built by my group over some years – with rather extensive use
> of ad hoc and (ironically) informal constructs; initially, the informality was borderline
> enjoyable but more formalised constructs (e.g., via deltas) may be an appropriate way to
> bring order to such taxonomies. (Bruce Watson, Stellenbosch University)

And an industrial collaborator says about the adoption of delta modelling:

> We as an industry partner got involved into delta modelling when we realised, that most of
> the time proactive product line engineering or variant management cannot be implemented
> because, when starting a product line development, it is not clear which parts of the solution
> are variable. More than that, in the beginning you don't want to invest additional effort
> beyond the core engineering task. So we appreciated the idea to rather reengineer the variant
> structures by computing deltas of created modelling artifacts. (An industrial collaborator)

6   Conclusion

Delta modelling has gone a long way in the last years. We have applied delta
modelling for model-based development, used it for efficient test, analysis and
verification purposes, and proposed approaches to refactor existing sets of (cloned)
variants into a delta model to make them amenable to managed reuse and future
evolution.

But of course, we are not quite there yet. There are a number of open questions
and future research challenges in order to make delta modelling more applicable
to large-scale systems and in industrial practice: First, delta modelling needs to
be integrated into mainstream modelling and programming languages or DSLs,
such as already done for the ABS [3] or DeltaJ [5]. Deltas have been generalised
to also work language independently, e.g., in the DeltaEcore framework [18].
However, in order to make delta modelling applicable to large-scale software system
development, we indeed need approaches how to improve the comprehensibility
of delta models, e.g., by providing editors and visualisations for dependencies
between delta modules, accompanied with appropriate analyses and type systems.

The high flexibility and invasiveness of delta modelling is boon and bane at the same time. Hence, we are currently looking at approaches how to move from delta modelling for fine-grained software variability of early software product lines to more coarse-grained component-based composition approaches as a software product line matures.

Acknowledgements I would like to thank Christoph Seidl for his valuable comments on an earlier version of this work.

References

1. Apel, S., Batory, D.S., Kästner, C., Saake, G.: Feature-Oriented Software Product Lines - Concepts and Implementation. Springer (2013)
2. Haber, A., Kolassa, C., Manhart, P., Nazari, P.M.S., Rumpe, B., Schaefer, I.: First-class variability modeling in matlab/simulink. In: The Seventh International Workshop on Variability Modelling of Software-intensive Systems, VaMoS '13, Pisa , Italy, January 23–25, 2013, pp. 4:1–4:8 (2013)
3. Hähnle, R.: The abstract behavioral specification language: A tutorial introduction. In: Formal Methods for Components and Objects - 11th International Symposium, FMCO 2012, Bertinoro, Italy, September 24–28, 2012, Revised Lectures, pp. 1–37 (2012)
4. Hunsen, C., Zhang, B., Siegmund, J., Kästner, C., Leßenich, O., Becker, M., Apel, S.: Preprocessor-based variability in open-source and industrial software systems: An empirical study. Empirical Software Engineering **21**(2), 449–482 (2016)
5. Koscielny, J., Holthusen, S., Schaefer, I., Schulze, S., Bettini, L., Damiani, F.: Deltaj 1.5: delta-oriented programming for java 1.5. In: 2014 International Conference on Principles and Practices of Programming on the Java Platform Virtual Machines, Languages and Tools, PPPJ '14, Cracow, Poland, September 23–26, 2014, pp. 63–74 (2014)
6. Kowal, M., Tschaikowski, M., Tribastone, M., Schaefer, I.: Scaling size and parameter spaces in variability-aware software performance models. In: 30th IEEE/ACM International Conference on Automated Software Engineering, ASE 2015, Lincoln, NE, USA, November 9–13, 2015, pp. 407–417 (2015)
7. Lity, S., Kowal, M., Schaefer, I.: Higher-order delta modeling for software product line evolution. In: Proceedings of the 7th International Workshop on Feature-Oriented Software Development, FOSD@SPLASH 2016, Amsterdam, Netherlands, October 30, 2016, pp. 39–48 (2016)
8. Lochau, M., Lity, S., Lachmann, R., Schaefer, I., Goltz, U.: Delta-oriented model-based integration testing of large-scale systems. Journal of Systems and Software **91**, 63–84 (2014)
9. Lochau, M., Schaefer, I., Kamischke, J., Lity, S.: Incremental model-based testing of delta-oriented software product lines. In: Tests and Proofs - 6th International Conference, TAP 2012, Prague, Czech Republic, May 31 - June 1, 2012. Proceedings, pp. 67–82 (2012)
10. Meinicke, J., Thüm, T., Schröter, R., Benduhn, F., Leich, T., Saake, G.: Mastering Software Variability with FeatureIDE. Springer (2017)
11. Nieke, M., Engel, G., Seidl, C.: Darwinspl: an integrated tool suite for modeling evolving context-aware software product lines. In: Proceedings of the Eleventh International Workshop on Variability Modelling of Software-intensive Systems, VaMoS 2017, Eindhoven, Netherlands, February 1–3, 2017, pp. 92–99 (2017)
12. Schaefer, I.: Variability modelling for model-driven development of software product lines. In: Fourth International Workshop on Variability Modelling of Software-Intensive Systems, Linz, Austria, January 27–29, 2010. Proceedings, pp. 85–92 (2010)

13. Schaefer, I., Bettini, L., Bono, V., Damiani, F., Tanzarella, N.: Delta-oriented programming of software product lines. In: Software Product Lines: Going Beyond - 14th International Conference, SPLC 2010, Jeju Island, South Korea, September 13–17, 2010. Proceedings, pp. 77–91 (2010)

14. Schaefer, I., Damiani, F.: Pure delta-oriented programming. In: Proceedings of the Second International Workshop on Feature-Oriented Software Development, FOSD 2010, Eindhoven, Netherlands, October 10, 2010, pp. 49–56 (2010)

15. Schaefer, I., Rabiser, R., Clarke, D., Bettini, L., Benavides, D., Botterweck, G., Pathak, A., Trujillo, S., Villela, K.: Software diversity: state of the art and perspectives. STTT **14**(5), 477–495 (2012)

16. Schaefer, I., Seidl, C., Cleophas, L.G., Watson, B.W.: Splicing TABASCO: custom-tailored software product line variants from taxonomy-based toolkits. In: Proceedings of the 2015 Annual Research Conference on South African Institute of Computer Scientists and Information Technologists, SAICSIT '15, Stellenbosch, South Africa, September 28–30, 2015, pp. 34:1–34:10 (2015)

17. Schaefer, I., Worret, A., Poetzsch-Heffter, A.: A model-based framework for automated product derivation. In: In Workshop on Model-driven Approaches in Software Product Line Engineering (MAPLE2009 (2009)

18. Seidl, C., Schaefer, I., Aßmann, U.: Deltaecore - A model-based delta language generation framework. In: Modellierung 2014, 19.-21. März 2014, Wien, Österreich, pp. 81–96 (2014)

19. Thüm, T., Apel, S., Kästner, C., Schaefer, I., Saake, G.: A classification and survey of analysis strategies for software product lines. ACM Comput. Surv. **47**(1), 6:1–6:45 (2014)

20. Wille, D., Runge, T., Seidl, C., Schulze, S.: Extractive software product line engineering using model-based delta module generation. In: Proceedings of the Eleventh International Workshop on Variability Modelling of Software-intensive Systems, VaMoS 2017, Eindhoven, Netherlands, February 1–3, 2017, pp. 36–43 (2017)

Are Synchronous Programs Logic Programs?

Klaus Schneider and Marc Dahlem

Abstract Synchronous languages have been introduced as programming languages that directly reflect the nature of reactive systems: Their execution is divided into discrete reaction steps such that in each reaction step, inputs are read from the environment and outputs are instantaneously computed. Reaction steps, which are also called macro steps, consist thereby of a set of atomic micro step actions that are executed in the variable environment associated with the macro step. At the beginning of the macro step, only the values of the input variables are known in this variable environment, and the values of the remaining variables have to be computed according to the data-dependencies. Since the micro step actions depend on the variable environment that they also create, it might be the case that there are cyclic dependencies. Whether such cyclic dependencies can be constructively resolved has to be checked by a compile-time causality analysis which will ensure that there is for all inputs a suitable schedule of the micro steps. If the synchronous programs are converted to guarded actions as done in the author's Averest system, some relationships with logic programs can be found: In particular, the concepts of reaction-to-absence of synchronous languages and negation-to-failure of logic programs seem to be the same; another analogy is found for the generation of equation-based code of synchronous programs and the completion of logic programs, and also for the fix-point analyses defined in both paradigms. This paper outlines these analogies between the two paradigms of programming languages and discusses whether further known semantics of logic programs like well-founded and stable models may find useful counterparts in the synchronous world in future.

K. Schneider (✉)
TU Kaiserslautern, Kaiserslautern, Germany
e-mail: schneider@cs.uni-kl.de; https://es.cs.uni-kl.de

M. Dahlem
Insiders Technologies GmbH, Kaiserslautern, Germany
e-mail: m_dahlem@cs.uni-kl.de; https://insiders-technologies.de

© Springer Nature Switzerland AG 2018
P. Müller, I. Schaefer (eds.), *Principled Software Development*,
https://doi.org/10.1007/978-3-319-98047-8_16

251

1 Introduction

In contrast to *transformational systems* that read inputs only at starting time and provide their outputs only at termination time, *reactive systems* [29, 30] have an ongoing computation that is divided into so-called reaction steps. Within every reaction step, the reactive system reads inputs given by its environment and instantaneously computes the outputs for the environment in the same macro step. Reactive systems occur in many areas, in particular, most embedded systems are reactive in nature, and also many distributed systems have a notion of rounds that correspond to reaction steps. While the idea of reactive systems seems very simple, it turned out that the semantics of reactive programming languages turned out to be a challenge as was early realized by the family of statechart languages [4, 22, 28, 43].

Synchronous languages [2, 27] have been introduced as a new class of programming languages for reactive systems. Classic synchronous languages were Esterel [3, 8], Lustre [15, 31], and Signal [23, 26] that followed different paradigms: While Esterel is an imperative language, Lustre is data-flow oriented, and Signal is even declarative. Still, all of these languages have a notion of a reaction step where input signals are given by the environment, and where output signals have to be instantaneously computed by the synchronous program. These reaction steps are defined by a set of atomic actions that are in the programmer's view executed in zero time, i.e., in the same reaction step. As a consequence, the atomic actions of a reaction step have an instantaneous feedback to the variable environment of their reaction step. Reaction steps and atomic actions are also often called macro and micro steps, respectively.

The *distinction between macro and micro steps* is an elegant abstraction that allows programmers to reason about their programs in terms of macro steps so that there is no need to worry about the schedules of the micro steps. However, the compilers have to make sure that this abstraction is meaningful: Due to the instantaneous feedback of the atomic micro step actions to their variable environment, reaction steps may have for one and the same input no consistent behavior or even several consistent behaviors. To ensure determinism, compilers for synchronous languages have to analyze the programs for consistency. Depending on the synchronous language, the main consistency analyses are clock consistency and causality analysis [5, 46, 47, 51].

Causality problems arise from the fact that synchronous programs can read—and therefore instantaneously react to—their own outputs. This way, they may assign a value to a variable *because* that variable is already seen to have this value, or they may instantaneously assign another value to a variable *because* that variable has another value in this step. Of course, these cyclic dependencies may be also transitive via other variables, and they may involve arbitrary data-dependent conditions as well. Causality problems arise also in other areas where abstractions to reaction steps were made: For example, the composition of Mealy automata suffers from the same problems, and also in the synthesis of digital hardware circuits, the *false cycle problem* is well-known.

A simple solution to *avoid causality problems* is to forbid all cyclic dependencies of micro step actions. This is, for example, done in STATEMATE and also in the Lustre language, and it can be easily achieved by either syntactic checks of the data-dependencies or by simply delaying the outputs by one reaction step. However, it was already observed in the early seventies [35, 36, 44] that digital hardware circuits can have meaningful combinational feedback loops. It was also already known that there are circuits with combinational feedback loops that are smaller than all equivalent circuits without such loops. This is also exploited today in hardware synthesis in that operands and results are shared using multiplexers, and this may lead to *false loops* [40, 41, 53]. False loops are pseudo-cycles in the sense that they syntactically appear as cyclic dependencies that will however never show up at runtime. One reason may be that different multiplexers will make always the same or opposite selections with is not easily seen without knowing all the reachable states.

Malik [40, 41] was the first who introduced *algorithms to analyze whether feedback loops in circuits are combinational or lead to unwanted states*. Malik's analysis is based on the ternary symbolic simulation of the circuits due to Bryant [14] that was also used for the analysis of asynchronous circuits [9, 11–13, 50] by Brzozowski and Seger. Since the abstraction from asynchronous circuits to synchronous circuits is comparable to the abstraction from micro steps to macro steps in general, Shiple, Berry, and Touati [52] realized that the causality analysis of synchronous languages can be dealt with the same algorithms and introduced thereby the notion of *constructive circuits* [5, 52] which are circuits whose output values stabilize for all possible gate and wire delays. The third truth value $\bot$ has the meaning that the value has not yet been determined and it may change in the progress of the macro step to one of the two boolean truth values 0 or 1. It was conjectured that a logical definition based on a constructive logic, a semantic definition based on three-valued lattices, and the electrical definition should be equivalent.

Berry defined then the semantics of Esterel based on a ternary analysis of control-flow conditions that can also be formulated using *abstract interpretation* by a may/must analysis. We also followed this great idea and defined the semantics of our Quartz language [49] using SOS transition and reaction rules which are based on a multivalued logic that directly reflects the information flow during macro steps. Hence, semantics of synchronous programs—like Esterel and Quartz—are defined by multivalued logics where the truth value $\bot$ is used for not yet determined variables.

In ternary logic, where we define $\neg\bot := 0\bot$ and $\bot \vee x := x \vee \bot := 1$ if $x = 1$ and $\bot$ otherwise, we cannot prove certain two-valued theorems like $\varphi \vee \neg\varphi$. If φ evaluates to $\bot$, then also $\neg\varphi$ does so, and no information has yet arrived at this place. Causality demands however that some partial information will trigger the computation of further information which is not possible in these examples.

Similarly, $\varphi \vee \neg\varphi$ cannot be proved in constructive logic. A proof for φ in constructive logic would require a way/algorithm to construct φ, and a proof for $\neg\varphi$ would require to prove that no such algorithm exists. Even though this suggests that multivalued logic and constructive logic have some similarities, there are good arguments why the relationship between causality analysis and constructive logic [42] cannot be as simple as suggested at first: Kurt Gödel already proved that constructive logic is not equivalent to any multivalued logic. Since causality analysis is defined by ternary logic, it cannot be equivalent to constructive logic. Another argument to see this difference is the double negation theorem of constructive logic due to Glivenko: Any propositional formula φ is valid in classic logic if and only if $\neg\neg\varphi$ is valid in intuitionistic logic. However, in ternary logic, $\neg\neg\varphi$ is equivalent to φ and thus, makes no difference. In constructive logic, also other forms of negation have been considered like 'negation as implication of impossibility' also known as 'strong negation'. We therefore see that while there are similarities to constructive logic, there are also many differences, so that there is no simple equivalence to constructive logic.

The main motivation of the use of ternary logic for causality analysis was to describe with the value $\bot$ that the information flowing from the known input values has not yet been sufficient to generate the considered variable's value. Besides this *positive flow of information*, there is another very important concept in synchronous languages: Due to the notion of macro steps, there is logical notion of time, and if a value does not arrive within such a time step, we can conclude that no action is there to determine it in this step. For this reason, the *reaction to absence* is applied and determines the variable's value as a default value like 0 for boolean values.

In the Averest system, the Quartz programs are first translated to *synchronous guarded actions* which are essentially pairs (γ, α) with a control-flow condition γ and an atomic action α having the simple meaning that whenever $\gamma = 1$ holds, then α must be instantaneously executed. In previous work [10, 49], we have shown how Quartz programs can be compiled to such guarded actions, and in further work [6, 54], we also showed how other synchronous languages can be converted to that intermediate representation. This has also been observed by other researchers in the field [7, 55].

In this paper, we therefore abstract away from a particular synchronous language and consider synchronous guarded actions as a representative for any synchronous language. Causality analysis can be done on the guarded actions as well, and to this end, we have to proceed in rounds within a macro step where in each round, those actions α are executed whose trigger condition γ is 1 ('must' actions). Also, all guarded actions (γ, α) are removed whose trigger condition γ is 0 ('cannot' actions). If no action to assign a value to a variable x that is still having the value $\bot$ is left, we perform the reaction to absence in that we assign that variable a default value. A little tool for teaching to illustrate this can be found at http://es.cs.uni-kl. de/tools/teaching.

Looking at the causal execution of guarded actions, we found many similarities to logic programs. In particular, the information flow of known conditions γ to compute new information by firing actions α is similar to the *resolution steps done by logic programs*. Moreover, the reaction to absence seems to be equivalent to the concept of *negation as failure* that exists for logic programs. For this reason, we discuss in this paper the relationship between synchronous programs and logic programs. The first author of this paper remembers a discussion he had with Arnd

Poetzsch-Heffter about these relationship that turned out to be very interesting, but has not yet been published. We are not aware of any paper discussing these interesting relationships. We therefore want to address this point here, and will discuss in the following some details about the relationship between synchronous and logic programs.

2 Semantics of Logic and Synchronous Programs

In the following, different kinds of semantics of logic programs are considered to compare these semantics with the constructive semantics of synchronous programs. For the sake of simplicity, we restrict the consideration to only propositional variables. There are some obvious goals like the computation of a model of a set of clauses/guarded actions by a polynomial algorithm, and one wants to make sure that either a *unique model* exists or that at least a *canonical model* is chosen among the existing ones.

To this end, we first start with basic definitions like *Horn clauses* and their minimal models that can be computed by a fixpoint analysis that is exactly the same as the one used for synchronous programs. The addition of negation generalizes Horn clauses to *logic programs*, which also increases their expressiveness. In general, any propositional formula can be written as a logic program (with goal clauses as explained below), but in addition to simple clauses, the rules of a logic program also follow some causality, i.e., *because* the subgoals/guards are satisfied, the conclusion holds, and *if there is no rule to derive the truth of a variable, then this variable is considered to be false*. It is therefore not allowed that variables become true without such a *justification*, which is also a similar point of view as taken in synchronous programs (and in constructive logic).

To consider this justification, one defines the *completion of a logic program*, which is in essence *an equation system that exists in exactly the same form for synchronous programs*. The equation system formalizes that a variable is false if no rule will justify it, and true otherwise. However, one loses the causality with the equation system, at least if the equations are read in a logical sense, where equations have no causal direction (in contrast to guarded actions).

The models of the equation system are therefore a general frame to determine the semantics of a logic program, and the same holds for synchronous programs. However, it is disturbing that for given inputs, there might be more than one solution, and therefore one aims at choosing a canonical model for logic programs. For this reason, several attempts were made to define canonical models, and in the following, we review the fixpoint semantics by Fitting [21], which is the same as the constructive semantics of synchronous programs. A generalization of this is the well-founded semantics [25], where a stronger form of the 'reaction-to-absence' is used to define the unique fixpoint, and therefore more programs can be given a unique meaning. A recommended survey of this material is [18], and of course, the original references [20, 21, 24, 25, 39] are worth to be read.

2.1 Horn Clauses

A clause is a set of literals, i.e., variables or negated variables, and the meaning of this set is the disjunction of these literals. Thus, a set of clauses can be considered as a propositional logic formula in conjunctive normal form.

A *Horn clause* is a clause with at most one positive literal, i.e. $\{\neg x_1, \ldots, \neg x_n\}$ or $\{\neg x_1, \ldots, \neg x_n, y\}$. These clauses are named after the logician Alfred Horn and play an important role in logic programming and constructive logic.

A Horn clause with exactly one positive literal like $\{\neg x_1, \ldots, \neg x_n, y\}$ is called a *definite clause*; a definite clause without negative literals like $\{y\}$ is called a *fact*; and a Horn clause without a positive literal like $\{\neg x_1, \ldots, \neg x_n\}$ is called a *goal* clause. Since the literals of a clause are disjunctively connected, one may also write a Horn clause as an implication $x_1 \wedge \ldots \wedge x_n \rightarrow y$. This implication written in the Prolog and Quartz programming languages are shown in the following table.

y :- x1,...,xn	```module P1(event y,x1,...,xn) {```
	``` if(x1 and ... and xn) emit(y);```
	```}```

The *resolvent* of two Horn clauses is also a Horn clause: To compute a resolvent, one of the clauses must contain a negated literal of the other one. Thus, at least one of the two clauses must have a positive literal, say $\{\neg x_1, \ldots, \neg x_n, y\}$, while the other one contains that literal y negatively, say $\{\neg y, \neg z_1, \ldots, \neg z_m, u\}$ or $\{\neg y, \neg z_1, \ldots, \neg z_m\}$. The resolvent is in the first case the clause $\{\neg x_1, \ldots, \neg x_n, \neg z_1, \ldots, \neg z_m, u\}$ and $\{\neg x_1, \ldots, \neg x_n, \neg z_1, \ldots, \neg z_m\}$ in the second case which are both Horn clauses.

Checking the satisfiability of a set of propositional Horn clauses is P-complete [17], and it can be even solved in linear time. Moreover, Emden and Kowalski showed that every set of definite clauses has a *unique minimal model* [19], and an atomic formula is logically implied by a set of definite clauses if and only if it is true in its minimal model. The minimal model semantics of Horn clauses is the basis for the semantics of logic programs.

2.2 Minimal Models of Horn Clauses and the Marking Algorithm

Minimality of a model is defined in terms of the number of variables made true. If a satisfying assignment is associated with the set of variables it makes true, then minimality refers to minimal cardinality of these sets of variables. Thus, the least assignment is the one where all variables are false, and the greatest one is that one that makes all variables true.

As already stated above, every set of Horn clauses has a minimal model. A minimal model of a set of Horn clauses can be constructed by the *marking algorithm* [17] which distinguishes again between facts, definite clauses, and goal clauses that can be alternatively written as follows:

- facts: $\{\} \to y$
- goal clauses: $\{x_1, \ldots, x_n\} \to$ false
- definite clauses: $\{x_1, \ldots, x_n\} \to y$

Given a set of Horn clauses, the marking algorithm first assigns all variables y of facts the value true and propagates these values in the remaining clauses, i.e., it simplifies the remaining clauses using a partial assignment as follows:

- A definite clause of the form $\{x_1, \ldots, x_n\} \to y$ where y occurs on the right is thereby removed (since it is already satisfied).
- A definite clause of the form $\{x_1, \ldots, x_n, y\} \to z$ where y occurs on the left is replaced with $\{x_1, \ldots, x_n\} \to z$, i.e., y is removed from the premises.
- A goal clause $\{x_1, \ldots, x_n, y\} \to$ false is replaced with $\{x_1, \ldots, x_n\} \to$ false if $n > 0$ holds. The goal clause $\{y\} \to$ FALSE leads to a contradiction so that the considered set of Horn clauses is then seen to be unsatisfiable.

This procedure is repeated as long as new facts are derived. If no new facts are derived, the algorithm terminates and returns the so far obtained assignment (meaning that all other variables are interpreted as false). Note that the marking algorithm only makes variables true if needed, i.e., to satisfy new facts, otherwise variables are made false. It therefore obviously generates a minimal model if a model exists at all. Using appropriate data structures, this algorithm can be implemented with a linear runtime [17]. It only returns unsatisfiable if the empty clause $\{\} \to$ false is detected.

2.3 Selective Linear Definite Clause (SLD) Resolution

Proving that the addition of a goal clause G to a set of definite clauses and facts P makes this set inconsistent is the same as proving that P implies $\neg G$, i.e., P implies all literals that occur in G, i.e., all variables $y \in G$ are contained in the minimal model (note that all other models include the minimal model).

There is also a syntactic characterization of this logical implication: Based on *selective linear definite clause (SLD) resolution* [37], one can prove that G is implied by P: The leftmost literal y of the goal clause is replaced as follows: if it is a fact, it is simply removed (since proved), otherwise, if there is a definite clause with right hand side y, then y is replaced with the left hand side of that definite clause. Note that there is some freedom in choosing one of the available definite clauses having this right hand side. If the goal clause becomes finally empty, the goal has been proved. In principle, SLD resolution is a backward reasoning in correspondence to the marking algorithm.

2.4 Introducing Negation (Logic Programs)

Horn clauses are not as powerful as general clauses; it is not difficult to find a propositional formula whose conjunctive normal form contains clauses that are no Horn clauses. For this reason, one may wish to introduce 'some kind' of negation in the Horn clauses. If this kind of negation would be treated as the usual logical negation, one would no longer deal with a restricted set of clauses, thus with general propositional logic, and thus, the satisfiability problem would become NP-complete. For this reason, special forms of negations are preferred, as the 'negation by failure' [16] meaning that $\mathtt{not}(x)$ is considered to be proved if and only if x cannot be proved.

In the following, Horn clauses where negated literals are used are called *logic programs* to avoid confusion with sets of Horn clauses. For example, consider the following logic program on the left hand side and its corresponding Quartz program on the right hand side:

p r :- p,q s :- p,not(q)	```module P2(event p,q,r,s) {``   `` emit(p);``   `` if(p and q) emit(r);``   `` if(p and not q) emit(s);``   ``}```

Let us first consider the logic program: Clearly, p is provable since p is a fact. However, q is not provable, since q is neither a fact nor is there a rule having q as conclusion. Thus, q is viewed as being false, and therefore $\mathtt{not}(q)$ is declared to be provable. For this reason, s holds, and r is false since the premises of the only rule having r as conclusion are not all true. Thus, negation as failure determines the assignment {p, s}. However, considering 'not' as logical negation, there would be also the following further satisfying assignments {p, s}, {p, r, s}, {p, q, r}, {p, q, r, s}.

The Quartz program given on the right hand side makes similar conclusions: It generates the three guarded actions $(\mathtt{true}, \mathtt{emit}(p))$, $(p\ \&\ q, \mathtt{emit}(r))$, and $(p\&!q, \mathtt{emit}(s))$ and first starts with the assignment where all variables have the value $\bot$. In the first iteration, $\mathtt{emit}(p)$ fires, so that the value of p is changed to $\mathtt{true}$. Moreover, it is seen that there is no action that will assign q any value, so q is given the default value $\mathtt{false}$. These changes will now satisfy the trigger of $(p\&!q, \mathtt{emit}(s))$ so firing its action will make s true. The trigger of $(p\ \&\ q, \mathtt{emit}(r))$ is however false, so that also r cannot be assigned any other value than the default value $\mathtt{false}$. The same unique model is found by the causal semantics of Quartz which ignores the logically possible other models.

2.5 Completion of Horn Clauses

Keith Clark showed in [16] an explanation of the 'negation as failure' in that he considered the *completion* of a logic program. The completion is obtained by computing for each variable y an equivalence $y \leftrightarrow \varphi_y$ where φ_y is the disjunction of all premises of clauses with conclusion y. Thus, for the above example, we obtain the following completion:

p <-> true
q <-> false
r <-> p & q
s <-> p & !q
	```module P2(event p,q,r,s) {```
	   ```emit(p);```
	   ```if(p and q) emit(r);```
	   ```if(p and not q) emit(s);```
	```}```

In the above example, the model found by negation as failure is the model of the completion of the logic program (meaning the conjunction of the equivalences).

For Quartz programs, a hardware synthesis has been defined in [48] similar to the circuit semantics given by Berry in [5]. In essence, circuits define nothing else than equation systems in that outputs of gates are determined by a Boolean expression in terms of the inputs of the gate. The synthesis of circuits from synchronous program can also be used for software synthesis and has the nice advantage that in contrast to automaton-based code generation, programs of only polynomial size are obtained. For this reason, [49] explicitly describes how to generate from the guarded actions of a Quartz program a corresponding equation system. For Boolean variables this is exactly the Clark completion shown above.

However, there are still some differences between the completion and the semantics of logic programs, and also between the equation systems and the semantics of Quartz programs: for example, consider the following logic program and Quartz programs:

p :- not(p)	```module P3(event p,q) {```
	   ```if(not(p)) emit(p);```
	```}```

For the above single clause p :- !p, we obtain the completion p <-> !p which has no two-valued models, so all formulas are implied by it. However, Prolog answers 'no' to the query q and 'yes' to !q. The corresponding Quartz on the right hand side is declared to be not constructive by the compiler which still can derive that q is false, but it cannot assign a value different than $\bot$ to p. So, while the completion does not yet give a complete characterization of the semantics of logic programs, the Quartz programs still behave in exactly the same way.

2.6 Fitting's Fixpoint Semantics is Causal Synchronous Semantics

To characterize the semantics of logic programs, Fitting [21] suggested to use three-valued logic to denote whether a variable is true, false or unknown ($\bot$). To compare this iteration with *well-founded models*, we formally introduce two transformations of environments. To this end, an environment $\mathscr{I}$ is represented as a set of literals with the meaning that $x \in \mathscr{I}$ means that x is true, $\neg x \in \mathscr{I}$ means that x is false, and if neither is the case, then x is unknown.

For a given logic program P and an environment $\mathscr{I}$, we then define the following two functions:

(1) $\mathscr{T}_P(\mathscr{I})$ is the set of variables y that have a rule $\ell_1, \ldots, \ell_n \rightarrow y$ in P such that all literals $\ell_1, \ldots, \ell_n$ are true in $\mathscr{I}$.
(2) $\mathscr{F}_P(\mathscr{I})$ is the set of variables y where all rules $\ell_1, \ldots, \ell_n \rightarrow y$ in P have at least one literal ℓ_i that is false in $\mathscr{I}$.

Note that (2) also applies if there is no rule with conclusion y. In [21], it has been shown that the minimal model of Horn clauses is the least fixpoint of the function $f_P(\mathscr{I}) := \mathscr{T}_P(\mathscr{I}) \cup \{\neg x \mid x \in \mathscr{F}_P(\mathscr{I})\}$. Moreover, it has been proved in [21] that a three-valued interpretation is a model of an equation system of a program P if and only if it is a fixpoint of f_P. For this reason, the meaning of a logic program P has been defined as the least fixpoint of this function f_P.

Again, we find exactly the same kind of reasoning for the synchronous programs: The above function $\mathscr{T}_P(\mathscr{I})$ corresponds with that part of the causality analysis that determines the 'must' actions of a program, i.e., those guarded actions (γ, α) where γ is true under $\mathscr{I}$. The function $\mathscr{F}_P(\mathscr{I})$ determines the variables that 'cannot' be assigned a value, since for all existing guarded actions (γ, α) where α could assign a value to them, the guard γ is false under $\mathscr{I}$. The causality analysis computes these two sets and then updates the environment by applying the above function $f_P(\mathscr{I})$. Thus, causality analysis of Quartz programs is exactly what is defined by Fitting as the meaning of a logic program.

Let P be an arbitrary logic program, E be its Clark completion, and let $\mathscr{I}$ be the least fixpoint obtained as the meaning of P. One may wonder whether one can say that $x \in \mathscr{I}$ implies that x holds in all two-valued models of E, and that $\neg x \in \mathscr{I}$ implies that x is false in all two-valued models of E, i.e., that the computed fixpoint is the minimal model in the sense that it determines the minimal Boolean requirements. However, this is not the case, as shown by the following example:

x1 :− !x1 , !x2
x2 :− x3
x2 :− x4
x3 :− x3
x4 :− x4

```
module P4(event x1,x2,x3,x4) {
    if(!x1 & !x2) emit(x1);
    if(x3) emit(x2);
    if(x4) emit(x2);
    if(x3) emit(x3);
    if(x4) emit(x4);
}
```

Considering Boolean variable assignments, there are the three models $\mathscr{I}_1 = \{x2, x3\}$, $\mathscr{I}_2 = \{x2, x4\}$, and $\mathscr{I}_3 = \{x2, x3, x4\}$. Their 'agreement' is $\mathscr{I} = \{\neg x1, x2\}$, i.e., all models agree on the values for $x1$ and $x2$. However, the agreement $\mathscr{I}$ is not a three-valued model of the equation system. The least fixpoint is the variable assignment where all variables are unknown (and of course that is also computed by the Quartz simulator for the program on the right hand side). Thus, it is not the case that if a variable has a Boolean value in all two-valued models of the equation system, then it must also have this value in the three-valued fixpoint.

Since the least fixpoint is however the infimum of all other fixpoints, and a three-valued interpretation is a model of the completion of a program if and only if it is a fixpoint of f_P, it follows that x in contained in the least fixpoint of f_P holds if and only if all three-valued models $\mathscr{I}$ contain x (same for $\neg x$). Note that the above equation system is satisfied by assigning all variables the value unknown.

2.7 Beyond Causal Synchronous Semantics: Well-Founded Semantics

Van Gelder et al. [25] introduced the *well-founded semantics of logic programs*. To this end, again a three-valued interpretation of variables is used as in the previous section. As above and in [25], these three-valued interpretations are represented by consistent sets of literals, i.e., sets that do not contain both a variable and its negation.

A canonical model is also computed by a fixpoint computation. However, the function $g_P(\mathscr{I})$ used here instead of $f_P(\mathscr{I})$ is a stronger one so that the well-founded semantics can be defined for programs where Fitting's fixpoint semantics cannot be defined. The part where the assignment of a variable is changed from unknown to true is thereby the same, i.e., function $\mathscr{T}_P(\mathscr{I})$ is also used, but the changes from unknown to false are done using a function $\mathscr{U}_P(\mathscr{I})$ instead of $\mathscr{F}_P(\mathscr{I})$. The definition of $\mathscr{U}_P(\mathscr{I})$ is the greatest unfounded set, which is defined as follows:

Definition 1 (Greatest Unfounded Set) Given a partial interpretation $\mathscr{I}$ and a logic program P, a set of variables A is called unfounded, if for all variables $x \in A$ one of the following conditions holds for each rule with conclusion x:

- Some positive or negative subgoal x_i of the body is false in $\mathscr{I}$.
- Some positive subgoal of the body occurs in A.

Intuitively, an unfounded set of variables A is a set of variables that can be simultaneously made false based on a partial interpretation, i.e., changing $\mathscr{I}$ such that all variables in A will be assigned false is justified either by $\mathscr{I}$ or A.

The important observation is now that the union of unfounded sets is also an unfounded set, and therefore there is always a greatest unfounded set (which is the union of all unfounded sets). This greatest unfounded set of a program P w.r.t.

an three-valued interpretation $\mathscr{I}$ is denoted as $\mathscr{U}_P(\mathscr{I})$, and can be computed as a greatest fixpoint as follows: First, we remove all rules from P where at least one subgoal is false in $\mathscr{I}$ (it is clear that these rules cannot fire since they are already disabled by the so-far determined interpretation $\mathscr{I}$). Let the remaining rules be the subset P' of P. We now seek the greatest set of variables $\mathscr{U}_P(\mathscr{I})$ such that x is in $\mathscr{U}_P(\mathscr{I})$ if and only if for each rule $x_1, \ldots, x_m, \neg y_1, \ldots, \neg y_n \to x$ one of the x_i is in A as well.

Thus, we start with the set of all variables $\mathscr{V}_0$, and successively remove variables x from this set if there is a rule $x_1, \ldots, x_m, \neg y_1, \ldots, \neg y_n \to x$ either without positive subgoals x_i or where none of the positive subgoals is in the current set.

	module P5(event x1,x2,x3,x4,x5,x6) {
x1	emit(x1);
x2 :− x4,not(x5)	if(x4&!x5) emit(x2);
x2 :− x5,not(x6)	if(x5&!x6) emit(x2);
x3 :− not(x2)	if(!x2) emit(x3);
x4 :− x2	if(x2) emit(x4);
x5 :− x4	if(x4) emit(x5);
	}

For example, for $\mathscr{I} = \{\}$ and the above program P, we obtain the greatest unfounded set $\mathscr{U}_P(\mathscr{I}) = \{x2, x4, x5, x6\}$ so that these variables could now be made false. Note that we remove x1 and x3 since these variables have a rule without positive subgoals.

For a fixed program P, let $\mathscr{U}_P(\mathscr{I})$ denote the greatest unfounded set, and let $\mathscr{T}_P(\mathscr{I})$ denote the set of variables x whose truth values can be derived from the rules in P instantiated by the truth values of $\mathscr{I}$ (as in the fixpoint semantics). The well-founded model of a logic program is then obtained as the least fixpoint of the function $g_P(\mathscr{I}) := \mathscr{T}_P(\mathscr{I}) \cup \{\neg x \mid x \in \mathscr{U}_P(\mathscr{I})\}$, i.e., starting with $\mathscr{I} = \{\}$ and iterating with g_P yields in the limit the well-founded model of P.

For the above program, we obtain $\mathscr{I}_0 = \{\}$, $\mathscr{I}_1 = \{x1, \neg x2, \neg x4, \neg x5, \neg x6\}$, and $\mathscr{I}_2 = \{x1, \neg x2, x3, \neg x4, \neg x5, \neg x6\}$. Fitting's fixpoint semantics, however, computes $\mathscr{I}_0 = \{\}$ and $\mathscr{I}_1 = \{x1, \neg x6\}$ which is also the result of the Quartz simulator for the corresponding program on the right hand side above.

The two-valued models of the completion are $\mathscr{M}_1 = \{x1, \neg x2, x3, \neg x4, \neg x5, \neg x6\}$, $\mathscr{M}_2 = \{x1, \neg x2, x3, \neg x4, \neg x5, x6\}$, and $\mathscr{M}_3 = \{x1, x2, \neg x3, x4, x5, \neg x6\}$ so that the well-founded semantics determined the minimal model (in the sense that the fewest variables are made true)!

It is not difficult to see that the well-founded semantics always computes a minimal model, since $\mathscr{U}_P(\mathscr{I})$ determines the largest set of variables that can be consistently made false (not true). Now, consider the following extension of the above program with two further rules:

```
x1                          module P5'(event x1,x2,x3,x4,x5,x6,x7,x8){
x2  :-  x4,not(x5)              emit(x1);
x2  :-  x5,not(x6)              if(x4&!x5) emit(x2);
x3  :-  not(x2)                 if(x5&!x6) emit(x2);
x4  :-  x2                      if(!x2) emit(x3);
x5  :-  x4                      if(x2) emit(x4);
x7  :-  not(x8)                 if(x4) emit(x5);
x8  :-  not(x7)                 if(!x8) emit(x7);
                                if(!x7) emit(x8);
                            }
```

The well-founded semantics computes $\mathscr{I}_0 = \{\}$, $\mathscr{I}_1 = \{x1, \neg x2, \neg x4, \neg x5, \neg x6\}$, and $\mathscr{I}_2 = \{x1, \neg x2, x3, \neg x4, \neg x5, \neg x6\}$ as before, and is therefore not able to determine values for x7 and x8 that depend on each other via negations. If the negations of the last two rules were omitted, the new variables x7 and x8 are made false.

Since $f_P(\mathscr{I})$ is a subset of $g_P(\mathscr{I})$, it follows that the least fixpoint of f_P is a subset of the least fixpoint of g_P, thus the fixpoint semantics is weaker than the well-founded semantics. Moreover, it can be proved that the least fixpoint of g_P is also a fixpoint of f_P (although not necessarily the least one). Thus, it is a three-valued model of the equation system of P.

Again, we see that the semantics of Quartz is equivalent to Fitting's fixpoint semantics, and therefore weaker than the well-founded semantics. It is therefore also possible to define a well-founded semantics of Quartz programs in the same sense as van Gelder et al. [25] defined for logic programs. Similar to the existing semantics, a canonical model will be chosen this way that can be computed by fixpoints, and programs like the one above which do not have a semantics with the current definitions will be given a semantics with the well-founded approach.

From the computational perspective, the computation of the well-founded reaction is still polynomial in the size of the program, but requires the evaluation of an alternating fixpoint instead of a simple least one. It is therefore more expensive, i.e., it no longer runs in linear time, but it is still polynomial and therefore might scale well also for larger programs.

A generalization to non-boolean programs could be made such that as few as possible rules should be fired by the well-founded semantics.

3   Summary and Future Directions

As shown in the previous section, there is a strong relationship between the semantics of synchronous programs and logic programs. For our discussion, we restricted the programs to Boolean variables only, and furthermore, only considered one macro step where all variables are output variables. In particular, Fitting's fixpoint semantics for logic programs can be easily seen to be equivalent to the current definition of the causal semantics of synchronous Quartz programs. We have also seen that more powerful semantics known for logic programs like the well-founded semantics of van Gelder et al. [25] can be defined for synchronous programs so that more synchronous programs can be accepted by the compilers as constructive programs so that deterministic code can be generated also for them.

The list of semantics discussed for logic programs in this paper is by far not complete. In particular, there is the *stable model semantics* [24] which is based on the definition of a 'reduct' of a logic program. Another direction is the concept of *stratified and locally stratified programs* [38]. These and more alternatives allow to compute models for logical programs which cannot be found with the semantics discussed in this paper.

A recent interest in new ways to define causal semantics for synchronous programs like [1, 32–34, 45] might be also influenced by the already existing work done for logic programs through the past decades. However, just defining semantics for synchronous programs is not sufficient, it also has to be shown by future work that code can also be efficiently generated for these semantics. We are looking forward to further research in that direction to see the fields of logic and synchronous programs being cross-fertilized in the future.

References

1. J. Aguado et al. "Grounding Synchronous Deterministic Concurrency in Sequential Programming". In: *Programming Languages and Systems* Ed. by Z. Shao. Vol. 8410. LNCS. Grenoble, France: Springer, 2014, pp. 229–248.
2. A. Benveniste et al. "The Synchronous Languages Twelve Years Later". In: *Proceedings of the IEEE* 91.1 (2003), pp. 64–83.
3. G. Berry and L. Cosserat. "The Esterel Synchronous Programming Language and its Mathematical Semantics". In: *Seminar on Concurrency (CONCUR)* Ed. by S.D. Brookes, A.W. Roscoe, and G. Winskel. Vol. 197. LNCS. Pittsburgh, Pennsylvania, USA: Springer, 1985, pp. 389–448.
4. M. von der Beeck. "A Comparison of Statecharts Variants". In: *Formal Techniques in Real-Time and Fault-Tolerant Systems (FTRTFT)* Ed. by H. Langmaack, W.-P. de Roever, and J. Vytopil. Vol. 863. LNCS. Lübeck, Germany: Springer, 1994, pp. 128–148.
5. G. Berry. *The Constructive Semantics of Pure Esterel*. July 1999.
6. J. Brandt et al. "Embedding Polychrony into Synchrony". In: *IEEE Transactions on Software Engineering (TSE)* 39.7 (July 2013), pp. 917–929.
7. J.-P. Bodeveix, M. Filali-Amine, and S. Kan. "A Refinement-based compiler development for synchronous language". In: *Formal Methods and Models for Codesign (MEMOCODE)* Ed. by J.-P. Talpin, P. Derler, and K. Schneider. Vienna, Austria: IEEE Computer Society, 2017, pp. 165–174.
8. F. Boussinot and R. de Simone. "The Esterel language". In: *Proceedings of the IEEE* 79.9 (1991), pp. 1293–1304.
9. J.A. Brzozowski and C. Ebergen. "On the Delay-Sensitivity of Gate Networks". In: *IEEE Transactions on Computers (T-C)* 41.11 (Nov 1992), pp. 1349–1359.
10. J. Brandt and K. Schneider. "Separate Compilation for Synchronous Programs". In: *Software and Compilers for Embedded Systems (SCOPES)*. Nice, France: ACM, 2009, pp. 1–10.
11. J.A. Brzozowski and C.-J.H. Seger. *Advances in asynchronous circuit theory part I*. Bulletin of the European association of Theoretical Computer Science. Oct. 1990.

12. R.E. Bryant and C.-J.H. Seger. "Formal Verification of Digital Circuits Using Symbolic Ternary System Models". In: *Computer Aided Verification (CAV)*. Ed. by E.M. Clarke and R.P. Kurshan. Vol. 531. LNCS. New Brunswick, New Jersey USA: Springer, 1991, pp. 33–43.

13. J.A. Brzozowski and C.-J.H. Seger. *Asynchronous Circuits* Springer, 1995.

14. R.E. Bryant. "Boolean Analysis of MOS Circuits". In: *IEEE Transactions on Computer Aided Design of Integrated Circuits and Systems (T-CAD)*. CAD-6.4 (July 1987), pp. 634–649.

15. P. Caspi et al. "LUSTRE: A declarative language for programming synchronous systems". In: *Principles of Programming Languages (POPL)* Munich, Germany: ACM, 1987, pp. 178–188.

16. K.L. Clark. "Negation as Failure". In: *Logic and Data Bases* Ed. by H. Gallaire and J. Minker. Toulouse, France: Plemum Press, New York, 1977, pp. 293–322.

17. W.F. Dowling and J.H. Gallier. "Linear-time algorithms for testing the satisfiability of propositional Horn formulae". In: *The Journal of Logic Programming* 1.3 (Oct. 1984), pp. 267–284.

18. T. Eiter, G. Ianni, and T. Krennwallner. "Answer Set Programming: A Primer". In: *Reasoning Web Semantic Technologies for Information Systems* Ed. by S. Tessaris et al. Vol. 5689. LNCS. Brixen-Bressanone, Italy: Springer, 2009, pp. 40–110.

19. M. van Emden and R. Kowalski. "The semantics of predicate logic as a programming language". In: *Journal of the ACM (JACM)* 23.4 (Oct. 1976), pp. 733–742.

20. F. Fages. "Consistency of Clark's completion and existence of stable models". In: *Methods of Logic in Computer Science* 1.1 (1994), pp. 51–60.

21. M. Fitting. "A Kripke-Kleene Semantics for Logic Programs". In: *Journal of Logic Programming* 2.4 (Dec. 1985), pp. 295–312.

22. H. Fecher et al. "29 New Unclarities in the Semantics of UML 2.0 State Machines". In: *International Conference on Formal Engineering Methods (ICFEM)* Ed. by K.-K. Lau and R. Banach. Vol. 3785. LNCS. Manchester England, UK: Springer, 2005, pp. 52–65.

23. T. Gautier, P. Le Guernic, and L. Besnard. "SIGNAL, a declarative language for synchronous programming of real-time systems". In: *Functional Programming Languages and Computer Architecture* Ed. by G. Kahn. Vol. 274. LNCS. Portland, Oregon, USA: Springer, 1987, pp. 257–277.

24. M. Gelfond and V. Lifschitz. "The Stable Model Semantics for Logic Programming". In: *Logic Programming*. Ed. by R.A. Kowalski and K.A. Bowen. Seattle, Washington, USA: MIT Press, 1988, pp. 1070–1080.

25. A. van Gelder, K.A. Ross, and J.S. Schlipf. "The Well-Founded Semantics for General Logic Programs". In: *Journal of the ACM (JACM)* 38.3 (July 1991), pp. 620–650.

26. P. Le Guernic et al. "Programming real-time applications with SIGNAL". In: *Proceedings of the IEEE* 79.9 (1991), pp. 1321–1336.

27. N. Halbwachs. *Synchronous programming of reactive systems*. Kluwer, 1993.

28. D. Harel and A. Naamad. "The STATEMATE Semantics of Statecharts". In: *ACM Transactions on Software Engineering and Methodology (TOSEM)* 5.4 (1996), pp. 293–333.

29. D. Harel and A. Pnueli "On the development of reactive systems". In: *Logic and Models of Concurrent Systems*. Ed. by K.R. Apt. Springer, 1985, pp. 477–498.

30. D. Harel. "Statecharts: A visual formulation for complex systems". In: *Science of Computer Programming* 8.3 (1987), pp. 231–274.

31. N. Halbwachs et al. "The Synchronous Dataflow Programming Language LUSTRE". In: *Proceedings of the IEEE* 79.9 (Sept. 1991), pp. 1305–1320.

32. R. von Hanxleden et al. "SCCharts: sequentially constructive statecharts for safety-critical applications: HW/SW-synthesis for a conservative extension of synchronous statecharts". In: *Programming Language Design and Implementation (PLDI)* Ed. by M.F.P. O'Boyle and K. Pingali. Edinburgh, United Kingdom: ACM, 2014, pp. 372–383.

33. R. von Hanxleden et al. "Sequentially constructive concurrency: a conservative extension of the synchronous model of computation". In: *Design, Automation and Test in Europe (DATE)*. Ed. by E. Macii. Grenoble, France: EDA Consortium/ACM, 2013, pp. 581–586.

34. R. von Hanxleden et al. "Sequentially Constructive Concurrency A Conservative Extension of the Synchronous Model of Computation". In: *ACM Transactions on Embedded Computing Systems (TECS)* 13.4s (July 2014), 144:1–144:26.
35. D.A. Huffman. "Combinational circuits with feedback". In: *Recent Developments in Switching Theory* Ed. by A. Mukhopadhyay Academic Press, 1971, pp. 27–55.
36. W.H. Kautz. "The necessity of closed circuit loops in minimal combinational circuits". In: *IEEE Transactions on Computers (T-C)* C-19.2 (Feb 1970), pp. 162–166.
37. R. Kowalski. "Predicate Logic as Programming Language". In: *IFIP Congress* Stockholm, Sweden, 1974, pp. 569–574.
38. K. Kunen. "Signed data dependencies in logic programs". In: *Journal of Logic Programming* 7.3 (Nov 1989), pp. 231–245.
39. F. Lin and Y. Zhao. "ASSAT: Computing answer sets of a logic program by SAT solvers". In: *Artificial Intelligence* 157 (2004), pp. 115–137.
40. S. Malik. "Analysis of Cyclic Combinational Circuits". In: *International Conference on Computer-Aided Design (ICCAD)*. Santa Clara, California USA: IEEE Computer Society, 1993, pp. 618–625.
41. S. Malik. "Analysis of cycle combinational circuits". In: *IEEE Transactions on Computer Aided Design of Integrated Circuits and Systems (T-CAD)* 13.7 (July 1994), pp. 950–956.
42. G. Mints. *A Short Introduction to Intuitionistic Logic* The University Series in Mathematics. Kluwer, 2000.
43. A. Pnueli and M. Shalev. "What is in a step: On the semantics of statecharts". In: *Theoretical Aspects of Computer Software (TACS)* Ed. by T. Ito and A.R. Meyer. Vol. 526. LNCS. Sendai, Japan: Springer, 1991, pp. 244–264.
44. R.L. Rivest. "The Necessity of Feedback in Minimal Monotone Combinational Circuits". In: *IEEE Transactions on Computers (T-C)* C-26.6 (1977), pp. 606–607.
45. K. Rathlev et al. "SCEst: Sequentially Constructive Esterel". In: *Formal Methods and Models for Codesign (MEMOCODE)* Austin, Texas, USA: IEEE Computer Society, 2015, pp. 10–19.
46. K. Schneider et al. "Maximal Causality Analysis". In: *Application of Concurrency to System Design (ACSD)* Ed. by J. Desel and Y. Watanabe. Saint-Malo, France: IEEE Computer Society, 2005, pp. 106–115.
47. K. Schneider, J. Brandt, and T. Schüle. "Causality Analysis of Synchronous Programs with Delayed Actions". In: *Compilers, Architecture and Synthesis for Embedded Systems (CASES)*. Washington, District of Columbia, USA: ACM, 2004, pp. 179–189.
48. K. Schneider. "A Verified Hardware Synthesis for Esterel". In: *Distributed and Parallel Embedded Systems (DIPES)* Ed. by F.J. Rammig. Kluwer, 2000, pp. 205–214.
49. K. Schneider *The Synchronous Programming Language Quartz*. Internal Report 375. Kaiserslautern, Germany: Department of Computer Science, University of Kaiserslautern, Dec. 2009.
50. C.-J. Seger and J.A. Brzozowski. "An optimistic ternary simulation of gate races". In: *Theoretical Computer Science (TCS)* 61.1 (Oct. 1988), pp. 49–66.
51. E.M. Sentovich. "Quick conservative causality analysis". In: *International Symposium on System Synthesis (ISSS)* Ed. by F. Vahid and F. Catthoor. Antwerp, Belgium: ACM, 1997, pp. 2–8.
52. T.R. Shiple, G. Berry, and H. Touati. "Constructive Analysis of Cyclic Circuits". In: *European Design Automation Conference (EDAC)* Paris, France: IEEE Computer Society, 1996, pp. 328–333.
53. L. Stok. "False Loops Through Resource Sharing". In: *International Conference on Computer-Aided Design (ICCAD)* IEEE Computer Society 1992, pp. 345–348.
54. J.-P. Talpin et al. "Constructive Polychronous Systems". In: *Logical Foundations of Computer Science (LFCS)* Ed. by S.N. Artëmov and A. Nerode. Vol. 7734. LNCS. San Diego, California, USA: Springer, 2013, pp. 335–349.
55. Z. Yang et al. "A verified transformation: from polychronous programs to a variant of clocked guarded actions". In: *International Workshop on Software and Compilers for Embedded Systems (SCOPES)*. Ed. by H. Corporaal and S. Stuijk. Sankt Goar, Germany: ACM, 2014, pp. 128–137.

Illi Isabellistes Se Custodes Egregios Praestabant

Simon Bischof, Joachim Breitner, Denis Lohner, and Gregor Snelting

Abstract We present two new results in machine-checked formalizations of programming languages. (1) *Probabilistic Noninterference* is a central notion in software security analysis. We present the first Isabelle formalization of low-security observational determinism ("LSOD"), together with a proof that LSOD implies probabilistic noninterference. The formalization of LSOD uses a *flow-sensitive* definition of low-equivalent traces, which drastically improves precision. (2) We present the first full and machine-checked proof that Launchbury's well-known semantics of the lazy lambda calculus is correct as well as adequate. The proof catches a bug in Launchbury's original proof, which was open for many years.

Both results continue the work of the "Quis Custodiet" project at KIT, which aims at machine-checked soundness proofs for complex properties of languages, compilers, and program analysis. We thus include a short overview of earlier "Quis Custodiet" results.

1 Introduction

"Quis custodiet ipsos custodes?"[1] is the motto of a long-standing project at KIT and TUM, where Isabelle is used to verify complex properties of programming languages, compilers, and program analysis methods. At KIT, "Quis Custodiet" provided the following major results:

---

[1] "Who will guard the guards?", a question by the roman satirist Juvenal, ca. 100 A.C.

S. Bischof · D. Lohner · G. Snelting (✉)
Karlsruhe Institute of Technology (KIT), Karlsruhe, Germany
e-mail: simon.bischof@kit.edu; denis.lohner@kit.edu; gregor.snelting@kit.edu

J. Breitner
DFINITY Stiftung, Zug, Switzerland
e-mail: joachim@dfinity.org

© Springer Nature Switzerland AG 2018
P. Müller, I. Schaefer (eds.), *Principled Software Development*,
https://doi.org/10.1007/978-3-319-98047-8_17

- The semantics of multiple inheritance in C++ was formalized in Isabelle, and type safety was proven [33, 36];
- Program dependence graphs were formalized in Isabelle, and PDG-based information flow control—a specific form of software security analysis—was proven to be sound [34, 35];
- The Java memory model was completely formalized in Isabelle, and sequential consistency was proven; this project included a full semantics for threads and a verified Java compiler [17–19];
- A new code optimization for Haskell, called call arity, was implemented, proven correct and integrated into the GHC [2, 3, 6].

Altogether, the "Quis Custodiet" project at KIT produced over 100,000 lines of Isabelle code, distributed over 14 publications in the Archive of Formal Proofs.

In this contribution, we present two new results in the "Quis Custodiet" project:

1. *Probabilistic Noninterference* (PN) is a central notion in software security. In particular, information flow control (IFC) algorithms check program code for confidentiality and integrity leaks, and guarantee noninterference. We present a formalization of the well-known low-security observational determinism IFC criterion ("LSOD"), which is flow-sensitive and thus much more precise than previous approaches. We provide an Isabelle proof that our flow-sensitive LSOD implies PN.
2. We present the first full and machine-checked proof that Launchbury's well-known semantics of the lazy λ-calculus is correct as well as adequate. In particular, Launchbury's original adequacy proof had a bug, which could not be fixed for many years. Using Isabelle, a new proof approach was discovered, which allowed a machine-checked adequacy proof.

Together with our earlier work, we can thus answer the original question" *Quis custodiet ipsos custodes?*" by stating: "*Illi Isabellistes se custodes egregios praestabant!*".[2]

2 Providing Software Security Guarantees: Isabelle Soundness Proofs for Noninterference

2.1 Background

"Quis Custodiet" was originally founded with the goal to provide machine-checked soundness proofs for certain software security analysis algorithms, in particular algorithms for *information flow control* (IFC). IFC analyses program code, and checks it for *confidentiality* ("no secret values can leak to public ports") and

---

[2]We leave the translation as an exercise to the reader.

integrity ("critical computations cannot be manipulated from outside"). A *sound* IFC guarantees that all potential leaks are discovered, while a *precise* IFC does not cause false alarms.[3] To prove soundness of an IFC analysis, the notion of *noninterference* is essential [25]. In particular, for multi-threaded programs, subtle leaks resulting from scheduling and nondeterminism must be found resp. prohibited, which requires that IFC guarantees *probabilistic noninterference* (PN) [26].

Many authors investigated properties and variations of PN definitions, and some built IFC tools that check program code for confidentiality leaks based on PN. At KIT, Snelting et al. developed the JOANA system, which can handle full Java with unlimited threads, scales to 250 kLOC, guarantees PN, produces few false alarms, has a nice GUI, and is open source [12]. JOANA achieves scalability and precision by using sophisticated program analysis technology such as program dependence graphs (PDGs), points-to analysis, exception analysis, and may-happen-in-parallel analysis. In particular, the analysis is flow-sensitive, context-sensitive, and object-sensitive, which drastically improves precision [13]. JOANA was successfully used to guarantee confidentiality of an experimental e-voting system [15], and to analyse the full source of the HSQLDB database [11].

JOANA can handle unlimited threads and provides a new algorithm for PN. This "RLSOD" algorithm is more precise than competing methods, while avoiding limitations or soundness bugs of previous algorithms [1, 7, 10]. RLSOD is based on the classical "low-security observational determinism" (LSOD) approach, but, for the first time, allows secure low-nondeterminism. RLSOD again exploits modern program analysis, thus being much more precise than LSOD [1].

In the scope of "Quis Custodiet", PDGs and the PDG-based sequential noninterference were formalised in Isabelle, and a machine-checked soundness proof was provided [35]. For PN however, noninterference and its analysis are more demanding. While soundness proofs for PN checkers based on *security type systems* have successfully been provided [22, 26], the PDG-based approach is, due to its flow- and context-sensitivity, much more complex to formalize. A machine-checked soundness proof for RLSOD has just begun. As a first step, the next sections describe the Isabelle formalization of flow-sensitive LSOD and its PN guarantee. To keep this article self-contained, we begin with a summary of technical PN properties.

2.2 Technical Basics

IFC guarantees that no violations of confidentiality or integrity may occur. For confidentiality, all values in input, output, or program states are classified as "high"

---

[3]Note that "100% soundness + 100% precision" cannot be achieved simultaneously: Rice's famous theorem states that such perfect program analysis is undecidable.

```
1   void main ():        1   void main ():        1   void main ():
2      read (H);          2      fork thread_1 ();  2      fork thread_1 ();
3      if (H < 1234)      3      fork thread_2 ();  3      fork thread_2 ();
4         print (0);      4   void thread_1 ():    4   void thread_1 ():
5      L = H;             5      read (L);          5      longCmd ();
6      print (L);         6      print (L);         6      print ("AR");
                          7   void thread_2 ():    7   void thread_2 ():
                          8      read (H);          8      read (H);
                          9      L = H;             9      while (H != 0)
                                                   10         H--;
                                                   11      print ("ND");
```

Fig. 1 Some leaks. Left: explicit and implicit, middle: possibilistic, right: probabilistic. For simplicity, we assume that read (L) reads low variable L from a low input channel; print (H) prints high variable H to a high output channel

(secret) or "low" (public), and it is assumed that an attacker can read all low values, but cannot see any high value.[4]

Figure 1 presents small but typical confidentiality leaks. As usual, variable H is "High" (secret), L is "Low" (public). Explicit leaks arise if (parts of) high values are copied (indirectly) to low output. Implicit leaks arise if a high value can change control flow, which can change low behaviour (see Fig. 1 left). Possibilistic leaks in concurrent programs arise if a certain interleaving produces an explicit or implicit leak; in Fig. 1 middle, interleaving order 5, 8, 9, 6 causes an explicit leak. Probabilistic leaks arise if the probability of low output is influenced by high values. For example in Fig. 1 right, there are no explicit or implicit leaks; but if the value of H is large, probability is higher that "ARND" is printed instead of "NDAR". Thus the attacker may gather information about H from public output.

The simplest (sequential) noninterference definition assumes that a global and static classification $cl(v)$ of all program variables v as secret (H) or public (L) is given. The attacker can only see public variables and values. Noninterference then requires that for any two initial state with identical L variables, but perhaps varying H variables, the final states also coincide on L variables. Thus an attacker cannot learn anything about H variables, and confidentiality is guaranteed.[5]

Formally, the simplest form of (sequential) noninterference is defined as follows. Let $\mathscr{P}$ be a program. Let s, s' be initial program states, let $[\![\mathscr{P}]\!](s)$, $[\![\mathscr{P}]\!](s')$ be the final states after executing $\mathscr{P}$ in state s and s', resp. Noninterference holds iff

$$s \sim_L s' \implies [\![\mathscr{P}]\!](s) \sim_L [\![\mathscr{P}]\!](s') \ .$$

---

[4]A more detailed discussion of IFC attacker models can be found in, e.g., [10]. Note that JOANA allows arbitrary lattices of security classifications, not just the simple $\perp = L \leq H = \top$ lattice. Also note that integrity is dual to confidentiality, but will not be discussed here; JOANA can handle both.

[5]Note that noninterference covers security only on the program level, it does not cover side channel attacks, compromised hardware, etc. The latter must be handled by other security techniques.

The relation $s \sim_L s'$ means that two states are low-equivalent, that is, coincide on low variables: $cl(v) = L \implies s(v) = s'(v)$. Program input is assumed to be part of the initial states s, s', and program output is assumed to be part of the final states ("batch-mode behaviour").

In multi-threaded programs, fine-grained interleaving effects must be accounted for, thus traces are used instead of states. A trace is a (possibly infinite) sequence of events $t = (s_0, o_0, s_1), (s_1, o_1, s_2), \ldots, (s_v, o_v, s_{v+1}), \ldots$, where the o_v are operations (i.e. dynamically executed program statements), and s_v and s_{v+1} are the program states before and after execution of o_v, resp.

For PN, the notion of low-equivalent traces is essential. In the simplest definition, traces t, t' are low-equivalent if for all low-observable events $(s_v, o_v, s_{v+1}) \in t$, $(s'_v, o'_v, s'_{v+1}) \in t'$ it holds that $s_v \sim_L s'_v$, $o_v = o'_v$, and $s_{v+1} \sim_L s'_{v+1}$. For low-equivalent traces, we write $t \sim_L t'$. Obviously, $\sim_L$ is an equivalence relation. The low-class of t is $[t]_L = \{t' \mid t' \sim_L t\}$. Note that the $t' \in [t]_L$ cannot be distinguished by an attacker, as all $t' \in [t]_L$ have the same public behaviour. Thus $[t]_L$ represents t's low behaviour.

PN is called "probabilistic" because it depends on the probabilities of certain traces under certain inputs. Probabilistic behaviour is caused by program nondeterminism (e.g., races), scheduler behaviour, interleaving, and other factors. We write $P_i(T)$ for the probability that a trace $t \in T$ is executed under input i. Thus, $P_i([t]_L)$ is the probability that some trace $t' \sim_L t$ is executed under i. In practice, the $P_i([t]_L)$ are very difficult or impossible to determine—fortunately, for our soundness proof explicit probabilities are not required.

The following PN definition uses explicit input streams instead of initial states. For both inputs the same initial state is assumed. Inputs consist of a low and a high stream of values. Inputs are low-equivalent ($i \sim_L i'$) if their low streams are equal.

Now let i and i' be inputs; let $T(i)$ be the set of all possible traces of program $\mathscr{P}$ for input i. Obviously, we have $P_i(T(i)) = 1$. In the following definition, we use $P_i([t]_L \cap T(i))$ instead of $P_i([t]_L)$. Note that $[t]_L \setminus T(i)$ is a subset of all impossible traces, which is a null set for P_i. Let $\Theta = T(i) \cup T(i')$. PN holds iff

$$i \sim_L i' \implies \forall t \in \Theta : [t]_L \cap T(i) \text{ is measurable for } P_i$$

$$\wedge \; [t]_L \cap T(i') \text{ is measurable for } P_{i'}$$

$$\wedge \; P_i([t]_L \cap T(i)) = P_{i'}([t]_L \cap T(i')) \; .$$

That is, if we take any trace t which can be produced by i or i', the probabilities that a $t' \in [t]_L$ is executed are the same under i and i'. In other words, **probability for any public behaviour is independent from the choice of i or i'** and thus cannot be influenced by secret input. Note that for the equality of probabilities to have a meaning, both sets must be measurable. It is easy to prove that PN implies sequential noninterference, as the proof is independent of specific P_i (see [1, 7]).

Applying this to Fig. 1 right, we first observe that all inputs are low-equivalent as there is only high input. For any $t \in \Theta$ there are only two possibilities:

```
...print("AR")...print("ND")...∈t or
...print("ND")...print("AR")...∈t.
```

Thus, there are only two equivalence classes

$[t]_L^1 = \{t' \mid \ldots \text{print("AR")} \ldots \text{print("ND")} \ldots \in t'\}$ and

$[t]_L^2 = \{t' \mid \ldots \text{print("ND")} \ldots \text{print("AR")} \ldots \in t'\}$.

Now if i contains a small value and i' a large value, as discussed earlier we have $P_i([t]_L^1) \neq P_{i'}([t]_L^1)$ as well as $P_i([t]_L^2) \neq P_{i'}([t]_L^2)$, hence PN is violated.

LSOD is the oldest and simplest criterion which enforces PN. LSOD is independent from specific P_i, and thus independent of specific scheduler behaviour. This attractive feature made us choose LSOD as a starting point for JOANA's PN. LSOD demands that low-equivalent inputs produce low-equivalent traces. It is intuitively secure: changes in high input can never change low behaviour, because low behaviour is enforced to be deterministic. This is however a very restrictive requirement. To address this, RLSOD, as used in JOANA, relaxed this restriction and led to a powerful and precise analysis [1, 7].

Formally, let i, i' be inputs, Θ as above. LSOD holds iff

$$i \sim_L i' \implies \forall t, t' \in \Theta : t \sim_L t' \ .$$

Under LSOD, all traces t for input i are low-equivalent: $T(i) \subseteq [t]_L$, because $\forall t' \in T(i) : t' \sim_L t$. If there is more than one trace for i, then this must result from high-nondeterminism; low behaviour is strictly deterministic.

Lemma 1 *LSOD implies PN.*

Proof Let $i \sim_L i', t \in \Theta$. W.l.o.g. let $t \in T(i)$.

Due to LSOD, we have $T(i) \subseteq [t]_L$ and thus $[t]_L \cap T(i) = T(i)$. As $P_i(T(i)) = 1$, the set $[t]_L \cap T(i)$ is measurable. Therefore, we have

$$P_i([t]_L \cap T(i)) = P_i(T(i)) = 1.$$

Likewise, the set $[t]_L \cap T(i')$ is measurable and $P_{i'}([t]_L \cap T(i')) = 1$, so we have $P_i([t]_L \cap T(i)) = P_{i'}([t]_L \cap T(i'))$. $\quad\square$

The proof makes obvious that LSOD does not care for specific P_i—which is both its strength (scheduler independence) and its weakness (lack of precision).

2.3 Giffhorn's Flow Sensitive LSOD

The above simple definition for $\sim_L$ is extremely restrictive and causes many false alarms. Not only does it require an unrealistic "lock-step" execution of both traces, it is also based on a static H/L classification of program variables, which is neither flow- nor context- nor object-sensitive.

Using security type systems, more refined definitions of $\sim_L$ have been investigated (see, e.g., [24, 26, 37]). In 2012, Giffhorn discovered that PDGs can be used to define low-equivalent traces in such a way that (a) lock-step execution is not necessary; (b) infinite traces are covered, and soundness problems of earlier approaches to infinite traces are avoided; (c) PN checking is flow-, context- and object-sensitive. This insight fits nicely with JOANA's PDG-based IFC. We will know sketch Giffhorn's approach; more details and explanations can be found in [10].

Giffhorn observed that due to flow sensitivity, the same variable or memory cell can have different classifications at different program points i.e. corresponding trace operations (because it has multiple occurrences in the PDG) without compromising soundness.[6] For a low event (s, o, s'), its (flow-sensitive!) low projection is $(s|_{use(o)}, o, s'|_{def(o)})$, where $s|_{use/def(o)}$ denotes the restriction of s to the variables read and written in operation o, resp.[7] Giffhorn allows infinite traces and defines low-equivalent traces as follows:

Let t, t' be two traces. Let t_L, t'_L be their low-observable behaviours, which are obtained by deleting high events and using the low projections for low events. Let $t_L[n]$ be the n-th event in the low-observable behaviour of t, $k_t = |t_L|$, $k_{t'} = |t'_L|$. Then $t \sim_L t'$ iff

1. $\forall 0 \le i < \min(k_t, k_{t'}) : t_L[i] = t'_L[i]$, and
2. if $k_t \ne k_{t'}$, and w.l.o.g. $k_t > k_{t'}$, then t' is infinite and $\forall k_{t'} \le j < k_t : t'$ infinitely delays an operation $o \in DCD(op(t_L[j]))$, where $op(e)$ is the operation of event e.

The latter condition is new and makes sure that operations $op(t_L[j])$ missing in the shorter low-observable trace t'_L can only be missing due to nontermination before o, where o is transitively dynamically control dependent (DCD) on $op(t_L[j])$. [10] explains (a) that this subtle definition avoids soundness problems known from earlier definitions of low-equivalent infinite traces; (b) that dynamic control dependence can be soundly and precisely approximated through PDGs. Giffhorn thus provides a static, PDG-based criterion which guarantees LSOD and thus PN. We will not go into the details of the static criterion and its soundness proof (see [9, 10]). Instead we now present an Isabelle proof that LSOD based on Giffhorn's $\sim_L$ guarantees PN.

2.4 Giffhorn's LSOD in Isabelle

The Isabelle formalization of Giffhorn's approach starts with definitions and lemmas about traces, postdominance, and dynamic control dependency (DCD). In fact, all events in a trace can be uniquely determined by their chain of dynamic control

---

[6]Note that in JOANA only input and output must be classified, all other classifications are computed automatically by a fixpoint operation [13].

[7]This flow-sensitive definition increases precision, see [10].

predecessors, which is expressed by a series of lemmas. Note there are no concrete definitions for dynamic control dependency and postdomination, but just minimal requirements, which can be instantiated in various ways. Next, low observable events and low-equivalence of traces are defined. Giffhorn's crucial innovation, the condition "t' infinitely delays $o \in DCD(o_j)$" reads as follows:

> **definition** *infinite-delay* :: *'trace* $\Rightarrow$ *'stmt operation* $\Rightarrow$ *bool* (- *id* -)
> **where** $T\ id\ o' \equiv \neg\ o' \in_t T \wedge (\exists o''.\ \textit{in-same-branch}\ o'\ o'' \wedge o'' \in_t T)$

where *in-same-branch* uses *DCD* chains to check if o', o'' are in the same branch, caused by some branching point b (e.g., a dynamic IF statement). If so, but $o' \notin_t T$, then U infinitely delays o' due to nontermination between b and o' [10].

Low-equivalency $\approx_{low}$ follows Giffhorn's original definition (see [10], definition 6). The final $LSOD$ definition reads

> **locale** $LSOD =$
>
> ...
>
> **fixes** *input-low-eq* :: *'input* $\Rightarrow$ *'input* $\Rightarrow$ *bool* (**infix** $\sim_L$ 50)
> **and** *possible-traces* :: *'input* $\Rightarrow$ *'trace set* $(T'(\text{-}'))$
>
> **definition** $\Theta\ i\ i' \equiv T(i) \cup T(i')$
> **definition** $LSOD$
> $\equiv \forall i\ i'.\ i \sim_L i' \longrightarrow (\forall t \in \Theta\ i\ i'.\ \forall t' \in \Theta\ i\ i'.\ t \approx_{low} t')$

Note that *input-low-eq* is a parameter of locale $LSOD$ and can again be instantiated in various ways. To prove that Giffhorn's LSOD implies PN, we originally planned to use the formalization of PN in Isabelle as described by Popescu and Nipkow [23]. Unfortunately, this work assumes that $\approx_{low}$ is an equivalence relation, while Giffhorn's $\approx_{low}$ is not transitive (more precisely, it is transitive only in the finite case). Therefore, we defined our own notion of PN in Isabelle using the *HOL-Probability* library [14].

We define PN in an abstract setting (independent of $LSOD$), which will be instantiated later. In this setting we assume the existence of *probability spaces* P_i and sets of possible traces $T(i)$ for each input i such that $P_i(T(i)) = 1$. As before, the definition is parametric in *input-low-eq*, and this time also in the low relation between traces.

> **locale** *Probabilistic-Noninterference* $=$
> **fixes** *input-prob* :: *'input* $\Rightarrow$ *'trace measure* $(P_\text{-})$
> **and** *input-low-eq* :: *'input* $\Rightarrow$ *'input* $\Rightarrow$ *bool* (**infix** $\sim_L$ 50)
> **and** *low-rel* :: *'trace* $\Rightarrow$ *'trace* $\Rightarrow$ *bool* (**infix** $\approx_{low}$ 50)
> **and** *possible-traces* :: *'input* $\Rightarrow$ *'trace set* $(T'(\text{-}'))$
> **assumes** *prob-space*: *prob-space* P_i
> **and** *prob-T*: $P_i\ T(i) = 1$

Let *sets* P_i denote the set of measurable sets of P_i. The PN definition then reads
definition $PN \equiv \forall\, i\, i'.\, i \sim_L i'$
$\longrightarrow (\forall\, t \in \Theta\, i\, i'.$
$\{t' \in T(i).\, t \approx_{low} t'\} \in sets\ P_i\ \wedge$
$\{t' \in T(i').\, t \approx_{low} t'\} \in sets\ P_{i'}\ \wedge$
$P_i\,\{t' \in T(i).\, t \approx_{low} t'\} = P_{i'}\,\{t' \in T(i').\, t \approx_{low} t'\})$

Connecting the abstract PN definition to $LSOD$ is straightforward by equating the possible traces of both formalizations and instantiating *low-rel* with Giffhorn's low-equivalency. The proof of the soundness theorem
theorem *LSOD-implies-PN*: **assumes** *LSOD* **shows** *PN*

follows the handwritten proof in Lemma 1 (we would like to point out that Isabelle's Sledgehammer tool was quite helpful in finding the right lemmas from the probability library). The reader should keep in mind that this soundness theorem is only the first step for an RLSOD soundness proof in Isabelle. For a manual proof of RLSOD soundness, see [1].

To justify the assumptions made by the abstract settings above, we adopted Popescu and Nipkow's [23] construction of the trace space using a discrete time markov chain (see [14]) and instantiated *input-prob* of our locale *Probabilistic-Non-interference* with the resulting trace space.[8]

Further, we formalized *multi-threaded CFGs* as a set of CFGs (as presented by Wasserrab [33]) extended with fork edges,[9] for which we defined a multithreaded small-steps semantics. The state is modelled as a tuple consisting of the memory and, for each thread, a list of the executed edges—this implies that there is no thread local memory. We then define the semantics to be the intra-thread semantics (that is annotated to the edges, see [33]) on each thread, spawning new threads for each fork edge.

As there are only finitely many threads in each state, we can compute a discrete probability distribution for the successor states of a given state and use that as the transition distribution (see [14]) for our discrete time markov chain. For that we used *pmf-of-multiset* on the multi-set of possible successor states, thus modelling a uniform scheduler.

In addition to the trace semantics of the discrete time markov chain, we defined a second trace semantics using possibly infinite lists (type $'a$ *llist*) and traditional interleaving of threads to model finite and infinite executions explicitly. We then proved the two semantics to be equivalent.[10]

---

[8]In contrast to Popescu and Nipkow, our traces include the initial state.

[9]We currently don't support any form of synchronization primitives such as join/wait.

[10]Note that in the case of finite traces, the discrete time markov chain remains in the finished state forever.

We instantiated the multi-threaded CFGs with two simple multi-threaded toy languages, a structured while language, and a goto language, both extended with a fork operation.

The complete formalization of flow-sensitive LSOD and PN, including parallel CFGs, dominance, dynamic dependences, and the toy languages, comprises about 10 kLOC of Isabelle text.[11]

3 An Old Proof Completed, Finally

Formal semantics provide the underpinning for proofs in language-based security, as without them, many theorems cannot even be stated, let alone be proved in a rigorous, machine-checked manner. All (standard) semantics describe mathematically what a program does, but they vary in style (e.g., operational big-step semantics vs. denotational semantics) and in detail (i.e. which details of the actual program execution are modelled and which are abstracted over).

Launchbury's seminal paper "A Natural Semantics for Lazy Evaluation" [16] introduces two such semantics for a lambda calculus with lazy evaluation:

1. An operational semantics where the relation $\Gamma : e \Downarrow \Delta : v$ indicates that the expression e, evaluated within the heap Γ, evaluates to the value v while changing the heap to Δ, where a heap is modeled as a partial map from variable names to expressions. The relation is inductively defined by the rules in Fig. 2.
   Because the shape of the heap is explicit in this formulation, the semantics allows us to represent expressions as graphs instead of trees, and thus express sharing, lazy evaluation and memory usage. This is indeed relevant for an IFC analysis of functional programming languages with lazy evaluation, as sharing can cause hidden channels [8].
2. A denotational semantics $[\![e]\!]$ which translates an expression e into a mathematical object (an element of a cpo, to be precise) that captures its functional behaviour. This semantics is more abstract than the operational, as it does not model the evolution of the heap.

$$\frac{}{\Gamma : \lambda x.e \Downarrow \Gamma : \lambda x.e}\text{LAM} \qquad \frac{\Gamma : e \Downarrow \Delta : \lambda y.e' \qquad \Delta : e'[y{:=}x] \Downarrow \Theta : v}{\Gamma : e\,x \Downarrow \Theta : v}\text{APP}$$

$$\frac{\Gamma : e \Downarrow \Delta : v}{x \mapsto e, \Gamma : x \Downarrow x \mapsto v, \Delta : v}\text{VAR} \qquad \frac{\operatorname{dom}\Delta \cap \operatorname{fv}(\Gamma) = \{\} \qquad \Delta, \Gamma : e \Downarrow \Theta : v}{\Gamma : \textbf{let } \Delta \textbf{ in } e \Downarrow \Theta : v}\text{LET}$$

Fig. 2 Launchbury's natural semantics for Lazy Evaluation

---

[11]The complete formalization can be found at http://pp.ipd.kit.edu/git/LSOD/.

In order to prove that the operational semantics makes sense, and to allow transferring results from one semantics to the other, they are connected by two theorems: *Correctness* states that given $\Gamma : e \Downarrow \Delta : v$, the denotational semantics assigns the same meaning to **let** Γ **in** e and **let** Δ **in** v. *Adequacy* states that every program that has a meaning under the denotational semantics (i.e. $[\![e]\!] \neq \bot$) also evaluates in the operational semantics.

3.1 A Sketchy History

Launchbury's paper comes with a detailed proof of correctness, which translates nicely into an Isabelle proof. For the proof of adequacy, the story is not quite so simple.

In his paper, Launchbury outlines an adequacy proof via two intermediate semantics:

1. He introduces the variant ANS of his operational semantics which differs in three aspects (Fig. 3):

   a. In the rule for function application $(\lambda y.\, e)\, x$, instead of substituting x for y in e, the binding $y \mapsto x$, called an *indirection*, is added to the heap.

   b. In the rule for evaluating a variable x, the original semantics removes the binding for $x \mapsto e$ from the heap until e is evaluated. This models the *blackholing* technique that is employed by language implementations such as the Haskell compiler GHC in order to detect some forms of divergence. It also allows the garbage collector to free unused memory in a more timely manner [20]. The alternative operational semantics does not perform blackholing.

   c. Also in the rule for evaluating a variable x that is bound to e, after evaluating e to v, the original semantics binds x to v, so that further uses of x will not recalculate this value. This *updating* is essential to lazy evaluation, and differentiates it from the call-by-name evaluation strategy, where e would be re-evaluated for every use of x. Again, the alternative operational semantics omits this step.

The intention is that these changes make ANS behave more similarly to the denotational semantics and thus simplify the adequacy proof.

$$\frac{\Gamma : e \Downarrow \Delta : \lambda y.\, e' \qquad y \mapsto x, \Delta : e' \Downarrow \Theta : v}{\Gamma : e\, x \Downarrow \Theta : v}\text{App'} \qquad \frac{x \mapsto e, \Gamma : e \Downarrow \Delta : v}{x \mapsto e, \Gamma : x \Downarrow \Delta : v}\text{Var'}$$

Fig. 3 Launchbury's alternative natural semantics

2. He introduces a variant of the denotational semantics $\mathcal{N}[\![e]\!]$, dubbed the *resourced denotational semantics*, which expects as an additional parameter an element of $C := \mathbb{N} \cup \omega$, and decreases this argument in every recursive call. When the argument is ω, this does not actually limit the number of recursive calls, and the semantics coincides with the regular denotational semantics. If the argument is a natural number, the semantics might run out of steam before it fully calculates the meaning of the given expression.

Launchbury's adequacy proof sketch then proceeds with little more detail than the following list:

1. If $[\![e]\!] \neq \bot$, then, because the semantics coincide, we have $\mathcal{N}[\![e]\!] \, \omega \neq \bot$.
2. Because the resourced denotational semantics are continuous, there is an $n \in \mathbb{N}$ such that $\mathcal{N}[\![e]\!] \, n \neq \bot$.
3. From that we can show that in the alternative operational semantics, there exist Δ and v such that $\{\} : e \Downarrow \Delta : v$. The step is performed by induction on n, and justifies the introduction of the resourced denotational semantics.
4. Finally, because the two operational semantics obviously only differ in the shape of the heap, but otherwise reduce the same expressions, we also have such a derivation in the original operational semantics.

Given the impact of the paper as the default big-step operational semantics for lazy evaluation, it is not surprising that there are later attempts to work out the details of this proof sketch. These turned up a few hurdles.

The first hurdle is that it does not make sense to state the coincidence of the denotational semantics as $[\![e]\!] = \mathcal{N}[\![e]\!] \, \omega$, since these semantics map into different cpos. The regular denotational semantics maps into the cpo D defined by the domain equation

$$D = [D \to D]_\bot$$

where every element is either $\bot$ or a continuous function from D to D. The resourced denotational semantics map into the cpo E defined by the domain equation

$$E = [(C \to E) \to (C \to E)]_\bot \; .$$

This problem was first discovered by Sánchez-Gil *et al.*, and just fixing this step, by defining a suitable similarity relation between these cpos, was a notable contribution on its own [28].

The same group also attempted to complete the other steps of Launchbury's proof sketch, in particular step 4. They broke it down into two smaller steps, and starting from the alternative semantics, they proved that removing indirections from the semantics does indeed yield an equivalent semantics [29]. But to this date, the remaining step resists rigorous proving, as Sánchez-Gil et al. report [27]. It seems that without blackholing and updates, the difference in heap evolution are too manyfold and intricate to be captured with a sufficiently elegant and handleable relation.

3.2 Denotational Blackholing

Considering the difficulties of following Launchbury's proof sketch directly, we revisited some of his steps. If it is so hard to relate the two operational semantics, maybe it is better to work just with the original operational semantics, and try to bridge the apparent mismatch between the operational semantics and the denotational semantics on the denotational side?

The first of the differences listed on page 277—substitution vs. indirection—can be readily bridged by a substitution lemma ($[\![e]\!]_{\rho(y \mapsto \rho\, x)} = [\![e[y := x]]\!]_{\rho}$), which is needed anyways in the correctness proof.

The third of the listed differences—whether updating is performed or not—is even easier to fix, as it does not affect the adequacy proof at all. In an adequacy proof we need to produce evidence for the *assumptions* of the corresponding natural semantics inference rule, which is then, in the last step, applied to produce the desired judgement. The removal of updates only changes the *conclusion* of the rule, so the adequacy proof is unchanged. There is an indirect effect, as in the adequacy proof we use the corresponding correctness result, and the correctness proof needs to address updates.

The remaining difference is the tricky one: how can we deal with blackholing in the adequacy proof? As during the evaluation of a (possibly recursive) variable binding the binding itself is removed from the heap, the denotation of the whole configuration changes. This is a problem, as there is no hope of proving $\mathcal{N}[\![e]\!]_{\mathcal{N}\{x \mapsto e, \Gamma\}} = \mathcal{N}[\![e]\!]_{\mathcal{N}\{\Gamma\}}$.

But what we could hope for is the following statement, which indicates that if a recursive expression has a denotation, then the expression has some (likely less defined) denotation even when all recursive calls are $\bot$:

$$\mathcal{N}[\![e]\!]_{\mathcal{N}\{x \mapsto e, \Gamma\}}n \neq \bot \implies \mathcal{N}[\![e]\!]_{\mathcal{N}\{\Gamma\}}n \neq \bot$$

This lemma follows from the following, also quite natural proposition, which expresses that if we allow the resourced semantics function to take at most $n + 1$ steps, then the environment only matters in so far as at most n steps are passed to it:

$$\mathcal{N}[\![e]\!]_{\sigma}|_{(n+1)} = \mathcal{N}[\![e]\!]_{(\sigma|_n)}|_{(n+1)}$$

It turned out, however, that the resourced denotational semantics as introduced by Launchbury does not fulfill this property! By carefully capping the number of steps passed in the function equation for lambda expressions, we could fix this, and indeed prove adequacy of the resourced denotational semantics.

3.3   Gaining Assurance

These systems and proofs are, as the discussions in the previous sections showed, abundant with pitfalls. We would not believe our own proofs, had we not implemented all of them in Isabelle.

This includes a formalization of the similarity relation between the two denotational semantics from [28]. As it is a non-monotonous relation, we cannot simply define it as an inductive relation, but have to first define finite approximations and then manually take the limit. Once constructed, however, the details of the construction are no longer relevant—a blessing of the extensionality of Isabelle's logic.

Throughout our development we used the Isabelle implementation [32] of Nominal Logic [21] to elegantly deal with the contentious issues involving name binding. The interested reader can find full details in [4] and Breitner's award-winning thesis [3].

We have since extended our formalization [5] with boolean values and it has served as the target for a formal verification that a transformation performed by the Haskell compiler does not increase the number of allocations performed by the program [2, 6]—a property that can only be proven with a semantics as operational as Launchbury's.

4   Conclusion

Juvenal's question "Quis custodiet ipsos custodes?" can from a science-theoretic viewpoint be interpreted as an early precursor of later "constructivist" positions, which deny the possibility of objective knowledge and sound methodology. While we dismantled constructivist positions in the field of software technology [30, 31], we interpreted Juvenal's question as a challenge to produce soundness guarantees for various program analysis and software security techniques. Today we are satisfied to state our answer to Juvenal: "Illi Isabellistes Se Custodes Egregios Praestabant!".

References

1. Simon Bischof et al. "Low-Deterministic Security For Low-Deterministic Programs". In: *Journal of Computer Security* 26 (2018), pp. 335–336. https://doi.org/10.3233/JCS17984
2. Joachim Breitner. "Formally proving a compiler transformation safe". In: *Proceedings of the 8th ACM SIGPLAN Symposium on Haskell, Haskell 2015, Vancouver BC, Canada, September 3–4, 2015*. 2015, pp. 35–46.
3. Joachim Breitner. "Lazy Evaluation: From natural semantics to a machine-checked compiler transformation". PhD thesis. Karlsruher Institut für Technologie, Fakultät für Informatik, Apr. 2016.

4. Joachim Breitner. "The adequacy of Launchbury's natural semantics for lazy evaluation". In: *J. Funct. Program.* 28 (2018), e1. https://doi.org/10.1017/S0956796817000144.
5. Joachim Breitner. "The Correctness of Launchbury's Natural Semantics for Lazy Evaluation". In: *Archive of Formal Proofs* (Jan. 2013). ISSN: 2150-914x. http://afp.sf.net/entries/Launchbury.shtml.
6. Joachim Breitner. "The Safety of Call Arity". In: *Archive of Formal Proofs* (Feb 2015).
7. Joachim Breitner et al. "On Improvements Of Low-Deterministic Security". In: *Proc. Principles of Security and Trust (POST)* Ed. by Frank Piessens and Luca Viganò. Vol. 9635. Lecture Notes in Computer Science. Springer Berlin Heidelberg, 2016, pp. 68–88.
8. Pablo Buiras and Alejandro Russo. "Lazy Programs Leak Secrets". In: *NordSec* Vol. 8208. Lecture Notes in Computer Science. Springer, 2013, pp. 116–122.
9. Dennis Giffhorn. "Slicing of Concurrent Programs and its Application to Information Flow Control". PhD thesis. Karlsruher Institut für Technologie, Fakultät für Informatik, May 2012.
10. Dennis Giffhorn and Gregor Snelting. "A New Algorithm For Low-Deterministic Security". In: *International Journal of Information Security* 14.3 (Apr 2015), pp. 263–287.
11. Jürgen Graf. "Information Flow Control with System Dependence Graphs — Improving Modularity Scalability and Precision for Object Oriented Languages". PhD thesis. Karlsruher Institut für Technologie, Fakultät für Informatik, 2016.
12. Jürgen Graf et al. "Tool Demonstration: JOANA". In: *Proc. Principles of Security and Trust (POST)* Ed. by Frank Piessens and Luca Viganò. Vol. 9635. Lecture Notes in Computer Science. Springer Berlin Heidelberg, 2016, pp. 89–93.
13. Christian Hammer and Gregor Snelting. "Flow-Sensitive, Context-Sensitive, and Object-sensitive Information Flow Control Based on Program Dependence Graphs". In: *Interna- tional Journal of Information Security* 8.6 (Dec. 2009), pp. 399–422.
14. Johannes Hölzl. "Construction and Stochastic Applications of Measure Spaces in Higher Order Logic". Dissertation. München: Technische Universität München, 2013.
15. Ralf Küsters et al. "Extending and Applying a Framework for the Cryptographic Verification of Java Programs". In: *Proc. POST 2014* LNCS 8424. Springer, 2014, pp. 220–239.
16. John Launchbury "A Natural Semantics for Lazy Evaluation". In: *Principles of Programming Languages (POPL)* ACM, 1993. DOI: 10.1145/158511.158618.
17. Andreas Lochbihler "A Machine-Checked, Type-Safe Model of Java Concurrency : Language, Virtual Machine, Memory Model, and Verified Compiler". PhD thesis. Karlsruher Institut für Technologie, Fakultät für Informatik, July 2012.
18. Andreas Lochbihler. "Making the Java Memory Model Safe". In: *ACM Transactions on Programming Languages and Systems* 35.4 (2014), 12:1 12:65.
19. Andreas Lochbihler. "Verifying a Compiler for Java Threads". In: *Proc. 19th European Symposium on Programming ESOP 2010* Vol. 6012. Lecture Notes in Computer Science. 2010, pp. 427–447.
20. Simon Peyton Jones. "Implementing Lazy Functional Languages on Stock Hardware: The Spineless Tagless G-Machine". In: *Journal of Functional Programming* 2.2 (1992), pp. 127–202. https://doi.org/10.1017/S0956796800000319.
21. Andrew M. Pitts. "Nominal logic, a first order theory of names and binding". In: *Theoretical Aspects of Computer Software (TACS) 2001* Vol. 186. Information and Computation 2. Elsevier, 2003, pp. 165–193. https://doi.org/10.1016/S08905401(03)00138X
22. Andrei Popescu, Johannes Hölzl, and Tobias Nipkow. "Formal Verification of Language- Based Concurrent Noninterference". In: *J. Formalized Reasoning* 6.1 (2013), pp. 1–30.
23. Andrei Popescu, Johannes Hölzl, and Tobias Nipkow "Formalizing Probabilistic Noninterference". In: *Proc. Certified Programs and Proofs CPP* Vol. 8307. Lecture Notes in Computer Science. 2013, pp. 259–275.
24. Andrei Popescu, Johannes Hölzl, and Tobias Nipkow. "Noninterfering Schedulers When Possibilistic Noninterference Implies Probabilistic Noninterference". In: *Proc. Algebra and Coalgebra in Computer Science (CALCO)* Lecture Notes in Computer Science. 2013, pp. 236–252.

25. A. Sabelfeld and A. Myers. "Language-Based Information-Flow Security". In: *IEEE Journal on Selected Areas in Communications* 21.1 (Jan. 2003), pp. 5–19.
26. Andrei Sabelfeld and David Sands. "Probabilistic Noninterference for Multi-Threaded Programs". In: *Proceedings of the 13th IEEE Computer Security Foundations Workshop, CSFW '00, Cambridge England, UK, July 3–5, 2000.* 2000, pp. 200–214.
27. Lidia Sánchez-Gil, Mercedes Hidalgo-Herrero, and Yolanda Ortega-Mallén. "Launchbury's semantics revisited: On the equivalence of context-heap semantics (Work in progress)". In: *XIV Jornadas sobre Programación y Lenguajes* (2014), pp. 203–217.
28. Lidia Sánchez-Gil, Mercedes Hidalgo-Herrero, and Yolanda Ortega-Mallén. "Relating function spaces to resourced function spaces". In: *Symposium on Applied Computing (SAC)* ACM, 2011, pp. 1301–1308. https://doi.org/10.1145/1982185.1982469
29. Lidia Sánchez-Gil, Mercedes Hidalgo-Herrero, and Yolanda Ortega-Mallén. "The role of indirections in lazy natural semantics". In: *Perspectives of System Informatics (PSI) 2014* Vol. 8974. LNCS. Springer, 2015. https://doi.org/10.1007/9783662468234$\delimiter"026E30F$_24
30. Gregor Snelting. "Paul Feyerabend and software technology". In: *International Journal on Software Tools for Technology Transfer* 2.1 (Nov 1998), pp. 1–5.
31. Gregor Snelting. "Paul Feyerabend und die Softwaretechnologie". In: *Informatik-Spektrum* 21.5 (Oct. 1998), pp. 273–276.
32. Christian Urban and Cezary Kaliszyk. "General Bindings and Alpha-Equivalence in Nominal Isabelle". In: *Logical Methods in Computer Science* 8.2 (2012). DOI: 10.2168/LMCS8(2:14)2012.
33. Daniel Wasserrab. "From Formal Semantics to Verified Slicing – A Modular Framework with Applications in Language Based Security". PhD thesis. Karlsruher Institut für Technologie, Fakultät für Informatik, Oct. 2010. http://digbib.ubka.uni-karlsruhe.de/volltexte/1000020678.
34. Daniel Wasserrab. "Information Flow Noninterference via Slicing". In: *Archive of Formal Proofs* (2010).
35. Daniel Wasserrab, Denis Lohner, and Gregor Snelting. "On PDG-Based Noninterference and its Modular Proof". In: *Proc. PLAS '09* ACM. Dublin, Ireland, June 2009. http://pp.info.unikarlsruhe.de/uploads/publikationen/wasserrab09plas.pdf.
36. Daniel Wasserrab et al. "An Operational Semantics and Type Safety Proof for Multiple Inheritance in C++". In: *21th Annual ACM Conference on Object-Oriented Programming Systems, Languages, and Applications* ACM, Oct. 2006, pp. 345–362.
37. Steve Zdancewic and Andrew C. Myers. "Observational Determinism for Concurrent Program Security". In: *Proc. CSFW.* IEEE, 2003, pp. 29–43.

Reasoning About Weak Semantics via Strong Semantics

Roland Meyer and Sebastian Wolff

Abstract Verification has to reason about the actual semantics of a program. The actual semantics not only depends on the source code but also on the environment: the target machine, the runtime system, and in the case of libraries the number of clients. So verification has to consider weak memory models, manual memory management, and arbitrarily many clients. Interestingly, most programs are insensitive to the environment. Programs are often well-behaved in that they appear to be executed under sequentially-consistent memory, garbage collection, and with few clients—although they are not. There is a correspondence between the actual semantics and an idealized much simpler variant. This suggests to carry out the verification in two steps. Check that the program is well-behaved. If so, perform the verification on the idealized semantics. Otherwise, report that the code is sensitive to the environment.

Arnd is one of the few researchers who is able to switch with ease between the practice of writing code and the theory of defining programming interfaces. Discussions with him had substantial influence on the above verification approach, which we started to develop in Kaiserslautern, two offices next to his. In this paper, we give a unified presentation of our findings.

Happy Birthday, Arnd!

1 Introduction

Writing code is difficult. The programmer has to reason about the actual semantics of a program. The actual semantics not only depends on the code but is influenced to a great extent by the program's environment: the underlying hardware, the runtime system, and the clients. This influence results in a complexity that virtually no

R. Meyer · S. Wolff (✉)
TU Braunschweig, Braunschweig, Germany
e-mail: roland.meyer@tu-bs.de; sebastian.wolff@tu-bs.de

© Springer Nature Switzerland AG 2018
P. Müller, I. Schaefer (eds.), *Principled Software Development*,
https://doi.org/10.1007/978-3-319-98047-8_18

programmer can fully understand. For example, to speed-up execution, modern processors employ weak memory models, like total store ordering (TSO). Under TSO, every processor is equipped with a store buffer. Memory writes are put into that buffer and eventually written to memory in batches. A processor can read from its own buffer but cannot see the other buffers. Hence, each processor may observe a different memory valuation. For another example, to avoid the runtime penalty of garbage collection (GC) many programming languages require memory to be managed manually (MM). Programmers have to explicitly reclaim memory that is no longer used to prevent the system from running out of available memory. As a consequence, programs can behave unexpectedly due to unknowingly accessing reallocated memory or crash due to accessing memory no longer available. Weak memory models and manual memory management thus introduce intricate program behaviors that lead to subtle bugs which are typically hard to debug.

The intricacy of such *weak semantics* makes reasoning about programs difficult. To still argue about correctness, programmers consider, sometimes unknowingly so, a *stronger* semantics. They assume sequential consistency (SC) and garbage collection. That is, they assume memory operations to be atomic and ignore bugs due to flawed memory management.

This approach to program development is widely spread and successful. Most industrial programs lack formal correctness proofs. Instead, programmers reason informally about the strong semantics and use tests to support their reasoning. This leads to the following conjecture: reasoning about the strong semantics is sufficient. Phrased differently, correctness of a program under the simpler strong semantics entails correctness of the program under the actual weak semantics.

Obviously, our conjecture cannot be true in general. There are programs where the difference between weak and strong semantics becomes evident [9, 29], where TSO reorderings result in behavior not present under SC and where GC prevents reallocations harmful under MM. Surprisingly, this seems to be the case exclusively for performance-critical applications where experienced programmers are proficient in the weak semantics and deliberately exploit system-specific characteristics. For the majority of programs, however, the conjecture does hold. This claim is supported by the so-called *DRF theorem* [3]. It states that TSO and SC coincide, i.e., admit the exact same behaviors, provided the program is *data race free (DRF)*. Similarly, there is a *PRF theorem* [18] stating that MM and GC coincide provided the program is free from *pointer races*—roughly speaking, if no dangling pointers are used.

Interestingly, the applicability of both the DRF and the PRF theorems can be checked in the strong semantics. This is crucial since reasoning about the weak semantics—whether it is about correctness or about race freedom—is infeasible. This allows programmers to solely reason in the strong semantics and be sure that their reasoning carries over to the actual semantics.

Our verification approach can be formulated as automating the programmer's manual reasoning. In the strong semantics, we check (1) properties like DRF and PRF and (2) correctness. If any of the checks fails, verification fails. That is, we consider programs that do not adhere to rules like DRF buggy. Note that automation allows us to consider properties more complex than DRF and PRF that would be hard to establish manually. This makes the approach applicable to more programs. We have successfully instantiated the approach for weak memory, concurrent data structures, and heap-manipulating programs.

For weak memory, the goal is to show that TSO does not admit more behaviors than SC. In literature, this is also known as *robustness* [7] or *stability* [4]. The main insight required for the result observes that non-robustness becomes evident in computations of a particular form [5, 7]: if a program is not robust, then there is a TSO computation which is infeasible under SC where only one thread delays stores. That the computation is infeasible under SC can be detected by searching for a happens-before path from the last load of the delaying thread to the first delayed store. Finding such a path can then be done under SC. The reason for this is that the store buffer of the delaying thread is used in a restricted way during the time frame that needs to be analysed. Hence, the store buffer can be elided altogether. To that end, the original program is instrumented: instead of putting a write to the store buffer and flushing it to memory later, we modify the thread such that it performs the write to another memory location and immediately flushes it. This memory location is fresh in that no other thread reads it. Then, the delaying thread performs reads from the elided location to mimic reads from its own store buffer. Other threads are not affected by the elision. They would not observe the delayed write in the original program and also do not observe the write in the instrumented program as they do not load the elided location. Since this instrumentation does not affect the happens-before relation involving actions of the non-delaying threads, the instrumented program contains the happens-before path in question if and only if the original program does. Altogether, this means that robustness can be checked under SC.

The above instrumentation allows to check robustness of programs. So for robust programs, correctness can be checked under the simpler SC semantics. For non-robust programs, however, verification remains impossible; correctness results of SC do not carry over to TSO and an analysis of full TSO is intractable. To overcome this limitation, one can iteratively enrich the SC computations with TSO relaxations (delayed stores) via an instrumentation [8]. To that end, one uses the robustness decision procedure from above. If it terminates with a negative answer, one extracts a TSO computation that is infeasible under SC. As described above, at the heart of such a computation is a delayed store that introduces a happens-before cycle. Then, one instruments the program to explicitly buffer that store in a local register and flush it to memory later. This introduces TSO behavior of the original program into the SC behaviors of the instrumented version. Repeating this procedure yields a semi-decision procedure. If the instrumented program is eventually found robust, it can be used to check correctness because its SC behaviors coincide with the TSO behaviors of the original program. However, it is not guaranteed that there is a finite set of instrumentations that lead to a positive robustness result.

For heap manipulating programs, we showed the PRF theorem mentioned above [18]. Intuitively, the theorem states that if no dangling pointers are used, then a program cannot detect whether or not memory is reclaimed and reused. The reason for this is the following. In order to detect whether a memory cell has been reclaimed and reused, a program needs to acquire a pointer to that memory cell, wait for it to be reclaimed, and then observe that it is in use again. After the reclamation, however, any pointer to that memory becomes *dangling*. Those pointers remain dangling when the referenced memory is reused. We consider any subsequent usage of a dangling pointer as a bug. We call those bugs *pointer races*. They are indeed races because the access is not synchronized with the preceding deletion—the program uses a pointer after it's referenced memory was deleted and is thus prone to crash due to a *segmentation fault* or a *bus error* because the memory might as well be returned to the underlying operating system instead of being reused. However, if pointers are never dereferenced and used in conditionals after they become dangling, then a program cannot find out whether another pointer holds the same value. In particular, it cannot decide whether the result of an allocation is already referenced by a dangling pointer. Hence, it cannot know whether an allocation reuses reclaimed or fresh memory. As a consequence, the behavior is the same if memory is reused or not at all. That is, the program behaves identical under both GC and MM.

Another result for concurrent heap manipulating programs studies the interaction of threads communicating via a shared memory [22]. In particular in fault-tolerant implementations, like lock-free programs, threads typically do not rely on other threads having finished their work. This means that if a thread starts to alter a shared structure but does not finish its update due to an interruption or a failure, then any thread can *take back* the shared structure to a consistent state (wrt. to a sequential execution). Put differently, after every atomic update every thread can continue and finish its operation even though the update left some shared structure in an inconsistent state. Using standard data flow analyses one can collect a set of atomic updates that are likely to over-approximate the updates of the original program. We call a sequential program which repeatedly executes those updates a *summary*. Such a summary is then a candidate program for over-approximating the behavior of the original program on the shared heap. Hence, if correctness can be judged solely by the contents of the heap, then the sequential summary can be used for checking correctness of the concurrent program under scrutiny. For this approach to be sound, the summary must cover all possible updates of the original program. We showed that this can be done by considering the parallel composition of the summary and a single thread of the program: if the summary can mimic every shared heap update of the retained thread in this two-threaded program, then the summary indeed over-approximates the shared heap updates of the original program.

The results presented above simplify the analysis. Instead of performing an expensive analysis, one proves that a simpler analysis implies the desired results. In the automated program verification literature, a standard framework for this kind of results is *abstract interpretation* [11]. Abstract interpretation is a powerful tool for reasoning about a weak semantics using a strong semantics. The correspondence of the semantics is then guaranteed by the underlying theory. More specifically, to use abstract interpretation one has to show—in a manual proof—that the strong semantics is a *safe approximation* of the weak semantics. That is, one has to show that every behavior of the weak semantics is *mimicked* by a behavior of the strong semantics. Note that this property is shown independently of the program under scrutiny. On the one hand, this allows the framework to be applicable to any program once shown that the strong semantics is a safe approximation. On the other hand, however, it may not leverage properties that hold only for a fragment of programs. In particular, abstract interpretation cannot reason about properties like the soundness check for summaries because it is a property of the entire state space rather than a (safety) property of an individual computation. The reason for this is that abstract interpretation shows the reduction *statically*; it holds for any program. We, however, suggest to add a *dynamic* check at verification time which ensures that the simpler analysis indeed provides a correct result. That is, we sacrifice universal applicability to provide more efficient analyses for a fragment of programs.

Our experience shows that relying on dynamic checks to judge whether a simpler analysis is correct makes verification much more efficient than classical approaches, like abstract interpretation. Moreover, we found that the concept is very flexible; even performance critical code can be handled with the concepts discussed above.

The rest of the paper is structured as follows. Section 2 introduces a general framework for reasoning about programs using strong semantics. This framework is then instantiated in Sects. 3–5 for TSO programs, shared memory programs, and pointer programs, respectively. Section 6 concludes the paper.

2   From Weak Semantics to Strong Semantics

In this paper we consider the task of verification. More specifically, we consider the problem of checking a safety property *safe* for a set of computations $\mathcal{W}$. Intuitively, $\mathcal{W}$ contains all computations of a given program where a computation is a sequence of executed actions. Formally, we refrain from making this set any more precise; we will appropriately instantiate it as needed. The safety property is given as a predicate *safe* over computations. That is, the task is to check whether $safe(\tau)$ holds for every computation $\tau \in \mathcal{W}$, denoted by $safe(\mathcal{W})$ for brevity.

It is well known that the above verification task is undecidable for most interesting programs. To fight this theoretical limitation, abstractions and approximations are applied. A standard approach for program abstraction is *abstract interpretation* [11, 12]. The goal of abstract interpretation is to execute a given program in an *abstract semantics*. Roughly, this means that rather than using actual (concrete) values the program uses abstract values. An abstract value represents a set of concrete ones, potentially infinitely many. To guarantee soundness of such an approach, abstract interpretation requires the abstract semantics to be a *safe approximation* of the concrete semantics. Intuitively, this means that every action a program can take in a concrete execution can be mimicked in the corresponding abstract run. That is, one has to show for all possible programs that abstract computations over-approximate the reachable control states of concrete computations.

Abstract interpretation has proven to be a powerful tool for verification. However, the state space $\mathcal{W}$ might be too large to enumerate despite aggressive finite abstractions. In particular, weak memory and concurrent shared memory programs suffer from a severe state space explosion. Our goal is to provide reductions that allow verification for cases where abstract interpretation alone cannot. To that end, we suggest to identify a simpler semantics to conduct the verification in. That is, we suggest to consider a smaller/simpler state space $\mathscr{S}$ the successful verification of which implies the desired property of $\mathscr{W}$. Intuitively, we want to identify $\mathscr{S} \subset \mathscr{W}$ such that $\mathscr{S}$ can be verified efficiently with existing abstract interpretation techniques. Technically, we do not require $\mathscr{S} \subset \mathscr{W}$. In fact, we do allow $\mathscr{S}$ to stem from another program than the one under scrutiny. In any case, the analysis of $\mathscr{S}$ may *skip* computations of $\mathscr{W}$. Hence, one has to show that the verification result of $\mathscr{S}$ carries over to $\mathscr{W}$ indeed. In the spirit of abstract interpretation, we perform an over-approximation: we require that a *successful* verification of $\mathscr{S}$ implies correctness of $\mathscr{W}$. More formally, we require that *safe*($\mathscr{S}$) implies *safe*($\mathscr{W}$). The reverse needs not hold.

However, the above reduction idea is flawed. The problem is that we require *safe*($\mathscr{S}$) $\implies$ *safe*($\mathscr{W}$). In a manual proof for a specific program one can reason about the $\mathscr{W}$-computations that are skipped by $\mathscr{S}$. For automated techniques, however, the above implication needs to be established for *every* program. To simplify this task, we weaken the requirement. We allow a reduction to supply a predicate ρ which judges whether or not an analysis of the simpler $\mathscr{S}$ is sound. For example, ρ could check for data races to judge whether or not the DRF theorem applies.

Intuitively, in terms of abstract interpretation, ρ characterizes those computations for which the abstract semantics is a safe approximation of the concrete semantics. That is, in computations for which ρ evaluates to *true* any action performed in $\mathscr{W}$ can be mimicked in $\mathscr{S}$. Consider Fig. 1 for an illustration. Consequently, an analysis has to additionally check whether or not $\rho(\mathscr{S})$ holds. If it does hold, then the

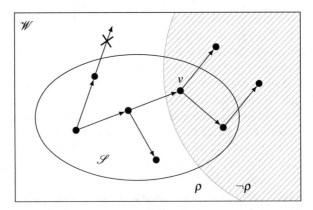

Fig. 1 A borderline computation, like v, is a computation that may *leave* $\mathscr{S}$. More specifically, v can perform actions under $\mathscr{W}$ that are not discovered by (not included in) $\mathscr{S}$. This jeopardizes sound verification. To detect such situations, we use a predicate ρ over $\mathscr{S}$. This predicate is evaluated at analysis-time, e.g., after $\mathscr{S}$ has been enumerated

analysis is guaranteed to be sound. Otherwise, there are *borderline* computations (cf. v in Fig. 1) that can perform actions under $\mathcal{W}$ not captured by $\mathcal{S}$. Since ρ is checked dynamically, the result may differ from program to program. Those programs for which ρ cannot be established we deem buggy and verification fails.

Technically, we require $\rho(\mathcal{S}) \wedge \mathit{safe}(\mathcal{S}) \implies \mathit{safe}(\mathcal{W})$ to hold. As we will see in more detail later, this has two advantages. On the one hand, this weakened property can be established for arbitrary programs. It is thus amenable for automated techniques as it need not be re-proven for every program of interest. On the other hand, the soundness check $\rho(\mathcal{S})$ can be done by the actual analysis. Typically, it can be implemented efficiently, taking insignificant time compared to the actual analysis of $\mathcal{S}$. Lastly, note that we do not pose any restriction on ρ. In particular, we allow ρ to be any predicate over *sets* of computations rather than just a predicate over *single* computations. This renders ρ strictly more powerful than a safety property.

The following summarizes how we reduce the verification of $\mathcal{W}$ to $\mathcal{S}$.

Reduction I

Given: A set of computations $\mathcal{W}$ and predicate *safe*.

Task: Find a set of computations $\mathcal{S}$ and a predicate ρ over $\mathcal{S}$ such that:

$$\rho(\mathcal{S}) \wedge \mathit{safe}(\mathcal{S}) \implies \mathit{safe}(\mathcal{W}) . \tag{R}$$

With such a reduction at hand, we suggest the following approach: (1) enumerate $\mathcal{S}$, (2) check $\mathit{safe}(\mathcal{S})$, and (3) check $\rho(\mathcal{S})$. Verification fails if one of the checks fails. Otherwise it succeeds because (R) guarantees that $\mathit{safe}(\mathcal{W})$ holds.

The main goal in establishing a reduction is to prove property (R) once $\mathcal{S}$ and ρ are chosen. The following is a promising proof strategy for this task. Introduce a relation $\approx\ \subseteq\ \mathcal{W} \times \mathcal{S}$ among computations. Intuitively, $\tau \approx \sigma$ states that σ mimics in $\mathcal{S}$ the behavior of τ in $\mathcal{W}$. So if τ is a safety violation, then also σ is a safety violation. Now, if there is such a σ for every τ, denoted $\mathcal{W} \prec \mathcal{S}$, then $\mathcal{S}$ covers all behaviors of $\mathcal{W}$. That is, if there is a safety violation $\tau \in \mathcal{W}$, then there must be a safety violation $\sigma \in \mathcal{S}$. Hence, it is sufficient to verify $\mathcal{S}$.

Altogether, we suggest to refine the reduction approach from above as follows.

Reduction II

Given: A set of computations $\mathcal{W}$ and predicate *safe*.

Task: Find $\mathcal{S}$, $\prec$, and ρ such that:

$$\rho(\mathcal{S}) \implies \mathcal{W} \prec \mathcal{S} \tag{R1}$$

and $\qquad \neg\mathit{safe}(\mathcal{W}) \wedge \mathcal{W} \prec \mathcal{S} \implies \neg\mathit{safe}(\mathcal{S}) . \tag{R2}$

As noted before, an analysis may find that the provided reduction does not allow to soundly verify a program. In the case of TSO programs, for instance, the analysis may explore the SC executions and find a data race. Following the approach so far, the analysis must deem the program incorrect even if no *proper* correctness violation was found. This makes verification imprecise. To fight the false-positives of such an analysis, one can dynamically weaken $\mathscr{S}$ to include computations that make the soundness check fail. To that end, we adapt the verification procedure suggested above. If the check $\rho(\mathscr{S})$ fails, then we extract a witness computation. Such a computation is a borderline event, as depicted in Fig. 2. The computation is borderline because it allows behavior under $\mathscr{W}$ which $\mathscr{S}$ does not allow. Put differently, the borderline computation can *leave* $\mathscr{S}$ and thus harms soundness. Instead of deeming the program incorrect, we can extend $\mathscr{S}$ to include the missing behavior. The adding process can be guided by ρ: ρ detects a borderline action that can be done under $\mathscr{W}$ but not under $\mathscr{S}$. Then, we add this missing behavior to $\mathscr{S}$ and repeat the analysis. In the next iteration, either the analysis can be shown sound or ρ reveals another missing behavior. Repeating the above approach thus yields a semi-decision procedure. If a bug is found or the analysis becomes sound eventually, then the procedure stops with a definite result. However, the above process may loop indefinitely because there is no guarantee that there are only finitely many behaviors missing in $\mathscr{S}$ in general.

In the remainder of the paper, we discuss several instantiations of the above framework to ease reasoning about weak memory models, concurrent shared memory programs, and concurrent pointer programs.

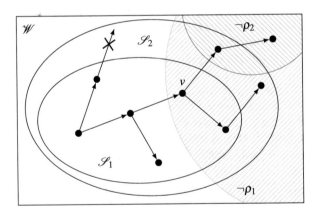

Fig. 2 One-step extension $\mathscr{S}_2$ of $\mathscr{S}_1$. The extension $\mathscr{S}_2$ includes the borderline events of $\mathscr{S}_1$. The borderline events are given by ρ_1, like v. The extended $\mathscr{S}_2$ has another borderline event according to ρ_2

3   From Total Store Ordering to Sequential Consistency

A natural memory model is sequential consistency (SC) [26]. Under SC, all operations appear instantaneous and atomic. That is, the effect of an operation is immediately visible to all threads. This simplicity makes it easy to reason, both manually and automatically, about SC executions. For performance reasons, however, SC is not implemented in today's processors. Instead, weak memory models are used which may reorder or buffer operations. A widespread weak memory model is total store ordering (TSO) [34], which is used on x86 machines, for example. TSO relaxes the atomicity of SC for memory writes. Instead of writing directly to memory, store operations are placed in a per-thread FIFO *store buffer*. Eventually, the store buffer is flushed and the memory is updated. Only after the buffer has been flushed, other threads see the memory update that may have happened much earlier. However, for the thread executing the store, the processor establishes the illusion that it was already performed—technically, this *early read* lets threads read from their own store buffer. Altogether, this causes every thread to have its own local perception of the shared memory. For a program to synchronize the individual perceptions of threads, TSO provides *fence* instructions which force flushing the store buffer to memory. It is then the programmer's (or compiler's) task to introduce fences such that the program does not read stale values and behaves correctly. This task can be cumbersome and requires an understanding of how the underlying weak memory affects a programs behavior. To address this obstacle, we discuss two reductions that allow for reasoning about TSO under SC. The first reduction comes in the form of a programming guideline and is amenable for manual reasoning. The second reduction is built for automated reasoning and focuses on more complex programs that cannot be handled with the first reduction. Before we go into the details of those reductions, we give a characterization of SC and distinguish it from TSO.

Characterization In the literature, the most common approach to reason about weak memory models is to consider the *trace* [35] of a computation, rather than the sequence of executed instructions. The trace of a computation is a graph. Its nodes correspond to the executed operations. The arcs represent the *happens-before (hb)* relation. Intuitively, $(o_1, o_2) \in hb$ means that o_2 relies on the result of o_1. Technically, hb is a union of four different relations: *program order (po), store order (st), source relation (src)*, and *conflict relation (cf)*. The program order implements the per-thread sequence of executed operations. The store order is a per-address serialization of all store operations. A store is in source relation to a load if the load reads the value written by the store. The conflict relation, intuitively, relates loads to stores if the value read was over-written by the store. With this, SC traces are guaranteed to be acyclic due to the operations being instantaneous and atomic.

Lemma 1 ([35]) *A trace is acyclic iff it is induced by an SC computation.*

On the other hand, TSO computations can produce cycles due to store buffering. More precisely, a thread can load a value that was already over-written by a

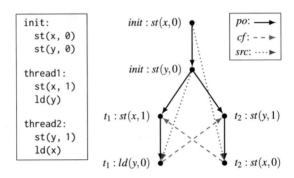

Fig. 3 A program and a possible TSO trace. The load of t_1 and the store of t_2 are in conflict relation because the load is executed after the store is put into the store buffer but before it was flushed. Hence, the load reads a stale value—the program is not properly synchronized. The behavior here is not present under SC because the store would immediately be visible and thus read by the other thread

store of another thread. Loading the over-written value is indeed possible under TSO because the store may have been buffered and only flushed after the load is performed—a scenario not possible under SC. For an example, consider Fig. 3.

DRF Theorem To tackle the complexity of TSO computations, one can rely on the well-known DRF theorem [3]. It states that every TSO trace is acyclic provided the program is *data race free (DRF)* under SC. A data race occurs if there are two unsynchronized accesses to the same memory location at least one of which is a store. Intuitively, they are unsynchronized if at one point the program could execute either of the operations. Formally, one introduces a *synchronizes with (sw)* relation to explicate the behavior of synchronization primitives, such as fences. (We omit a more formal discussion of sw for brevity.) Then, two actions are unsynchronized if they are not related by $(po \cup sw)^+$. The key insight here is that conflict arcs stem from data races; indeed, the program is free to choose whether to execute the load or to flush the store involved in a conflict. So if a program is DRF, then it contains no conflict arcs. One can easily see that the absence of such arcs makes *hb* acyclic.

Theorem 1 ([3]) *Data race freedom implies that the SC and TSO traces coincide.*

With this theorem, we can come up with a reduction following the format from Sect. 2. For $\mathcal{W}$ and $\mathcal{S}$ we choose the sets of traces induced by TSO and SC, respectively. Then, we instantiate the predicate ρ such that it checks for data races. And we use equality as a relation among computations. Then, property (R2) follows immediately assuming there is a dedicated *unsafe* control location. For (R1) we have to show that data race freedom of a program can be judged by its SC traces. To see this, consider a shortest TSO computation τ which raises a data race. By minimality, there is exactly one conflict arc. This arc relates some load and store instruction. Again by minimality, the store is the *po* latest operation of the executing thread (because actions of the same thread are never in conflict). Hence, we can remove that store and get a DRF trace. Then, there must be an SC computation σ with the same trace. Moreover, the store can be executed after σ because trace equality implies that all threads are in the same control state. This establishes the same conflict arc in the resulting trace as in the trace for τ. Altogether, this means that scanning SC for data races suffices to show a program DRF.

Theorem 2 *A program is data race free under SC iff it is so under TSO.*

This justifies our choice of ρ and proves our reduction sound. That is, one can rely on the simpler SC semantics to check for data races and to perform an actual analysis.

Robustness Against TSO The above development works well for general purpose programs because they tend to be data race free. However, there are many areas where data races cannot be avoided, for example, in concurrency libraries and performance-critical code [13, 20, 25, 31]. Despite the data races, we observe that there are programs that do not show non-SC behavior. This is the case because DRF does not characterize SC—it is strictly stronger. To see this, consider Fig. 3: if we remove one of the conflict arcs there we retain a data race but get an acyclic and thus SC trace. So we seek a method for *precisely* identifying under SC if a program is *robust*, i.e., allows only SC behavior even if executed under TSO. We do this in two steps. First, we establish a characterization of robustness. Then, we show how to employ this characterization for an SC-based robustness check.

For a characterization of robustness we show that if a program is not robust, then it allows for an *attack* [5, 6]. An attack is a computation of a particular form that exhibits TSO behavior, as shown in Fig. 4. The rational behind attacks is the following. If a program has non-SC behavior, then it must be due to a delayed store, st_A. Moreover, the delayed store must be on a happens-before cycle due to Lemma 1. Now, assume for a moment that there is only one delayed store. Then, this delay must overtake a load of the same thread, ld_A, for otherwise the store would be flushed immediately. Similarly, ld_A must be on the happens-before cycle since the store could be flushed immediately otherwise. This means that the happens-before cycle is of the form $ld_A \rightarrow_{hb}^+ st_A \rightarrow_{po}^+ ld_A$. (For Fig. 4 note that isu_A represents the store being buffered and st_A the store being flushed; hence, st_a is indeed *po*-earlier than ld_A although the figure suggests otherwise; in the trace isu_A and st_A appear as one node.)

This cycle, however, is based on the assumption that there is only one delayed store. Our reasoning remains valid if only one thread delays stores. Intuitively, st_A is the first delayed store on the happens-before cycle. Any prior store can be flushed

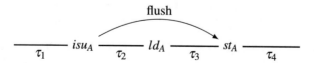

Fig. 4 A TSO attack [5]. Instructions isu_A, ld_A, and st_A are executed by the attacker. The pair (isu_A, st_A) makes visible when the delayed store is executed and flushed, respectively

immediately because it is in the *SC prefix* of the computation. Any later delayed store cannot participate in the $ld_A \rightarrow_{hb}^{+} st_A$ part of the happens-before cycle because the FIFO property of the TSO store buffer guarantees that it is flushed only after st_A is. Interestingly, one can show the needed property, namely, if a program is not robust then there is a non-SC computation where only one thread delays stores [7]. Due to its technical nature, we refrain from elaborating on this result and refer the reader to [6, 7] instead. Altogether, this means that if a program is not robust, there is an attack. Due to the happens-before cycle in an attack, the revers holds too. The following theorem summarizes the characterization result.

Theorem 3 ([5]) *A program is robust iff there is no attack.*

Towards a practical reduction, it remains to check for attacks under SC. This requires to find a delayed store and a subsequent load that are on a happens-before cycle. Such a cycle cannot be observed under SC as postulated by Lemma 1. However, an attack makes only limited use of the store buffer: only a single thread, the *attacker*, delays stores. To mimic such delays under SC we make the store buffer of the attacker explicit [5, 6]. To that end, we instrument the program under scrutiny. To delay a store to address a of the attacker, we replace it with a store to an auxiliary address a' which is not used by any other thread. The attacker can read the value early as it knows of address a'. All other threads continue to read the stale value at address a. We do not need to handle flushes, because the instrumentation can stop execution if the happens-before cycle is *closed*. To do that, we instrument all other threads, the *helpers*. Technically, we force the computation to produce a happens-before cycle. That is, with respect to Fig. 4, we require every action in τ_3 to participate in the cycle and prevent any other instruction from being executed. More precisely, we require each action act of a helper to satisfy $ld_A \rightarrow_{hb}^{+} act$. If a helper thread already contributed an action, then any subsequent action continues the happens-before path using program order. Whether an action has already been contributed can be kept in the control state of helpers threads. Otherwise, act cannot continue the happens-before path from ld_A using program order. Let a denote the address which is accessed by act. If a has been loaded on the happens-before path, then act has to be a store to a because only the conflict relation allows it to continue the hb path. Otherwise, if a has seen a store, then any access allows to continue the hb path through act: using the store relation in case of a store, and the source relation in case of a load. The access information can be kept in a per-address auxiliary address. Altogether, a helper thread closes the happens-before cycle if it accesses the address targeted by st_A. In such a case the program jumps to a dedicated goal state. So if an instrumented program reaches this goal state, then the program is guaranteed to contain a hb cycle and thus to be not robust. Otherwise, the program is robust and shows the exact same behavior as the original program under TSO.

Theorem 4 ([5]) *A program is not robust iff its instrumentation reaches the goal state.*

The above development allows us to formulate the approach as a reduction. The set $\mathcal{W}$ contains the TSO traces of the program under scrutiny. For $\mathcal{S}$ we choose the set of SC traces that stem from an instrumented version of the program. The predicate ρ simply checks if the goal state was reached. And we use equality as relation among traces. Then, both (R1) and (R2) follow from the above theorems.

Supporting Non-robust Programs The above method handles all robust programs and allows their verification to rely on the simpler SC semantics. Programs that are not robust, however, do not profit from that development. That is, the above method does not guarantee soundness for non-robust programs. Unfortunately, TSO resists efficient automated reasoning [23, 30]. To overcome this problem, we can patch non-SC behavior into the SC semantics using the approach described in Sect. 2 paired with the above insights [8]. So consider a program that is not robust. The above instrumentation makes visible the delayed store which allows for a happens-before cycle and thus non-SC behavior. More precisely, non-robustness yields as witness an attack like the one from Fig. 4—a borderline computation in the wording of Sect. 2. From such an attack, we can extract the attackers sequence of actions performed while st_A was in the store buffer. That is, we can extract which store is delayed and when it is flushed. Then, we instrument the program to make the delay explicit. To that end, upon arriving at the to-be-delayed store, the thread makes a non-deterministic choice. Either it continues it's original computation, or it executes the instrumentation. The instrumentation writes the store into an auxiliary register instead of writing it to memory. Then the actions from the extracted sequence follow. However, they are adapted such that early reads of the buffered value are read from the auxiliary register. After the sequence is executed, the write is flushed to memory, i.e., copied from the auxiliary register to the original target address. Then, the thread jumps back into its original program. Technically, the instrumentation has to handle further stores that are delayed during the extracted sequence. They are handled in the same way as described above. Note that since the extracted sequence is finite, the instrumentation requires only finitely many auxiliary registers. Altogether, this allows to patch finite sequences of delayed stores into SC. The stores we choose here stem from attacks making the program non-robust. Hence, the instrumented program is guaranteed to contain more behaviors than the original one.

Repeating the above patching allows to continuously enrich the SC behavior with TSO behavior. This yields a semi-decider for safety. If there is a safety violation under TSO, then this behavior is eventually added to the instrumentation and thus explored under SC. Otherwise, it may not terminate at all; there may be infinitely many non-SC behaviors that are iteratively added. So the algorithm will not converge to an instrumentation that is robust.

4 From Many Threads to Few

For concurrent programs, informal reasoning and testing techniques can only explore a fraction of all possible program behaviors and are likely to miss delicate corner cases [10]. The reason for this are the many thread interleavings and the severe state space explosion of concurrent programs. This problem becomes worse when considering lock-free code. There, correctness arguments require rigorous formal proofs due to the subtle thread interactions. Providing a manual proof is a cumbersome task and requires a deep understanding of the program to be verified [14–16, 24, 32, 33, 37]. Hence, we strive for automation. For practicality, we need techniques that can handle parametrized programs. That is, we need techniques that can establish correctness of a given lock-free program for any number of threads. Our goal is to develop a reduction from parametrized programs to programs with few threads. We focus here on lock-free programs. It is an inherent characteristic of lock-freedom that allows for the desired reduction. Towards the result, we discuss the working principles of lock-free programs first.

Lock-Freedom Lock-freedom is a progress property of programs [20]. It guarantees that a thread can make progress even if arbitrary other threads stall or fail. To see how this influences the way in which programs are written, consider as an example a program which maintains a shared structure, like a stack or a list, that is used for inter-thread communication. A logical update of the structure, like adding or removing elements, may (and in most cases does) require multiple physical updates, i.e., multiple memory writes [14, 17, 20, 27–29, 38]. The naive solution would use a critical section to guard the sequence of memory updates from interference of other threads. Lock-free programs, however, do not allow the usage of locks. Now assume a thread wants to perform a sequence of updates but fails half-way through, that is, performs only some of its updates. With respect to lock-based programming, this means that the thread executed only a part of its critical section. This typically leaves the shared structure in an *inconsistent* state wrt. the invariants of the lock-based implementation. Now, to achieve lock-freedom, other threads must still be able to progress. That is, they have to anticipate the incomplete sequence of updates and either roll back or finish that sequence. In the literature, this is commonly referred to as *helping* [20]. And indeed, this is what other threads do. They first make sure that the structure is in a consistent state, helping another thread updating the structure if necessary, before they continue with their own operation. For an example, consider a lock-free singly-linked queue which maintains a shared pointer to the last list segment. Appending a new segment requires to link the new segment and to update the shared pointer. This requires two subsequent updates. Hence, a thread may find that the shared pointer does not point to the last element. If so, it will first move it to the last segment before it continues to, e.g., add another element to the end of the list.

Summaries It is this helping that we exploit for the desired reduction. It is typically implemented in such a way that a thread, by inspecting a shared structure, can find out whether or not the structure is in a consistent state and what actions are required to make it consistent if it is not. That is, inconsistencies and the required fixes can be deduced from the shared structure itself—a thread does not need knowledge about other threads nor of the history of the structure. Hence, we say that the process of helping is *stateless* [21, 22]. Consequently, those updates can be collectively executed by a single thread which we call *summary*. So assume for a moment we had such a summary thread. Then, that summary could produce any shared heap the original program can produce. Hence, if correctness can be judged by the contents of the shared heap (which is a reasonable assumption[1] in practice), then it suffices to analyse this single thread. In the following, we discuss how to generate a candidate summary and check whether it is a proper summary [21, 22].

A candidate summary can be generated by inspecting the program under scrutiny. As mentioned before, lock-free programs update shared structures on a memory-word level. In practice, the prevalent pattern to update the content of a single memory location is the following [14, 17, 20, 27–29, 38]: (1) read the memory contents of the location to be updated, (2) compute a new value for the location (based on the previously read value), and (3) atomically write the new value to memory if the valuation has not changed (typically implemented using Compare-And-Swap) or retry otherwise. Instances of this update mechanism can be found by a syntactic analysis of the program under consideration. The summary is then simply an indefinite loop every iteration of which non-deterministically chooses and atomically executes one of those update instances. It is worth stressing that the resulting program is sequential. Moreover, executing the instances of the above pattern atomically allows to apply standard compiler optimizations resulting in a summary that is much shorter and more easily understandable than the original program. While understandability of the summary is not important for an automated technique, reducing its code size can be beneficial. To sum up, we create a candidate summary by syntactically identifying shared updates in the original program assuming atomicity.

Summaries in Verification An instantiation of the framework from Sect. 2 exploiting summaries is in order. To that end, let $P = \prod_{i=1}^{k} T_i$ be the original program, a parallel composition of k identical threads T_i, and let Q be a candidate summary. Then, $\mathscr{S}$ is the set of all computations of P. For $\mathscr{S}$ we choose the set of computations of the program $T_1 \parallel Q$, a parallel composition of a single thread T_1 from P and the single thread Q. Predicate ρ checks whether Q is a proper summary of P. We discuss how to do this later. As a relation among computations we choose an equivalence relation $\approx$ such that τ and σ are related if they coincide on the shared structures and the thread-local state of T_1. Property (R2) follows immediately provided safety can be concluded from the state of the shared structures as assumed initially. For (R1), we proceed as follows. Given a computation $\tau \in \mathscr{W}$, we replace all actions of threads $T_2, \ldots, T_k$ that update a shared structure by actions of Q that have the same effect and simply remove all other actions of threads $T_2, \ldots, T_k$. The replacement is feasible since Q is a proper summary due to the premise of (R1). The removal is feasible because actions that do not change the shared structures cannot influence other threads by assumption. Altogether, this process yields a computation $\sigma \in \mathscr{S}$ with $\tau \approx \sigma$, as required for (R1). The intuition behind this construction is

---

[1]For linearizability proofs, for example, one encodes the sequence of linearization points in the shared heap [2] and checks whether a non-linearizable sequence can be produced by the program.

the following: thread T_1 can be influenced by other threads only through updates of the shared structures; however, it cannot detect which entity performs the updates of those structures. Hence, T_1 cannot detect whether it runs in parallel with $T_2, \ldots, T_k$ or just with Q; it's behavior is the same. To conclude the reduction, it remains to discuss ρ.

Checking Summary Candidates As shown by our experiments, the procedure for generating candidate summaries works well for common lock-free implementations from the literature [21, 22]. Nevertheless, the process may give a candidate summary which is *missing* updates of the original program. This can be the case, for instance, if the read value is changed back and forth such that the final check of the pattern erroneously concludes that the structure was not changed, known as the *ABA problem* in the literature [29]. Hence, we require a method for checking whether a candidate summary is indeed a proper summary. In the remainder of this section we present such a check and embed it into the framework from Sect. 2. For simplicity, we assume that the only way threads can influence each other are updates of shared structures.[2]

We now turn towards checking whether or not the candidate summary Q is a proper summary, as required to be done by ρ. So let Q be a candidate summary that misses some required update of the program under scrutiny. That is, there is a shortest computation $\tau = act_1 . \ldots . act_n . act_{n+1}$ from $\mathscr{W}$ such that action act_{n+1} performs an update of a shared structure that Q cannot perform. Let us denote the state of the shared structures after $\tau_i = act_1 . \ldots . act_i$ by s_i. That is, no sequence of Q-actions can transform s_n into s_{n+1}. Wlog. the last action act_{n+1} is performed by thread T_1.[3] Since τ is the shortest such computation, Q can mimic all updates in the prefix τ_n. So we can perform for τ_n the same construction we used to establish (R1) above. That is, we construct a computation $\sigma \in \mathscr{S}$ with $\tau_n \approx \sigma$. Since act_{n+1} is performed by T_1, we get $\tau \approx \sigma . act_{n+1} \in \mathscr{S}$. This means, every missing update, like the one from s_n into s_{n+1}, can be found in $\mathscr{S}$. So, ρ can simply collect all updates from $\mathscr{S}$ and check whether Q can perform them too.

Missing Updates Altogether, it suffices to analyse the two-threaded program $T_1 \parallel Q$ instead of the much more complicated P. This allows us to use existing techniques for programs with a fixed number of threads. Moreover, note that Q has a particular form which may allow for further optimizations.

Although our experiments showed that the summaries generated by the above approach work well in practice [22], they may miss updates. A missing update is a transformation of the shared heap. Instead of aborting the analysis in such a case, one can collect those updates in a set Up. Then, one repeats the analysis. This time,

---

[2]Technically, one separates the memory into a shared and a per-thread owned part and checks whether threads comply to this separation, that is, ensure that threads never read/write from/to the parts owned by other threads. The actual separation is a parameter to our result and can thus be instantiated as needed [22].

[3]This can be achieved by a simple renaming of threads.

however, the updates from Up are applied in addition to the summary. Applying an update $s \rightsquigarrow s'$ from Up to a computation means to replace the shared heap s with s'. This procedure is repeated until saturation of Up. This yields a semi-decider because it is not guaranteed that there are finitely many missing updates. Nevertheless, this approach has been shown effective and efficient in [36].

5 From Manual Memory Management to Garbage Collection

A major obstacle in reasoning about programs relying on manual memory management is the fact that memory is explicitly deleted and can be reused immediately after the deletion. This allows for pointers to become *dangling* after the memory they reference is deleted. After a subsequent reuse of the deleted memory, the dangling pointer can still be used to modify the memory contents without the reusing thread knowing. As shown in the literature [28, 29], this can lead to corruption of program invariants and thus to undesired behavior. Under garbage collection, this problem does not arise. Any reference would prevent the memory from being reused. Put differently, an allocation guarantees exclusive access under GC but does not do so under MM. This makes it significantly harder to reason about MM than about GC [1, 2, 18, 39]. To tackle the problem, we establish a practical reduction from MM to GC [18, 19]. Let $\mathscr{W}$ and $\mathscr{S}$ be the sets of computations of a program under MM and GC, respectively.

General Purpose Programs The main idea of the result is to allow dangling pointers but prevent them from begin used. Later, we generalize this result to allow for certain accesses of dangling pointers. Towards the result, we need to characterize what it means for a pointer to be dangling. Technically, it is easier to define when a pointer is *not* dangling. We call such non-dangling pointers *valid* pointers. Initially, no pointer is valid. A pointer becomes valid, if it is the target of an allocation or if it is assigned from a valid pointer. A valid pointer becomes invalid if its referenced memory location is deleted or if it is assigned from an invalid pointer. Basically, this means that allocations make pointers valid, deletions make pointers invalid (or dangling), and all other operations simply *spread* (in)validity. We stress that an allocation makes valid the receiving pointer only; every other invalid pointer remains invalid even if its referenced address is reallocated. With this definition, using an invalid pointer is said to yield a *pointer race*.

Definition 1 ([18]) A computation $\tau.act$ raises a pointer race if action act (i) dereferences, (ii) compares, or (iii) deletes an invalid pointer.

Now, we observe that pointer race free (PRF) programs are invariant to memory reuse. That is, a PRF program cannot detect whether the result of an allocation is fresh, i.e., has never been allocated before, or if it was already in use and has been deleted. To see this, assume a program seeks to draw such a conclusion. To do so, it requires a pointer p to address a before a is deleted and a pointer q to a that wlog. receives the address from an allocation. To tell whether or not the allocation for q reused the deleted a the program has to compare the addresses held by p and q. However, the deletion of a rendered p invalid. And it remains invalid through the reallocation involving q. So the comparison of p and q raises a pointer race. Altogether, this means that pointer race free programs indeed cannot distinguish fresh and reused memory. Our goal is to instantiate the framework from Sect. 2 to reduce MM to GC for pointer race free programs. We use for ρ a predicate that decides whether or not a given computation is pointer race free. We showed that such a check is effective and can be implemented efficiently with low overhead to an actual analysis [18]. Also note that this reduction allows to use existing tools which rely on exclusivity of allocated memory as discussed above.

Towards a reduction result we need to find an appropriate relation among computations as suggested by (R1). A non-trivial relation is required because in general GC yields a proper subset of MM computations. In the above example, MM allows to reallocate a for q. Under GC this is not possible. Instead, an allocation would give a fresh address b. In order to find an appropriate relation, recall that invalid pointers cannot be used. Hence, their valuation does not matter. It suffices to relate the valid pointers. Those pointers coincide with respect to an isomorphism which states how memory reuse is elided (mapped) to fresh memory. So we introduce an equivalence relation $\approx$ such that two computations are related if they end up in the same program counter and in the same valid heap up to an isomorphism. For this relation, one can show the desired first part, (R1), of the reduction.

Theorem 5 ([18]) *If the program under scrutiny is pointer race free then* $\mathscr{W} \approx \mathscr{S}$.

To establish this result, one proceeds by induction over the structure of computations and constructs a new computation with an appropriate isomorphism to elide reallocations. For the technical details of that construction we refer the reader to [18, 19]. With this main result, the second part, (R2), of the reduction follows easily. If there is an unsafe computation in $\mathscr{W}$, then $\mathscr{W} \approx \mathscr{S}$ yields a related computation from $\mathscr{S}$. By the definition of $\approx$ both computations end up in the same program counter. Wlog. this implies that also $\mathscr{S}$ is unsafe.

Performance-Critical Programs Unfortunately, the restriction to pointer race free programs is too strong to handle performance-critical code. Lock-free programs, for instance, typically perform memory reads optimistically to avoid synchronization overhead on the read side. Such optimistic accesses patterns, however, use dangling pointers and thus suffer from pointer races. To prevent harmful accesses that can lead to system crashes or integrity corruption, those patterns include checks to guarantee that if a dangling pointer was used it was used in a *safe* way. These checks necessarily need to compare dangling pointers. Therefore, we adapt the notion of pointer races from above to tolerate such optimistic access patterns. To that end, we mark the result of memory reads which dereference an invalid pointer as strongly invalid and require those strongly invalid values never to be used. The development then follows the one from ordinary pointer races.

Definition 2 ([18]) A computation $\tau.act$ raises a strong pointer race (SPR) if action *act* (i) deletes, or (ii) writes to memory dereferencing an invalid pointer, or if *act* (iii) contains a strongly invalid value otherwise.

The relaxation to strong pointer races does not allow for a reduction of MM to GC. The reason is, as seen before, that eliding reuse does not allow to maintain equivalence among invalid pointers. Hence, assertions involving invalid pointers (which raise no SPR) may not have the same outcome in an MM-computation from $\mathcal{W}$ and the corresponding GC-computation from $\mathcal{S}$ which elides reuses. Nevertheless, the relaxation to strong pointer races eases verification efforts. We found that SPR freedom provides an allocating thread with exclusivity [18]. This exclusivity is a write exclusivity rather than a read/write exclusivity as in GC. Exploiting this observation improves the efficiency of existing techniques [18].

In the future we want to establish a reduction for programs using optimistic access patterns. A promising approach is a *mixed semantics* where only a few memory locations can be reused like in MM and the remaining ones cannot like in GC. To guarantee soundness then, one has to show that the aforementioned comparisons involving invalid pointers can be mimicked in the mixed semantics. We believe that this boils down to showing that the program under scrutiny does not suffer from the ABA problem. This can be decided in the simpler mixed semantics.

6 Conclusion

We presented various approaches for reasoning about correctness wrt. to a complicated weak semantics by solely relying on a simpler strong semantics. The approaches exploit properties satisfied by *most but not all* programs. In other word, they facilitate that programs for a certain (application) domain typically adhere to the same principles or programming patterns. Consequently, not all programs can be handled because the usage of the pattern is not enforced, for example, by the programming language. Experiments show two interesting things. First, most programs of interest can be handled despite relying on domain specific assumptions. Second, exploiting those assumptions allows for much more efficient analyses. The stronger semantics can be verified much easier and a soundness check for the reduction can be performed without much overhead too. Altogether, this line of research highly suggests to give up completeness and focus on specific program domains in order to make verification possible where it is highly needed but not yet successful.

References

1. Parosh Aziz Abdulla, Bengt Jonsson, and Cong Quy Trinh. "Automated Verification of Linearization Policies". In: *SAS* Vol. 9837. LNCS. Springer, 2016, pp. 61–83.
2. Parosh Aziz Abdulla et al. "An Integrated Specification and Verification Technique for Highly Concurrent Data Structures". In: *TACAS* Vol. 7795. LNCS. Springer, 2013, pp. 324–338.
3. Sarita V. Adve and Mark D. Hill. "A Unified Formalization of Four Shared-Memory Models". In: *IEEE Trans. Parallel Distrib Syst.* 4.6 (1993), pp. 613–624.
4. Jade Alglave. "A shared memory poetics". PhD thesis. Université Paris 7, 2010.
5. Ahmed Bouajjani, Egor Derevenetc, and Roland Meyer. "Checking and Enforcing Robustness against TSO". In: *ESOP* Vol. 7792. LNCS. Springer, 2013, pp. 533–553.
6. Ahmed Bouajjani, Egor Derevenetc, and Roland Meyer. "Checking Robustness against TSO". In: *CoRR* abs/1208.6152 (2012).
7. Ahmed Bouajjani, Roland Meyer, and Eike Möhlmann. "Deciding Robustness against Total Store Ordering". In: *ICALP (2)*. Vol. 6756. LNCS. Springer, 2011, pp. 428–440.
8. Ahmed Bouajjani et al. "Lazy TSO Reachability". In: *FASE* Vol. 9033. LNCS. Springer, 2015, pp. 267–282.
9. Sebastian Burckhardt and Madanlal Musuvathi. "Effective Program Verification for Relaxed Memory Models". In: *CAV* Vol. 5123. LNCS. Springer, 2008, pp. 107–120.
10. Edmund M. Clarke. "The Birth of Model Checking". In: *25 Years of Model Checking*. Vol. 5000. LNCS. Springer, 2008, pp. 1–26.
11. Patrick Cousot and Radhia Cousot. "Abstract Interpretation: A Unified Lattice Model for Static Analysis of Programs by Construction or Approximation of Fixpoints". In: *POPL* ACM, 1977, pp. 238–252.
12. Patrick Cousot and Radhia Cousot. "Systematic Design of Program Analysis Frameworks". In: *POPL* ACM Press, 1979, pp. 269–282.
13. Edsger W. Dijkstra. "Cooperating Sequential Processes". In: *The Origin of Concurrent Programming: From Semaphores to Remote Procedure Calls*. Ed. by Per Brinch Hansen. Springer New York, 2002, pp. 65–138.
14. Simon Doherty et al. "Formal Verification of a Practical Lock-Free Queue Algorithm". In: *FORTE*. Vol. 3235. LNCS. Springer, 2004, pp. 97–114.
15. Tayfun Elmas, Shaz Qadeer, and Serdar Tasiran. "A calculus of atomic actions". In: *POPL* ACM, 2009, pp. 2–15.
16. Tayfun Elmas et al. "Simplifying Linearizability Proofs with Reduction and Abstraction". In: *TACAS* Vol. 6015. LNCS. Springer, 2010, pp. 296–311.
17. Timothy L. Harris. "A Pragmatic Implementation of Non-blocking Linked-Lists". In: *DISC* Vol. 2180. LNCS. Springer, 2001, pp. 300–314.
18. Frédéric Haziza et al. "Pointer Race Freedom". In: *CoRR* abs/1511.00184 (2015).
19. Frédéric Haziza et al. "Pointer Race Freedom". In: *VMCAI* Vol. 9583. LNCS. Springer, 2016, pp. 393–412.
20. Maurice Herlihy and Nir Shavit. *The art of multiprocessor programming*. Morgan Kaufmann, 2008.
21. Lukás Holík et al. "Effect Summaries for Thread-Modular Analysis". In: *CoRR* abs/1705.03701 (2017).
22. Lukás Holík et al. "Effect Summaries for Thread-Modular Analysis Sound Analysis Despite an Unsound Heuristic". In: *SAS* Vol. 10422. LNCS. Springer, 2017, pp. 169–191.
23. Thuan Quang Huynh and Abhik Roychoudhury. "A Memory Model Sensitive Checker for C#". In: *FM* Vol. 4085. LNCS. Springer, 2006, pp. 476–491.
24. Bengt Jonsson. "Using refinement calculus techniques to prove linearizability". In: *Formal Asp. Comput.* 24.4-6 (2012), pp. 537–554.
25. Leslie Lamport. "A Fast Mutual Exclusion Algorithm". In: *ACM Trans. Comput. Syst.* 5.1 (1987), pp. 1–11.

26. Leslie Lamport. "How to Make a Multiprocessor Computer That Correctly Executes Multi-process Programs". In: *IEEE Trans. Computers* 28.9 (1979), pp. 690–691.
27. Maged M. Michael. "High performance dynamic lock-free hash tables and list-based sets". In: *SPAA* 2002, pp. 73–82.
28. Maged M. Michael and Michael L. Scott. "Nonblocking Algorithms and Preemption-Safe Locking on Multiprogrammed Shared Memory Multiprocessors". In: *J. Parallel Distrib Comput.* 51.1 (1998), pp. 1–26.
29. Maged M. Michael and Michael L. Scott. "Simple, Fast, and Practical Non-Blocking and Blocking Concurrent Queue Algorithms". In: *PODC* ACM, 1996, pp. 267–275.
30. Seungjoon Park and David L. Dill. "An Executable Specification, Analyzer and Verifier for RMO (Relaxed Memory Order)". In: *SPAA*. 1995, pp. 34–41.
31. Gary L. Peterson. "Myths About the Mutual Exclusion Problem". In: *Inf Process. Lett.* 12.3 (1981), pp. 115–116.
32. Pedro da Rocha Pinto, Thomas Dinsdale-Young, and Philippa Gardner. "TaDA: A Logic for Time and Data Abstraction". In: *ECOOP* Vol. 8586. LNCS. Springer, 2014, pp. 207–231.
33. Gerhard Schellhorn, John Derrick, and Heike Wehrheim. "A Sound and Complete Proof Technique for Linearizability of Concurrent Data Structures". In: *ACM Trans. Comput. Log.* 15.4 (2014), 31:1–31:37.
34. Peter Sewell et al. "x86-TSO: a rigorous and usable programmer's model for x86 multipro-cessors". In: *Commun. ACM* 53.7 (2010), pp. 89–97.
35. Dennis E. Shasha and Marc Snir. "Efficient and Correct Execution of Parallel Programs that Share Memory". In: *ACM Trans. Program. Lang Syst.* 10.2 (1988), pp. 282–312.
36. Viktor Vafeiadis. "RGSep Action Inference". In: *VMCAI* Vol. 5944. LNCS. Springer, 2010, pp. 345–361.
37. Viktor Vafeiadis and Matthew J. Parkinson. "A Marriage of Rely/Guarantee and Separation Logic". In: *CONCUR* Vol. 4703. LNCS. Springer, 2007, pp. 256–271.
38. Martin T. Vechev and Eran Yahav. "Deriving linearizable fine-grained concurrent objects". In: *PLDI* ACM, 2008, pp. 125–135.
39. Eran Yahav and Shmuel Sagiv. "Automatically Verifying Concurrent Queue Algorithms". In: *Electr Notes Theor Comput. Sci.* 89.3 (2003), pp. 450–463.

Recipes for Coffee: Compositional Construction of JAVA Control Flow Graphs in GROOVE

Eduardo Zambon and Arend Rensink

Abstract The graph transformation tool GROOVE supports so-called *recipes*, which allow the elaboration of composite rules by gluing simple rules via a control language. This paper shows how recipes can be used to provide a complete formalization (construction) of the control flow semantics of JAVA 6. This construction covers not only basic language elements such as branches and loops, but also abrupt termination commands, such as exceptions. By handling the whole JAVA 6 language, it is shown that the method scales and can be used in real-life settings. Our implementation has two major strengths. First, all rule sequencing is handled by recipes, avoiding the need to include extraneous elements in the graphs for this purpose. Second, the approach provides rules modularization: related rules are grouped in recipes, which in turn can be used again to form larger, more elaborated recipes. This gives rise to an elegant, hierarchical rule structure built in a straightforward, compositional way.

1 Introduction

This paper presents two contributions: a fully formalised *control flow specification* for JAVA (language version 6), and an extensive case study demonstrating the concept of *recipes*, which is a mechanism for rule composition in the graph transformation (GT) tool GROOVE [7, 11].

Control Flow Specification Our first contribution addresses the issue of control flow specification for the imperative, object-oriented language JAVA. The step of generating a control flow graph from the source code of a program is a very

E. Zambon (✉)
Federal University of Espírito Santo (UFES), Vitória, ES, Brazil
e-mail: zambon@inf.ufes.br

A. Rensink
University of Twente (UT), Enschede, The Netherlands
e-mail: arend.rensink@utwente.nl

© Springer Nature Switzerland AG 2018
P. Müller, I. Schaefer (eds.), *Principled Software Development*,
https://doi.org/10.1007/978-3-319-98047-8_19

well-known one: it lies at the core of both compiler optimisation and formal program analysis; see, for instance, [1, 9]. The control semantics of basic imperative statement types, such as `while`, `if`, `switch`, `for` and the like, is very well-understood, and it is not difficult to come up with an efficient, compositional algorithm for their construction. It is quite a bit more tricky to do the same in the presence of *abrupt termination* (as it is called in JAVA); that is, for `break`, `continue`, `throw` and `return` statements occurring anywhere in a block. The presence of abrupt termination firstly requires an extension to the notion of control flow itself—for instance, a flow transition taken because of a thrown exception needs to be treated differently from an ordinary control flow transition—and secondly mandates an overhaul of the construction algorithm.

The challenge involved in control flow generation can be made precise as follows: to devise an algorithm that, given the abstract syntax tree (AST) of an arbitrary (compilation-correct) JAVA program, generates a control flow graph (CFG) that captures all feasible paths of execution, with minimal over-approximation. (Some over-approximation is unavoidable, as the question whether an execution path can actually be taken by some real program run generally involves data analysis and is ultimately undecidable.)

In this paper we aim for a solution to this challenge that satisfies the following criteria:

- It is based on a declarative, rule-based formalism that manipulates (abstract syntax, respectively control) graphs directly; thus, one can alternatively understand our algorithm as a *specification* of the JAVA control flow semantics.
- It covers all of JAVA, rather than just a fragment; thus, we cannot take shortcuts by ignoring the more "dirty" language features.
- It is implemented and executable using a state-of-the-art graph transformation tool.

Recipes as a Rule Composition Mechanism Our second contribution is specifically directed at rule-based specification languages in general, and graph transformation in particular. In rule-based formalisms, it is quite common (as we also point out in the related work discussion below) to offer a way of scheduling rules sequentially or as alternatives; essentially, this comes down to adding imperative control to a declarative formalism. However, this form of composition results in constructs that cannot themselves be regarded as rules: their execution does not show up as a single, atomic step. Thus, one composes *from* rules but not *into* new rules. Instead, in this paper we demonstrate the concept of *recipes*, which are essentially named procedures with atomic behaviour. Recipes can for all intents and purposes be regarded as rules; in particular, they themselves can again be composed and recursively form new recipes.

The grammar for control flow specification presented in this paper very extensively uses the concept of recipes as implemented in the GT tool GROOVE, and hence serves as a demonstrator for their viability.

Related Work On the topic of (explicitly) dealing with abrupt termination in a formal setting, we can point to [8], which extends assertional reasoning to abrupt termination. The notion of control flow is implicitly treated there (as it must be, because the notion of pre- and post-conditions is inextricably bound to control flow) and the paper is rather comprehensive, but does not share our ambition of actually dealing with, and providing tool support for, any complete version of JAVA.

A much earlier version of the approach reported here is given in [14]: there also, graph transformation is used to construct flow graphs for programs with abrupt termination, but the construction is not compositional, relying instead on intricate intermediate structures that cause it to be far less elegant than what one would hope for in a declarative formalism.

On the topic of controlled graph rewriting, i.e., using control constructs for rule composition, quite some work has been done in the field of graph transformation. For instance, many GT tools, such as PROGRES [13], GRGEN [6] and VIATRA [4] include textual control languages, some of which are quite rich. Other tools such as HENSHIN [3] rely on the visual mechanism of *story diagrams* (developed in [5]) for specifying control. In [10] it is investigated what the minimal requirements are for a control language to be, in a strict sense, complete, and [2] generalises the notion of control composition itself. However, none of these approaches explicitly include the notion of atomicity that is essential to be able to regard a control fragment as a rule, as we do in our recipes. In fact, we argue that this is a dimension not covered by Plump [10] that identifies an incompleteness of other control languages.

2 Background

In this section we set the stage by providing some necessary background information.

2.1 Graph Grammars

We use graph transformation as our basic formalism for specifying computations. This means that we rely on *typed graphs* to describe states—in this case, ASTs and flow graphs—and *transformation rules* to describe how the states change, and under what conditions—in this case, how flow graphs are incrementally built on top of ASTs. Without going into full formal detail, we pose the following:

- A problem-specific *type graph* $\mathscr{T}$ that describes all the concepts occurring in the domain being modelled, in terms of node types (which include primitive data types and carry a subtype relation) and edge types. The possible connections between nodes and edges are restricted to those explicitly contained in $\mathscr{T}$.

- A universe of graphs $\mathscr{G}$, consisting of nodes and edges that have an associated (node or edge) type, subject to the restrictions imposed by $\mathscr{T}$.
- A universe of rules $\mathscr{R}$, with each rule r associated with a *signature* $sig(r)$, consisting of possibly empty sequences of input and output parameter (node) types.
- An application relation, consisting of tuples of the form

$$G \xrightarrow{r(\mathbf{v},\mathbf{w})} H$$

where G, H are graphs, r is a rule and $\mathbf{v}, \mathbf{w}$ are sequences of nodes from G and H, respectively, typed by $sig(r)$: these represent the actual input and output parameters and have to satisfy the rule signature.

An application instance such as the one above is called a *transformation step*, with G as *source graph* and H as *target graph*. A rule is called *applicable* to a given graph G if there exists an application step with G as source.

As a toy example, consider the rule fib depicted in Fig. 1a, with two example applications shown next to the rule in Fig. 1b. This specifies (in GROOVE syntax):

- A third **Cell** is created and appended to two existing next-linked **Cell**-nodes; the new **Cell** gets a val-attribute that is the sum of the val-attributes of the existing **Cell**s. In GROOVE syntax, element creation is indicated by fat, green outlines.
- The first of the two existing **Cell**s is deleted, together with its outgoing edges. In GROOVE syntax, this is indicated by blue, dashed outlines.

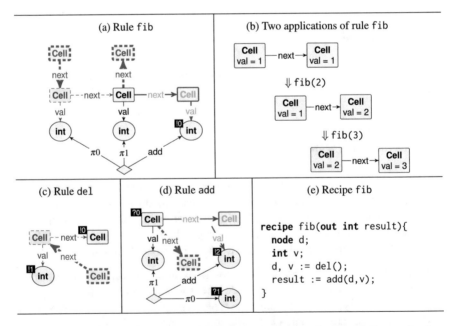

Fig. 1 From simple GT rules to recipes. (**a**) Complete simple GT rule fib. (**b**) Two applications of rule fib. (**c**) Ingredient rule del. (**d**) Ingredient rule add. (**e**) Recipe fib

- However, this only occurs if there is not a third **Cell** already. In GROOVE syntax, this is indicated by the red, dotted **Cell** nodes on top, which are so-called *negative application conditions*.
- The rule has a single output parameter, and no input parameters. In GROOVE syntax, this is indicated by the black adornment with the inscribed parameter number preceded by the exclamation mark **!**. An input parameter has a **?**-prefix instead.

A graph *grammar* is essentially a set of graph transformation rules, together with a start graph. We say that a graph grammar defines the "language" of graphs that can be derived through a sequence of rule applications from the start graph. One of the ways in which this can be used is to define transformations from one graph to another, namely by setting one graph as start graph and then considering all reachable graphs in which no more rules are applicable.

2.2 Recipes for Rule Composition

One of the attractive aspects of graph transformation (which it shares with other rule-based formalisms) is its declarative nature: each rule describes a particular change combined with conditions under which it can be applied, but there is typically no a priori prescription on how that change is effected or how different changes are combined. However, in practice it does occur quite frequently that an algorithm encoded in a set of transformation rules requires some dependencies between rules, resulting in a certain built-in order for their application. Moreover, it is also quite common that different rules contain similar parts, in which case it is desirable to be able to share those as sub-rules. Both are scenarios which can benefit from a notion of *rule composition*, meaning that a notion of control is imposed on top of the declarative rules, restricting the order in which rules may be applied and allowing the same rule to be applied in different contexts. Rule parameters can then be used to pass information between rule applications, circumventing the need to artificially put control information into the graphs themselves.

The GT tool GROOVE supports such rule composition in the form of *recipes*, which are procedure-like constructs with:

- A signature, consisting (like for rules) of a name and sequences of input and output parameters;
- A body, which specifies rule sequencing, repetition and choice.

A recipe is guaranteed to have atomic (transaction-like) behavior: it either finishes completely, in which case its effect, which may consist of many consecutive rule applications, is considered to be a single step; or it is aborted if at some point during its execution the next scheduled rule is inapplicable, in which case the recipe is considered to not have occurred at all.

As an example, Fig. 1c–e show how the rule from Fig. 1a can be specified instead as a recipe, by composing two ingredient rules (del and add) and using rule parameters to ensure that the second rule is applied using the **Cell**- and **int**-nodes obtained from the first. The atomic nature of recipe execution implies that, if rule add is not applicable because the **Cell** already has a next, the execution is aborted and the graph is "rolled back" to the one before the del-transformation.

As stated in the introduction, for all intents and purposes a recipe itself behaves like a rule. The concept of a grammar is therefore extended to consist of rules, recipes and a start graph.

2.3 Constructing Abstract Syntax Trees

As explained in the introduction, the first contribution of this paper is to specify the construction of JAVA CFGs on top of ASTs; but in order to do so, first we have to obtain the ASTs themselves. The overall picture of how this is done can be seen in Fig. 2. For a more detailed discussion on the topics of this section we refer the interested reader to [15].

To bridge the world between JAVA source code and GROOVE graphs we built a specialized *graph compiler* that receives as input one or more .java files and produces a corresponding AST in GROOVE format for each compilation unit. The graph compiler was created by replacing the back-end of the Eclipse JAVA compiler with one that outputs the AST in the GXL format used in GROOVE. Our restriction to JAVA version 6 in this work stems from the Eclipse compiler used, which is limited to this language version. As future work, we plan to update the graph compiler to the latest JAVA version, namely version 10 at the time of writing.

As explained above, our graphs and rules are *typed* by a problem-specific type graph $\mathcal{T}$ that describes the allowed graph elements and their connections. In particular, program ASTs generated by the graph compiler conform to a JAVA AST type graph (see also Fig. 2), the node types of which are shown in Fig. 3. This type graph was manually constructed based on the AST structure produced by the Eclipse compiler. Additional typing structure is present in the form of edge types, which are omitted from Fig. 3 but presented in detail in [12].

Flow graph construction adds extra elements on top of the AST, which are also typed, this time by a JAVA CFG type graph (see Fig. 4), which extends the AST type

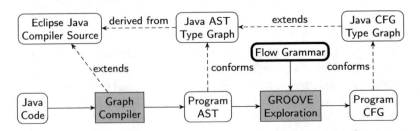

Fig. 2 Overview of the conversion from JAVA sources to GROOVE graphs

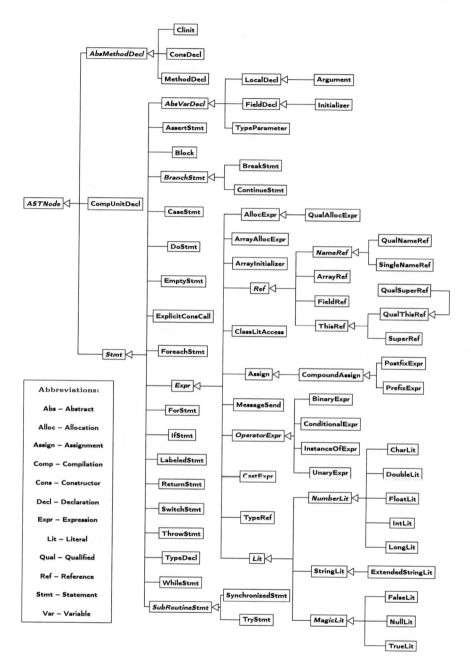

Fig. 3 JAVA AST type graph

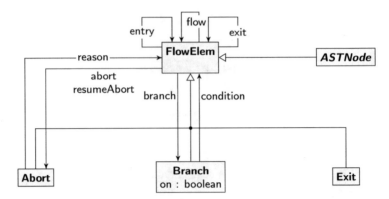

Fig. 4 JAVA CFG type graph

graph. Node type **FlowElem** is the top super-type of all possible elements that can occur in a CFG. Every executable block of code, such as a method body, has an entry point marked by an entry-edge. Execution then follows flow-edges until the **Exit** node is reached. Additional elements in Fig. 4 are **Branch** nodes, which are used in the over-approximation of loops and conditional statements, and **Abort** nodes, which point to commands that cause abrupt termination (see Sect. 3.2).

3   Building JAVA Control Flow Graphs with Recipes

In this section we give an overview of the GROOVE grammar for JAVA CFG construction. The grammar is composed of over 50 recipes and more than 250 simple GT rules, and therefore, a complete discussion in this paper is unfeasible. Instead, we focus on key aspects of grammar design and on some representative recipe cases. In Sect. 3.1, we give a simple example that shows the general idea of CFG construction for sequential execution of statements. Subsequently, Sect. 3.2 discusses the more elaborate case of dealing with abrupt termination commands. Finally, Sect. 3.3 presents the basic guidelines followed during grammar construction.

3.1   Basic Construction of CFGs from ASTs

Given an AST representing a valid JAVA program, we construct the CFG by adding flow-edges between AST nodes. The fundamental aspect of this construction is similar to the operation of a recursive descent parser. The AST is visited in a top-down manner, starting at the AST root node and traversing down the children nodes by recursive calls to appropriate recipes. Recursion stops at the AST leaf nodes, where recipes terminate and return to their caller. When the entire calling sequence is finished, i.e., when the recipe for the root node completes, the entire AST was visited and the whole CFG was constructed.

Suppose a simple JAVA assignment expression, such as x = 2+3*4. Assuming that x is a simple local int variable, language semantics states that the right-hand side expression must be evaluated left-to-right[1] and the resulting value should be stored in x. Considering the usual operator precedence, the expression in post-fix notation corresponds to (2 (3 4 *) +).

In JAVA, a *method* is the usual unit for grouping statements. Hence, the control flow grammar builds one CFG for each method in the AST. Commands inside a method are normally executed first-to-last, left-to-right. However, our recursive descent on the AST visits its nodes from right-to-left. In other words, the construction of the CFG is done in reverse order. This choice was made to limit the need for additional elements in the program graph.

The construction of a method CFG starts at a **MethodDecl** node, the root of the method in the AST. Upon visiting such node, a special **Exit** node is created, to indicate the method exit point (both for normal and abrupt termination). Then, method statements are visited last-to-first.

Every recipe for CFG construction has the following signature:

```
recipe SomeCommand(node root, node exit, out node entry) { ... }
```

Thus, recipe SomeCommand receives as input the root node of the sub-tree being visited and the exit node where the execution should flow after SomeCommand finishes. The recipe is responsible for constructing the CFG of SomeCommand and of all its composing sub-commands, by recursively descending in the AST starting at root. Finally, once this part of the CFG is constructed, the entry point of the entire sub-tree is known. This node is assigned to the entry parameter, and is returned to the caller.

To illustrate the process explained above, we present a step-by-step construction of the CFG for the assignment x = 2+3*4. The AST for this command is depicted in Fig. 5a. The Assign recipe (not shown) starts by calling BinaryExpr(n2, n0), meaning that the CFG construction traverses down the AST, to the root node of the right-hand side expression (node n2), whose exit point is the **Assign** node (n0). Execution then continues inside the BinaryExpr recipe, given in Listing 1.

---

[1] For the argument's sake we assume the compiler does not perform optimizations such as *constant folding*, which would simplify the expression during compile time.

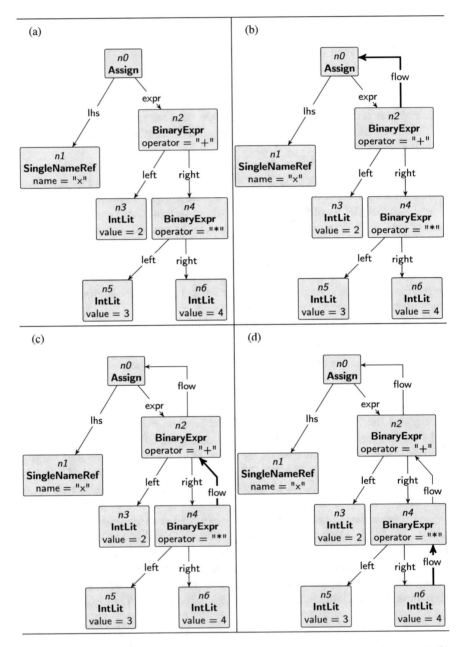

Fig. 5 Step-by-step construction of the CFG for x = 2+3*4. (**a**) BinaryExpr(n2, n0), (**b**) create-FlowEdge(n2, n0), (**c**) BinaryExpr(n4, n2), (**d**) Lit(n6, n4)

Fig. 6 Rule `get-Children`, used by recipe `BinaryExpr`

Listing 1 Recipe for a binary expression

```
1  recipe BinaryExpr(node root, node exit, out node entry) {
2      create-FlowEdge(root, exit);
3      // Match the left and right components of the expression.
4      node lroot, rroot := get-Children(root);
5      // Build the flow for the right sub−expression.
6      node rentry := Expr(rroot, root);
7      // Build the flow for the left sub−expression.
8      entry := Expr(lroot, rentry);
9  }
```

In line 2 of Listing 1, the simple GT rule `create-FlowEdge` is applied to create a flow-edge from node n2 to node n0, resulting in the graph presented in Fig. 5b. The recipe then continues in line 4, where rule `get-Children`, shown in Fig. 6, is invoked.

Rule `get-Children` is a common kind of simple GT rule used in our solution. Its sole role is to traverse along the AST, according to the given parameters, as can be seen from its signature in Fig. 6. (Recall from Sect. 2.1 that adornments with symbol **?** indicate an input parameter node, whereas **!** marks an output node.) Thus, given the root for the binary expression, the rule in Fig. 6 matches and returns the two roots for the left and right sub-expressions.

Execution of Listing 1 then continues on line 6, with recipe `Expr` being called on the right sub-expression (`rroot` node). This recipe (given in Listing 5 in an abbreviated form) just dispatches the call to the appropriate recipe, depending on the type of root node given as input. This dispatch leads to the recursive call `BinaryExpr(n4, n2)`, which starts by creating the flow-edge between n4 and n2, leading to the graph shown in Fig. 5c.

The second call of `BinaryExpr` continues in the same vein as previously explained, until leaf node n6 is reached with a call to recipe `Lit`, presented in Listing 2.

Listing 2 Recipe for all types of Literals

```
1  recipe Lit(node root, node exit, out node entry) {
2      // A literal is always a leaf in the AST, so we close the recursion here.
3      create-FlowEdge(root, exit);
4      entry := root;
5  }
```

Since literals do not have children in the AST, the recursion stops at the Lit recipe, which just flows to the exit and returns the literal node itself as the entry point, yielding the graph in Fig. 5d.

The current BinaryExpr reaches line 8, where the left sub-expression is constructed. Note that the entry of the right sub-expression (rentry) is now used as the exit point. This leads to call Lit(n5, n6), and the resulting graph from Fig. 7e. The second BinaryExpr call returns, leading to the traversal of node n3 with call Lit(n3, n5), and the corresponding graph in Fig. 7f. Finally, the right-hand side expression of the assignment was traversed and node n3 was identified as the entry point, as can be seen in Fig. 7g. By following the flow-edges starting from the entry, we obtain exactly the post-fix expression (2 (3 4 *) +) from the beginning of this example.

Construction of a CFG for sequential statements is as straightforward as that of expressions. When dealing with branching commands and loops, however, it is necessary to generate **Branch** nodes in the CFG, to mark the possible paths of execution. The overall method for handling branching is quite similar to the idea discussed above, and thus it will be skipped for brevity's sake. Instead, in the following we show the more complex case of abruptly terminating commands.

3.2 Handling Abrupt Termination

In JAVA, four statements cause abrupt termination, viz., **break, continue, throw** and **return**. These are so named because they "break" the normal execution flow of a program, causing a block to terminate early. The semantics of these commands can get quite convoluted due to nesting and the possibility of abrupt termination inside **try-finally** blocks. The JAVA method m() given in Listing 3 illustrates this complex case.

Listing 3 Method with **return** in **try-finally** block

```
1  void m() {
2          ;  // C1
3          try {
4                  ;  // C2
5                  return;
6          } finally {
7                  ;  // C3
8          }
9          ;  // Unreachable
10 }
```

We use empty statements (;) in method m() to simplify the example, but these can be seen as place-holders for any block of commands. JAVA semantics states that a **finally** block must always be executed, even in the case of an abrupt termination. Thus, execution of m() starts at command C1, enters the **try** block and executes

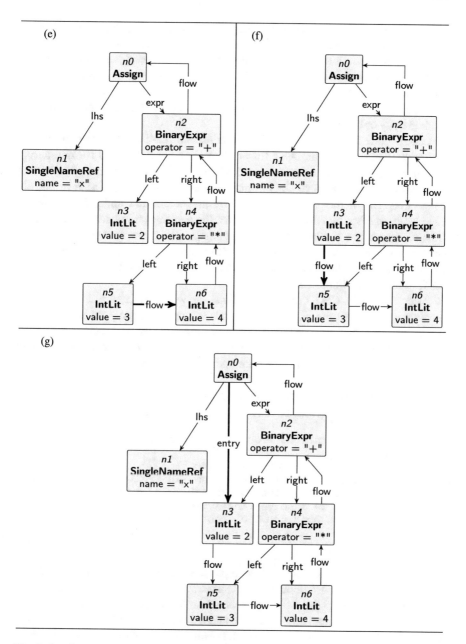

Fig. 7 Step-by-step construction of the CFG for x = 2+3*4 (cont'd). (**e**) Lit(n5, n6), (**f**) Lit(n3, n5), (**g**) create-EntryEdge(n0, n3)

C2, and is *aborted* by the `return` statement. Control then flows to the `finally` block, causing the execution of C3. Lastly, the abortion is *resumed* on the enclosing scope, where execution flows immediately to the method exit point, bypassing the command indicated as unreachable. The AST of method `m()` is shown in Fig. 8a, where **EmptyStmt** nodes are marked with the same comments as in Listing 3. Integer attribute index is used in the AST to record the ordering of statements within a method body or block.

Control flow for abrupt termination requires information about flow in normal execution. Thus, during the AST traversal, we construct the CFG for non-abrupt statements as usual, and create **Abort** nodes in the CFG to mark abruptly terminating commands. An intermediate CFG in our running example can be seen in Fig. 8b, where node n10 marks the abort caused by the **ReturnStmt** node. The resolving-edge between these two nodes indicates that the abortion still needs to be handled. Control flow is now extended with abort-edges, which can be traversed as, but have priority over flow-edges, leading to **Abort** nodes and their associated reason for abrupt termination. On a complete CFG, **Abort** nodes flow to some point of the AST, so that execution can continue.

After the basic CFG construction finishes, we enter a phase called *abort resolution*, where all the aborted commands are properly analyzed and the CFG is finalized. As long as possible, **Abort** nodes are matched and recipes are called to resolve them. All these recipes are neatly contained in a control package called `Abort`, and Listing 4 shows the code for one of such recipes.

Listing 4 Recipe for resolving pending Return commands

```
1  package Abort;
2  recipe ResolveReturn(node root, node aroot) {
3    do {
4      choice root := propagate(root, aroot);
5      or root,aroot := resolve-ReturnStmt-In-TryBlock(root, aroot);
6      or root,aroot := resolve-CatchBlock(root, aroot);
7      or root,aroot := resolve-FinallyBlock(root, aroot);
8    } until (resolve-AbsMethodDecl(root, aroot))
9  }
```

Recipe `ResolveReturn` receives as input a **ReturnStmt** node (parameter root) and its associated **Abort** node (aroot). The recipe enters a loop, where abort resolution traverses up the AST, by means of rule `propagate`, shown in Fig. 9a. This rule receives as input an **Abort** node and the current **FlowElem** being resolved, and returns the parent statement in the AST. This rule is used to propagate abortions along nested blocks, for example, in Fig. 8b, from node n7 to node n4.

Abort propagation continues until it hits the method root node, when the abort is finally resolved by rule `resolve-AbsMethodDecl`, shown in Fig. 9b, which immediately flows to the method exit point. Lines 5–7 in Listing 4 handle the cases when abort propagation cannot go up, due to an enclosing `try` statement. Rule `resolve-ReturnStmt-In-TryBlock` is given in Fig. 9c. When reaching the outer

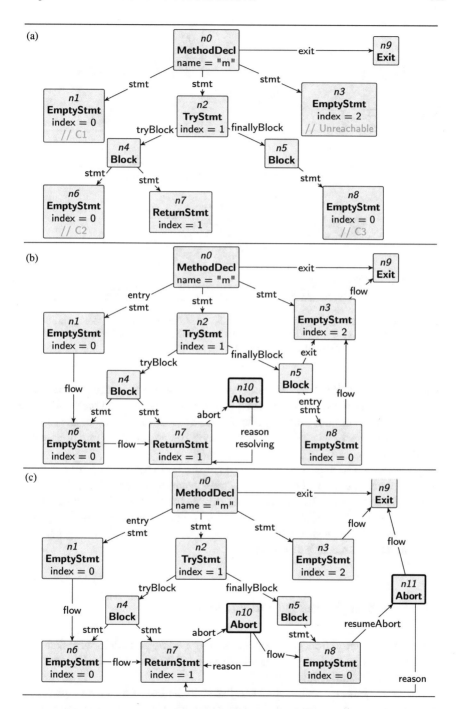

Fig. 8 Handling abruptly terminating commands. (**a**) Start state. (**b**) CFG after traversal with pending **Abort** node. (**c**) Final CFG after resolution

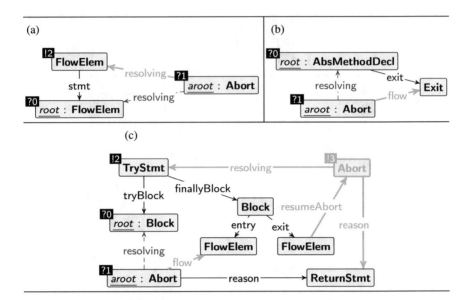

Fig. 9 Three rules used in recipe `Abort.ResolveReturn`. **(a)** `Abort.propagate`, **(b)** `Abort.resolve-AbsMethodDecl`, **(c)** `Abort.resolve-ReturnStmt-In-TryBlock`

scope of a `try` block that has an associated `finally` block, the given **Abort** node flows to the entry point. However, abort propagation does not end there, otherwise execution would continue normally after the `finally` block. Therefore, the rule also creates a new **Abort** node in the enclosing scope and returns it, so that propagation can proceed.

The rules used in lines 6–7 of Listing 4 are similar to the one in Fig. 9a and thus are not shown. The final CFG for this running example is given in Fig. 8c, with an additional **Abort** node (n11) created. Edge resumeAbort has the same semantics and priority as an abort-edge. It is interesting to note that some code analysis can now be performed on the finished CFG. For instance, node n3 has no incoming flow edge and is therefore unreachable (as expected).

3.3 Rationale for Recipe Elaboration

Given that the control flow grammar is quite large, some guidelines were defined to rationalize its construction. We present these guidelines here with the hope that they will be useful in similar case studies.

The entire grammar construction was based on the JAVA AST type graph (Fig. 3) that was previously published in [12] and later updated in [15]. By looking at type nodes, the following guidelines were applied:

Fig. 10 Part of the AST type
graph showing the abstract
type **Expr** and some of its
subtypes

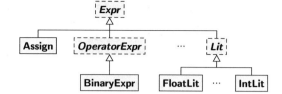

1. Types that are not composed by other elements, i.e., that cannot have children in
   the AST, are the base case for the recursive descent of recipes on the AST. An
   example of such type is **Lit**, with its recipe given in Listing 2. Other types that
   also fit into this category are **EmptyStmt, NameRef**, and **ThisRef**, which follow
   the exact same recipe structure from Lit.
2. Abstract types lead to recipes that only dispatch the call to the correct recipe,
   based on the type of the given root node. For example, Fig. 10 shows part of
   the type graph from Fig. 3 zoomed in the hierarchy of abstract type **Expr**. The
   associated recipe is given in Listing 5.

Listing 5 Part of the recipe for an Expression

```
1  recipe Expr(node root, node exit, out node entry) {
2      choice entry := Assign(root, exit);
3      or entry := OperatorExpr(root, exit);
4      or entry := Lit(root, exit);
5      [...]
6  }
```

This recipe sequentially tries to call each of the recipes associated with the direct
subtypes of **Expr**. If node root passed to Expr has type **Assign**, then the call to
recipe Assign succeeds and Expr returns. If the node has a different type, the
call to Assign fails and the Expr recipe tries the next line, until a successful call
is made. It is interesting to note that recipe Lit does not follow this structure,
despite **Lit** being an abstract type, because it falls in case 1.
3. Types that have one or more sub-trees in the AST give rise to the standard type
   of recipe, of which the BinaryExpr recipe in Listing 1 is a prime representative.
   Elaborating this type of recipe was the core of this work, and basically amounted
   to constructing the CFG for each sub-tree in the reverse order, following the JAVA
   semantics.

As a passing note, we should point that one of the recipe features highlighted
in Sect. 2.2, namely the possibility to "rollback" a failing recipe is not needed in
the CFG constructing grammar. Since we work with syntax-correct ASTs, the only
place where a recipe can fail is on "dynamic recipe dispatching", i.e., on recipes
for abstract types such as **Expr**, where we know we have an expression but we have
yet to determine its concrete type. The **choice-or** construction sequentially calls
recipes until one succeeds, but even in this case there is no real need of rollback,

because a recipe can only fail when inspecting the type of its given root node, and we are sure that exactly one of the recipes in the `choice-or` construct will succeed. (Since we are at an abstract node and it can only have one of the subtypes prescribed by the type graph, which are all potentially tested by the corresponding recipe.)

4 Conclusions and Future Work

This paper presented a GROOVE recipe-based solution for the problem of generating control flow graphs over abstract syntax trees of JAVA programs. Recapping the contributions stated in the introduction:

- The CFG generating grammar can be seen as an alternate, formal, executable specification of the control flow semantics of JAVA, which is presented in the language manual in plain English.
- The use of recipes provides an elegant, hierarchical rule composition mechanism. Although we tried in the text to make this point across, it can only be fully grasped when handling the real grammar in GROOVE. A previously attempted, non-recipe-based solution quickly became unwieldy, as one was forced to work in an unstructured set of several hundred rules, which could interact in complex ways and "polluted" the CFG with extraneous elements to ensure rule composition. In contrast, in this solution, rule composition and sequencing lend themselves neatly to a recipe-based implementation. This, in turn, simplifies the rules used in the grammar, making it easier to understand and maintain. We refer the interested reader to http://groove.cs.utwente.nl/downloads/grammars/, where the complete grammar here described is available for download.

As future work, the most pressing task is to update the graph compiler to JAVA version 10. No major obstacles are foreseen in lifting this approach to the latest JAVA version, given that new language constructs (such as lambdas) are defined in terms of existing ones to ensure backwards language compatibility. After a new compiler is available, the grammar here presented must be updated, but again no major hurdles are expected.

Having the ability to import real-life JAVA code to a GT tool such as GROOVE opens up a myriad of possibilities. One possible extension would be the creation of an optimizing grammar that does dead code elimination and other types of code analysis. Another would be the creation of a simulating grammar, that can follow the constructed CFG and "execute" the program, effectively rendering GROOVE a GT-based JAVA Virtual Machine. Since the major functionality of GROOVE is state space exploration, this could in turn allow for the model-checking of JAVA code. We plan to follow this line of investigation in the future.

References

1. F.E. Allen. "Control Flow Analysis". In: *ACM SIGPLAN Notices* 5 (7 1970), pp. 1–19.
2. M. Andries et al. "Graph Transformation for Specification and Programming". In: *Sci. Comput. Program.* 34.1 (1999), pp. 1–54. https://doi.org/10.1016/S01676423(98)000239
3. T. Arendt et al. "HENSHIN: Advanced Concepts and Tools for In-Place EMF Model Transformations". In: *Model Driven Engineering Languages and Systems (MODELS), Part I*. Vol. 6394. Lecture Notes in Computer Science. Springer, 2010, pp. 121–135.
4. A. Balogh and D. Varró. "Advanced model transformation language constructs in the VIATRA2 framework". In: *Proceedings of the 2006 ACM Symposium on Applied Comput- ing (SAC)*. ACM, 2006, pp. 1280–1287. ISBN: 1-59593-108-2. https://doi.org/10.1145/1141277.1141575.
5. T. Fischer et al. "Story Diagrams: A New Graph Rewrite Language Based on the Unified Modeling Language and JAVA". In: *Theory and Application of Graph Transformations (TAGT)*. Vol. 1764. Lecture Notes in Computer Science. Springer, 2000, pp. 296–309. ISBN: 3-540-67203-6. https://doi.org/10.1007/9783540464648_21.
6. R. Geiß and M. Kroll. "GrGen.NET: A Fast, Expressive, and General Purpose Graph Rewrite Tool". In: *Applications of Graph Transformations with Industrial Relevance (AGTIVE)*. Vol. 5088. Lecture Notes in Computer Science. Springer, 2008, pp. 568–569. ISBN: 978-3-540-89019-5. https://doi.org/10.1007/9783540890201_38.
7. A. Ghamarian et al. "Modelling and analysis using GROOVE". In: *STTT* 14.1 (2012), pp. 15–40.
8. M. Huisman and B. Jacobs. "JAVA Program Verification via a Hoare Logic with Abrupt Termination". In: *FASE*. LNCS 1783. 2000, pp. 284–303. https://doi.org/10.1007/3-540-46428-X_20.
9. C. Ouyang et al. "Formal semantics and analysis of control flow in WS-BPEL". In: *Science of Computer Programming*. 67.2 (2007), pp. 162–198.
10. D. Plump. "The Graph Programming Language GP". In: *Third International Conference on Algebraic Informatics (CAI)*. Vol. 5725. Lecture Notes in Computer Science. Springer, 2009, pp. 99–122. ISBN: 978-3-642-03563-0. https://doi.org/10.1007/9783642035647_6.
11. A. Rensink. "The GROOVE Simulator: A tool for state space generation". In: *AGTIVE*. LNCS 3062. 2003, pp. 479–485.
12. A. Rensink and E. Zambon. "A Type Graph Model for JAVA Programs". In: *FMOODS/-FORTE* LNCS 5522. Full technical report: Centre for Telematics and Information Technology TR-CTIT-09-01, University of Twente. Springer, 2009, pp. 237–242.
13. A. Schürr. "Internal Conceptual Modeling: Graph Grammar Specification". In: *Building Tightly Integrated Software Development Environments: The IPSEN Approach*. Ed. by M. Nagl. Vol. 1170. Lecture Notes in Computer Science. Springer, 1996. Chap. 3, pp. 247–377. ISBN: 3-540-61985-2.
14. R. Smelik, A. Rensink, and H. Kastenberg. "Specification and Construction of Control Flow Semantics". In: *2006 IEEE Symposium on Visual Languages and Human-Centric Computing (VL/HCC)*. IEEE Computer Society, 2006, pp. 65–72.
15. E. Zambon. "Abstract Graph Transformation – Theory and Practice". PhD thesis. Centre for Telematics and Information Technology University of Twente, 2013.

Printed in the United States
By Bookmasters